פנינים על התורה
PENINIM ON THE TORAH

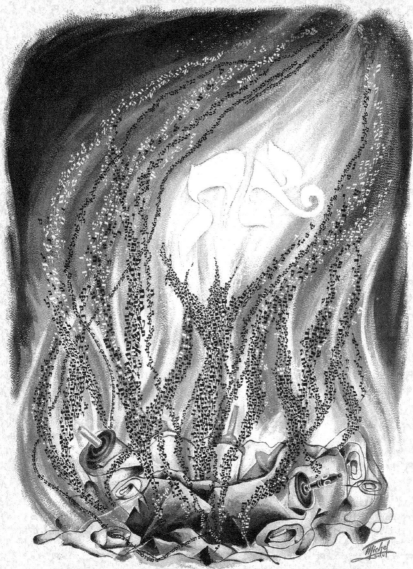

AN ANTHOLOGY OF THOUGHT PROVOKING IDEAS
AND PRACTICAL INSIGHTS ON THE WEEKLY PARSHA

BY RABBI A.L. SCHEINBAUM

FOURTEENTH SERIES

PENINIM AL HATORAH
Copyright 2009
By Rabbi A.L. Scheinbaum

Published and Distributed by Peninim Publications
in conjunction with *The Living Memorial*
a project of the **Hebrew Academy of Cleveland**
1860 S. Taylor Road, Cleveland Heights, Ohio 44118
216-321-5838 Ext. 165 / Fax 216- 321-0588

ISBN: 0-9635120-0-5

TYPOGRAPHY AND PAGE LAYOUT
Kisvei Publications, Detroit MI, 48075, 248-559-5005

COVER DESIGN
KENNY FIXLER, K.F. GRAPHICS, Cleveland, Ohio 44106,
216-421-8520

COVER PHOTO
"The Indestructible Letters" by Michel Shevach Schwartz
Touching upon an incident which occurred in Jerusalem during the Roman
conquest, the great sage, Rabbi Chanina ben Teradyon was being burnt alive
with a Torah scroll wrapped around his body. When asked by his students
what he saw, he replied, *Gevillin nisrafin v'osiyos porchos b'avir*, "The
parchment is ablaze, but the *osiyos*, the holy letters, are soaring up to
Heaven." Also depicted is Moshe *Rabbeinu* shattering the *Luchos*, Tablets,
with the letters rising up to Heaven. This scene signals the indestructibility of
the Jewish People, as long as we are bound up with the Eternal Torah.
For information about this and other prints:
www.Jewdaica.com
Exclusive distributor of "cali-graphic" Judaica by Michel.
Lenny@Jewdaica.com Phone (203) 912-5254

Printed in the United States of America

With joy and gratitude to the Almighty,
we dedicate this volume
in honor of the marriage of our children

Captain Peter & Major Liat Reisman
(Israel Defense Forces)

Who have devoted their lives
to serving their people
and their country – Eretz Yisrael.

We are proud of their individual achievements
and their sensitivity to their fellow man.

May they be blessed with
ששון ושמחה – joy and happiness,
good health and success as they build a
בית נאמן בישראל
in the tradition of their forebears.

With love,
Sidney and Phyllis Reisman

Pepper Pike, OH
Jupiter, FL

בס"ד

בס"ד

ר"ח שבט תשס"ט

הנה כבר איתמחי גברא המחנך הותיק הרה"ג ר' אברהם לייב שיינבויים,שליט"א,
נודע בשערים עם הדפסת י"ג חלקים פנינים על פרשיות התורה שזכה להפצה
מרובה בכל רחבי תבל ועכשיו עלה במחשבתו לסדר ולהדפיס סדרה י"ד "יד
חזקה" של "פנינים על התורה".

יברכהו השי"ת ויזכה לברך על המוגמר להדפיס ולהפיץ על התורה מעיינות
רבותינו ז"ל שמפיהם אנו חיים ומימיהם אנו שותים להגדיל תורה ולהאדירה.

נחום זאב דסלר

"A People Survives As Long As It Transmits Its Heritage From One Generation To The Next"

למזכרת נצח בהיכל הספר

לז"נ הורי היקרים

ר' נח ב"ר יהודה אריה ז"ל שיינבוים

נפטר כ"ב כסלו תשכ"ו

הא' גליקא בת ר' אברהם אלטר ע"ה

(שיינבוים) באגען

נפטרה ח' אדר ב' תש"ס

לז"נ מר חמי

ר' שלמה זלמן ב"ר יצחק ז"ל ברינגער

נפטר ב' דר"ח אייר תשכ"ח

חמותי

הא' פיגא רחל בת ר' משה צבי ע"ה

(ברינגער) פעלדמאן

נפטרה ערב פסח תשס"ג

לז"נ אחיותי שנקטפו בילדותן ע"י הנאצים הארורים ימ"ש

רחל לאה ע"ה

פריידא ע"ה

שרה אסתר ע"ה

שיינבוים

נשמתן עלו בטהרה י"ג תשרי תש"ב

PREFACE

The first copy of *Peninim* was distributed in the greater Cleveland community eighteen years ago. Since that day, this endeavor has been blessed with amazing *siyata d'Shmayah*, as it is disseminated weekly in dozens of synagogues and schools throughout the country. I am humbled by this *zechus* and fervently pray to *Hashem Yisborach* that I merit the ability to continue promulgating authentic *Torah* thoughts and values.

Peninim presents a broad-based anthology of thought-provoking ideas, homilies, and practical insights. These are based upon the *Parashas HaShavua*, but are applicable to varied situations. The concepts presented reflect authentic *Torah* perspective on life. We take great pride in presenting to the public the fourteenth volume in the *Peninim* series.

The comments and insights compiled in this volume are geared to beginner and scholar alike, as many practical messages may be gleaned from this work. It is our sincere hope that the insights anthologized in this book will give effective expression to the mind and soul of its readers, affording them the opportunity for personal development and educational enrichment through *Torah* study.

ACKNOWLEDGMENTS

The obligation to appreciate, acknowledge and extend gratitude to those from whom we have benefited is compelling. Indeed, one's humanness is defined in accordance with his ability to be *makir tov*. My parents and mentors are clearly the one's who have fostered and stimulated my growth both as a human being and as a student of *Torah*. My parents were Holocaust survivors who came to these shores with one goal and objective: to rebuild their lives and raise a family that was true to *Torah* and *mitzvos*. With their uncompromising integrity and sterling character they devoted their lives to this mission. My in-laws *Shlomo Zalmen* and *Faige Rochel Brunner* were individuals of singular devotion to *Klal Yisrael*. They imparted a legacy of *ahavas Yisrael* and *ahavas chesed* – a legacy that has been emulated by their many descendants.

During my *yeshiva* and *kollel* years spent studying at the Telshe Yeshiva, I had the privilege to learn under *Roshei Yeshiva* whose very lives epitomized *gadlus ba'Torah*. *Horav Chaim Mordechai Katz, zl,* and *Horav Refael Boruch Sorotzkin, zl,* left a lasting impact on my life.

I have been fortunate to be the recipient of both professional and personal reinforcement from *Rabbi N. W. Dessler, Shlita*, Dean and founder of the Hebrew Academy of Cleveland. His understanding, concern and uncompromising standards have been a source of guidance. *Rabbi Simcha Dessler*, the Academy's Educational Director and *Rabbi Eli Dessler*, its Financial Director, have assumed the leadership of this institution. Together they have maintained the standards of excellence imparted to them by their forebears. I will always be indebted to *Morry Weiss* whose vision and encouragement catalyzed my venture in writing. *Sidney Reisman* and *Ivan Soclof* are continuing sources of support and counsel. *Dr. Louis Malcmacher*, the current president of the Academy, is a longtime valued friend.

Peninim is not the work of one individual. It is a concerted team effort of an untiring, devoted support staff who nurture its success. My gratitude to *Mrs. Sharon Weimer and Mrs. Tova Scheinerman.* They are resourceful, dedicated and above all, patient. *Mrs. Marilyn Berger* carefully edits the original manuscript making it presentable.

Rabbi Malkiel Hefter is a colleague and friend whom I call upon at all hours of the day to solve a problem, correct an error, or simply to enhance a project. *Mrs. Ethel Gottlieb* is able, erudite, meticulous and a special human being. She has proofread, copy edited and coordinated the entire manuscript. *Rabbi Doniel Neustadt* is a *talmid chacham* par excellence whose area of expertise extends far beyond the aesthetically appealing *sefer* which he has produced. *Kenny Fixler* has designed a beautiful cover which adds the crowning touch to this project.

My greatest source of strength, encouragement, support and understanding has always been my wife, *Neny* מנב"ת. She is knowledgeable, proficient, concerned, but above all, always there. Throughout our years together, she has always been the anchor of stability and support. Her rationale and ability to see clearly through the ambiguities of life have steered the course for our family. She proofreads the weekly *Peninim,* often under extenuating circumstances. She has devoted herself, often single-handedly, towards raising our children and imbuing them with her unique imprimatur. In regard to her the famous words of Rabbi Akiva ring true: "All that I have accomplished really belongs to her." May she have good health and may we, together with our children and grandchildren, merit that the love of *Torah*, its study and dissemination, be the hallmarks of our home.

Avraham Leib Scheinbaum
T"u B'shvat 5769, Cleveland Hts., Ohio

Approbations for the Peninim Al HaTorah series

from

Horav Mordechai Gifter, *z.l.*

Horav Shmuel Kamenetsky, *shlita*

Horav Yaakov Perlow, *shlita*

Horav Mattisyahu Solomon, *shlita*

appear in previous volumes of

Peninim Al HaTorah

Table of Contents

Sefer Bereishis

Sefer Shemos

Sefer Vayikra

Sefer Bamidbar

Sefer Devarim

The Living Memorial is pleased to pay tribute
to our sponsors and benefactors who have enabled us to
create an everlasting memorial to "The World That Was",
and to the Patrons of Peninim who have each dedicated
one Sefer of the five Chumashim.

Sefer Bereishis

Neil and Marie Genshaft

Sefer Shemos

Mendy and Ita Klein

Sefer Vayikra

Dr. Marijah McCain

Sefer Bamidbar

Dr. Sam and Ruthie Salamon

Sefer Devarim

Stephen McCain

ספר בראשית
SEFER BEREISHIS

Dedicated in loving memory of our dear
father and grandfather

Arthur I. Genshaft

יצחק בן נחום ישראל ז"ל
נפטר ח' חשון תשל"ט

By his family

Neil and Marie Genshaft
Isaac and Naomi

בראשית ברא אלקים את השמים ואת הארץ

In the beginning of G-d's creating the heavens and earth. **(1:1)**

The *Baal HaTurim* notes that the last letters of the words *Bereishis bara Elokim* — *taf, aleph, mem* — spell out (when rearranged) the word *emes*, truth. This teaches us that the world was created via the attribute of *emes*. Interestingly, the *Torah* alludes to the word *emes* in an indirect manner, since the sequence of the letters is out of order. *Horav Shmuel David Walkin, zl,* infers a profound lesson from here. The *Torah* teaches us that one must strive for the truth, regardless of the situation. One is not obligated to be truthful only during times of smooth sailing in which he has no extenuating circumstances or financial troubles. One must be truthful, even under circumstances that overwhelm and distress him, when life has no *seder*, order, and the demands on him are overpowering. Even when he is under stress, one must act with integrity. Indeed, the only thing that can guide him to maintain a straight course through the ambiguities and vicissitudes that confront him is the truth.

The *Brisker Rav, zl,* was known to be the paragon of integrity. The attribute of *emes* was his benchmark in every endeavor in his life. He demonstrated this trait when an individual whom he held in esteem would visit. The Brisker *Rav* showed him the greatest reverence, regardless of the person's station in life. Conversely, if he was visited by a person for whom he had very little respect, it did not matter whether the individual had a large following or not, the *Rav's* greeting was only cordial and diplomatic.

Indeed, the Brisker *Rav* was once asked if a person's stature can be measured by his following. He responded that one's following is not an indication of his true character. He substantiated this with *Rashi's* comment concerning the multitude of stars that accompany the moon. These stars are present to appease the moon after its size had been diminished by Hashem. This teaches us that one's following is not a sign of his essence. On the contrary, it might indicate the converse. A weak person needs a strong backing. A strong person does not need the accolades and the "pat on the back" that are quite often false anyway.

The *Rav* cited the following analogy to explain this further. A man walks down the street and notices a large tree. Regardless of how many people come along to support his "view," he is clearly aware that there is a tree in this place, because he sees it with his own two eyes. Let us look at another scenario. The same person stands in the street and does not see a tree. Then, even if another person comes along and says he sees a tree, he will not believe his peer. If ten people come and declare that they see a tree, the first person might begin to question his own ability to see clearly. After all, ten people say that they see a tree! If one hundred people come along and verify that they see a tree, then the first person who had not seen a tree might even begin to believe that he is losing his eyesight. If one hundred people see something and he does not, then something must be wrong. His "inability to see" will increase as more and more people exclaim that they see a tree.

The same idea applies to *Torah* leadership. The true *Torah* giant does not need a large community to pay him homage. The *Chafetz Chaim* was *rav* in Radin, a small community in Poland. *He* made the town great. *He* gave it distinction. *He* gave it greatness. The *Chafetz Chaim* and so many like him were distinguished in their own right. They did not need others to substantiate the reality of their *gadlus*. There are others, however, who are like the elusive tree that one believes exists only because so many say they see it. If the tree is not there, the fact that people say it is there will not bring it into existence. *Gadlus baTorah* is inherent within the person. It is not subject to public acclaim.

וירא אלקים את כל אשר עשה והנה טוב מאד

And G-d saw all that He had made and behold it was very good. (1:31)

L ife is comprised of successes and failures. Some of us have a greater number of successes. Others look at failure more often than at success. This is not a perfect world, but our perspective on life and the world can make a "world" of difference. Hashem created the world that we know in Six Days of Creation. He made some subtle changes during Creation in order to offset some of the problems that arose.

Hashem first created light. This was a powerful, intense and very spiritual light. In fact, it was so spiritually illuminating that the wicked would never be worthy of experiencing it. Hashem, therefore, separated this light from this world and set it aside for the righteous to enjoy in the World to Come.

On the third day, there was once again a disappointment, when Hashem created fruit trees whose bark would taste the same as the fruit. The trees produced a bark, but it did not taste like the fruit. The earth was later punished for not conforming to Hashem's command.

On the fourth day, the two illuminations, the sun and the moon, had a "situation." At first, they were both the same size — until the moon complained about having to share its dominion over the world with the sun. In response, Hashem decreased the size of the moon. Once again, the creation produced disappointment.

Yet, as we see from the *Torah*, despite the shortcomings and disappointments, Hashem said that His creation was *tov me'od*, very good. It could have been better. It could have been perfect. There could have been an absence of strife, no disagreement, no complaints. There might have been — but there was not. Yet, Hashem says that it was very good. Why? *Horav Avraham Pam, zl,* cited in *The Pleasant Way*, explains that Hashem accentuated the positive. He focused upon the successes — not the disappointments.

Emphasize success; accentuate the positive; focus on winning: these are phrases that we hear all the time. How often do we listen to them? We listen to a *shiur*, lecture, or speech. The speaker/lecturer has presented a powerful and brilliant discourse. Yet there were a few short moments when his presentation seemed to drag. During the sixty-minute lecture, eight minutes were boring. Does that diminish the value of the rest of the speech? Just because a small part of an endeavor does not reach the apex of our expectations does not — and should not — decrease its total accomplishment.

Having said this, we are enjoined to make every effort to praise the positive efforts of those with whom we come in contact on a regular basis. This is a reference to those whom we take for granted, the *chazzan* or *baal tefillah* in *shul*, the cook who prepared our food, the one who gives a daily *shiur*, and of course, our wives and mothers, etc. We tend to ignore the basic expression of gratitude for services rendered, either because we take them for granted or because we do not focus on their positive aspects. We have constant opportunities to perform *chesed* with a simple good word, a smile, a gesture of recognition. Some of us, regrettably, find it difficult to pay a compliment. We conjure up all forms of excuses for not rendering this common courtesy, but, after all is said and done, it is the result of an insecurity on our part. What we do not realize is that a subtle compliment can make a distinct difference in someone's life, as evidenced by the following story:

The story is told about a famous author who was walking along the East River promenade in New York City, feeling very depressed. He felt at the end of his rope. His life's work, his writing, was of no value. His life felt empty and meaningless. Had his writing really accomplished anything? At that point there seemed to be only one thing to do. Suicidal, he thought about climbing over the railing that divided the promenade from the river and throwing himself in.

He stood there, staring at the dark waters, about to make his final move, when he suddenly heard an excited voice, "Excuse me, I am sorry to impose on your privacy, but are you Christopher D'Antonio, the author?" He could only nod in return. "I hope you do not mind my approaching you, but I had to tell you what a difference your books have made in my life! They have helped me incredibly, and I just wanted to thank you!"

"No, it is I who should be offering gratitude to you," he replied, as he turned around, walking away from the East River and heading home.

Space does not permit me to add many more vignettes of *chesed* through words. As someone who has spent many years in the field of *chinuch*, however, I can say unequivocally that nothing does more for a student than positive recognition from his *rebbe*. This equally applies with regard to the *rebbe*. Parental recognition of a *rebbe's* efforts on behalf of their child is crucial for the *rebbe*, the child, and the *parents*.

✻ ✻ ✻ ✻ ✻ ✻

ועץ החיים בתוך הגן ועץ הדעת טוב ורע

***And the Tree of Life in the midst of the garden, and the Tree of Knowledge of good and bad.* (2:9)**

S*forno* explains that *daas*, knowledge, means to focus one's heart on (what is) good and evil. This explanation of the word *daas*, is also found in the phrase *v'haAdam yoda*, "and Adam knew," i.e., he became aware and now concentrated his heart on her (Chavah). This is also why a relative is called a *moda*, as it says in *Rus* 2:1, *moda l'ishah*, "a relative of her husband," for it is natural that one concerns himself with the needs of his relative. *Horav Shmuel David Walkin, zl,* infers from here that a relative is a *moda,* because the foundation of closeness and love is the knowledge and concern for the needs of his relative. This is also why a friend is referred to as *meyuda*, as it is written in *Tehillim* 31:12, *u'fachad l'myudoai*, "and a fright to those who know me (my friends)." A friend is someone who understands my needs and focuses upon them.

Any love, any relationship in which the two parties are not sensitive to the needs of one another, is not a relationship. Love cannot exist unless there is an awareness of each other's needs and sensitivities. *Horav Moshe Leib Sossover, zl,* was wont to say that he learned *ahavas Yisrael*, love for all Jews, from an itinerant farmer. A farmer who was totally inebriated asked his friend, "Do you love me?" The friend responded, "Of course I do," and he immediately proceeded to demonstrate his affection by embracing and kissing him. The drunken farmer continued, "Do you know what I am missing? Do you know what I need?" "How should I know what you need?" the other farmer/friend retorted. "Well, if you are not aware of my needs, how can you say that you are my friend?"

This story sums it up. A friend is aware; a friend cares. One who is not aware of his friend's needs is not much of a friend.

******

בזעת אפיך תאכל לחם... כי עפר אתה ואל עפר תשוב. ויקרא האדם שם אשתו
חוה כי היא היתה אם כל חי. ויעש ד׳ אלקים לאדם ולאשתו כתנות עור

"By the sweat of your brow shall you eat bread... For you are dust and to
dust you shall return." The man called his wife's name Chavah, because
she had become the mother of all the living. And Hashem G-d made for
Adam and his wife garments of skin. (3:19,20,21)

T he commentators question the sequence of the *pesukim*. The fact
that Adam named Chavah should have been written earlier, at the
end of *Perek bais*, where the *Torah* relates how Adam gave names
to all the creatures. Why is the naming of Chavah juxtaposed to Hashem
making garments for Adam and Chavah? The *Kehillas Yitzchak* explains that
when Adam realized what Chavah's act had catalyzed, when he understood
that his death and the deaths of all future generations was the result of
Chavah's eating and sharing of the *Eitz HaDaas*, he immediately became
severely depressed and angry. After awhile, it dawned on him that anger
would be to no avail. It would not rescind the decree. Death was now an
inevitable part of the human condition. At the same time, Adam was acutely
aware of Chavah's role in propagating life. He decided to be *maavir al
midosav*. He overlooked his anger and decided to forgive Chavah. He
transcended, passed over, his natural character traits that would predispose
him to anger. This character trait was Adam's distinction.

Imagine what we have just said. A man discovers that his wife has
put poison into everyone's food. She is about to feed this preparation to him
and all of their descendants. Is there any question as to his reaction? He
would undoubtedly call her a murderess at best and immediately go out to
publicize his wife's invidious act.

Is that not what Chavah did? She caused death to become a part of
our lives. Everyone returns to dust as a result of Chavah's actions. Should
she be lauded for this act? Yet, Adam controlled himself and overlooked her
error. He did not call her an evil serial killer or murderess. Instead, he
accentuated her positive attributes. While it was true that she brought death
to the world, she also brought life. Without Chavah there would be no life, no
future — nothing! We must remember her positive contributions and name
her accordingly.

When Hashem saw how Adam transcended his anger and harbored

no enmity towards his wife, He made holy garments for them — an indication of His favor. This teaches us that when one transcends his natural inclination for anger, revenge and hatred, Hashem overlooks his transgressions and gazes favorably upon him.

Great people are able to act in this manner. The *Ohr HaChaim Ha'kadosh* writes that Moshe *Rabbeinu* had every reason to be upset with *Klal Yisrael*. They caused his death. Because of them, he would never enter *Eretz Yisrael*. Yet, he still blessed them prior to his death. Great people overlook their contemporaries' shortcomings. They transcend slander and disparagement. They look beyond the pettiness that has become a major component in the daily endeavor for so many of us.

Horav Yitzchak Zilberstein, Shlita, relates that this *middah*, character trait, the ability to transcend anger and hurt in order to pursue peaceful reconciliation, was the hallmark of the previous *Bobover Rebbe*, *Horav Shlomo Halberstam, zl.*

The Bobover *Rebbe* was a wellspring of sensitivity for all Jews. His activities during and after World War II saved the remnants of Galician Jewry, both physically and spiritually. Men of distinction, however, will inevitably have detractors who are filled with envy, glory-seekers who resent sharing the limelight with anyone other than their own shadow. Shortly after the *Rebbe* emerged on the American scene, a rabbi who felt threatened by the Bobover *Rebbe's* activities on behalf of world Jewry lashed out strongly against the *Rebbe*. He did not mince words in his character assassination of the *Rebbe*. The Bobover *Rebbe* did not respond. It was only after the slanderous remarks were becoming downright humiliating that the *Rebbe* called together all of his *chassidim* in his *bais ha'medrash*.

The large *shul* was filled to capacity. There was not an empty seat, as everyone crammed the room to hear the *Rebbe's* response to the insults hurled at him. Everyone expected a fiery rejoinder that would put the rabbi in his place. The *Rebbe* entered the *bais ha'medrash*, ascended to the lectern in front of the *Aron Kodesh*, and, after kissing the *Paroches*, ark cover, turned to the gathering and spoke for fifteen seconds! He said, "I am declaring to everyone assembled, as I stand in front of the *Aron Kodesh,* that I absolutely forbid anyone from battling on my behalf. My honor is my honor — and it will remain my honor, if everyone acts appropriately and does not take sides.

Whoever does not obey me has no place in my *bais ha'medrash*." The *Rebbe* then descended the podium and left the *bais ha'medrash*.

A few hours later, the *Rebbe* asked his *gabbai*, attendant, to take him to the rabbi's home. Word of the *Rebbe's* response had already circulated throughout the community. The *Rebbe* arrived at the rabbi's home and ascended the steps to his apartment. He knocked lightly on the door until the rabbi himself answered. Ashen-faced, the rabbi realized who was standing before him. Words were not necessary, nor would they suffice. It was action that was needed. The Bobover *Rebbe* took the rabbi in both his arms, embraced and kissed him. He said, "You may go to any one of my *chassidim* and they will attest to the fact that I harbor no ill feelings towards you. As once we were friends, we will continue to remain friends."

Rav Zilberstein notes that the Bobover *Rebbe* left this world on *Rosh Chodesh Av*, the same *yahrtzeit* as Aharon *HaKohen*. They had one thing in common: *ohaiv shalom v'rodef shalom*; they were both individuals who loved peace and pursued peace. The common thread that coursed between them was their love of all Jews and unswerving desire to promote harmony within *Klal Yisrael*.

Parashas Noach

קץ כל בשר בא לפני כי מלאה הארץ חמס מפניהם והנני משחיתם את
הארץ

"The end of all flesh has come before Me, for the earth is filled with robbery through them; and behold, I am about to destroy them from the earth." (6:13)

R ashi notes that whenever you find promiscuity, catastrophe comes to the world. As a result, both good and evil people perish. Yet, the ultimate judgment of destruction was sealed as a result of robbery. The *Gur Aryeh* reconciles this apparent contradiction with the idea that although robbery catalyzed the destruction, once it occurred the good and the evil both died because promiscuity was also involved. We wonder why robbery has an effect only on the evil, while the consequence of promiscuity radiates to the good people as well?

Horav Shmuel Walkin, zl, explains that like a *physical* disease, in which certain illnesses are highly contagious while others affect only the immediate victim, *spiritual* disease has similar characteristics. One of those sins that is contagious and spreads quickly throughout a group is promiscuity. The far-reaching effect of this sin is obvious throughout history. Contemporary society is plagued by this spiritual disease to the point that its greatest and most illustrious leaders have fallen prey to it. The slightest vestige of promiscuity arouses the *yetzer hara*, evil-inclination, granting it the power to bring us down spiritually.

Yes, robbery sealed the sentence of destruction. Yet this sentence would have been executed only against the actual perpetrator. Once promiscuity entered the picture, both the sin and its consequence became more widespread.

Rashi's statement that the "good" are also affected means that the good are no longer good. In other words, the *yetzer hara* of *znus*, promiscuity, is difficult to overcome. It has an effect on everyone, unless a person is stoic and maintains a strong footing against the blandishments of the *yetzer hara*. This is the reason that *tznius*, modesty/moral chastity, plays such an integral role in the *weltenshauung* of the Jewish People.

Interestingly, as noted by *Horav Eliyahu Munk, zl*, the first time that the *Torah* refers to the descendants of Avraham, Yitzchak and Yaakov by the name, *Yisrael*, is in regard to morality. When Shechem violated Dinah, daughter of Yaakov *Avinu*, her brothers exclaimed their outrage with the words, *Ki nevalah asah b'Yisrael*, "He had committed a disgraceful act against *Yisrael*" (*Bereishis* 34:7). This occurred even before the name *Yisrael* had officially been proclaimed as exemplifying our strength and ability to overcome challenge. This name denotes the priestly people, who will "fight for G-d." To paraphrase *Rav* Munk, "What a lofty conception of duty, virtue, and moral nobility is already connected with this august name!" It is particularly significant that the first "struggle for G-d" with which the name, "*Yisrael*," is connected is in defense of the sacred ideal of moral purity. The primary mission of those who are *Bnei Yisrael* is to safeguard this ideal.

כי אתך ראיתי צדיק לפני בדור הזה
"For it is you that I have seen to be righteous before Me in this generation." (7:1)

What did Noach do during the year that he and his family spent on the *Teivah*, Ark? *Chazal* teach us that Noach immersed himself in *chesed*, acts of kindness, as he saw to the needs of the thousands of creatures that were in his care. The *Midrash Tanchuma* tells us that the *Torah* refers to Noach as a *tzaddik* due to his extraordinary care of the animals. Indeed, Noach was unable to sleep because the schedules for feeding the various animals did not coincide. Noach's devotion to performing *chesed* was a *kaparah*, atonement, for the selfishness and depravity of the members of his generation. They lived for themselves. Noach lived for others. They preached cruelty, injustice and apathy. Noach exemplified love, sensitivity and hope.

Feeding the hungry is a form of *chesed* that many of us ignore, because we do not know what it means to be hungry. Sensitivity towards others can often be expressed once the beneficiary has himself experienced the "other side of the coin," once he has been sick or hungry or poor and in need. We live in a country where people do not usually experience the hunger that is commonplace in Third World countries. Yet, there are people among us who, although they do not starve, do not have the money to put meat and chicken on the table — even on *Shabbos*! There are people who do not have enough to eat. They might not go to bed hungry, but how do we measure hunger? Noach taught us the significance of caring for the simple material needs of *all* creatures. Surely what he did is a lesson for us all in our concern for our fellow man.

I would like to share with the reader an analogy, a story that pertains to this subject: A man had two distinctly different dreams. In the first dream, he saw hundreds of sad, expressionless people, sitting at a large banquet table that was filled with large platters of the most delectable foods. Regrettably, not a morsel of food had been touched. The people simply stared at the tables.

He wondered, "Why are these people not eating? They appear to be hungry. The food is there for the taking. What is preventing them from availing themselves of this feast?"

His guide told him, "They cannot feed themselves. If you will look, you will notice that the people have no joints in their arms. They can hold their arms straight out, but they cannot bend them. No matter how hard they try, they cannot bend their arms to bring the food to their mouths."

In his second dream, the man saw a similar vision: same room, same table, same people with no joints in their arms. Everything was the same, except in this vision the people all appeared to be well-fed and happy. "How could this be?" he wondered. "How can these people appear to be well fed if they cannot feed themselves?"

The guide gave a quick response, "Look again, carefully, and tell me what you see."

He looked again and saw an astonishing sight. While each person could not feed himself, he could grasp the food in his outstretched hand and place it in to his neighbor's mouth. They could not feed themselves, but they could feed one another!

What a powerful analogy! To the extent that we do for others, we do for ourselves. When we feed only ourselves, we all starve. When we think of others, we are all satiated. A wise man once said, "This world is comprised of two kinds of people: the givers and the takers. The takers eat well, but the givers sleep well.

The following story happened to Fiorella LaGuardia in 1933: The future legendary mayor of New York was then a presiding judge in police court. A trembling old man was brought before him. The charge: stealing a loaf of bread. The man broke down and conceded his guilt, adding, "What can I do? My family is starving."

LaGuardia turned to the man and said, "I have no recourse but to fine you ten dollars for your crime." He then reached into his pocket and said, "Well, here is the ten dollars to pay for your fine." He proceeded to place the ten-dollar bill on the table. "Furthermore," he declared, "I am going to fine everybody in this courtroom fifty cents for living in a town where a man has to steal bread in order to eat. Will the bailiff please collect the fines and give them to the defendant!"

The bailiff went around the room collecting the fines and gave the defendant the money. The shocked old man, who was originally brought to the judge for stealing a loaf of bread, left with tears in his eyes and forty-seven dollars and fifty cents to help feed his starving family.

This story teaches us the value of human compassion; the importance of caring about others; and the extent of our responsibility towards our fellow man.

✻ ✻ ✻ ✻ ✻ ✻

וירא חם אבי כנען את ערות אביו ויגד לשני אחיו בחוץ

And Cham, the father of Canaan, saw his father's nakedness, and told his two brothers outside. (9:22)

*H*orav S.R. Hirsch, zl, observes that Cham should have remained respectfully outside, as his brothers did. Entering the tent with the intent to look already identified him as the degenerate that he was. Cham should have known better. After all, he was also a father. Nevertheless, he went in and saw what he wanted to see. When he came out to his brothers he did not simply tell them, he related in detail what he had seen. *Vayaged*, he painted the story in words to get the most out of it. He gloated on the shocking effect of his words.

Cham fathered Canaan and Mitzrayim, two nations that descended to the nadir of depravity. The social degeneration that characterized Egypt and the moral decadence that personified Canaan had their source in Cham's behavior towards his father. All of humanity is built on the relationship of children to their parents.

Veritably, parents are there for their children: "the mother, is the condition for their existence; the father as the one whose life should be given up for the well-being of his children. Children must see in their parents the repository of Hashem's mission in this world." If respect for a parent is absent, then the stem that connects the sapling to the tree is severed. The younger generation then considers itself only a *yoreish*, inheritor, of the previous generation. The more vital supplants the older weaker generation and steps into its place. We are taught differently. The Jew's relationship to the previous generation is one of *nachalah*, a form of inheritance, a word derived from *nachal*, stream, a flow. Thus, the older generation hands over its strength and powers, material and spiritual treasures, to the younger generation. While others seek to divorce themselves from the past, we see our parents as a source of strength, power and experience. As a stream flows from above, the spiritual mission of the Jew is transmitted from one generation to the next.

Cham denigrated the pivotal *mitzvah* of *Kibbud Av,* honor for a parent. The degeneration that followed was the consequence of his iniquity. The ensuing moral disintegration of his descendants was a direct outgrowth of that first act of disrespect towards a father. Cham set the standard of behavior for his children throughout the following generations.

הבה נרדה ונבלה שם שפתם אשר לא ישמעו איש שפת רעהו

"Come, let us descend and there confuse their language, that they should not understand one another's language." (11:7)

*R*ashi tells us how their failure to communicate in a common language resulted in confusion and discord. One person would ask for a brick. The other one, as a result of a lack of comprehension, returned with plaster. The first one would rise up and kill the other person for not bringing him the brick. We wonder why *Rashi* has to go so far as to say that the lack of communication resulted in murder? The original purpose of confusing the language was to undermine their building project. If they could not communicate, they would not be able to build. Why did they resort to murder?

The *Brisker Rav, zl,* explains that unity can have a negative as well as a positive effect. Furthermore, when the wicked unite with a common objective, they find an avenue to succeed. The cause of the downfall of the *d'or haflagah,* generation of the dispersal, was that they used the harmony that existed between them to focus on the wrong thing. If their goal was to build a tower, they would find a way to see their goal reach fruition. Nothing would stand in the way of their *collective* efforts. This is why it was essential that the confusion brought about by the language problem had to be so great that it resulted in a complete breakdown of society, even murder. The greatest proof is the fact that even after they killed one of their own, they continued building the tower. It was only when they were dispersed that the *Torah* writes that work on the tower came to a halt.

✻ ✻ ✻ ✻ ✻ ✻

ויקח תרח את אברם בנו... ויצאו אתם מאור כשדים ללכת ארצה כנען ויבאו
עד חרן וישבו שם

Terach took his son Avram... and they departed with them from Ur Kasdim to go to the land of Canaan; they arrived at Charan and they settled there.
(11:31)

*H*orav Yitzchak Zilberstein, *Shlita,* notes that the *Torah* reveals to us that Terach originally had set a destination to reach Canaan. In the end, he did not reach his goal; he settled midway in Charan.

He cites the *Arugas Habosem* that explains this occurrence in the following manner: Terach set a goal to reach Canaan. Like so many other weak people, Terach did not achieve his goal. The *yetzer hara*, evil inclination, challenges us midway, seeking a way of preventing us from bringing our goal to fruition. This is what happens to the wicked: they undertake glorious endeavors; they make grandiose plans, all with good intentions. Yet, along the way, they fall prey to their *yetzer hara* which misleads them. *Tzaddikim*, the righteous, are not like that. They set sail on a mission, and nothing obstructs their way. They triumph over the challenges and obstacles that lie in their path, because they are focused on their objective. Regardless of the difficulties, once they have accepted a task upon themselves, they complete it.

The *Chassidic Seforim* distinguish between angels and man in that angels manifest the virtue that they cannot deteriorate. Their concomitant flaw is that they cannot improve. They cannot go forward and grow. Man, regrettably, can deteriorate, but he also possesses the virtue that he can improve. Man can set goals for himself which he can drive himself to achieve. A wise man once said, "Humanity cannot be measured by what it is; only by what it is trying to become." When people set a goal before themselves, and they adhere to the path towards achieving that goal, their success is determined by their achievement. They can only achieve their goal, however, if they feel a sense of mission.

One of our most common human failings is a lack of persistence. We set before ourselves lofty goals, which we initially attack with great enthusiasm, but we do not persevere. When we lose the will to go forward, we have lost the most significant line of defense against failure — persistence. And a lack of persistence is the natural consequence of losing our sense of mission.

How often do we throw up our hands in defeat at a time when — with just a bit more effort, a bit more patience — we would have succeeded? With a little more perseverance and a little more effort, what previously might have seemed hopeless, may yet turn into a glorious success. The greatest failure is in no longer trying. There is no barrier more insurmountable than our own lack of purpose, our own lack of mission.

Hasmadah, diligence, in *Torah* study produces *Torah* leaders. One does not have to be a genius to achieve this status. Indeed, many talented geniuses have not achieved this zenith in *Torah*. It is those who plug away every day, all the time, who are undiscouraged and indefatigable, who achieve the mark of success.

A person who is on a mission works at achieving his goal on a constant basis. He looks for every way to enhance his work and grow in his endeavor. He does not slack off and take the easy way out. Nothing stands in his way. He is on a constant mission. The story is told about a firm that sought to hire a man for a top executive position. They had bypassed the man next in line and chosen an outsider for the position. This individual who had seniority was understandably upset, so he decided to take his case to the company's CEO. In very hurt tones he said, "But I had fifteen years of experience with this firm." The CEO replied, "That is not so. You had one year of experience fifteen times."

In every endeavor, in every field, especially in the field of *Torah chinuch*, education, one must be creative, vital and fresh. The success of a teacher is determined by his excitement, energy and sense of mission. *Horav Shraga Feivel Mendlowitz, zl,* the legendary *menahel* of *Mesivta Torah Vodaath* and primary architect of *Torah* in America, instilled this sense of mission in his *talmidim,* students. He understood that the transformation of American Jewry was dependent on the creation of a cadre of teachers who had a passion for their work, a burning sense of mission. He imbued them with a love for each Jew, with a sensitivity to their physical and spiritual needs, by having them identify personally with each one. *Rav* Shraga Feivel once sent one of his close students to a distant community for the *Yamim Noraim*, High Holy Days. When the student returned, he asked him, "How many *shomrei Shabbos* did you find there?" The *talmid* responded, "I highly doubt if there is even one *shomer Shabbos* in the community." *Rav* Shraga Feivel quickly asked in amazement, "Did you not cry bitterly because of this?" He felt that only those capable of weeping over the sorry spiritual state of American Jewry were capable of changing it. The situation required sensitivity, determination, diligence and a sense of mission.

לך לך מארצך

"Go for yourself from your land." (12:1)

*C*hazal note that *"Lech Lecha"* is repeated a second time, when Hashem once again instructs Avraham *Avinu* to go forth (22:2). This time he is to go *to Har Moriah* to offer his son, Yitzchak, as a sacrifice. They add that the second *Lech Lecha* was more beloved to Hashem. What are *Chazal* teaching us? Is there a question about the relative significance of *Akeidas Yitzchak* compared to Avraham's moving from his home to go out into the world?

In his *sefer, Simchas HaTorah, Horav Simcha Hakohen Sheps, zl,* distinguishes between the two commands, offering a practical insight into *Chazal's* query and response. Both commands to Avraham had a definite purpose: to sanctify Hashem's Name in the world. The difference between the two concerns the immediate focus of the *Kiddush Hashem.* When Avraham was told to leave his home, his family, his past, and go forth to build the future of Monotheism in the world, the goal was *Kiddush Shem Shomayim b'rabim, public* sanctification of Hashem's Name throughout the world. *Akeidas Yitzchak* also centered on *Kiddush Hashem,* but it was intended for a different audience. It was for Yitzchak alone. The next link in the chain of transmission of belief in the *Ribono Shel Olam* had to concretize his own beliefs.

Chazal wonder which trial is more beloved to Hashem: sanctifying His Name to the world, or *chinuch,* teaching and transmitting *emunah,* faith, in the Almighty to his son. They respond that *chinuch* — transmitting the message of Hashem's Oneness to one's own flesh and blood — eternalizes it, guaranteeing its continued application. Avraham *Avinu* converted many people, reaching out to the world. How many remained committed to his teachings? How many followed in his pathway? Very few, if any, continued on the road charted by the first Patriarch. His son, however, not only adhered to his father's teachings, he became the next Patriarch, assuring that the *Kiddush Shem Shomayim* that he experienced was disseminated to the next generation.

Teaching a world is all-important. For some, it is their lifelong ideal. However, it should not be at the expense of one's own children. Many educators have successfully transmitted the message of Judaism to the wider community, but regrettably have neglected to reach their very own. There are also individuals who refuse to go out and teach the world for fear that they will harm their own children. This selfish excuse has kept some of the most talented potential teachers from spreading Hashem's *Torah* to the greater community. There is no doubt, *chinuch* of one's own children takes precedence, but how should he weigh the relative importance of the two goals? Educating one's own children does not take the place or absolve one of *chinuch ho'rabim*.

ויעבר אברם בארץ עד מקום שכם
Avram passed into the land as far as the site of Shechem. **(12:6)**

*R*ashi explains that Avraham *Avinu* went to Shechem by design. He prayed there for Yaakov's sons, Shimon and Levi, who would wage war there. Interestingly, it was necessary for Avraham to go into Shechem to pray for them. Could he not have prayed elsewhere for his descendants? *Horav Shmuel Walkin, zl,* derives from this that in order to pray appropriately for another person's anguish, it is critical that the individual himself *experience* the pain. Prayer is the result of sensitivity. This idea is manifest in a number of places.

Rachel *Imeinu* was buried on the road near Bais Lechem, not in Chevron — which would have been her rightful burial place — so that she would be able to help her descendants when Nevuzaradan exiled them. They would pass by her tomb, and Rachel would *go out* onto her grave, weeping and seeking mercy for them. Why did Rachel have to "go out" of her grave to weep? Certainly, she was aware of her children's travail. She could have wept from within her grave. Once again, we see that in order to empathize, one must observe, one must sensitize himself to the pain.

Likewise, we see that when Moshe *Rabbeinu* went out to his brethren, the *Torah* writes, "Moshe grew up and went out to his brethren and observed their burdens" (*Shemos* 2:11). *Rashi* comments that Moshe went out to *see* their suffering and grieve *with* them. It would have been so natural, so practical, even so understandable for Moshe to remain secure and protected within the confines of the palace. He could have chosen not to notice his brothers' travail, to claim no kinship with the Jewish slaves. Moshe's growing "up" was really his act of going "out." Growing up is growing out — going out of ourselves and identifying with the needs of others, reaching out beneficently to others. Regrettably, many of us become self-absorbed as we grow older, failing to recognize that as one matures, he should begin to shoulder greater responsibility from without.

Avraham *Avinu* knew that Shechem was a place destined for punishment; the evil permeated the air. It suffused the environment. By going there, by being within the confines of the area, he could identify with and sensitize himself to the future needs of his descendants. This is the essence of empathy.

A poor man once approached *Horav Bunim, zl, m'Peshischa*, and asked him for a donation. *Rav* Bunim immediately gave him a considerable amount of money. As the poor man began to leave, *Rav* Bunim called him back and gave him some more money. Overcome with curiosity, the man asked *Rav* Bunim why he had called him back.

"The first donation was in response to the pity I felt for you," said *Rav* Bunim. "The second one was to fulfill Hashem's command to give to the poor."

One has to give *tzedakah* to fulfill the *mitzvah*. One must also understand and empathize with the needy. In fact, it is especially important that one give to suit the needs of the recipient, not simply as a response to his own feelings of guilt.

Giving does not always have to be of a material nature. There was once a famine in Russia. People literally starved to death. One day a poor, emaciated beggar came up to a man and begged for alms. The man searched his pockets for a coin, to no avail. He did not have even one copper coin in his possession. Taking the beggar's worn hands between his own, he said, "Do not be angry with me, my brother, I have nothing with me." The thin, lined face of the beggar lit up as from some inner light, and he whispered in reply, "But you called me 'brother'! That was a gift in itself."

People are starving all around us — not for bread, but for recognition. I would suggest that much of the depression that we see could have been prevented had the individual been exposed to kindness. While we readily give a check to the poor, how many of us have the time, thoughtfulness, or compassion to say a kind word, perform a gracious act, or actually give a piece of bread to an emaciated spirit?

Horav Shraga Feivel Mendlowitz, zl, imbued his students with a sense of responsibility for their fellow Jew. No subject so dominated his teachings as the obligation imposed upon every Jew towards his brother. Among the most important words in his lexicon were *Klal Yisrael.* His constant question was: "What are you doing for *Klal Yisrael?*"

Rav Shraga Feivel would interpret the *pasuk* in *Tehillim* (145:4), *Dor l'dor yeshabach maasecha,* "Each generation will praise Your deeds/creations to the next," to mean that each generation has an obligation to improve Hashem's world, rendering it more praiseworthy. He emphasized that a Jew may not make himself the primary focus of his own life. To be concerned only with oneself — apart from the community — is wrong.

In *Pirkei Avos* 2:18, *Chazal* say, "Do not judge yourself to be a wicked person." *Rav* Shraga Feivel interpreted this to mean that anyone who limits his efforts to himself alone — who is *bifnei atzmecha,* for himself — is derelict in his obligation. *Torah* is called *Toras chesed,* the *Torah* of kindness. This is *Torah* that is taught to others, not just kept selfishly to oneself.

The *Sefas Emes* teaches us that a Jew must be prepared to sacrifice everything, even his personal share in the World to Come, on behalf of *Klal Yisrael.*

Rav Shraga Feivel sensitized his students to the needs of other students. Younger students in the *Mesivta* learned to be sensitive to the needs of those sitting next to them in the *bais ha'medrash.* Better students were "encouraged" to study with weaker students.

He once noticed two *talmidim* carrying chairs to a classroom. He asked one of them, "For whom are you bringing this chair?" The student answered, "For myself." He then asked the same question of the other boy, and the response was the same. *Rav* Shraga Feivel chided, "*You* brought a chair for yourself, and *you* brought a chair for yourself. So you are both *shleppers*. Had each one of you brought a chair for the other, each of you would have performed a *chesed*."

Mesivta Torah Vodaath students were never allowed to forget that, regardless of how happy they personally were to be able to sit and study *Torah* in the *bais ha'medrash*, they represented a small fraction of the Jewish world — a world that regrettably was far-removed from the walls of the *bais ha'medrash*. This situation has lamentably not changed significantly. While the number of students in the *bais ha'medrash* has certainly increased, the Jewish world outside the *bais ha'medrash* has also grown. As *bnei Torah*, we have a moral obligation not to ignore that world. Indeed, what greater act of *chesed*, kindness, is there than bringing a Jew back into the spiritual fold?

✻ ✻ ✻ ✻ ✻ ✻

והקמתי את בריתי... להיות לך לאלקים ולזרעך אחריך
"And I will uphold My covenant...to be a G-d to you and to your offspring after you." (17:7)

To be a G-d to you and to your offspring after you. Why could the *Torah* not simply have said, "To be a G-d to you and to your offspring"? It seems that the two do not necessarily go together. Rather, Hashem must first be a G-d to the father, and then *afterwards*, He can be a G-d to the son. That is the natural order. A child observes a role model in his father. He senses his father's level of commitment, and he becomes inspired. Regardless of whether it is a parent or a gifted *rebbe*, a child/student needs a positive role model, someone that inspires him, infusing him with a desire to grow in *Torah*. We never know when that inspiration will occur or who will be the source, but invariably it is an important part of the child's growth process.

The *Ben Ish Chai, Horav Yosef Chaim, zl, m'Baghdad*, was a brilliant *Torah* giant, who inspired thousands with his writings and lectures. Each *Shabbos*, he would lecture for two hours in the main *shul* in Baghdad to thousands of Jews. The pearls of wisdom that left his mouth were treasured by his listeners. Among those who came to listen every *Shabbos* was a young boy, Sulamon Mutzafi. His father, *Rav* Tzion Meir, was one of Baghdad's known *Torah* scholars.

After the *drashah*, lecture, the child held onto his father's cloak as the assemblage went over to the *rav* to receive his blessing. It was finally Sulamon's turn to greet the *rav*. Shaking with awe and trepidation, holding onto his father's sleeve, the child went forward and kissed *Rav* Yosef Chaim's hand. This was the high point of the week. "It should be the will of Hashem that you grow up to become great in *Torah*," said *Rav* Yosef Chaim, as he placed his hands on young Sulamon's head. Everyone responded with a resounding *Amen*! This was no mere *brachah*, blessing — this was inspiration at its apex. Sulamon was already on the path to *gadlus b'Torah*, distinction in the field of *Torah* erudition.

On the thirteenth day of *Elul*, 1898, *Rav* Yosef Chaim's pure soul returned to its Maker. The funeral cortege left from the *shul* on *Motzoei Shabbos*, followed by thousands of broken-hearted Jews. Their beloved *rebbe*, their leader, mentor and guide, was gone. The eulogies were powerful portrayals of his life of dedication to *Torah*. Unparalleled mourning and grief were manifest. The Mutzafi family also attended, everyone but young Sulamon. He was too young.

Sulamon Mutzafi could not remain in his home. He had to attend the funeral of the *rebbe* that had left such a powerful impact on him. He had to say good-bye. He joined the assemblage of grief-stricken mourners. Like a young orphan, his cries shattered the sounds of silence, as he stood there watching *Rav* Yosef Chaim's mortal remains being lowered into the earth. At that very moment, he accepted upon himself greater sanctity, greater sublimity and purity. *Torah* would be his guide, his friend with whom he would share every minute of the day. He began to study every night from midnight until dawn. His parents attempted to dissuade him, claiming that such practice was set aside for great *tzaddikim*. Yet, the child was not swayed. He was not deterred from his mission. He was inspired to achieve greatness.

Our children have many such opportunities for inspiration. If they do not find it at home, they find it in the *yeshivah*, or in stories of *Gedolim* — who achieved distinction because they followed their own inspiration. When you bring up the subject of achieving greatness to a parent, the immediate response is, "Today is different." *Heintiga tzeiten*, today's times/society has greater demands. It is more difficult to get inspired. I recently read a story which was related by the *Voideslaver Rav, zl.*

When the *Voideslaver* was a young boy, he met an elderly *rebbetzin* who was a granddaughter of the *Chasam Sofer, zl.* She explained that as a young girl she would often eat the *Shabbos* meal with her grandfather. She remembered something the *Chasam Sofer* once said at the meal. He asserted that in each generation the *yetzer hara*, evil-inclination, takes on a new identity. This is done for a practical reason, since in each ensuing generation, people become increasingly aware of the dangers of associating with known evil, so they stay away. As they become aware of one evil disguise, the *yetzer hara* quickly dons a new one, so that his evil is always one step ahead. He then added that in their generation, the disguise/*yetzer hara's* new name could very well be *heintiga tzeiten*, today's world.

The *Voideslaver* continued his story, saying that he asked the *rebbetzin* what she felt was the *yetzer hara* of their day. At first, she demurred, claiming that she was nothing more than an elderly woman. Then after some cajoling, she said, "It may very well be *l'shem Shomayim*, for the sake of Heaven."

In other words, deception is all around us. We find excuses for our children's lack of inspiration, rejection of discipline, and absence of respect. In truth, however, it is all part of the *yetzer hara's* deceptive powers. This is similar to those times when we are prepared to resort to anything, even character assassination, all in the name of *l'shem Shomayim*.

Parashas Vayeira

וירא אליו ד'

Hashem appeared to him. (18:1)

ashi tells us that Hashem appeared to Avraham *Avinu* in order to visit him during his recuperation from his *Bris Milah*. Man is instructed to cleave to Hashem. *Chazal* explain that we cling to Hashem by following in His ways. As He visits the sick, so should we emulate this great act of *chesed* and see to it that we care for the ill and infirm. Visiting the sick means more than sending flowers and a card. While this gesture certainly has value, the essence of the *mitzvah* requires that one pray for the sick person. In fact, the *Shulchan Aruch Yoreh Deiah* (335:4) advises us when is the most propitious time to visit the sick. Therefore, we should perform the *mitzvah* at a time that will inspire the greatest outpouring of *tefillah*, prayer.

In his inimitable manner, *Horav Avraham Pam, zl,* focuses on this *mitzvah*. What is most inspirational about his *shmuess*, ethical discourse, is the sensitivity, caring and love that the venerable *Rosh HaYeshivah* displays toward his fellowman. *Rav* Pam gave a *shmuess* about what he felt was important for his *talmidim* to learn. Some may feel that *Bikur Cholim*, visiting the sick, is relegated to the female gender; Hashem *Yisborach* demonstrates otherwise. *Rav* Pam's *shmuess* delves into the minutiae of this *mitzvah* from a practical standpoint, something he sought to infuse in his *talmidim,* students.

Bikur Cholim means more than mere visitation. It compels us to assess the needs of the sick person and to address them. In some situations, this may involve seeking appropriate medical attention. In other circumstances, it means providing for simple necessities such as *seforim*, tapes and various items that can occupy the patient's time. The *Perishah* emphasizes the importance of making sure that the patient's room is clean and orderly, for a person's mind is clear when everything around him is neat, clean and in its proper place. Incidentally, this applies equally to the classroom. A student studies best in a clean, organized environment.

One who is a *Kohen* has a problem visiting the sick in a hospital which also has a morgue. Nonetheless, there are other ways to enliven the patient's spirits, as evidenced by *Rav* Pam himself, who was a *Kohen*.

There was an elderly Jew who *davened* with *Rav* Pam in the neighborhood *shul*. The man was hospitalized with a serious illness. *Rav* Pam really wanted to visit him, but due to his status as a *Kohen,* he was not able to do so. What did the saintly *Rosh HaYeshivah*, whose sensitivity to other Jews was his hallmark, do? He wrote the man a three-line note wishing him a *refuah sheleimah* and expressing his hope that the man would soon return to his place in *shul*.

Can we imagine what such a simple note from *Rav* Pam could do for an elderly Jew who was alone in the hospital? To be told that he was missed in *shul* and to be given a *brachah* for a *refuah sheleimah* by one of the spiritual giants of the generation could raise a person's spirits from the depths. Indeed, the note did so. The man was strengthened by it. He displayed the note that the "Rabbi" sent to everyone who came to visit. It became his most treasured possession during his last months on earth. When the man passed away, the family hired a rabbi to deliver a eulogy at the funeral service. Not knowing the deceased, the rabbi based his remarks on the salutation *Rav* Pam wrote in the note. The salutation was *Rav* Pam's characterization of the man!

Rav Pam emphasized the great kindness a little gesture of sincerity can affect. This note, which meant so much to the sick Jew, became the basis for his own eulogy. He would often express his fear that this *kleine tzetele*, small note, would someday be held against him by the Heavenly Tribunal, which would accuse, "If you saw how much one small note can accomplish, why did you not do this more often?" What amazes this writer is the nature of *Rav* Pam's thoughts. Instead of the customary pat on the back for which we all yearn, he was concerned that he either did not do enough or did not do it often enough.

In closing, *Rav* Pam explains that besides the *halachic* aspects of the *mitzvah*, there is a crucial emotional aspect to recognize. Many people feel that their achievements and qualities are underestimated, a fact which is regrettably true. We are into ourselves and it is basically our own accomplishments that mean something to us. This attitude misses the mark and is harmful to others. People crave recognition. While this is true on a regular basis, one who is bedridden or hospitalized, forcibly removed from his daily endeavor and contact with the outside world, is even more miserable. Loneliness, lethargy and feelings of depression quickly set in. This can even delay the recuperative process. Hence, someone who finds it difficult to visit the sick should make it a point to call or write, to convey a few words of hope and encouragement. At least the patient will not think he has been forgotten. When a sick person sees that people care about him, it increases his desire to live, to fight the illness. Indeed, *Bikur Cholim* can spell the difference between life and death.

✷ ✷ ✷ ✷ ✷ ✷

וד׳ אמר המכסה אני מאברהם אשר אני עשה. ואברהם היו יהיה לגוי גדול...
כי ידעתיו למען אשר יצוה את בניו ואת ביתו אחריו... ויגש אברהם ויאמר
האף תספה צדיק עם רשע

*And Hashem said, "Shall I conceal from Avraham what I do…And
Avraham will surely be a great nation…For I have cherished him, because
he commands his children and his household after him…" Avraham came
forward, and said, "Will You even obliterate righteous with wicked?"*
(18:17-19,23)

*H*orav Yaakov Moshe Charlap, zl, posits that Avraham *Avinu's* dialogue with Hashem serves as a cogent lesson in how to educate future generations in the area of *middos tovos*, positive character refinement. To this end, Hashem said, "Shall I conceal from Avraham what I am about to do to Sodom?" After all, he is the educator par-excellence, whose devotion to his progeny sets the standard for others to emulate. Therefore, it is essential that he know what I am about to do to Sodom, so that he will transmit the information — to his descendants, concerning the dangers of negative character traits. Furthermore, Avraham will derive from My actions that one must be patient with his children. Give them space and time to return, to mend their ways. At the same time, however, he must realize that there is a time when enough is enough. Sodom had reached the point of no return. The residents were beyond education. Punishment was the only recourse.

Avraham *Avinu* countered, "Will You even obliterate righteous with wicked?" If the purpose of the destruction of Sodom was not specifically for its pedagogic value, I would never question it. Since it is to serve as a lesson for the future, would it not be a greater lesson if the city was spared because of the righteous? This way, future generations would realize the overwhelming role the righteous play and the inspiration they infuse in a community. Regrettably, the number of righteous was inconsequential.

❋ ❋ ❋ ❋ ❋ ❋

וירא לוט ויקם לקראתם
And Lot saw and (he) stood up to meet them. (19:1)

*R*ashi tells us that Lot learned from the house of Avraham the significance of seeking out guests. In other words, Lot, by his very nature and deed, was not a person who enjoyed performing acts of loving-kindness. Opening his home to wayfarers was not only against his nature, but, in Sodom, it was also against the law and thus dangerous. Yet, he did so because of the *chinuch*, education, that he received from Avraham. This teaches us the far-reaching effect of education. Lot spent his early years in the home of Avraham and Sarah. There he imbibed the spiritual lessons from the paragons of education. Avraham *Avinu* was the *amud ha'chesed*, pillar of loving-kindness. He exemplified this attribute in his every demeanor. Lot was inculcated with this *middah*, and it stayed with him in his later years, when his "other" character traits were manifest.

We suggest that it was no simple education that inspired Lot. True, it was Avraham as the *rebbe* that should have made the difference. There was something else, however. *Rashi* says that Lot learned *chesed* in Avraham's home. This does not mean that Avraham *Avinu* gave classes in *chesed* in his house. It means that Lot saw by personal example that *chesed* reigned supreme. When one observes the lesson, it has greater and more enduring value than when it is simply taught in the classroom. When the *rebbe's* demeanor is the classroom of instruction, its effect has a greater impact on the student. Avraham's home was the natural classroom, because he lived and breathed his lessons.

ויתמהמה ויחזיקו האנשים בידו

Still he lingered — so the men grasped onto his hand. **(19:16)**

ot is an enigma. Throughout the entire episode of his rescue, from the destruction of Sodom and the ensuing relationship with his daughters, back to the previous *parsha* where he severed himself from Avraham and his G-d, Lot perplexes us. On the one hand, he risked his life for the safety of the angels. On the other hand, he offered his children to the wild mob outside his door. As he was being rescued, he lingered to save his money, the sole reason that he came to Sodom. In the end, in a state of inebriation, he fathered his grandsons. Previously, he had been Avraham *Avinu's* close disciple, absorbing not only his teachings, but even his mannerisms. Yet, when the going became intolerable between his shepherds and Avraham's, he left, as the *Torah* relates (13:11), "And Lot journeyed from the east." *Chazal* say that the word *kedem*, usually translated as east, can also be understood as *kadmono shel olam*, "the Ancient One of the world," its Creator. Lot separated himself from Avraham, saying, "I want neither Avraham, nor his G-d." So what was he, a saint or a sinner? If he was both, how did this reality unfold?

Horav Yechezkel Levenstein, zl, explains how a person can grow up in the presence of Avraham and Sarah, be witness to the glorious endeavors on behalf of the monotheistic belief, absorb their *Torah* and ethics, and, yet, descend to the nadir of depravity, as evidenced in Lot's relationship with his daughters and his rejection of everything that his *rebbe* Avraham stood for. He explains that Lot possessed *middos ra'os*, negative character traits, and an overwhelming passion for materialism that had not been expunged during his tenure with Avraham and Sarah. True, he succeeded in covering it up out of shame. He did not want Avraham to discover his true essence, so he put on a show. The moment that the chains were off, however, Lot reverted to his true self. Immediately, he expressed his disdain for Avraham and his monotheistic belief.

This idea applies equally to anyone who does not work on developing his character traits. *Rav* Chatzkel asserts that one can study for years in a *yeshivah gedolah* and develop into a God-fearing *Torah* scholar. Yet, when he leaves, he may suddenly transform into a stranger to *Torah*. What happened to his learning? What happened to his *yiraas Shomayim*?

Nothing happened to it. It was all built upon a shaky foundation. As long as he disregarded his *middos*, character traits, his *Torah* study and fear of Heaven were baseless. *He* did not change. He *acted* differently, but *he* remained the same.

The following story serves as a powerful analogy to the above thesis. A distinguished *rav* came to a community for a visit. In an attempt to understand the nature of the community, he sought out various individuals and asked them probing questions about the character and activities of the citizenry. "Young man, tell me, what is the state of *mitzvah* observance in this town?" the *rav* asked the first person he met.

"*Rebbe*, our town has people that are truly righteous," the young man responded. "You will never find a thief or murderer, or, indeed, anyone whose character traits are deficient."

The *rav* met another person and asked him, "Tell me about the interpersonal relationships among the members of this community." "*Rebbe*, in this city everyone loves one another," the man said. "No one would ever testify falsely. Never would someone raise a hand to his fellow man. Indeed, if every Jew was like us, *Moshiach* would surely come."

When the *rav* heard this, he was greatly impressed. He still had one more question to ask to determine the essence of the community. "Can you tell me about the community's observance of the *mitzvos* of *Tefillah*, prayer, *Tefillin*, *Shabbos*, and other such *mitzvos* that define man's relationship with the Almighty?"

"*Rebbe*," the third man answered, somewhat incredulously. "Why are you so negative? Is it not sufficient that the members of our community are fine, upstanding citizens who are active in all sorts of charitable endeavors? They get along with and care for each other. Why do you have to bog them down with all these *mitzvos*? Is it not enough that they do nothing wrong?"

The *rav* was dumbfounded. These people really had it all wrong. How was he to impress upon them that *sur meira*, refraining from doing evil, was not enough? One also had to be *asei tov*, be proactive and perform positive *mitzvos*.

While the *rav* was thinking, a foul odor seemed to fill the air. He looked around and noticed that the carcass of a dead mule had been flung to the side of the road. Suddenly, a brilliant idea dawned on him. He knew how to convey the message to the townspeople. He turned to his *shamash*, assistant, and asked him to go to the tailor and purchase a large black sheet. The *shamash* went and bought a black sheet, which the *rav*, in turn, draped over the dead mule. He then instructed the *shamash* to go throughout the community and publicize that everyone should gather in the street for the funeral of a *meis mitzvah*, someone who had died and had no one to be involved in his funeral. This *mitzvah* takes precedence over all other *mitzvos*.

Word got out that someone had been tragically killed, and his funeral was presently taking place. Everyone should attend the service. The whole town, men and women, gathered to hear the *rav* eulogize the deceased.

The *rav* began his eulogy with a broken voice, "My brethren, the deceased was holy. His life was tragically cut short. He did not deserve to die. He never spoke *lashon hara*, slanderous speech, nor was he a talebearer. In fact, throughout his life, he never spoke — period." The people were stupefied. Who could this great person be?

The *rav* continued, "He was among those who accept their humiliation and do not respond negatively. He was constantly being beaten, taking each lash stoically. Material necessities meant nothing to him. He never ate meat or fish. He suffered the cold with whatever covering he had. He never slept in a bed, laying down on the ground or on some straw. He was the paragon of humility. Who can replace him?"

Everyone cried bitter tears for the exalted deceased. He apparently was no simple human being, but who was he? "My friends, we must all ask his forgiveness. Little were we aware that in our midst lived such a great *tzaddik*. *Oy*, we were so wrong. How did we ignore such a great presence in our community?"

Suddenly, to everyone's shock the *rav* pulled off the black sheet. Everyone took a step back when they saw that the "great *tzaddik*" was none other than a foul-smelling dead mule. They, of course, began to mumble. "How could you have fooled us so?" they asked the *rav*.

"I did not fool you," the *rav* countered. "Everything that I said was absolutely true. The mule meticulously fulfilled the concept of *sur meira*. He never wavered from not doing evil. Yet, he remained a mule all of his life, because it is not enough merely to distance oneself from evil. One must act positively and perform *mitzvos*. Without *mitzvah* observance, one remains a mule."

Yes, Lot distanced himself from evil. On the other hand, he did nothing positive to refine his character. He was a donkey in many ways. When he left Avraham, his true character was manifest. An observant Jew is one who distances himself from anything negative, while simultaneously acting in a positive manner to perform *mitzvos* and refine his character.

פרשת חיי שרה
Parashas Chayei Sarah

ויהיו חיי שרה... שני חיי שרה

Sarah's lifetime was...the years of Sarah's life. (23:1)

T here is an element of redundancy in repeating the phrase, "the years of Sarah's life," at the end of the *pasuk*. Obviously, these are the years of Sarah's life; the *pasuk* began, "Sarah's lifetime was." The *sefer Shevus Yehudah,* explains that since *Chazal* teach us that Sarah *Imeinu's neshamah* left her as a result of hearing the news of the *Akeidas Yitzchak,* one might think that Sarah died before her time. The *Torah,* therefore, reiterates that Sarah died at her predetermined time — the time of death that had been designated for her prior to her birth. In other words, Sarah would have passed away when she did, regardless of *Akeidas Yitzchak.* Hashem provided her with a death integrated with a *mitzvah*: the seminal event of *Akeidas Yitzchak.*

This thesis can help a person who has caused harm — or even *chas veshalom* death — to another to cope with the experience and the feelings of guilt that are intrinsic to it. A person must recognize that all that occurs in this world is part of a Divine plan. The individual merely serves as a vehicle in the plan, an agent of the Almighty.

In the *sefer Yeshuah u'Nechamah*, the author cites an episode that occurred concerning one of the distinguished *roshei yeshivah* of our generation. When he was a young man, he heated up a large pot of water and carried it across the room. A tragic accident occurred and he spilled the burning contents on his young daughter. The child was burned over most of her body and, after a short while, she succumbed to her injuries and died.

One cannot imagine the grief and guilt sustained by the father. Overcome with depression, he could not function. He could not continue his studies. He drew into himself, as his deep melancholy prevented him from eating and sleeping. In short, he lost his will to go on. When word reached the *Chazon Ish* regarding the *rosh yeshivah's* condition, he immediately sent for him. He told him the following: "Man thinks that he is in control of the world. He is wrong. *Chazal* teach us in the *Talmud Chullin* 7b, "A person does not prick his finger in this world unless it has been originally decreed (to occur) in Heaven." Everything that happens is the result of a Heavenly decree. You should, therefore, forget everything that occurred. Remove it from your mind as if it never took place." The *rosh yeshivah* took heed of the *Chazon Ish's* words and went back to a life of normalcy.

We cannot go through life second-guessing everything that we do. The "what if I did not do that or go there" syndrome distresses people. We have to live our lives as it is handed to us. We all have our parts in the Heavenly script. Our problem is that we think that our roles go beyond merely being supportive.

✻ ✻ ✻ ✻ ✻ ✻

ויהיו חיי שרה מאה שנה ועשרים שנה ושבע שנים שני חיי שרה

Sarah's lifetime was one hundred years, and twenty years, and seven years; the years of Sarah's life. (23:1)

*R*ashi explains why the term *shanah*, years, is written after each category: to teach that each one is expounded on its own. When Sarah was one hundred years, she was so pure that she was like a twenty-year–old with respect to sin. When she was twenty-years-old, she was like a seven-year-old with regard to beauty. Last, all of her years were equal for goodness. At the beginning of the *pasuk*, we establish some insight into the amazing personality of Sarah. The end of the *pasuk*, however, does not seem to be conveying any significant message to us. What praiseworthy attribute do we find in the fact that all her years were equal for goodness?

Horav Sholom Schwadron, zl, explains that from an outsider's point of view, Sarah's life can be divided into two parts: before she conceived Yitzchak and after Yitzchak's birth. By her natural condition, Sarah *Imeinu* was not able to conceive. As she approached old age, the chances of her ever having a child became even more remote. At the age of ninety years, when she probably should have reached the point of depression and hopelessness, she conceived and gave birth to Yitzchak. Can we imagine the unparalleled joy and excitement that suddenly became a part of her life? Everything had changed. She was now like everyone else. She was a mother!

Two lives: before she was ninety and afterwards. That is what would be expected of a lesser person. Not so, Sarah — *kulam shavin l'tovah*, "they were all equal for goodness." Her *entire* life was filled with goodness and joy. There was no difference. There was no "before" and "after." She did not sense any deprivation before she became a mother, because she understood that the greatest *tov*, good, for a *tzaddik* in this world is the knowledge that he is fulfilling the *ratzon*, will, of Hashem. Sarah understood that if she was an *akarah*, a barren woman, it was Hashem's will that she be so. If this is what Hashem wanted for her, then so be it. She accepted His decree with joy. When Yitzchak was born, it was a continuation of her joy, because she was serving as a vehicle of Hashem's will. This, indeed, was the *matarah*, sole purpose, of each of the *Imahos*, Matriarchs: to serve Hashem in accordance with His will.

Rav Sholom points out that while Sarah accepted the Divine decree with complete equanimity, she nonetheless yearned for — and did everything possible to conceive — a child. Man's obligation in this world is to be *mishtadel*, endeavor, to act accordingly. At the same time, we are to accept that, at times, the answer is no. It is not that Hashem does not listen to our entreaty. He definitely does listen, but the response is not always what we would like.

Sarah *Imeinu* exemplified greatness and perfection. On the one hand, she entreated Hashem, doing everything in her power to bring a child into this world. On the other hand, she acquiesced to Hashem's decree that she remain barren. It was His will, and she saw only goodness in Hashem's will. The years of her life were all on the <u>same</u> level of goodness, because she was always carrying out the will of Hashem.

ותמת שרה
And Sarah died. (23:2)

The *Midrash* on *Megillas Esther* relates that when Haman conceived his diabolical plan to kill the Jews, he employed a series of lots to determine the most propitious month to execute his decree. He began with *Nissan*, but discarded it due to its merit in "hosting" the festival of *Pesach*. He excluded *Mar Cheshvan* because of the merit of Sarah *Imeinu*, who died in this month. When he reached *Adar*, he noted that Moshe *Rabbeinu* died during this month. It would be the perfect time to issue the decree against the Jews. He erred, because Moshe also happened to be born in the month of *Adar*. We wonder why Moshe's death represented a bad omen for the Jewish nation, while Sarah's did not. Indeed, her death served as a great merit for *Klal Yisrael*.

Pri Haaretz explains that Moshe *Rabbeinu's* demise after Hashem completed his days did not incur any benefit for *Klal Yisrael*. Indeed, *Chazal* state that on that day the Jewish people forgot three hundred *halachos*. Sarah's death, in contrast, epitomized a Jewish mother's conviction and dedication to the point of self-sacrifice. She was prepared to give up her only son for whom she had waited and yearned for so long, in order that he go study *Torah* — or at least that is where she thought he was going. The entire night before he left for the *Akeidah*, Sarah *Imeinu* stayed up embracing, caressing and kissing Yitzchak. "Who knows if I will ever see you again?" Yet, she was prepared to send him off, because she understood true *mesiras nefesh*, dedication, to *Torah*. Her death reflected a paradigm of commitment and dedication to *Torah*. Hence it is a *zchus*, merit, for *Klal Yisrael*.

Haman understood that to select the month during which Sarah died would be foolhardy. He understood that Sarah's death symbolized the self-sacrifice of a Jewish mother, a devotion that has withstood the test of time. Both Avraham and Sarah imbued in their descendants an inexorable sense of dedication to the ideals of *Torah* and *mitzvos*. They taught us how to set our priorities. It was this deep faith and conviction that has given Jewish fathers and mothers throughout the millennia the strength to overcome adversity, trial and tribulation.

It has been over sixty years since the beginning of the Holocaust, and we still read and hear stories of the superhuman, spiritual strength that the Jewish People demonstrated. *Horav Yehoshua Moshe Aronson, zl,* a *rav* in Poland, kept a diary in which he recorded the events of the Holocaust that he and members of his ghetto experienced. He writes that never did his faith in Hashem ever waver, nor did his spirit become depressed. He did not question the Almighty's decree. He was even able to inspire many people with his belief in Hashem. In his diary, he describes everyday life in the ghetto and how the Jews survived emotionally and spiritually, despite the persecution and deprivation to which they were subjected. What impressed him most was the sense of camaraderie that was evidenced in the ghetto. Everyone agreed to care for one another, understanding that not only was this the correct way to live, but it was also the only way they would survive as human beings.

Rav Aronson writes that in the beginning, most Jews did not realize what was happening. They believed the ruse that they were being sent away to "work" camp, where they would receive proper food and care. Little did they know the real function of these camps. *Rav* Aronson was acutely aware of the German's real intentions, and he did everything within his capabilities to publicize this. He sent a letter to his *rebbe,* the *Chasdei David* of Sochatshov, employing a Jewish boy who had the appearance of a German peasant, as a messenger.

He wrote the following note: "Aunt Esther from *Megillah* Street, number seven, apartment four, has arrived." To the German censor, the letter was innocuous. To his *rebbe,* it was a reference to *Megillas* Esther, *perek zayin,* chapter seven, *pasuk daled,* verse four, which reads, "For we have been sold, I and my people, to be destroyed, slain and annihilated." *Rav* Aronson was alluding to the real purpose of the German ghetto: to annihilate Jews. After he had begun writing the first letters of his note, his pen ran out of ink. *He continued writing, using blood collected from the wounded Jews as ink!* Not only did the note convey a message, but the ink emphasized its meaning.

The *Chasdei David* responded with a similar message when he wrote, "David from street number twenty three, apartment four, is with me." This alluded to *Sefer Tehillim,* chapter twenty-three, verse four, "Though I walk in the valley overshadowed by death, I will fear no evil, for You are with me."

Jewish resiliency is a character trait that is intrinsically Jewish. We live with the fear of attack in *Eretz Yisrael* in much the same way that the Jew has always been the unwanted neighbor wherever we have lived. Our history is marked with pogroms and persecutions. It is part of our heritage. We risk our lives because being Jewish means just that — risking one's life due to his belief in Hashem. This is the legacy of Avraham, Sarah and Yitzchak.

We do what is demanded of us. If we get dirty, we shake off the dirt and continue. Indeed, the tribulations spur our growth as a nation of Hashem.

There is a story told of a farmer whose donkey fell into a well. The animal cried piteously for hours, as the farmer tried to figure out what action to take. Finally, the farmer decided that since the donkey was old and the well was not producing that much water anyway, it was not worth freeing the donkey to remove the obstruction from the well. So he called together his friends and neighbors to help him shovel dirt into the well. At first, as the donkey realized what was happening, it cried out in horror. A few minutes later, when the farmer no longer heard the donkey's cries, he looked into the well to observe the most astonishing sight. With each load of dirt that hit the donkey's back, the donkey shook it off and took a step up. As they continued to shovel dirt into the well, the donkey continued to step higher and higher until he was able to climb out of the well.

Life is always throwing us a curve. It is a test from Hashem. We just need to shake it off and take another step forward and upward towards spiritual perfection. Alternatively, we could stay in the well buried by the dirt — and complain. We would be just one step behind the donkey.

✻ ✻ ✻ ✻ ✻ ✻

ותלד שרה אשת אדני בן לאדני אחרי זקנתה

"Sarah, my master's wife, bore my master a son after she had grown old."
(24:36)

Why was it necessary for Eliezer to add that Yitzchak was born to Sarah after she had aged way beyond her child-bearing years? Did it make a difference when Yitzchak was born? The *Brisker*

Rav, zl, explains that Eliezer was alluding to the fact that in regard to Avraham, Sarah and Yitzchak, everything was carried out and lived *l'maalah min ha'teva,* above the course of nature. Their lives were conducted in such a manner that they transcended the laws of nature. Therefore, if Rivkah's family acquiesced to the *shidduch,* match, between Rivkah and Yitzchak, it would be good. If not, it would make no difference. She would become his wife in a manner outside of the laws of nature. In other words, it was not in their hands. Rivkah was going to marry Yitzchak whether they agreed to it or not, because Hashem wanted it so — and He had the only say in the matter. *Rashi* (24:55), implies that when Besuel, Rivkah's father, sought to interfere with the *shidduch,* Hashem dispatched an angel to kill him! Nothing stands in the way of Hashem's plan.

The *Brisker Rav* was wont to say that *hishtadlus,* endeavoring, does not really make a difference in regard to a *shidduch.* One's own effort only serves to calm his nerves so that he feels that he is taking action. In truth, the *shidduch* will take effect at its predetermined time.

The *Steipler Rav, zl,* posits that the fulfillment of *bas ploni l'ploni,* the predetermined decree that "the daughter of so-and-so will wed so-and-so," is basically in the hands of man. If he seeks those attributes and virtues that will promote and enhance his ability to carry out *Torah* and *mitzvos,* then the decree will remain intact. If, however, he is foolish enough to make stipulations for the sole purpose of satisfying his own personal needs, such as money and other such superficial criteria, he may conceivably lose his predetermined match. Indeed, a young man once came to the *Steipler* and asked for a blessing to find his *zivug,* match. The *Steipler* told him, "You were once offered your correct *zivug,* but, regrettably, you pushed it aside, because the young lady did not meet your criteria." We must remember that in *shidduchim,* as well as in everything else, we must reckon with the "Hashem factor."

ואלה תולדת יצחק בן אברהם

And these are the offspring of Yitzchak ben Avraham. (25:19)

Whil e the narrative in *Parashas Toldos* addresses the life and accomplishments of Yaakov *Avinu*, its scope pales in comparison to the space devoted to the lives of Avraham *Avinu* and Yitzchak *Avinu*. Yitzchak lived longer than both his father and his son; yet, much less space is dedicated to his life. The *Rambam* reinforces this pattern, by devoting considerable space to Avraham's achievements in the area of outreach to the pagans. Similarly, he writes that Yaakov sanctified Hashem's Name through *harbotzas Torah*, dissemination of *Torah* teachings. Regarding Yitzchak, he writes simply that he studied and mandated his son, Yaakov, to transmit his teachings to the world. Thus, in comparison to Avraham and Yaakov, Yitzchak's spiritual activity in relation to the outside appears diminished. While Avraham and Yaakov reached out to thousands, Yitzchak had only one *talmid*, disciple: Yaakov.

Horav Yaakov Kaminetzky, zl, explains that the distinctions in the diversity of activities manifest by each of the *Avos*, Patriarchs, is to be understood in light of the differences in the manner that each spread *emunah*, faith in Hashem, which was an outgrowth of the uniqueness of his respective mission. We are accustomed to thinking that Avraham left his door open to the world, encouraging everyone to share his bread. When they conveyed their gratitude in response, he would instruct them to offer their gratitude to Hashem. While this is true, his manner of outreach was a little more complicated.

Avraham's *avodah*, service, was founded in his awe of Hashem's unceasing flow of *chesed*, kindness. Avraham saw his own role as exemplifying this character trait, teaching it to the world. When his guests expressed their gratitude for his generosity, they also marveled at his nobility of character. He would explain that his acts of altruism were a form of Divine service, which reflected the beneficence of the Almighty. This is a character trait that all of Hashem's creations should emulate. Indeed, the idea of a religion based upon kindness and altruism was attractive to the many thousands whom Avraham introduced to monotheism.

Yaakov's mode of *avodah* was *Torah* study as a pursuit of eternal truth. Although, his approach was clearly more restrictive than that of Avraham, he nonetheless did reach out to a multitude of adherents, people who came to form the first *yeshivah*.

Yitzchak's approach to *Avodas Hashem* reflected *middas HaDin*, the attribute of strict justice. This required total discipline, living life as fully as possible within the most exacting demands of Hashem's will, self-abnegation to the point that he was prepared to give up his life at the *Akeidah* — if this was Hashem's will. This type of service was certainly not as popular as that of the other two. Yitzchak attracted one faithful student — Yaakov. Yitzchak's *yeshivah* of "one" constituted the Patriarch's outreach to the world. Thus, his activities were not acknowledged with as much fanfare as those of Avraham and Yaakov.

The lifework of each *Av* is recorded in consonance with his individual success. The long-term success of the Patriarchs' dissemination of *emunah* in Hashem can be appreciated by noting how deeply the lessons of each has become indelibly ingrained in the Jew's national character. Yitzchak's lesson of self-negation to the point of self-sacrifice has surfaced in every era of Jewish history. Indeed, our readiness to sacrifice our lives for the Jewish ideal has been manifest in even the most dubious circumstances by the most improbable Jews. Our willingness to die for our beliefs has been the source of our survival.

A well-known incident that occurred in the early days of the Russian revolution demonstrates this idea. A band of outlaws entered the Russian hamlet of Machanov'ke, rounding up the town's thirty-seven Jews with one thing in mind: to kill them. The townspeople, who had no great love for the Jews, were all there to witness the atrocity. As the robbers picked up their rifles to begin the "proceedings," a voice shouted from the crowd, "I am also a Jew!" It was a pharmacist who had been living in town for years, whom no one, neither Jew nor gentile, had ever suspected of being Jewish. One wonders why this man, who had so completely assimilated into

Christian life, suddenly — after so many years of being estranged from his people — had returned to his roots, especially when doing so meant certain death. *Rav* Yaakov suggests that he was responding to his innate Jewish willingness to surrender his life to affirm his commitment to Hashem. Yitzchak's seminal act at the *Akeidah* imbued a spirit of self-sacrifice in the Jewish psyche that has remained integral until this very day.

The outlaws fired their guns in the air and released the Jews — only to gather them back to the village square once again to repeat the ruse. They repeated the charade, finally letting the Jewish citizens go free. Perhaps it was the *zechus*, merit, of the Jewish pharmacist, who dramatically awoke to his true identity, that saved the Jews that day.

✷ ✷ ✷ ✷ ✷ ✷

ויאהב יצחק את עשו... ורבקה אהבת את יעקב
Yitzchak loved Eisav...but Rivkah loved Yaakov. (25:28)

*H*orav Aharon Kotler, zl, asks a number of compelling questions concerning Yitzchak *Avinu's* relationship with Eisav. First, why did Yitzchak love Eisav? He certainly must have known that this son was far from the ideal. Why would he want to impart the *berachos*, blessings, to him — instead of Yaakov? Moreover, *Chazal* tell us that on the day Avraham died, Eisav transgressed five sins, among which was the sin of denying the existence of the Creator. Is this the kind of person that should have received the *berachos*? Second, how did Eisav turn into an apostate after being raised in Yitzchak's home? He was fifteen-years-old when Avraham *Avinu* died. He apparently had experienced an unparalleled exposure to *ruchniyus*, spirituality. Yet, he became an *apikores*, apostate. How did this happen? Last, if Eisav did not believe in Hashem, why did he grieve so bitterly over losing the *berachos*?

Rav Aharon explains that Eisav undoubtedly had developed an acute awareness of Hashem. He, therefore, realized that losing the *berachos* meant losing a treasure of inestimable value. As we have pointed out previously, one could not have grown up in a home that was so suffused with spirituality and not develop a strong understanding and appreciation of Hashem. Eisav was aware and understood but, nonetheless, he *did not care*. *Kofer b'Ikar* means that a person knows, yet denies. The reason for this is that in order for man to be a *baal bechirah*, have the ability to choose equally between right and wrong, good and evil, he must not be predisposed more to one side than to the other. Consequently, one who is very righteous, who has a profound understanding of Hashem, must have a *yetzer hara*, evil-inclination, that is equally powerful, that has the guile and ability to sway him away from his beliefs. How does a great person with a deep perception of the Almighty fall prey to the *yetzer hara*? The answer is clear: the *yetzer hara*, in his case, is armed with special weaponry. It can entice him to turn to his base desires to the point that he is prepared to throw away his opportunity for achieving eternity. *Chazal* teach us that the wicked are aware that in the end they must confront their own mortality. Despite this, their evil-inclination entices them to have a "good time" until the end.

Eisav's perception of the Almighty was sublime. Even so, he chose to live a life dedicated to materialism, debauchery and licentiousness. He knew better, but he did not care. He disregarded Hashem, because he wanted to live a lifestyle that was base and meaningless. This is why his "head" is buried in the *Meoras Ha'Machpeilah*. His mind was aware, but his body did not care. He had the "head" of a *Torah* Jew, but lived the life of a pagan. He chose to satisfy his physical desires. *He* was great, but so was his *yetzer hara*. The *yetzer hara* was victorious.

Yitzchak knew the difference between Yaakov and Eisav. He still, however, wanted to give the blessings to Eisav. Yaakov was spiritually pure, his sanctity unimpaired by any materialistic concerns or desires. His sons followed in his hallowed nature. They were destined to form the nation that would be a *mamleches Kohanim*, Nation of Priests, and *goi Kadosh*, Holy Nation. If Eisav and his descendants were to be bequeathed the material blessings of *Eretz Yisrael* they would be able to share in Yaakov's holy work by sustaining him and his descendants. In this way, Eisav would not be eternally severed from the Patriarchal heritage. He would not be a "Yaakov," but he still would not have descended to the nadir that he did.

Rivkah, however, saw that regardless of the positive influence on Eisav, it was not worth the risk for Yaakov to be subordinated and subservient to him in any way. Yaakov must be completely divorced from Eisav. This is why she wanted Yaakov to be independent of Eisav and be the sole beneficiary of Yitzchak's blessings. Apparently, Hashem agreed with her.

✻ ✻ ✻ ✻ ✻ ✻

ויקרא להן שמות כשמת אשר קרא להן אביו

And he called them by the same names that his father had called them.
(26:18)

Yitzchak *Avinu* dug the wells that the Philistines had stopped up. He then called them by the same names as his father, Avraham. *Horav Yechezkel Abramsky, zl,* compared the emergence of the "*yeshivos*" that were rebuilt after the Holocaust to Yitzchak's wells. In the first part of the *pasuk,* the *Torah* writes, "And Yitzchak dug anew the wells of water...the Philistines had stopped up." The *yeshivos* that taught *Torah,* the fountain of life of the Jewish People, which were originally founded in Europe by Avraham *Avinu's* descendants, the *Roshei HaYeshivah,* were "stopped up" by the Nazis. Those wellsprings of *Torah* were dug anew in *Eretz Yisrael* and were given the same names of *Mir, Slabodka* and *Ponevezh.* We may add that it was not only out of respect that these names were carried forward. It was to emphasize that the *derech ha'limud v'ha'chaim,* the manner of *Torah* study and the lifestyle that was inherent in these *yeshivos,* did not die. It had been transplanted to another place with renewed vigor and vibrancy.

In truth, these bastions of *Torah* constitute the fountainhead of *Torah* in *Eretz Yisrael* and throughout the world. They are what gives a place distinction. They are what gives it its "size" and influence. The *Alter, zl, m'Slabodka* was wont to say that just as there is a world map that points out where every country is located, so, too, is there a spiritual map. There is a difference between the two in regard to distinguishing one city/country from another. In the standard world map, many small cities/towns are either not marked or they are marked with a tiny dot. This is due to their miniscule population. The size of the dot denotes the population and significance of a place. The spiritual map is different: it does not place significance on population, but, rather, on spiritual influence. The dots on the global map for the cities of *Radin, Mir, Telz, Ponevezh* were probably very tiny, if they existed at all. On the spiritual map, in contrast, they were mammoth, because these small towns had a spiritual influence that outshined that of many of the largest cities. Furthermore, we may add that if a small town produces a *Torah* giant whose influence reaches out on a global level, he gives his hometown unparalleled distinction. Man's perspective must be guided by *Torah* orientation if he is to see any given situation with clarity and truth.

******

ותאמר רבקה אל יצחק קצתי בחיי מפני בנות חת

***Rivkah said to Yitzchak, "I am disgusted with my life on account of the daughters of Cheis."* (27:46)**

The way parents act — between themselves and in regard to their children — leaves an enduring impression. When Rivkah told Yitzchak that she wanted Yaakov to leave home, she said that there was no way he could find a suitable wife among the *Bnos Cheis*. On the other hand, she told Yaakov that she had instructed him to leave because Eisav sought to kill him. Why did she not tell Yitzchak the truth, that it was revealed to her *b'Ruach Hakodesh*, with Divine Inspiration, that Eisav was preparing to do away with his competition? The *Ohr Ha'Chaim HaKadosh* explains that Rivkah did not want to become a talebearer by relating to Yitzchak the evil intentions of their son, Eisav. If she could make do by simply telling him that it was for *shidduch* purposes, it would be more appropriate. To Yaakov, however, she told the primary reason: that Eisav was pursuing him. She could not take any chances what would happen if Yaakov remained. His life was in danger, and it was necessary to impress this upon him. When a mother is sensitive to <u>all</u> of the laws of the *Torah*, it is no wonder that she raises a son like Yaakov *Avinu*.

Horav Yitzchak Zilberstein, Shlita, derives a powerful lesson in how parents should speak to their children from the dialogue between Yitzchak and Yaakov. When Yitzchak "encouraged" Yaakov to leave home and go to seek a wife, he had specific criteria concerning who this wife should be. She could not be from the *Bnos Canaan,* and it would be best that she be from Rivkah's family in *Padan Aram*. Interestingly, when Yitzchak instructed Yaakov concerning whom not to marry, he preceded his negative command with a blessing. He then said, "Do not take a wife from the Canaanite daughters."

Why did he couch his instructions to leave with a blessing? Would it not have been more appropriate to first instruct him to leave and then to bless him prior to his trip?

Rav Zilberstein infers from here a valuable lesson in education and parenting. When Yitzchak commanded Yaakov to marry only from a specific milieu, he placed some very clear restrictions upon him. By limiting Yaakov to a specific group of people, Yitzchak was imposing a lot on his son. Perhaps he would not find a wife to his satisfaction among Rivkah's family. Who says that Lavan would agree to the match? Therefore, before Yitzchak could impose these restrictions on his son, he blessed him. Doing this would render his command more palatable and would insure its acceptance.

What a contrast to those parents who feel that the only way to raise their children is by exercising an iron fist. Placing restrictions and imposing obstacles every step of the way will only strain a relationship. While it is true that it is necessary to lay down the rules and that some rules must be inflexible, there is a way to present these rules on a positive note. Give the blessing of good will before you send the child to a corner. This way, he will at least realize that your intentions are noble.

※ ※ ※ ※ ※ ※

ועיני לאה רכות ורחל היתה יפת תאר ויפת מראה

Leah's eyes were tender, while Rachel was beautiful of form and beautiful of appearance. (29:17)

*C*hazal tell us that Leah's eyes were tender because she wept constantly in prayer that she would not have to marry Eisav. People would say that Rivkah had two sons and her brother, Lavan, had two daughters. The elder daughter would marry the elder son, and the younger daughter would marry the younger son. Leah's prayers were answered: Not only did she not marry Eisav, she even was the first to marry Yaakov. In his *sefer Simchas HaTorah, Horav Simchah Hakohen Sheps, zl,* notes that while Leah was the one who wept profusely because she was concerned about her fate, in the eternal scheme of things it was Rachel who was designated as the one who cries for her children. Her tears leave an impression. Hashem listens to her pleas. Why? Indeed, once she gave up her opportunity to wed Yaakov, she had every reason to fear that Eisav would seek to marry her. What is there about Rachel's tears that render their influence more favorable than those of any of the other Matriarchs?

Rav Sheps explains that the nature of Rachel's tears was different than Leah's because the two women had two distinct personalities. Leah worried; she feared that she would fall into Eisav's clutches. Rachel, by her very nature, was a *baalas bitachon*; she had incredible trust in Hashem that everything would work out for her. She did not cry; she did not fear. This is the underlying meaning of "Leah's eyes were tender." She did not have the fortitude, the stoicism, to confront challenges, trials and tribulations with tenacity, forbearance and conviction. She wept profusely out of fear and anxiety. Rachel was "beautiful of form and appearance." She never manifested hopelessness. One would look at her and see beauty in the way she carried herself — proud, hopeful, and filled with courage and resolution. When she wept, her tears were heard. She was, therefore, selected to serve as *Klal Yisrael's* advocate par excellence.

Rav Sheps notes that we have turned the tables around. In regard to routine, simple pressures, such as earning a livelihood, instead of being like Rachel and maintaining a sense of *bitachon*, we act like Leah and worry and cry. We demonstrate everything but *bitachon*. In regard to the important things, such as our children's education, we are like Rachel: filled with *bitachon* that everything will work out — eventually.

To expand a bit upon the above thesis, we may cite *Chazal* who teach us that after the destruction of the *Bais HaMikdash*, all the gates through which prayers travel to Heaven were closed, except for the *Shaarei Demaos*, Gates of Tears. This means that currently it is much more difficult for our prayers to penetrate the Heavenly Court. There is one set of gates, however, that remains open: the Gates of Tears.

If the Gates of Tears never close, why have gates altogether? The purpose of a gate is to lock someone out. If the gates never close, what is their purpose? The *Kotzker Rebbe, zl,* explains that some tears do not get through — regardless. Tears of desperation and hopelessness do not penetrate the Heavenly Court. These do not represent Jewish tears. The tears of a Jew should reflect the individual's innermost and purest thoughts. These are tears of hope. They have the power to pierce the Heavens. The gates are there to distinguish between tears of hope and tears of hopelessness.

Regardless of how overwhelming and desperate a situation may seem, a Jew cannot give up hope. *The Izbitzer Rebbe, zl,* explains that we are called *Yehudim,* after *Shevet Yehudah,* because when Yosef confronted his brothers with the planted incriminating evidence, all the brothers gave up hope — except Yehudah. He immediately approached Yosef. He drew near to him in order to establish a dialogue. Yehudah never gave up hope. This attitude must epitomize all Jews.

❈ ❈ ❈ ❈ ❈ ❈

ותאמר הפעם אודה את ד' על כן קראה שמו יהודה

And she declared, "This time let me gratefully thank Hashem." Therefore, she called his name Yehudah. **(29:35)**

In the *Talmud Berachos 7b, Chazal* say that no one paid gratitude to Hashem until Leah made this statement. Was Leah really the first to thank Hashem? Does this mean that the *Avos*, Patriarchs, did not show their appreciation to Hashem? The *Kesav Sofer* responds after first citing *Chazal's* maxim, "He who recites *Hallel* daily scoffs Hashem." Why should someone who praises Hashem be castigated? Apparently, *Chazal* are teaching us a significant lesson in regard to awareness of Hashem's daily miracles. One who is the beneficiary of a miracle that goes beyond the parameters of Hashem's daily caring for us is motivated to render his gratitude with the lofty praises of *Hallel*. What about the daily miracles, however, that are cloaked in what we call "nature?" Are they to be ignored? Ostensibly, this person thanks Hashem only for the "miracles," but not for the "nature." One who says *Hallel* daily, who appreciates the "*Hallel* type" miracles, but ignores the daily miracles which we take for granted, scoffs Hashem.

Surely, Avraham and Yitzchak thanked and praised Hashem for the miracles which He wrought for them. Indeed, their lives were filled with miracles. Leah, on the other hand, thanked Hashem for giving her a child — a seemingly "natural" gift. She understood the gift of a child. She understood that *teva*, nature, is really *neis*, miracle. She taught the world that one must offer gratitude for the natural as well as for the miraculous.

A man once came into *shul*, bringing with him a *l'chaim*, a bottle of whiskey to share with the members in honor of the great miracle that occurred in his life. He had been walking down the street, when a car went out of control and hit him. *Baruch Hashem*, it was a minor injury. In gratitude to Hashem, he was sharing his good fortune with others. The next day, another member came into *shul* and also brought a "*l'chaim*" to share with others. Assuming that he was also the beneficiary of a great miracle, they all wanted to know what had happened to *him*. "Nothing," he said, "absolutely nothing. I walked down the street, and nothing happened to me. Is that not also a miracle?"

Horav Eliyahu Eliezer Dessler, zl, in his Michtav M'Eliyahu, explains the concept of *teva* and *neis* in the following manner. He cites the famous statement made by the *Rambam* at the end of *Parashas Bo* that one must be aware and believe that everything that occurs is actually a miracle. Nothing is natural. It is all the result of Hashem's will. If so, how does one distinguish between *neis* and *teva*? *Rav* Dessler explains that while everything that occurs is really miraculous, Hashem has set forth a process in the world whereby some miraculous occurrences are guised in the cloak of nature, which means they adhere to the rule of cause and effect. Only in certain circumstances, for unique individuals, does Hashem act outside the parameter of cause and effect, causing what *we* refer to as a miracle, to occur.

Let us give an example of cause and effect. One plants a seed in the ground, and in a few weeks it begins to sprout. The cause is the planting and watering. The effect is the natural result. It *seems* natural, but is it really so? Does it make sense that when a living seed is buried in the ground, it decays and germinates, producing a living plant? Is this not some form of *techiyas ha'meisim*, resurrection of the dead? Indeed, it is; if it would happen with a human being, it would be called a miracle, while with a seed, it is called natural and taken for granted. In other words, there is no difference between *neis* and *teva*, other than what we have become accustomed to believing.

In our times, we should be aware of the daily miracles that pursue us. The places that we did not go — and something terrible happened; the places that we did go and to our good fortune — we "lucked out." It was just a couple of years ago following the 9/11 tragedy, that so many people became aware of the idea of *neis* and *teva*, and how what seemed to be an oversight, or a nuisance, was Hashem's gift of life — for some.

The following story caught my eye as an incident of *neis* which some might casually write off as *teva*. A group of Orthodox Jews prayed daily in a small, makeshift synagogue near the Twin Towers. Rarely was there a problem with a *minyan*, quorum. On September 11th, for *some reason,* they just could not put together a *minyan*. Perhaps the regular worshippers had opted to stay at their resident *shuls* for the *Selichos* services. Or, perhaps they were among the two hundred men who worked at the Twin Towers but were <u>late</u> to work that fateful day because they attended a *Shloshim*, one-month anniversary service, for a group of Jews killed in a helicopter crash over the Grand Canyon. Whatever the reason, only nine men were present for the *minyan*. It was getting late, and they *all* had to be at work at the World Trade Center well before 9:00AM. They looked at their watches and the time to leave for work was fast approaching. What should they do? They never missed *minyan*. Especially during *Selichos,* with *Rosh Hashanah* approaching, they had to try to get the proverbial tenth man.

As they were about to give up, an elderly gentleman shuffled in, asking, "Did you *daven* yet? I have to say *Kaddish*, the memorial prayer, for my father. It is his *yahrzeit*, the anniversary of his passing, and I would like to *daven* for the *amud*, lead the services."

Under normal circumstances, the members would have questioned the man: Who was he? Where did he come from? Was he observant? By now, however, they were frantic. It was late, and they had to move on — or they would be late for work. The man proved to be anything but a fast *davener*. He turned the pages and read the words at an agonizingly slow pace. The members were literally climbing the walls. Indeed, it seemed as if every gesture, every movement, every sound the man made was deliberate. The worshippers nonetheless respected his slow pace.

Suddenly, during their insistent complaining about being late for work, they heard the first plane explode! They heard the horrible blast that would forever cause their hearts and souls to shudder. They ran outside and saw the mass hysteria, the chaos and the thick smoke that lay before them.

"It should have been us," they thought. After the initial shock wore off, they realized that they had been *miraculously* spared from the jaws of death. Each and every one of them would have been there if not for the *minyan* and the elderly man who appeared from nowhere and who had *davened* so slowly. By the way, where was that man? They looked around, because they wanted to grab him and shower him with thanks. Where was that elusive mystery man who was probably the reason they were alive?

They would never know the answer to that question, however, because just as he had suddenly appeared — he disappeared. During the commotion, he must have slipped out of *shul*. Now is that *teva* or *neis*?

ויען לבן ...הבנות בנתי והבנים בני והצאן צאני וכל אשר אתה ראה לי הוא

Then Lavan spoke up... "The daughters are my daughters, the children are my children, and the flock is my flock, and all that you see is mine."

(31:43)

Lavan's response was to be expected: arrogant and insolent. It did not, however, respond to Yaakov's demand. Lavan pursued Yaakov and threatened him. Yaakov responded from the depths of over twenty years of frustration, describing his dedication and integrity beyond what was expected of him. He cited the many times that he had been mistreated and shortchanged by Lavan. How did Lavan respond to these claims? He said simply, "Your wives are mine; your children are mine; your sheep are mine; whatever you possess is mine." In other words, he did not respond to Yaakov. He ignored him — completely!

A famous incident occurred between the *Brisker Rav, zl*, and the *Chafetz Chaim, zl*. This dialogue serves as a portent for future relationships with our non-Jewish neighbors. The *Brisker Rav* once had a two-hour layover in Warsaw. As he was waiting in the station, he was notified that the *Chafetz Chaim* was presently in Warsaw. The *Brisker Rav* immediately ordered a wagon and driver, so that he could visit the *Chafetz Chaim*. During their conversation, the *Chafetz Chaim* shared the following incident with him. The *Chafetz Chaim* yearned to visit *Eretz Yisrael*. He decided to apply for an exit visa. The ministry of immigration said that he would have to produce a valid birth certificate before they could process his application. He told them that he had been born over ninety years ago, at a time when they were not issuing birth certificates. The only other alternative was to produce two witnesses from the same town who remembered his birth. The *Chafetz Chaim* looked at the minister incredulously, "The witnesses would have to be over one-hundred-years old!" To find two such witnesses was impossible.

"Now," continued the *Chafetz Chaim*, "what was the minister thinking? He certainly understood that his demand was impossible for me to fulfill. Why did he make such an impossible request of me? The answer lies in *Parashas Vayetzei* — and he cited the above *pasuk* in which Lavan basically dismissed Yaakov, saying, "Everything is mine. You have no claim on anything!" Lavan disregarded Yaakov's reasoning, overriding it with the notion that since everything is mine, you are a nobody and unable to demand anything of me.

"The same idea applies to our position in Polish society. We are nothing in their eyes. They view us as non-entities with no claim to anything. We are dismissed and ignored. Our feelings and sensitivities are totally meaningless to them."

Lavan did not consider himself arrogant. He viewed Yaakov as a nothing, someone whom he could dismiss without any compunction. This type of anti-Semitism is worse than blatant hatred. Not to be considered a people, to be regarded as a nonentity, to be dismissed without reason, to be relegated to a position of insignificance is worse than hatred. This demeaning view of our People is self-inflicted. We ask for it when we refuse to act like a *Torah* nation with pride and dignity. When we attempt to act like them, we become like them. What is there about us that is worthy of respect? We are not religious. We are not moral. We are not ethical. We are no different than the nations around us. Our assimilation indicates our insecurity. No one cares for an insecure person. Why should the nations of the world have regard for an insecure, vacillating nation? The cure for anti-Semitism is simple: act in the manner in which a Jew was created and instructed to act; the hatred will dissipate, and the respect will return.

Parashas Vayishlach

באנו אל אחיך אל עשו וגם הלך לקראתך וארבע מאות איש עמו

"We came to your brother, to Eisav; moreover, he is heading towards you, and four hundred men are with him." (32:7)

R ashi comments on the above *pasuk*, "You might think that he comes toward you as a brother. He is not. The four hundred men that he has gathered together are a war party, and you are to be the victim. Eisav is coming as Eisav!" Yet, despite Eisav's deep-rooted enmity toward Yaakov *Avinu*, when they met, Eisav embraced and kissed him. Was this accidental — or manipulative? *Rashi* cites the *Midrash*, that says that while it is a known axiom that Eisav despised Yaakov, at that moment, his feelings of brotherly love were stirred and, therefore, his embrace and the kiss were sincere. What brought about this total change of heart? Eisav left with one objective — to exact vengeance and kill Yaakov. Suddenly, his emotional disposition reversed and reconciliation was in the air. What happened? *Rashi* explains that when Eisav saw Yaakov bowing to him so many times, his compassion was moved. There is no question that if someone bows down to us a number of times, it leaves a strong impression. Was Eisav not above this? In the wake of a personal experience, *Horav Yosef Chaim Sonnenfeld, zl,* offers the following rationale for Yaakov's demonstration of reverence and Eisav's consequent transformation.

The old Orthodox Jewish community in *Yerushalayim* was boldly independent of the secular Zionist movement that viewed itself as the sole representative of the Jewish People inhabiting *Eretz Yisrael*. The Zionists harbored no love for the Orthodox Jew. More than once, the antagonism led to blatant physical hostility. One time, a group of thugs barged into *Rav* Yosef Chaim's house as he was studying with his grandson. They shouted all sorts of threats at him as the representative and leader of the "traitors" who dared to undermine the leadership of the Jews of Palestine. *Rav* Yosef Chaim did not budge. Instead, he sat calmly staring at them, with pity and sorrow for those who had estranged themselves from their noble heritage.

They became so unnerved by *Rav* Yosef Chaim's response, that they began to make physical threats. The aged *rav* arose from his chair and began to unbutton his shirt, until he bared his chest. He looked them defiantly in the eye and said, "I am prepared to give up my life to sanctify Hashem's Name. Shoot me — right here and now. I promise not to resist! We are not afraid of you or your threats. We seek only peaceful coexistence. As we have no influence on your sphere of activities, we ask that you not interfere in our matters of religion and permit us to operate independently. No threats will defeat us!"

It appeared as if they were about to attack the *rav*, when suddenly, they turned around and left. What happened that changed their minds?

Some time later, *Rav* Yosef Chaim explained that it was Yaakov *Avinu* and his behavior toward Eisav that inspired the way he acted toward the thugs. "*Chazal* tell us that it is axiomatic that Eisav hates Yaakov, but we must also remember that Yaakov hates Eisav as well." This is to be gleaned from the *pasuk* in *Tehillim* 139:21, "Those who hate you, I hate." Yet, when Yaakov saw Eisav coming towards him with four hundred men, he reacted by bowing down to the ground seven times. Yaakov acted wisely. He repressed his feelings of animosity toward Eisav, focusing instead on the positive aspects and character traits that Eisav possessed. He did this until he "reached his brother," figuratively it means that he overcame his feelings of hatred until he could feel a true sense of closeness and brotherhood with Eisav. This genuine attitude of brotherly love that emanated from Yaakov transformed Eisav's hatred into love.

This is how we must relate to our brethren that have alienated themselves from the *Torah* way. Look for their positive traits; seek out the good in them. By judging them favorably, we will dispel their animus toward us. When I look at those men as brothers, it compels them to change their attitude toward me. It is difficult to hate someone who loves you. Let us learn from our Patriarch Yaakov how to deal with those who demonstrate malice toward us.

✶ ✶ ✶ ✶ ✶

ויותר יעקב לבדו ויאבק איש עמו... ויגע בכף ירכו...

Yaakov was left alone and a man wrestled with him... he struck the socket of his hip. **(32:25,26)**

The confrontation between Yaakov *Avinu* and the *Sar Shel Eisav*, angel of Eisav, is a seminal event in the history of our nation. This is the foreshadowing of the many confrontations, trials and tribulations we have undergone throughout history. Yet, in the course of the many persecutions, we have survived and even thrived. *Horav S. R. Hirsch, zl,* observes that there are three levels of Jewish status in *galus*, exile. The first is analogous to the status of Avraham *Avinu*. "You are a prince of G-d in our midst" (*Bereishis* 23:5).The world respected him. He was free from jealousy, discrimination or harm. Not only was his Jewishness not a liability, it was actually beneficial to his maintaining a revered status in society.

The second type of status was that of Yitzchak *Avinu*. While he had great influence and was able to live a Jewish life among the pagans that surrounded him, he was nonetheless subject to envy, harassment and blatant bigotry — both economic and social. Yet, Yitzchak maintained his dignity. He continued prospering, but his profile was lower than that of his father. He saw the storm clouds of anti-Semitism gathering. He was acutely aware of what the future had in store for his descendants.

The third status is that of Yaakov *Avinu*. He suffered overt persecution, physical threats to his life, demeaning and derogatory remarks. He worked as a despised and lowly servant whose work was denigrated. Yaakov suffered, but persevered. He was obsequious, but persistent. He could not change the situation, living with enmity and derision all his life. What kept him going was his tenacity and faith. Indeed, the more he was hated, the more he was compelled to turn to his Jewishness for solace and strength.

We ask ourselves: Where are we today? We live more than sixty years after the perpetration of the greatest act of blatant anti-Semitism, the Holocaust. Regrettably, all too many of us tend — or seek — to forget that an entire world stood silent as we were brutally and mercilessly slaughtered. Our own host country, the United States, along with its president, turned a deaf ear to the pleas. The murder of the Jews elicited no sympathy in the media. There is no room in this book to record the many opportunities that would have helped our people. Moreover, we are discovering now that a U.S. President of that era, who *seemed* to be our friend, really viewed us as parasites.

Interestingly, the liberal *New York Times*, a paper not known for its support of the Jewish cause, some time ago ran an editorial that addresses the crux of German anti-Semitism. The editorial was entitled, "One Little Boy." It began by posing a series of questions: "Why the search for Nazis twenty years after World War II? Why does bitterness still burn as a hot coal in the hearts of millions throughout the world? Why are so many decent human beings unable to manage to find in their hearts the capacity to forgive and forget?

One of the reasons may be a story that was published in this newspaper. A book has recently been published, documenting the fate of the one and one-half million Jewish children under sixteen years of age in Hitler's concentration camps. The following few sentences from the story are sufficient:

"Then the guard ordered the children to fold their clothes neatly and march into the gas chamber and crematorium. One little boy, less than two–years–old, was too little to climb the steps. So the guard took the child in his arms and carried him into the chamber." There is the reason — one little boy.

Six million is a figure that is incomprehensible. While we say it in one breath, we really do not fathom the enormity of the statistic. One and one-half million children under the age of sixteen is a staggering figure. But it does not really tug at the emotions in the same manner that one little boy under the age of two who could not climb the stairs does. He was lifted up by the guard. This statistic bespeaks the fiendishness of the Nazis, the enormity of the outrage, the unspeakable magnitude of the disaster. If we are seeking insight into the hatred toward the Jews that embodied the Nazi, we have found it in the above article.

Today in the western world, this form of malignant hatred does not exist. *Bnei Yishmael*, the Arab nations, harbor a venomous hatred for everything Jewish, but "officially" they are not supported by the western world. Where does that leave us today? We might be tempted to say that we have achieved "Yitzchak" status. Some might even hypothesize that we are approaching "Avraham's" position. Time will tell whether this is true, or whether today is just another calm before the storm. The *Bais HaLevi* draws a parallel between assimilation and anti-Semitism. In other words, the more we attempt to acculturate and decrease the distinction between Jew and gentile, the more Hashem will turn the nations against us. We have the prescription for success. We now have to adhere to it.

What happened to the *yerech* Yaakov, the hip socket, where the angel seemingly bested Yaakov? What does that represent? Perhaps it refers to another form of enmity that is just as virulent and equally destructive — the hatred among brothers. The friction that exists between *frum* and non-*frum, chiloni* and *chareidi,* especially in *Eretz Yisrael,* is a new form of antagonism that has emerged. Moreover, the antagonism that reigns even among the various camps of the observant community is not only a *chillul Hashem,* it is delaying *Moshiach Tzidkeinu's* arrival. Regrettably, we have learned to cope with the external aggression, but the internal conflict seems to be eating away at the very core of our nation. Eisav's angel knew exactly where to strike to prevent Yaakov *Avinu* from moving forward. Throughout the darkness of night/*galus,* we prevailed — as Yaakov did. As light approaches — as the light of *Torah* becomes stronger and begins to illuminate the world — we become bogged down with petty *machlokes,* controversy, which prevents us from moving forward and reaching out to the wider community. Yes, Eisav's angel knew exactly where to strike.

וישבו בארץ ויסחרו אתה
"Let them settle in the land and trade in it." (34:21)

It seems like a simple vocation: settle in the land and apply yourself to commerce. It *seems* simple, but — as we may note from the following narrative — there is a profound lesson to be derived from every endeavor in life. To those who view the various occurrences in their lives as "simple" happenings, they present nothing more than the perspective of a "simple" person. We can and should learn a lesson from everything that occurs. Otherwise, we continue to remain "simple."

Prior to his being revealed as the great *tzaddik* and *rebbe, Horav Moshe Leib Sassover, zl,* lived with his wife and children in abject poverty. One wealthy person in the town provided the family's support. One day, his benefactor asked *Rav* Moshe Leib, "Is this going to go on forever? Do you really think that an individual of your scholarship should live from week to week from my support? I will give you a sizable amount of venture capital to go to the market and try your luck. Hashem will surely bless your endeavor, and you will succeed financially."

Rav Moshe Leib took the advice and went to the market together with all of the other businessmen. Each individual businessman sought out the wares that he would purchase for resale, while *Rav* Moshe Leib went to the *bais ha'medrash* to study *Torah*. At the end of the day, as everyone was packing up their wares, *Rav* Moshe Leib returned and wanted to purchase some commodities for resale. "Now you come!" they exclaimed. "The market hours are over. We are packing up to return home. You are too late." *Rav* Moshe Leib had no recourse but to return home — empty handed.

When he arrived home, his children ran out to greet him, asking, "Father, Father, what did you bring us from the marketplace?" As soon as *Rav* Moshe Leib heard this, he fainted and became ill. He took to his bed to recuperate. The benefactor who had originally given him the money came to visit. Noting *Rav* Moshe Leib's despondence, he asked, "*Rebbe*, what is wrong? Did you lose the money? Perhaps you gave it all away to the poor? Tell me, and I will give you more money."

After awhile, *Rav* Moshe Leib's color returned and he was ready to speak. He looked at his friend and said, "A person travels away from his home to the market for a day or two at the most. When he returns, his children ask him, 'Father, Father, what have you brought for us?' I had nothing to respond. How much more should I fear the day when I will have to go home to my final judgment, to the World of Truth where I will stand before the Heavenly Tribunal and be asked, 'What did you bring with you?' What will I answer then? Has my life been that replete with *Torah* and *mitzvos* that I am able to take off more time to spend in the market? What will I have to show for my stay in this world?"

"*Rebbe*, you are correct," said the man. "It is far better that you should spend your time immersed in *Torah*." It was soon after this incident that *Rav* Moshe Leib's reputation as a *tzaddik* began to spread and he became the famous *Sassover Rebbe*. He taught us not to ignore a simple occurrence. Furthermore, he *immediately* applied the lesson he gleaned to change the course of his life.

✽ ✽ ✽ ✽ ✽ ✽

וישב יעקב בארץ מגורי אביו

And Yaakov settled in the land of his father's sojournings. (37:1)

To settle implies permanency, while to sojourn denotes wandering. The contrast between Yaakov *Avinu's* "settling" and his father's "sojournings" prompts *Chazal* to state that, after Yaakov's arduous struggles, he finally sought to settle down in tranquility. The anguish of Yosef immediately overwhelmed him. *Chazal* explain that the righteous are not placed on this world to relax. They should be satisfied with what awaits them in the World to Come. This does not mean that Yaakov *Avinu* sought a vacation and was deprived of it. He just wanted to devote himself totally to spiritual perfection without confrontation. He thought that he had completed his task and laid the framework for the future of *Klal Yisrael*. Apparently, Hashem had other plans for him, plans that integrated the ensuing events and tribulations into the fiber of *Klal Yisrael*.

From a practical point of view, we note that as long as Yaakov's life hangs in the balance of Eisav's sword, peace reigns in the family. When the danger is from without, all of those within unify, remaining strong. When Eisav leaves us alone and we attempt a life of tranquility, the ideological confrontations between brethren prevail. Sometimes having "free time," peace and quiet, yields to anguish. It all depends how the added time is used.

The episode of Yosef and his brothers has repeated itself throughout the millennia under various guises and scenarios. Yosef's dreams were a source of dispute. Likewise, many of today's controversies center around nothing essential: dreams. The *Torah* writes that <u>first</u>, "they hated him" (v. 4) and <u>afterwards</u>, "the brothers were jealous of him" (v. 11). First comes the hatred; later, we seek a rationale to justify our feelings and actions. We are not prepared to sit down and talk. Dialogue appears to be a sign of weakness. "The brothers saw him [Yosef] from afar… They conspired against him to kill him" (v. 18). They did not give him a chance to talk, to explain himself.

They acted as witness, judge and jury simultaneously. An enmity that does not leave room for the option of dialogue leads to destruction.

True, the brothers had lofty reasons for their action, reasons steeped in *Halachah* that were unimpeachable — according to their arbitration of the law. Nonetheless, *mechiras Yosef*, the sale of Yosef, set the stage in history for intense controversy — even hatred — among brothers.

✱ ✱ ✱ ✱ ✱ ✱

וישראל אהב את יוסף מכל בניו כי בן זקנים הוא לו

Now Yisrael loved Yosef more than all of his sons, since he was a child of his old age. **(37:3)**

Yosef was born in Yaakov's old age, which was why he felt a greater affection for him. Although Binyamin was even younger than Yosef, Yaakov had developed this deep love for Yosef during the eight years prior to Binyamin's birth. This is hard to believe. If Yaakov's old age was the main factor, he should have harbored at least the same — if not greater — affection for Binyamin.

I once heard that it was not only Yosef himself that Yaakov loved; it was what Yosef represented and reminded him of. Yaakov *Avinu* loved his wife Rachel. Yosef was an extension of Rachel. He remembered the overwhelming love Rachel had for her only child. Yaakov loved Yosef because Rachel loved Yosef. Yosef brought back the memories of what Yaakov endured to marry his mother. This increased his love for him. Although Binyamin was also Rachel's son, he did not have the opportunity to be raised by his mother. Therefore, Yaakov did not view him in the same light as he did Yosef.

Perhaps this is the meaning of *ben zekunim*, child of his old age. Anguish and pain can age a person. Yaakov's marriage and eventual fathering of a child with Rachel did not come easily. It took time and was fraught with pain and tribulation. Finally, she had a son, but by that time Yaakov had aged prematurely. He went through so much to see this day. Yosef represented all that had aged him.

Bearing this in mind, the jealousy the brothers had towards Yosef had a more significant meaning. It was jealousy borne out of respect for the honor of their mother. They viewed Yaakov's exceptional love for Yosef as an affront to their mother, Leah. Indeed, the fact that Yaakov felt this way about Yosef and not Binyamin only served to validate their feelings. It was Rachel that Yaakov loved, and Yosef represented Rachel. Their mother was not loved by Yaakov in the same manner that he cared for Rachel.

It was not their own *kavod*, honor, for which they envied, hated and fought. It was for their mother's *kavod*. It was not for their own *kavod* that they would resort to killing or selling a brother into slavery. It was not for their own *kavod* that they would cause overwhelming pain and anguish to their aged father. It was all for their mother's *kavod*.

It might all have been true. Undoubtedly the *Shivtei Kah* were righteous and virtuous, so that their every action was well thought out — according to their perspective. Regrettably, over the generations, many have attempted to validate their own envies and hatred towards one another by using Yosef and his brothers as a precedent. All this demonstrates is how far we are from understanding what really occurred between Yosef and his brothers.

✳ ✳ ✳ ✳ ✳ ✳

וילכו אחיו לרעות את צאן אביהם בשכם

Now, his brothers went to pasture their father's flock in Shechem. (37:12)

*R*ashi notes that according to the *Masoretic* tradition, a dot is placed above both of the letters of the word *es* in the *Torah* scroll. This alludes to the fact that they went to the pasture only to indulge themselves. The *Gur Aryeh* explains that it was the brothers' indulgence in eating and drinking that led to their sin. The entire episode between Yosef and his brothers cannot be understood superficially. We are not dealing here with a band of thugs who casually tried to murder their brother out of envy and hatred. As *Sforno* explains, whatever they did was *halachically* correct. Indeed, years later when they were in Egypt and saw that things were not working out well for them, their only regret was for acting without compassion when Yosef entreated them to spare his life. Otherwise, they saw nothing wrong with their actions against Yosef. This was a spiritual battle over the right of the firstborn. After all was said and done, the brothers felt justified, but one question bothers us that must be addressed: Why did they not consult with Yaakov *Avinu*? He was the preeminent *Torah* authority of the day: speak to him; ask him for direction; act upon his guidance. Why did they act without asking?

Horav Yechezkel Abramsky, zl, explains that the brothers felt that Yaakov's objectivity was impaired in regard to Yosef. The greatest and most astute judge can only render the *halachah* as he sees it. If Yaakov's perspective had been limited, however, because he had fallen under the pervasive effect of Yosef's guile and charm, he could no longer adjudicate a fair and unbiased decision.

This is where they erred. They thought that *they* perceived objectively, while Yaakov's perspective was flawed. They were wrong. It was *their* perspective that was jaundiced, while Yaakov's vision was clear and unimpaired. Our *Gedolei Yisrael, Torah* luminaries, see farther, and their sight penetrates deeper because their line of vision is on a higher plane. It may be compared to a group of sailors who are on a boat searching for land. Suddenly, the sailor who is standing on top of the mast thirty feet in the air yells that he sees land. The sailors on the boat foolishly argue with him, questioning his ability to see. They fail to recognize that his lofty position affords him a greater range of view.

Rashi alludes to this idea when he says that the brothers went to Shechem to indulge *themselves.* This was their error. They thought of themselves. They saw only their needs. Yaakov, on the other hand, saw what they were not capable of seeing.

The brothers' inability to accept the advice of a *zakein,* elderly, experienced, erudite individual has repeated itself throughout history. In his commentary to *pasuk* 14, "And he (Yosef) arrived in Shechem," *Rashi* comments that "Shechem was a place prepared for adversity: there the tribes acted sinfully; there the *Shechemites* violated Dinah; there the kingdom of David *HaMelech* was divided." What is the relationship between these three incidents? In all three, the error reverts to one source: they thought only of themselves, acting alone without seeking or accepting advice. In the episode of Dinah, Shimon and Levi attacked the *Shechemites* with a bloody vengeance. They did not confer with their father, who would have vetoed their action.

When Rechavam, son of Shlomo *HaMelech,* ascended his father's throne, the people petitioned him to abolish some of the former king's harsher decrees. First, Rechavam took counsel with the elders who encouraged him to listen to the people. He later conferred with his young colleagues, who urged him to rule with an iron fist. Regrettably, Rechavam listened to them. As a result, the people revolted, and Yeravam was able to establish the kingdom of Yisrael. *Chazal* derive from here that the advice of elders is more beneficial because their vision has a wider and more penetrating perspective to it.

In his book, *Touched By A Story*, Rabbi Yechiel Spero relates a fascinating story that occurred concerning the *Ponevezher Rav, zl* It was during World War II when Nazi general Rommel stood poised to vanquish *Eretz Yisrael*. Success seemed imminent. It was at this time that the *Ponevezher Rav* had suffered what doctors suspected to be a stroke. Under his doctor's orders, he was confined to bed and not permitted to speak.

As soon as the *Rav* heard the latest news from the battlefront, he literally sprung into action. The man, who moments earlier had lain helpless, called over one of his students and wrote the following three instructions: "Inform *Rav* Shmuel Rosovsky that I want him to assume the position of *Rosh HaYeshivah* in *Eretz Yisrael*; a wealthy man has offered to give money to the *yeshivah*; tell him I accept the offer and I will repay him shortly; last, here is a list of ten *bachurim*, young men, I have spoken to regarding their attending the *yeshivah;* inform them that the *zman*, semester, begins the day after tomorrow."

Within a day, the messages were delivered, and the wheels were set in motion for the *yeshivah* to begin. The *Rav's* action paved the way for the future success of the Ponovezh Yeshivah in *Eretz Yisrael*. When the *Rav* was later queried concerning what inspired him to press forward at a time when the future of *Eretz Yisrael* appeared so bleak, he said, "I decided that regardless of what happened concerning the war, there had to be a living memorial to the original Ponevezh Yeshivah."

Here we have a classic example of two visions: the vision of those who saw tragedy, destruction and despair; and the perspective of the great visionary, the Ponevezher *Rav*, who saw hope, success and the future of

Torah in *Eretz Yisrael*. How lucky we are to be the beneficiaries of such perceptive vision!

✳ ✳ ✳ ✳ ✳ ✳

וישב ראובן אל הבור

Reuven returned to the pit. (37:29)

Where was Reuven this entire time? *Chazal* say that he was involved in penance, repenting for his part in the episode of Yaakov's bed (see *Rashi* 35:22). The *Midrash* tells us that Hashem said to him, "Never has there been a circumstance in which a person sinned and later repented. Since you are the first to begin with repentance, your reward will be that your descendant, the *Navi* Hoshea, will exhort *Klal Yisrael* to repent with the words: *Shuvah Yisrael*, Return O' *Yisrael*." *Chazal's* statement is enigmatic. Was Hoshea really the first to introduce *teshuvah*, repentance? Is there not a chapter in *Parashas Netzavim* that deals solely with the idea of *teshuvah*?

In the *sefer Kochvei Ohr,* the following analogy is cited to explain this *Midrash*. A scholar lost his mind and humiliated a venerable, pious sage. After the slanderer was healed and returned to his senses, he sought some way to apologize, but was overcome with shame. How could he face the *Torah* luminary that he had insulted so shamefully? Even to compel himself to go to the great man was overly difficult. If, however, the sage would send an agent specifically to ask him to come apologize — sort of to "break the ice" — he could bring himself to go.

The same idea applies in regard to *teshuvah*. True, the *Torah* dedicates a considerable amount of space to the concept of *teshuvah*, but what about the humiliation? Hashem wants us to repent, but repentance takes a certain amount of stoicism to overcome the shame that we feel regarding our transgression. The mere knowledge that the concept of repentance exists is not sufficient to bring the sinner to repent. He needs a push, a little nudge to help him get over the embarrassment. This is what Hashem did for us. Hashem introduced us to *teshuvah*. He also sent us Hoshea, whose clarion call invited us to repent. When Hashem sends His agent to help us along the way, it makes the repentance much more palatable. It gives us the courage to overcome our shame. Hoshea did not introduce *teshuvah*; he encouraged it.

ותאכלנה הפרות רעות המראה ודקת הבשר את שבע הפרות יפת המראה
והבריאת

The cows of ugly appearance and gaunt flesh ate the seven cows that were
of beautiful appearance and robust. **(41:4)**

There must be some purpose in having the ugly cows swallow up the healthy cows. It seems to be more than a minor detail. Yosef interpreted it to mean that the seven years of famine would be so severe and drastic that they would overshadow the years of plenty to the point that they would be completely forgotten. Yet, the seven lean cows swallowing up the seven robust cows does not seem to express this idea. While the seven years of famine might be ruinous, they did not interfere with the comfort level enjoyed during the seven years of abundance. Why was it necessary for the gaunt cows to *swallow up* the healthy cows?

Horav Yosef Chaim Sonnenfeld, zl, explains that there is a significant lesson about human nature to be derived from this dream. A person may be blessed with incredible bounty, but, if he knows that the time he has left for enjoying this gift is very short, his enjoyment will be limited, at best. One who is about to be executed hardly enjoys his last meal, regardless of how tasty it may be. The Egyptians were aware that the wonderful years of abundance were to last for a limited amount of time, to be followed by years of famine and disaster. How could they enjoy the gift, knowing fully well what was soon to befall them? Every time they ate a delicious, bountiful meal, they thought of the impending doom that would result in the upcoming famine. The dream was quite accurate in describing the years of famine. The seven years of famine would actually erode any remembrance of the years of bounty. *In anticipation* of the pain, the enjoyment could hardly be felt.

ויאמר פרעה אל יוסף... אין נבון וחכם כמוך. אתה תהיה על ביתי ועל פיך
ישק כל עמי

Then Pharaoh said to Yosef... "There can be no one so discerning and
wise as you...You shall be in charge of my house and by your command
shall all my people be sustained." (41:39,40)

Yosef certainly came across as wise, astute and knowledgeable. He
was wiser than anyone Pharaoh had previously employed as an
advisor. Yet, how does a king of Pharaoh's stature take a
"criminal" out of jail and almost immediately make him Viceroy over the
land of Egypt? Yosef was given the "keys" to the country! Is that the way a
wise king acts? Could he have not simply appointed Yosef as Secretary of
Finance and Agriculture? Why make him Viceroy?

Horav Chaim Shmuelevitz, zl, explains that the answer lies in one
word — *biladoi,* "this is beyond me" (41:16). Yosef could just as well have
said, *b'ezras Hashem,* with Hashem's help, I will interpret the dream. No! he
did not attribute any power to himself whatsoever. Everything came from
Hashem. He attributed all of his success to Hashem. A person such as this
was a unique find. Pharaoh had never met such an individual who took
absolutely no credit for himself. Such a person could be trusted to direct his
country.

In the ensuing years of bounty that Egypt would experience, there
was great opportunity for an enterprising individual to put a little away for
himself. Later on, during the years of famine, this person could make a
healthy profit from his foresight. Yes, this is what the average person might
do. A person who was prepared to give everything up and not take any credit
for himself, however, was above taking personal gain — albeit legal — from
the country's bounty. Such a person was unique. He was worthy of
immediately being put into place to govern the land.

As Jews, we should always realize that *biladoi* — everything comes
directly from Hashem. Whatever success we achieve has one source:
Hashem. This awareness should fortify our faith and trust in the Almighty as
it gives us the fortitude to confront life's challenges stoically, with
determination and courage.

✽ ✽ ✽ ✽ ✽ ✽

ויאמרו איש אל אחיו אבל אשמים אנחנו על אחינו אשר ראינו צרת נפשו
בהתחננו אלינו ולא שמענו על כן באה אלינו הצרה הזאת

*They then said one to another, "Indeed, we are guilty concerning our
brother inasmuch as we saw his heartfelt anguish when he pleaded with us
and we paid no heed; that is why this anguish has come upon us." (42:21)*

The brothers' regret and consequent confession regarding their lack
of compassion to Yosef's pleas constituted a turning point in the
story of *mechiras Yosef*, sale of Yosef. They acknowledged the
degree of their culpability and recognized that what was occurring to them,
the anguish caused by the Egyptian Viceroy, was the result of this previous
lack of compassion. *The Brisker Rav, zl,* was wont to say that every religious
decree that is enacted against us by those who seek to undermine our
religious observance is the direct result of <u>our</u> own failing in that area. When
we are complacent in regard to *tznius*, moral chastity, decrees are made that
endanger our ability to maintain proper morality. When edicts are legislated
that are harmful to *Torah* study, it is because we have been deficient in our
attitude toward *Torah* study. When we deprecate the value and sanctity of
Shabbos, injunctions will be made against our observance of *Shabbos*. In
other words, it is Hashem's way of conveying a message to us: you are not
acting properly.

When our *shemiras Shabbos, Shabbos* observance, is of a
heightened nature, when we study the laws of *Shabbos* and are proficient in
them, when our *Shabbos* is replete with *Torah* study, when our *Shabbos* table
is filled with song, then it will have a far-reaching effect on those around us.
Chillul Shabbos, desecration of *Shabbos*, is directly connected with our own
observance. Therefore, before we criticize and malign those of our brethren
who have strayed from the fold, let us focus the lens of condemnation on
ourselves. The *Brisker Rav* noted that we find that on *Yom Kippur* even those
who are usually non-observant will make an effort to fast, attend a *shul* and
refrain from traveling by car. Why? He explained that on *Yom Kippur* the
observant are on an unusually lofty spiritual plane, much more so than during
the year. This has a positive influence on the non-observant.

אבל אשמים אנחנו על אחינו אשר ראינו צרת נפשו בהתחננו אלינו ולא
שמענו

*"Indeed, we are guilty concerning our brother inasmuch as we saw his
heartfelt anguish when he pleaded with us and we paid no heed."* (42:21).

The brothers confessed their sin and indicated their contrition. This
is the beginning of the *teshuvah*, repentance, process. It seems like
they were properly motivated by heartfelt regret over their past
actions. If this was the case, why did Reuven involve himself, interjecting,
"Did I not tell you not to commit a sin with the child? You would not listen.
Now a (Divine) reckoning is being demanded for his blood" (42:22). Exactly
what was Reuven trying to do, add salt to their wounds? They apparently
regretted their lack of compassion for their brother's plea. Why make them
feel worse? Is this the way a would-be penitent is to be treated?

The commentators view Reuven's criticism in a different light. He
was not trying to hurt them, but rather to explain to them that the *teshuvah*
that they felt they had performed was incomplete. They were in error in
regard to their notion of the sin. It was not merely a lack of compassion on
their part that warranted this anguish. It was because they had "committed a
sin against the boy." Unquestionably, cruelty is a despicable character trait,
but Hashem does not punish people simply for being cruel. Divine retribution
is meted out against those who commit definite sins. *Teshuvah* is all-
important and necessary, but it is only effective if it is performed with the
correct sin in mind.

✽ ✽ ✽ ✽ ✽ ✽

אבל אשמים אנחנו על אחינו

"Indeed, we are guilty concerning our brother." (42:21)

Viddui, confession, is a primary component in the *teshuvah*,
repentance, process. Before one takes leave of his earthly
experience, he is enjoined to confess his sins so that he enters the
World of Truth pure and clean. *Ashamnu*, "we have become guilty," has
become the catchword of *Viddui*. I recently read a fascinating story of how
the *Klausenberger Rebbe, zl*, assembled thousands of Jewish survivors on
Erev Yom Kippur, immediately following the liberation from the infamous

death camps. The purpose: to speak to them about maintaining their religious observance. The method: he focused on the *Viddui* that we recite on *Yom Kippur*. The *Rebbe* had just undergone trial by fire in the camps. He had lost his wife and eleven children to the Nazis. Yet, his primary focus was on the deficiencies of faith in Hashem during the persecution that they had all experienced.

The *Rebbe* went up to the lectern and opened his *Machzor*. With bitter tears, he spoke not from the *Machzor*, but from the heart. Directing his monologue Heavenward, he began with *Ashamnu*. Rather than inflecting the word as a statement, he presented it as a question, "Did we sin? Did we rebel?

"Did we really sin? I hereby challenge the entire congregation. Is there one person here who was remiss in not repaying a loan? Nothing belonged to us — not even our bodies which were nothing more than receptacles for beatings and whippings. *Gozalnu*, we stole. Did we steal? From whom could we have stolen? No one owned anything. It was all confiscated by the Nazis. Wait — yes. I am guilty of theft! I admit that I stole. One day, upon returning from slave labor I collapsed into my bunk to rest, and my shriveled skin became caught between two boards. When I attempted to free myself, my skin tore from my bones. Blood streamed out, and I moaned softly. Regrettably, my moan was loud enough to wake up a fellow prisoner. Yes, I stole. I stole sleep from an exhausted prisoner. This is the only theft that I committed. I admit my iniquity!"

The *Rebbe* continued with his litany. "*Dibarnu dofi*, 'We spoke slander.' Did we slander? How could we? We did not even have the strength for idle conversation. If by chance we had any strength left, we saved it so that we could respond to the probing questions of our vicious tormentors. *He'evinu*, 'We caused perversion?' *Hirshanu*, 'We caused wickedness.' *Latznu*, 'We scorned.' Who could do such a thing here? We had no strength to do anything! *Moradnu*, 'We rebelled.' Against whom did we rebel? We could not muster enough strength to work. Rebellion was the last thing we could think of. We did not even have the strength to cry out as they beat us. We did not rebel against Hashem. We suffered in silence, accepting our fate."

The *Rebbe* finished the *Viddui*. After dismissing each and every sin as being physically impossible for them to have committed, he closed his *Machzor*. "We did not wrongfully sin. We committed no iniquity. This *Viddui* was not written for us!" The congregation just stood there, shock registering on their faces.

A few moments went by and the *Rebbe* raised up his voice again. "But we are guilty of sins that are not written in the *Machzor*. We did sin, perhaps in a minute and subtle manner, but we did sin. We sinned in our faith and trust in the Almighty. Did we not doubt Hashem out of despair and hopelessness in the camps? When we recited *Shma* at night, did we not hope it would be our last *Shma*, that the end to our suffering would finally come? How many times did we entreat Hashem, 'Master of the Universe, I have no more strength. Take my soul, so that I will no longer have to recite *Modeh Ani*.' And when daybreak came, and we were still alive and we were once again obligated to thank Hashem for 'returning my soul with great mercy,' were we not filled with rage? When we removed the corpses from the barracks, were we not envious that they no longer had to suffer?

"Yes, Hashem, this is how we sinned. We sinned with a lack of faith and trust. We should have held our heads up high, taking the suffering and pain, but we did not. And for this we beat our chests and confess our sins. Hashem, restore back our faith and trust in You. Help us to establish new families, so that we may perpetuate this faith in future generations. Above all, we must make *simchah*, joy, our foremost goal."

The *Rebbe's* words rang eternal for those in attendance. Everyone was moved beyond words. He brought out the inner yearning that every Jew has to return and be close with Hashem.

ויאמר יוסף אל אחיו אני יוסף... ולא יכלו אחיו לענות אתו

And Yosef said to his brothers, "I am Yosef"... But his brothers could not answer him. (45:3)

The episode of Yosef and his brothers finally reached its conclusion when Yosef revealed his identity with the words, "I am Yosef." Everything that had occurred during the past twenty-two years — the ambiguities and paradoxes, the strange, unexplained, unreasonable happenings — suddenly all had rationale and meaning. It had all come together. Yosef was truly a *Navi*, prophet, whose dreams were spiritual visions foreshadowing the future, not mere images of grandeur.

There is an important lesson to be derived from this twenty-two year incident. Nothing stands in the path of the Divine. Hashem has a plan, and it will reach fruition at its designated time. It was Hashem's will that Yosef become the viceroy of Egypt and that his father and brothers come down to Egypt and bow down to him. It happened — regardless of the brothers' machinations to thwart the plan. Not only did it materialize, but the brothers themselves provided the medium by which it became a reality.

Shlomo Ha'melech says in *Mishlei* (21:30), "There is neither wisdom, nor understanding, nor counsel against Hashem." *Ralbag* cites the episode of Yosef and his brothers as a paradigm of this idea. We conjure up ideas and prepare all kinds of plans, to no avail. Against Hashem's plan, our schemes are meaningless.

Horav Avraham Pam, zl, suggests that this concept has many practical applications. He cites one that is truly meaningful. An elderly parent becomes seriously ill. The children consult with a specialist to determine which course of treatment would be most beneficial. Two options are presented, each with its own risk and benefit potential. The family deliberates and makes a decision to follow one of the two approaches. Regrettably, the treatment fails, and the parent dies. The family is now besieged with guilt.

They blame themselves for choosing the wrong treatment, the wrong doctor, the wrong hospital. They begin to blame one another, imposing the onus of guilt on anyone but themselves.

This scenario is not unusual. In fact, it is common. What we fail to realize is that nothing — the doctor, the hospital, the therapy — would have made a difference, because it was not part of Hashem's plan. The family should do whatever is in line with their best understanding of the situation with the awareness that ultimately, if it does not coincide with Hashem's plan, it will not succeed.

Throughout the millennia, more than one wicked enemy has arisen to wipe us off the face of the earth. We are here today because it is part of Hashem's plan. It is a principle of our faith that this Divine protection will endure until the advent of *Moshiach Tzidkeinu*.

※ ※ ※ ※ ※ ※

ויפל על צוארי בנימן אחיו ויבך ובנימן בכה על צואריו

Then he fell upon his brother Binyamin's neck and wept; and Binyamin wept upon his neck. (45:14)

Rashi explains that the two brothers wept over the future destructions of the two *Bais HaMikdash*, which was to be situated on their portion in *Eretz Yisrael*. The two *Batei Mikdash* were to be built in Binyamin's territory, and the *Mishkon Shiloh* was to be erected in the territory of Yosef's son, Efraim. This commentary is enigmatic. In the very next *pasuk*, Yosef kisses his other brothers and also cries over them. Why does *Rashi* not explain over here that Yosef also cried over the destruction of the *Bais HaMikdash*? If the weeping was for the future, what does the crying over his brothers represent?

The *Piazesner Rebbe, zl,* cites the *Talmud* in *Rosh Hashanah* 28a that says, *Mitzvos laav l'hen'os nitnu*, "Commandments were not given to provide enjoyment." They were given to us as a yoke around our necks. The *mitzvos* engender a sense of discipline. This explains why the brothers cried on each other's neck. They each were lamenting the yoke of the *mitzvos* that would be shrugged off at the time of the destruction of the Holy Temple.

Each and every Jew has a yoke around his neck — *mitzvos*. He has responsibilities and obligations that he has to perform and fulfill as a Jew. Moreover, his thoughts and his speech must be holy. Even when he is physically prevented from carrying out the *mitzvos*, he must brace himself and remember that he has a yoke, a pending obligation to fulfill the Divine mandate.

In periods of catastrophe, when calamity and tragedy are a way of life, when suffering and pain overwhelm, and everything holy and Jewish is destroyed, people do not simply revoke their obligations due to the difficulty of observing the commandments. Yet, there are those who even shrug off the yoke of *mitzvos* in response to all of the pain and degradation that they endure. Yosef and Binyamin cried, each on the neck of the other, because they lamented shrugging off the yoke of *mitzvos* which was a result of the destruction of the *Batei Mikdash*. Yosef did not fall on his brothers' necks; he merely cried over them.

With this idea in mind, the *Piazesner* explains another anomaly. In the subsequent text, the *Torah* relates that when Yosef met his father, Yaakov *Avinu*, he fell upon his father's neck and cried, whereas Yaakov did not fall on Yosef's neck. *Rashi* explains that Yaakov, instead of falling upon Yosef's neck, was reciting *Krias Shma*. The famous questions echoed by all the commentators are: Why did Yaakov choose that particular moment to recite *Krias Shma*? And why did not Yosef also recite *Krias Shma*?

Considering that which has been suggested above, we can now understand the text. When Yosef met his father, he once again became cognizant of the spiritual calamity that would befall *Klal Yisrael* with the destruction of the Temple. He once again wept over the future shedding of the yoke of *mitzvos* associated with the catastrophe. This is the reason that the *Torah* refers to Yosef's weeping on his father's neck. The Jewish People were now entering the Egyptian *galus*, exile. Yosef wondered how, under these circumstances, they would be able to maintain the yoke of *mitzvos* around their necks.

Yaakov responded by reciting the *Shma*, the symbol of self-sacrifice. With *mesiras nefesh*, self-sacrifice, we will endure the trials and tribulations, the pain and persecution, that has so much been a part of our long exile. When we recite *Shma Yisrael*, we return our souls back to

Hashem, unconditionally and without reservation. The *Shma* recited in the morning sets the tone for the entire day. No one suggested that the exile would be easy, but with *mesiras nefesh*, we can and will triumph over the many challenges that arise.

When we think of *mesiras nefesh* for *mitzvah* observance, when we associate total dedication to *mitzvah* performance during the most difficult moments in Jewish history, we think of those who served Hashem during the most devastating and painful period of our history — the Holocaust years. One individual whose *mesiras nefesh* for *mitzvos* comes to the fore is the *Klausenberger Rebbe, zl,* who was the paradigm of total dedication to *mitzvah* observance — regardless of the danger and pain inflicted upon him. His devotion went beyond *mitzvah* observance. Indeed, any custom or tradition had to be maintained in the ghetto, even under the most trying conditions. This was *Yiddishkeit* — it could never be forgotten!

One incident that stands out among many, is the *Rebbe's* devotion to observing the Festival of *Shemini Atzeres.* This day, when Hashem communes exclusively with the Jewish People, is the crowning jewel of all the Festivals. It is the climax of the *Yamim Noraim*, High Holy Days, the zenith of the festival of *Succos.* It is the day when Hashem says to the Jewish People, "Come, let us celebrate together."

Although the *Rebbe* was a prisoner and, therefore, subject to the work detail, the camp doctor, Dr. Greenbaum, a Jew by birth, had agreed to grant the *Rebbe* an exemption, so that he could rest. In this way, the *Rebbe* did not have to work on *Succos. Shemini Atzeres* would be no different.

The Nazi *oberfuerher*, senior commander, had different plans. He decided to visit the camp together with Dr. Plukan, an evil woman, who was infamous for her selections, in which she would "weed out" the sick and infirm, immediately sending them to the crematorium in Dachau. Anyone missing at roll call was immediately sentenced to death. Word spread throughout the camp, and everyone immediately became concerned for the welfare of the *Rebbe.* Dr. Greenbaum was asked to change the *Rebbe's* dispensation. He would have to report for work, after all.

The *Rebbe*, however, had other plans. "Regardless of what happens to me, I will not work on *Shemini Atzeres*," he firmly declared. He remained in the barracks and celebrated *Shemini Atzeres* in the spirit of the day, with

Torah and *Tefillah*.

The prisoners were counted, and it became apparent that one prisoner was missing. Guards were immediately dispatched to the barracks to see who the missing person was. They found the *Rebbe* standing in the barracks immersed in prayer, oblivious to anything going on around him. The guards proceeded to handcuff the *Rebbe* and drag him to the lineup. Then two guards beat him mercilessly in front of the prisoners. They first beat him with truncheons, and then they kicked him fiercely with their metal tipped boots. The *Rebbe* just lay in a pool of his own blood, hardly breathing, barely alive. A few broken prisoners picked up their beloved *Rebbe* and took him to the camp infirmary for immediate medical attention.

The prisoners who witnessed the beating were distraught, certain that the *Rebbe* would not survive. When they returned at night, they were shocked to see that not only had the *Rebbe* survived, but he was back in his barracks. He was limping around a small stool, which served as a makeshift *Bimah*, holding onto a few pages from a torn *Mishnayos* in his hand. This was the *Rebbe's Hakofos* in honor of *Simchas Torah*! The sheer joy that illuminated the *Rebbe's* bruised face seemed to light up the room. This man epitomized a form of *mesiras nefesh* that our enemies could not destroy. This is specifically why we have endured and triumphed over every one of them.

❈ ❈ ❈ ❈ ❈ ❈

ואת יהודה שלח לפניו אל יוסף להורת לפניו גשנה

He sent Yehudah before him to Yosef, to instruct ahead of him in Goshen.
(46:28)

Rashi explains that *l'horos lefanav*, to instruct ahead of him, is to be understood as *Targum Onkelos* renders it, "to clear a place for him and to instruct how he will settle in it." In other words, Yehudah was sent to prepare housing for the family. In an alternative explanation, *Rashi* cites *Chazal* who say that Yehudah was sent to establish a house of study from which instruction would go forth. These are two meaningful reasons for sending Yehudah ahead of the family. It is especially noteworthy that Yaakov *Avinu* did not want to, even momentarily, be without his beloved *bais ha'medrash*. Thus, he sent Yehudah ahead to pave the way. What would have been wrong if he had spent a few weeks in Yosef's palace? Yosef had already demonstrated and confirmed his righteousness. Would it have been inappropriate if Yaakov had "moved in" for a few weeks until permanent housing was made available? What lesson does this convey to future generations?

Horav Yosef Zundel Salant, zl, suggests a powerful answer that teaches us an important principle. Yaakov was aware that while Yosef had maintained his piety and virtue, he was still the viceroy of Egypt. As such, he was compelled to exhibit a lifestyle that was not necessarily similar to one to which Yaakov would ascribe. As a government figure, the language spoken in his home was the native tongue, Egyptian. The palace, far from austere, was probably filled with portraits and figures that depicted Egyptian culture. In other words, the lifestyle of Yosef's home did not reflect an atmosphere to which the Patriarch would want his family exposed. Yaakov, therefore, sent Yehudah to establish for him and his family a Jewish home, the type of home they were used to — back home.

We must add that, regardless of the outer trappings of Yosef's palace, it was still the home of Yosef *HaTzaddik*, the righteous, saintly Yosef, who had triumphed over religious adversity and the blandishments of the *yetzer hara*, evil-inclination. Since his position in the Egyptian hierarchy demanded it, however, he had to present a home that in some way conformed to Egyptian culture. What an important lesson for us to make sure that the morals of contemporary society do not permeate our homes through the various conveyances of the media. While we choose to live here — and without a doubt, America is a wonderful country to whom we as Jews owe very much — we do not have to bring its societal pollution into our dining rooms.

✷ ✷ ✷ ✷ ✷ ✷

ואת יהודה שלח לפניו אל יוסף להורת לפניו גשנה

He sent Yehudah before him to Yosef, to instruct ahead of him in Goshen.
(46:28)

In one explanation, *Rashi* cites the *Midrash* that says that Yehudah was sent to establish the first *yeshivah* in Egypt. Yaakov was not going down to Egypt until he was assured that there was a *makom Torah,* place set aside for *Torah* study, for his family. Why was Yehudah selected for this position? He was the king of the brothers, while Yissachar was the *Rosh HaYeshivah*. He was the *yeshivah* man designate. Moreover, Levi, the individual to whom the transmission of our spiritual heritage was bequeathed, was also not asked to go establish the first *yeshivah*. Why was Yehudah asked as opposed to Yissachar or Levi?

The *Tiferes Shlomo* explains that earlier Yehudah had exhibited a character trait that is necessary for successfully preparing the next generation. To build a *yeshivah*, to maintain its function, to be a *Rosh HaYeshivah* and establish *talmidim*, students, that will continue as students, one must possess this trait. When Yaakov *Avinu* was reluctant to send Binyamin to Egypt for fear something would happen to him, Yehudah stepped forward and assumed responsibility. He said, "I will [personally] guarantee him" (*Bereishis* 43:9). To establish *talmidim*, to maintain a *yeshivah*, one must have a sense of *achrayos*, take responsibility.

When it comes to educating our children, *we* must assume responsibility. We cannot pass it off to someone else, claiming that we are too busy, too involved, too preoccupied. The greatest *roshei yeshivah* would first spend time studying with their own children, fulfilling their personal obligation as parents, before going out and teaching others. They were parents first and *rebbeim* second. How often are we too busy for our own children? We have *shiurim* to attend, *chavrusos* to study with — everything, but attending to our own children. The time we spend with our children engaged in *Torah* study is something that they will always remember.

Regrettably, some of us think that even playing a game with our children is too demanding. While he was in Bucharest, Romania, the *Skverer Rebbe, zl,* was the individual thousands came to for solace and encouragement following the devastation of the Holocaust. Yet, he found time to play with his daughters. He was acutely aware of the moral degradation of the "street." He could not expose them to the counter culture of the gentiles. If they were to stay, they had to have someone with whom to play. He was that someone. This great *tzaddik,* who founded one of the most incredible communities in this country, who was father figure and mentor to thousands of *chassidim*, found time to play with his daughters. He knew what his responsibilities were, and he did not look for an excuse to evade them. This was the root of his success.

Parashas Vayechi

ויאמר ליוסף הנה אביך חלה

And someone said to Yosef, "Behold! — Your father is ill." (48:1)

Visiting the sick is not easy. One must sensitize himself to the needs of the sick person and momentarily put himself in his shoes. The visitor must have in mind the varying degree of the person's illness and his own ability to confront the emotional and physical challenges that accompany it. The sick person is prone to moments of pain and depression. The one who visits him should address the issues that wreak havoc in the ill person's mind. *Horav Solumon Mutzafi, zl,* one of the great Sephardic *rabbanim* who lived in Yerushalayim prior to World War I, was known for his *chesed* in visiting the sick, as well as for his erudition in all areas of *Torah* jurisprudence.

It once happened that one of the *gedolei ho'rabbonim,* distinguished rabbinic leaders in Yerushalayim, became ill and was bedridden for an entire year. During that year, *Rav* Solumon would come over every *Erev Shabbos* and *Erev Yom Tov* on his way home from *shul* to visit for about one hour. He would discuss *Torah* thoughts and *halachic* questions that had been posed to the *Bais Din* for arbitration. He would seek the *rav's* advice on various issues. His family wondered why he would continue with his customary visit during the rainy season. Why did he not wait until *Motzoei Shabbos?* Furthermore, why did he subject his family to the trouble of waiting for him? It was not as if the *mitzvah* could not be performed the next day.

Rav Solumon explained, "When *Shabbos* night comes around, this great *rav* remembers how, when he was healthy and full of vigor, he would leave the *shul* accompanied by a large crowd of students and admirers, each one vying for his attention. He would arrive at home filled with joy and enthusiasm. Now that he is incapacitated, he must feel unwanted, unworthy and depressed. Perhaps his *Shabbos* is ruined by feelings of discontent and sadness. Such a distinguished *talmid chacham* should not be sad — ever, but certainly not on *Shabbos Kodesh*. My family can wait a little, so that this *rav* will not be let down on *Shabbos*."

This is what visiting the sick is all about. We are to visit someone for one purpose: to make *him* feel good, not ourselves. Regrettably, all too often we perform acts of loving-kindness because *we* are on a guilt trip. *Chesed* is for others — not to quell our own self-condemnation.

✹ ✹ ✹ ✹ ✹ ✹

המלאך הגאל אתי מכל רע יברך את הנערים ...וידגו לרב בקרב הארץ

"May the angel who redeems me from all evil bless the lads... and may they proliferate like fish within the land." (48:16)

The *Midrash* draws an analogy between a Jew's thirst for *Torah* and the unquenchable thirst a fish has for water. Fish grow and live in the water. Yet, as soon as a drop of new water is introduced into their environment, they seize it, as if they had never tasted water before. Likewise, a Jew grows and lives in the sea of *Torah*. Yet, when he hears a new *Torah* thought, he seizes upon it, as if he had never studied before. This was Yaakov *Avinu's* underlying idea when he blessed his descendants to proliferate as fish.

Horav Aharon Kotler, zl, derives a powerful lesson from here. We learn the overriding significance of each individual action that a person undertakes. *Chazal* say, "One who recites *Krias Shma* daily and misses one day, it is considered as if he never said *Krias Shma*." What is the meaning of this statement? *Rav* Aharon explains that just as every creation is composed of various components which can be viewed under the microscope, likewise, man is comprised of various elements. This applies not only to his essence, but also to his life and strength; everything is the sum total of various parts. Essentially, every minute, every second of his life is a separate, distinct unit. This unit exists forever and must be accounted for. Thus, if one did not recite *Krias Shma*, then that moment in time is left without *kabbolas ol malchus Shomayim*, a lapse in accepting upon himself the yoke of Heaven. There is a blemish forever, a lapse in his life, a moment that is without a *kabbolah*, a commitment. We are not to view this as one *kabbolah* among many thousands that do exist. No. For that moment, that individual component in time, this individual had not *committed* himself. That moment is left for posterity — without commitment.

We derive from here the importance of making use of every moment allotted to us. The moment we waste is lost to us — forever. This is the meaning of the *Midrash*. Every *dvar Torah*, every moment that we can study *Torah,* is unique and distinct. It has nothing to do with the past or the future. It stands alone. We should thirst to seize it, or it is lost to us forever.

✳ ✳ ✳ ✳ ✳ ✳

ארור אפם כי עז... אחלקם ביעקב ואפיצם בישראל

"Accursed is their rage for it is intense... I will divide them in Yaakov, and I will disperse them in Yisrael." (49:7)

The key word regarding Shimon and Levi's character fault is not "anger," but rather, "intense." *Ki az,* "for it is intense," describes an anger that overwhelms a person, that owns his actions, that controls his thoughts and moments. It is not the anger; it is the intensity that must be cursed. Anger is certainly not a good trait. *Chazal* tell us that anger is like idol worship. It consumes a person, takes over his identity, and distances him from Hashem. Yet, Yaakov *Avinu* wanted the descendants of these two "angry" brothers spread out throughout *Yisrael.* They became the scribes and *Torah* teachers of our children. Does this make sense? Did Yaakov have in mind to send an angry man into a classroom to teach our children?

Certainly not. There is another aspect to anger that is laudatory — stubbornness. When the anger is not *az,* "intense," when the *individual* is in control, then the stubbornness can give rise to a sense of mission, an ability to overcome overwhelming odds, to succeed where others would fail. Yes: Anger that gives way to *akshanus*, stubbornness, is commendable.

The *Skverer Rebbe, zl,* would relate that as a young boy he was known to have a stubborn streak. He once noticed a small object with which he immediately wanted to play. His grandfather took the object and placed it on the highest shelf of the bookcase, in order to keep it out of harm's way.

The little boy was not taking this lying down. He worked for an hour and devised a way to scale the bookcase and retrieve the object. When he finally succeeded, his grandfather patted him on the head, and said, *"Der yingel hot asach akshanus*, This little lad has a lot of stubbornness."

His grandfather was right. It was this stubbornness that helped him survive the Nazis and rebuild his *Kehillah*, community. He overcame pain, depravation and adversity to become a *manhig*, leader, that led and encouraged his flock. He was the prime architect of the idea of a *chassidic* community outside of New York. It was not easy, considering that many of the challenges that he had to overcome were not only from the secular community. Negativity among our own people has regrettably become natural, especially when someone else is doing what we *just decided* we would like to do. Despite the challenges and obstacles, he prevailed. It was then that he would relate his childhood prank and his grandfather's remark, saying, "I used up all that stubbornness to build this community."

ויעל יוסף לקבר את אביו
Yosef went up to bury his father. (50:7)

Although all the brothers went to the funeral of Yaakov *Avinu*, Yosef is singled out because he took personal responsibility for his father's burial, despite his exalted position as the Egyptian viceroy. In reward for this, Moshe *Rabbeinu*, the greatest Jewish leader, took personal responsibility for Yosef's remains when *Klal Yisrael* left Egypt. Being paid back *middah k'neged middah*, measure for measure, is the way Hashem metes out reward and punishment. When we perform a *chesed* for a person, we can be sure that it will be repaid in a like manner, at times many years later when we need it the most. I was especially moved by a selfless act of loving kindness performed by *Horav Elazar M. Shach, zl,* for an elderly woman who had *unknowingly* helped him as a young boy. The venerable *Rosh HaYeshivah's* remembering for a lifetime that he had a debt of kindness to repay — and the manner in which he repaid it — demonstrates his incredible character.

Rabbi Paysach Krohn, in his *Reflections of the Maggid*, relates the following story. It was a cold, dreary, stormy day when the aged *Rosh HaYeshivah* summoned his grandson to his house and said, "Please arrange a car for me. I have to travel to a town near Haifa to attend a funeral." Obviously, his grandson made every attempt to dissuade *Rav* Shach. His ill health and the inclement weather were both valid reasons for him to stay at home, but he knew that arguing with his grandfather would prove fruitless. In the car, during the two-hour trip, *Rav* Shach explained that he was attending the funeral of an elderly woman, who deserved great honor. While she might have deserved the great distinction, regrettably, there was barely a *minyan*, quorum, in attendance.

The funeral was short, sad and simple. After the funeral was over, *Rav* Shach still did not leave, but remained standing over the grave amidst the pelting cold rain. He stood there shivering, immersed in his thoughts for a short while, and then he was ready to go.

This scene was too much for his grandson. He needed an explanation, and *Rav* Shach promptly told him the following story: When he was only twelve-years-old, it was announced that a *yeshivah* was forming for *illuyim*, brilliant students. The *Rosh HaYeshivah* was meticulous in selecting only those students who had great academic potential. Also, their diligence and dedication to *Torah* had to be exceptional, since material conditions were meager, at best. The older students were given a hard bench to sleep on, while the younger ones had the "luxury" of sleeping on the floor. Food was edible, although very sparse. *Rav* Shach was accepted in this *yeshivah*, despite his young age.

During the spring and summer, the young prodigy was able to tolerate the physical conditions. Winter brought a new challenge, since there was no heat. The pangs of hunger, coupled with the bitter cold, took their toll on the young child. His commitment was challenged even more when he received a letter from his uncle, a successful blacksmith, asking him to "relocate" his vocation and join his burgeoning business. The letter arrived on Wednesday. By Friday, he was about to give up and join the "family" business. He decided that he would remain in the *yeshivah* for *Shabbos* and leave immediately thereafter.

Friday morning, a woman came to the *yeshivah* and shared her tale of sorrow with the *Rosh HaYeshivah*. Her husband had been a salesman who sold blankets. During his most recent trip, the horse and carriage that he was traveling in turned over, and he was killed. The woman had just gotten up from sitting *shivah,* and she wanted to donate the left-over blankets to the *yeshivah. Rav* Shach was one of the lucky students to be a beneficiary of her kindness. That blanket made the difference. He figured that he could survive the cold winter with the warm blanket. After that winter, the direction in which he would focus his life was clear.

Rav Shach continued, "That woman had a sad life. She never remarried. She later moved to Haifa and lived alone to a ripe old age. When I found out that she had passed away, I wanted to repay her kindness to me and attend her funeral. After the funeral, I waited around in the cold, rainy weather to remind myself how cold I was many years ago before this wonderful lady gave me the blanket. I wanted to have the proper *hakoras ha'tov,* gratitude, for all that she did for me."

The two lessons that we derive from this narrative are apparent. No kindness goes unnoticed. Every kind act will be repaid. We also note the depth of *hakoras ha'tov,* appreciation, that *Rav* Shach had to this woman and how he viewed her simple act of generosity as the turning point of his life.

※ ※ ※ ※ ※ ※

ויספדו שם מספד גדול וכבד מאד
And there they held a very great and imposing eulogy. (50:10)

Yaakov *Avinu* was accorded great honor as he was eulogized and lauded for his great virtue and accomplishment. Not everyone agrees with the concept of *hesped,* eulogy. In fact, many *gedolei Yisrael, Torah* giants, have insisted that after their demise, they be buried without eulogy or fanfare. *Horav Aryeh Levine, zl,* the distinguished *tzaddik* of *Yerushalayim,* wrote the following in his *tzavaah,* will: "I request in every language of entreaty that I not be eulogized at all... Woe is to him about whom great praises are rendered — and they are not true. Especially, me, that I do not possess any *Torah,* that I am not proficient even in a *perek* of *Mishnayos.* I do not even know *Chumash.* To my great anguish, I never had the opportunity to study with a *melamed,* primary *Torah* teacher."

More than once, *Rav* Aryeh would comment that when they praise the deceased in this world with appellations that are not necessarily true, in

Heaven it is demanded of him, "See, you could have been a *baal madreigah,* person of stature, listen to what they are saying about you!" When a person is lauded in this world, when his virtue and piety are being exalted, he had better be worthy of the distinction that is accorded to him, for in the World of Truth, the "other side of the story" is clear for all to see.

Rav Aryeh once explained why he was so insistent about not being eulogized. He related the following incident. It was at the time of the great famine that enveloped *Yerushalayim* during World War I. People suffered terribly, as they fell like flies to the overwhelming hunger. There was a *gabbai tzedakah,* charity distributor, in *Yerushalayim* who was in charge of disbursing to the poor the money he had received from America and Europe. Unfortunately, power sometimes goes to people's heads, and this man took his position a bit too seriously.

A close friend of *Rav* Aryeh's sent a sizeable amount of money designated specifically for *Rav* Aryeh's family. When the friend had not heard from *Rav* Aryeh, he wrote to him questioning if he had received the money. *Rav* Aryeh went to the *gabbai* and asked for *his* money. The *gabbai* responded, "I cannot give you the money until I ascertain that there is no other Aryeh Levine living in *Yerushalayim.*" *Rav* Aryeh retorted, "I know everyone in Yerushalayim, and there is no one else by this name. Furthermore, the benefactor has written to me that he had sent me a check. I am in dire need of these funds, as I have a number of hungry children at home who are literally starving!"

The man held his own and with great insolence said, "Nonetheless, before I give away someone's money, I must be absolutely sure that it is going to the correct address."

A few days later, *Rav* Aryeh's son passed away, a victim of the vicious famine. *Rav* Aryeh continued, "I will never forget my child looking up at me, pleading, '*Tateh!* Please give me a piece of bread.' I could not give him even a morsel, because I had nothing." During the *shivah,* seven-day morning period, the *gabbai* appeared at my house with the money, saying, "I researched it, and I have confirmed that the money is rightfully yours."

Rav Aryeh looked up with tear-streaked eyes and said, "You may take the money and give it to someone else. I no longer need it."

A number of days later, the *gabbai* passed away. The announcement went out all over Yerushalayim that the "distinguished" *gabbai tzedakah* had passed away and that everyone should attend his funeral. *Rav* Aryeh also attended the funeral and heard accolade after accolade about the man who had been so "meticulous" with his disbursement of allocated charities. *Rav* Aryeh knew first-hand how true this really was. His child was a sacrifice to the man's punctilious disbursement.

"It was after that funeral that I decided unequivocally that I did not want to be eulogized. I knew what I really was. Why should I have to suffer the humiliation in Heaven?" These were the words of the *Tzaddik* of Yerushalayim. What should we say?

✼ ✼ ✼ ✼ ✼ ✼

הבה נתחכמה לו

"Come, let us outsmart it." (1:10)

O ne of the most notorious incidents that occurred after World War II was perpetrated by secularists who were in charge of an absorption camp, Atlit, on the outskirts of Haifa. Here, groups of Jewish youths, mostly survivors of the Holocaust and Soviet Russia, were subjected to unimaginable mental and physical cruelty with one goal in mind: obliteration of Judaism. These children — mostly orphans from *frum*, observant, homes in Poland — were sent to Palestine through the auspices of the youth *Aliyah* division of the Jewish Agency, via Tehran. Hence, the name *Yaldei Tehran*. It was during the terrible incursion against the *Yaldei Tehran* that *Rav Moshe Blau* and *Rav Moshe Porush* came to the *Brisker Rav, zl,* to consult with him regarding the correct action to take to save these children from spiritual annihilation. When the *Brisker Rav* heard what was happening, he began to scream and cry uncontrollably. He enjoined them to do everything humanly possible to save the children. Seeing the *Rav* respond with such intensity, *Rav* Moshe Blau was concerned for his health. "Why does the *Rav* scream so much? It is not good for his health. Anyway, screaming is not going to solve the problem," said *Rav* Blau.

The *Brisker Rav* replied, "Whether screaming helps or not is not the issue. When it hurts, one screams. To hear about the tragedy hurts!" He continued by elucidating the *Midrash* that says that three advisors sat with Pharaoh to guide him concerning the decision about the "Jewish Problem": Iyov, Yisro and Bilaam. They each reacted differently and were punished accordingly. Bilaam, who advised Pharaoh to kill the Jewish boys, was himself killed. Yisro escaped. Because he fled, his descendants sat in *halachic* arbitration in the *Lishkas Hagazis*, Chamber of Hewn Stones. Iyov, who was silent, was punished by having to endure severe pain.

A person is repaid in the exact manner, measure for measure, as his actions. Hashem will repay accordingly the individual who gives charity to a poor man with a smile and shares his wherewithal unbegrudgingly with others. Bilaam and Yisro received their due *middah k'neged middah*, measure for measure. Bilaam advised Pharaoh to murder the Jewish boys, so he himself was later killed. Yisro was wealthy and famous. He was revered and exalted by all of Egypt. He turned his back on fame and fortune and ran away. For this, he was granted the great distinction of having descendants that arbitrated and adjudicated Jewish law. What, however, was the *middah k'neged middah* of Iyov's punishment? What relationship is there between pain and silence?

The *Brisker Rav* explained that Iyov had many reasons for keeping silent. He was acutely aware that he could not change the decree; therefore, screaming would be to no avail. Iyov felt that if he would not succeed in averting the decree, he might as well remain silent and be politically correct. Perhaps, he would be able to help the Jews later on.

Therefore, Hashem punished him with severe pain, so that Iyov would cry out in agony. Does crying out allay the pain? Does the pain diminish when one cries? No, but when it hurts, one cries. Any person who is in anguish cries out, because it is the normal reaction to pain. Likewise, when Iyov heard the terrible decree, it should have hurt to the point that he could not remain silent. Why did he not cry out? Apparently, the decree did not cause him sufficient anguish to invoke a scream. Therefore, Hashem gave him cause to scream.

וכאשר יענו אתו כן ירבה

But as much as they would afflict it, so it would increase. (1:12)

The *Midrash* interprets the *pasuk* in the following manner: *Ruach Hakodesh omeres kein*, the Holy Spirit is saying, "You say — *pen yirbeh*, lest it will increase, but I say — *kein yirbeh*, just so, it will increase." I once heard a homiletical rendering of this *Midrash*. You, enemies of *Yisrael*, think that your evil decrees will have an effect on increasing the *pen*, perhaps/the doubt factor, within the Jewish mind. You think that the more pain, the greater the persecution, the more intense the anguish, that the

Jew will give up hope, will fall into apathy. You are wrong! I say — *kein yirbeh*, the *kein*, yes, the Jew's unequivocal commitment and unbreakable bond with Hashem will only get stronger and more enthusiastic.

We have seen this demonstrated throughout the millennia. The more they have persecuted us, the greater and more steadfast was our dedication to *Torah* and *mitzvos*. They said "*Pen*"— and we responded, "*Kein!*"

✳ ✳ ✳ ✳ ✳ ✳

ויאמר מלך מצרים למילדת העברית אשר שם האחת שפרה ושם השנית
פועה

The king of Egypt said to the Hebrew midwives, of whom the name of the first was Shifrah and the name of the second was Puah. (1:15)

The *Midrash* cites a dispute between Rav and Shmuel as to the identity of the midwives. They both agree that Yocheved, Moshe *Rabbeinu's* mother, was one of them. Their point of contention is in regard to the second midwife. Was she Miriam, Moshe's sister, or Elisheva, the wife of Aharon *Hakohen*? Perhaps there is a message to be derived herein. Moshe *Rabbeinu*, the quintessential Jewish leader, the only human being who knew Hashem "face to face," was truly a unique individual with exemplary character traits, leadership qualities and a sanctity that paralleled the Heavenly beings. His parents must have had an incredible *zchus*, merit, to have such a child. Moreover, whose "gene" did he inherit?

The *Torah* tells us that Hashem rewarded the midwives by making for them *batim*, houses, a term that denotes families or distinguished offspring. While Amram was a distinguished scholar and the undisputed leader of the generation, it seems that he was a pacifist. We do not see him taking steps to impede Pharaoh's genocidal activities. He was resigned to doom. Thus, he discouraged any further procreation. He decided that *Klal Yisrael* should not bring new Jews into a world of suffering and death. Pharaoh cannot kill what does not exist. The image we have of Moshe is in direct contrast to that of Amram. Moshe burst on the scene proactively, exhibiting opposition to the man in whose palace he was raised.

It seems that Moshe inherited his activism and leadership role from his mother, who not only frustrated Pharaoh's efforts to decimate the Jewish male population, but even raised funds and collected food to sustain the impoverished Jewish mothers. Moshe was her reward. Furthermore, if we are of the opinion that Elisheva was the other midwife, we can understand from whom her grandson, Pinchas *Hakohen,* received his legacy.

I suggest that there is a great lesson to be derived from here. Scholarly pursuit has been our mainstay throughout the generations. We are the people of the book, not only in character, but also in demeanor. A Jew must take a stand for his people. Activism must be secondary to *Torah* ideals and values, but without *Torah* activism, indifference and apathy will reign.

✳ ✳ ✳ ✳ ✳ ✳

ויגדל משה ויצא אל אחיו וירא בסבלתם

Moshe grew up and went out to his brethren and observed their burdens.
(2:11)

Moshe *Rabbeinu* did not simply empathize with his persecuted brethren. *Rashi* says that *sum libo,* he applied his heart, to sensitize himself to their pain. He wanted to feel what they felt. In order to perform *chesed,* loving kindness, in the correct and proper manner, one must attune himself to his friends' needs, to those areas wherein he senses a deficiency. Even if he may not be on the same "wave length" as I, my act of kindness must address what my friend needs — not what I might need.

I recently read an exceptional example of this form of *'chesed'* cited by Rabbi Yechiel Spero, in his recent publication, *"Touched by a Story." Rav* Shraga Wollman, the *Mashgiach* of *Yeshivas Mekor Chaim* is the *Baal Musaf* for the *Yamim Noraim.* He has a unique ability to capture the essence of the day, and to convey its crucial message to all those assembled, as he inspires their *tefillos* with his melodious voice and fervent devotion. On *Yom Kippur,* he returns to the *amud* to lead the *Neillah* service. His passionate rendition and his beautiful voice turn the *Bais Hamedrash* into a sea of prayer. This particular *Yom Kippur,* when our story took place, was no different.

Well, it was no different as far as the *davening* was concerned.

There was something strange, however, about the *Tallis Rav* Shraga was wearing. It was not his. It was an old, tattered *Tallis* that he must have picked up somewhere. Was there something wrong with his own *Tallis*?

Neillah was concluded and the crowd broke into a joyous dance, singing *l'shanah habaah b'Yerushalayim*. This was followed by *Maariv,* and everyone began to leave for home. The question regarding the strange *Tallis* kept gnawing at a few people, until one of them decided that he would question *Rav* Shraga about why he had used this old *Tallis*.

At first, *Rav* Shraga refused to answer, attempting to avoid the question. The more he dodged the question, the more his friend pestered him, until *Rav* Shraga relented. He explained that shortly after *Mussaf,* as he walked back to his seat, he noticed an elderly woman whose husband has passed away that year. As he wished her a *"Gut Yom Tov,"* he noted that she was unusually depressed. She acknowledged that widowhood was not pleasant and that she missed her husband terribly. She was used to his company, especially on *Yom Kippur*. As she spoke, tears welled up in her eyes.

Rav Shraga then thought of an idea. He asked the woman if he could borrow her husband's *Tallis* for *Neillah*. This way, when she would gaze down on the *Chazzan*, she would see her late husband's *Tallis*. What greater remembrance could there be of her husband? This would bring her comfort and encouragement. Perhaps this *Tallis* was not as nice as his own, but what it represented was certainly more beautiful.

Chesed means identifying with another person's needs as if they are your own. Thus, if one's needs do not presently conform with those of his friends, he abnegates his own feelings for his friend. The following story concerning *Horav Moshe Mordechai Epstein, zl,* the venerable *Rosh HaYeshivah* of Chevron exemplifies this idea. It was 1929, and *Klal Yisrael* had sustained one of the most alarming atrocities of the Twentieth Century. A band of blood-thirsty Arabs, their hatred for the Jews aroused to a frenzy by their accursed leadership, ran through the streets of Chevron, murdering men, women and children in cold blood. Twenty-five students of the Chevron *Yeshivah* gave up their lives that fateful day *Al Kiddush Hashem,* to sanctify Hashem's Name. The *Rosh HaYeshivah, Rav* Moshe Mordechai, became physically ill as a result. His feelings of personal responsibility for the murder of his students never really left him. He took his fatherly feelings of guilt with him to the grave, never recovering from the tragedy.

His clarity of vision, however, never waned. The *Rosh HaYeshivah*, whose love for his *talmidim*, disciples, was legendary, never forgot his mission in life. It was the last day of his earthly existence and *Rav* Moshe Mordechai lay in bed, unable to move, surrounded by his closest students and his children. He asked that everyone but his son leave the room. When everyone had left, *Rav* Moshe Mordechai turned to his son and said haltingly, "My dear son, I know my time to leave this world draws close. One of the *talmidei ha'yeshivah*, students of the *yeshivah*, is to be married tonight. I ask you that <u>tonight</u>, regardless of what happens today, you will encourage the rest of the students to attend the wedding and dance with joy and enthusiasm. I do not want this young man's wedding to be marred in any way."

An hour later, the *Rosh HaYeshivah* returned his soul to its Maker. Thousands of Jews from all areas of the Jewish spectrum attended the funeral. Rivers of tears were shed for the man who loved all Jews and whose love was reciprocated. The funeral concluded right before *shkiah*, sunset, at which point *Rav* Moshe Mordechai's last request was announced to the *talmidim*. How could these broken students, bereft of their loving and exalted mentor, dance at a wedding? That is exactly what their *rebbe* had wanted. Indeed, that is what their *rebbe* epitomized. That evening, the crushed young men of the *yeshivah*, their eyes red with tears — the pain in their hearts still fresh and hurting — rejoiced at their friend's wedding, because that is what their *rebbe* wanted.

Parashas Vaeira

הוא אהרן ומשה אשר אמד ד׳ להם הוציאו את בני ישראל מארץ מצרים

This was the Aharon and Moshe to whom Hashem said, "Take Bnei Yisrael out of Egypt." (6:26)

D id *Klal Yisrael* need two leaders to liberate them from Egypt? In truth, for the *Geulah Ho'asidah*, the Future Redemption, when we will finally achieve ultimate redemption from the exile that is so much a part of our lives, there will also be two redeemers: *Moshiach ben Yosef;* and *Moshiach ben David*. The question remains: Why do we need two redeemers when one could do the job? I once heard a noteworthy reason. We need two redeemers to eradicate the concept of *galus*, exile, totally from our lives: one redeemer to take us out of *galus*; and the other redeemer, to take *galus* out of us!

Regrettably, the same idea that applied to the Jewish People as slaves in Egypt — in regard to the Egyptian culture and way of life — haunts us to this very day. Are we ready to be redeemed? Do we want to be redeemed? It is much easier to take the Jew out of Egypt than to take Egypt out of the Jew. We have become slaves to the society and culture in which we live. They way of life that prevails in modern society has, for the most part, controlled and reigned over our lives. Its mindset has become our mindset. Its art and culture has so captivated our lives that we have begun to accept what should be foreign to us as being a cultural necessity. Do we really want to be released from *galus*, or do we simply want *galus* relaxed?

It was not much different in Egypt. The Jews complained about the backbreaking labor and persecution. Did they want to leave Egypt? The decree of *galus* was accepted. They just wanted an "easier" *galus*. It was not Egypt that they wanted to leave; it was the hard work and torture that they could have done without. Have we accepted the state of *galus* as a way of life, as something with which we can live? Yes. We need two redeemers: one to take us out of *galus;* and one to remove the *galus* mentality from our minds.

With this idea in mind, we can better understand a compelling thought from *Horav Sholom, zl, m'Belz*. He notes that the word *p'dus*, distinction/redemption, is mentioned three times in *Tanach*: First, in our *Parshah* (8:19): Hashem says, "I will make a *p'dus*, distinction, between My People and your people;" second, in *Sefer Tehillim* 111:9: "He sent *p'dus*, redemption, to His nation," and last, in *Tehillim* 130:7: "For with Hashem is kindness, and with Him is abundant *p'dus*, redemption." These three promises of redemption correspond with these forms of *galus*.

The first *galus* is when the Jew is exiled among gentile nations. Hashem promises to make a distinction between Jew and gentile and redeem *Klal Yisrael* from their exile. The second exile is more difficult. It is when the Jew is in exile among Jews; when brother imposes his rule over brother; when a Jew is uncomfortable among his own brethren. When Jews disparage and hurt each other verbally, and even physically, we have a bitter *galus* that is far worse than when the persecution is directed at us by gentiles. To this form of exile, Hashem responds that He will send *p'dus*, redemption, to His nation — to His children that are enslaved by members of His own nation.

Last, is the *galus* to which we originally alluded: the Jew who is in exile within himself, who is subservient to his base nature and physical desires. The Jew who has no control over himself is in a deep exile. He can ascend from the depths of his self-inflicted exile only through his own efforts. It takes courage, strength, faith and incredible *siyata d'Shmaya*, Divine assistance. Hashem will grant abundant redemption to he who raises up his hands to Hashem and requests help.

ותעל הצפרדע ותכס את ארץ מצרים
And the frog infestation ascended and covered the land of Egypt. (8:2)

*R*ashi tells us that the plague of frogs started with only one frog which the Egyptians beat. As they beat the first one, it multiplied and became two frogs. This continued so that the more they beat them, the more they multiplied. The *Steipler Rav, zl,* asks a practical question: When they saw the result of their beating the frogs, why did they not stop? He explains that, indeed, rational thinking told them to stop, but they became enraged when they saw the result of their beating the frogs — and they lost control.

Anger does that to a person. When he becomes enraged, he loses control of his faculties. *Chazal* tell us that anger is like idol-worship. When one becomes angry, he indicates that Hashem does not control the world. Otherwise, why would he get angry? Whatever happened was the result of Hashem's decree. Control yourself! Idol worship abnegates Hashem's dominion; so does rage.

An angry person cannot sustain a relationship because he always places himself at the forefront. An individual may attempt to place the blame on others for a host of reasons, but, after all is said and done, it is himself who should be blamed. The angry person is insecure, and he takes his diffidence out on those around him in an attempt to conceal his troubled nature. The ones who suffer the most, after the spouse, are the innocent children, who become the punching bags for his feelings of inadequacy.

One must come to grips with his problem and overcome it before it envelops and possesses him. The worst thing one can do is to concede to the problem by ignoring it. Saying it is part of my nature to be angry is self-destructive and irresponsible. Taking hold of this negative character trait and using it for the common good will transform it in a positive way. Anger can be transformed into indignation when one sees that *Torah* or its causes are disparaged. In such a case, the negative undergoes a positive metamorphosis and is employed as a tool to combat indifference. So, after all is said and done, anger, like all other character traits, is something negative only when used in a destructive manner.

רק ביאר תשארנה

Only in the river shall they remain. (8:7)

W hy did Hashem not make a greater miracle and rid the land <u>and</u> the river of the frogs? Was there some reason that the frogs were left in the river? *Horav Yitzchak Zilberstein, Shlita*, cites the *Likutei Anshei Shem* who compares this to a father who, after disciplining his son with his belt, hangs up the belt on the wall, so that the boy will have a reminder. The belt on the wall will "motivate" him not to do anything that will incur his father's punishment again. Hashem kept frogs around as a constant reminder to the Egyptians of what had occurred and what could easily happen again if they were out of line.

Rav Zilberstein suggests that this is a practical idea to employ to spare an individual from repeating his mistakes. The constant reminder of the consequence of sin can be a powerful deterrent. Furthermore, one should maintain a remembrance of anything that Hashem does for him. If he was spared from a terrible fate, he should have some form of keepsake that will always serve as a reminder of what could have been.

Remembering and erecting memorials to the past are inherently Jewish actions. While one should not live in the past, one, nonetheless, should never forget it. *Zachor*, remember, whether it applies to *Shabbos*, the exodus from Egypt, or various incidents in our history. The *Torah* wants us to remember and never forget the lessons of the past. In our personal lives, a host of effective rituals are designed to help us to remember our loved ones who have passed on: *Kaddish, Yahrzeit; Yizkor*; naming our children and grandchildren after those that have died; erecting memorials; and giving charity in their names. Probably the most significant remembrance, however, is following in their righteous paths and not deviating from their legacy.

Following the death of his wife, a non-Jewish statesman took his three children to their mother's grave. The epitaph read: "Caroline Spencer, wife of J. Sterling Spencer, and mother of Joy, Frank and Mark." After reading the simple epitaph, the father turned to his children and said, "If any of you ever does anything that would have caused your mother grief or shame had she been alive, I will chisel your name off that stone." That is remembrance. That is motivation.

"And so that My Name may be declared throughout the land." (9:16)

The goal of universal recognition of Hashem's monarchy and ultimate sovereignty over the world requires that all nations recognize Him. The world would hear of the miracles He wrought against the Egyptian land, and a greater awareness of His powers would be realized. The word used for declaring Hashem's Name is *sapeir*, which means to tell over as a story (*Sipur*). This would suggest that there are many ways to relate Hashem's greatness, and the medium of a story is an effective one. A story is not only uplifting, it is an instrument of healing. *Horav Nachman, zl, m'Breslov*, a great proponent of the effectiveness of stories, notes that, prior to delving into the various *mitzvos* and the ensuing *halachos*, the *Torah* first relates the story of Creation and all the other stories of *Sefer Bereishis*. Our people carried their stories with them from exile to exile, giving them hope and inspiration. No enemy could destroy the emotion and faith achieved through an inspiring story; nor could the ravages of exile, persecution or disease. Yes, these stories of faith, Providence and Jewish resilience have kept many from succumbing to the despair and deprivation that have plagued us in *galus*.

There is a story that goes back a few hundred years that gives meaning to the concept of stories. When the *Baal Shem Tov* saw a decree threatening the Jewish People, he went into the solitude of the forest, lit a fire and poured out his heart in prayer to Hashem. The decree was averted.

Years later, when his primary *talmid*, disciple, the *Mezritcher Maggid* was compelled to advocate for the needs of the Jewish People, he would go to the same place in the forest that his revered *rebbe* had used and say, "*Hashem Yisborach*, I do not know how to light the fire, but I do know how to pray." Hashem listened to his prayer, and misfortune was avoided.

When his *talmid*, *Horav Moshe Leib Sassover*, went into the forest to intercede on behalf of *Klal Yisrael*, he would say, "*Ribbono Shel Olam*, I do not know how to light the fire; I do not know how to pray in the manner of my *rebbeim* that preceded me. One thing I do know, however, I know the place to go. I pray that just being in this holy site will effect salvation." He succeeded in turning the tide, and — again — the Jewish People were saved.

Last, the responsibility fell on the shoulders of his disciple the saintly *Rizhiner Rebbe*. Sitting in his home, he looked up and spoke to Hashem. "I have not achieved the spiritual plateau of my *rebbeim*. I neither know how to light the fire, nor do I know how to pray. I do not even know the place in the forest which is propitious for prayer. All I can do is relate the story and hope that this will be sufficient." It was, and he succeeded.

The story was all that was left. The analogy for us is that not all people have the ability to <u>convey</u> the message of truth through prayer or other forms of intellectual communication. Likewise, there are those who are not necessarily inclined to <u>derive</u> the message unless it is wrapped in a story. A story, when related properly, can have penetrating insight and touch a person in a way that no other means of communication can.

הירא את דבר ד' מעבדי פרעה הניס את עבדיו ואת מקנהו אל הבתים
*Whoever among the servants of Pharaoh feared the word of Hashem,
chased his servants and livestock into the houses.* (9:20)

The G-d-fearing Egyptians had the common sense to take their animals inside. Does this indicate *yiraas Shomayim*, fear of Heaven? This is the seventh plague to have struck Egypt. Moshe *Rabbeinu's* track record had been perfect. Whenever he foretold about a plague, it arrived on time and with intensity. Only a fool would leave his animals outdoors. In the *Zer Zahav* by *Horav Avraham, zl, m'Teshchinov,* the author distinguishes the G-d-fearing Egyptian who, upon hearing of the upcoming plague, immediately took action and brought his animals inside, from his counterpart, who waited until the hail came pounding down, wreaking havoc, before he gathered in his livestock.

Horav Yitzchak Zilberstein, Shlita, derives from here that a *yarei Shomayim* is not one who merely does not sin, but rather it is a person who is meticulous not to come in contact with anything that might lead him to sin. This may be compared to a person who fears fire. He will make sure not to have anything of a flammable nature in his possession. It goes without saying that he will not put his hands in the fire.

"And as for you and your servants, I know that you are not yet fearful of Hashem, Elokim." (9:30)

The Maharshdam, zl, notes that the dual terminology, Hashem *Elokim* is used only once prior to this instance. In the beginning of *Sefer Bereishis* 2:4, "These are the products of the heavens and earth when they were created, in the day that Hashem *Elokim*, made earth and Heavens." Is there some message to be derived from this? The *Maharshdam* explains that the term Hashem denotes *rachamim*, the Divine attribute of Mercy, while *Elokim* denotes *middas Ha'din*, the attribute of strict Justice. As Hashem was about to employ His *middas Ha'din* to punish the Egyptians, He preceded it with the attribute of Mercy, demonstrated by the fact that the wheat and spelt were not destroyed. Although the Egyptians were wicked, Hashem showed them compassion. If this is the case, why did Hashem not have any mercy on the Egyptians during the earlier plagues, such as the plague of blood?

Horav Mosuad ben Shimon, Shlita, explains that only concerning the plague of *barad*, hail, did the Egyptians manifest that they feared Hashem. It was during this plague that the G-d-fearing Egyptians took in their slaves and livestock, indicating that they believed in the plague's imminent occurrence. One who has *yiraas Shomayim* deserves Hashem's mercy.

Parashas Bo

ויאמר ד' אל משה בא אל פרעה כי אני הכבדתי את לבו ואת לב עבדיו

Hashem said to Moshe, "Come to Pharaoh, for I have made his heart and the heart of his servants stubborn." (10:1)

The concept of *hachbodas ha'lev*, hardening of the heart, and basically removing one's *bechirah chafshis*, free will, is a difficult idea to accept. G-d has endowed man with the ability to choose between right and wrong, good and evil. This concept plays a critical role in providing the correct balance for reward and punishment. Why did Hashem take this capacity from Pharaoh? In his *Sefer Simchas HaTorah, Horav Simchah HaKohen Sheps, zl*, applies the following analogy to explain and validate hardening Pharaoh's heart. A Jew once was in litigation with a gentile, which necessitated going to a secular court for adjudication. The Jew, realizing what he was up against, went to the gentile judge on the day of the trial and offered him a hefty bribe. The judge, understandably, was taken aback. "Is it not written in your Bible that one should not accept a bribe, because it blinds the eyes of even the most astute individual?" the judge asked indignantly. "How can you justify giving me a bribe?"

The Jew quickly responded, "Your honor, my behavior is really not inappropriate. After all, you and my litigant are both non-Jews. It makes sense, therefore, that you are predisposed to hear his side of the case with greater sensitivity than you would my claim. Thus, by giving you a bribe, I am only balancing the scales of justice by attempting to override your predisposition."

The same idea applies to Pharaoh's *hachbodas ha'lev*. The plagues wreaked havoc on Egypt. They left an indelible impact on the Egyptian psyche. Hence, Pharaoh and his people were partial to the Jewish cause. He was inclined to let the Jews leave the country, but for the wrong reason. He had no remorse; he did not regret the evil decrees that he had directed against the Jewish People. His contrition was insincere. Hashem, therefore, hardened his heart, in order to counteract the effect of the plagues.

ויהי חשך אפלה בכל ארץ מצרים שלשת ימים. לא ראו איש את אחיו ולא
קמו איש מתחתיו

There was a darkness of gloom throughout the land of Egypt for a three-day period. No man could see his brother, nor could anyone rise from his place. **(10:22,23)**

*R*ashi explains the rationale behind the intense darkness that lasted three days. It seems that among the Jews of that generation were wicked individuals who had no desire to depart the Egyptian exile. They perished during the three days of gloom, in order that the Egyptians should not be witness to their downfall and say, "They, too, are being smitten as we are." The obvious question is: Should the fact that they did not want to leave Egypt be sufficient reason to die? We see later, concerning the *eved Ivri*, Hebrew slave, who wants to extend his servitude beyond the required six years, that he goes to *Bais Din*, Jewish court, and has his ear "bored with an awl." That is it! One does not incur capital punishment because he is foolish enough to remain a slave. What is *Rashi* teaching us?

Horav Shmuel David Walkin, zl, explains this pragmatically. How could there have been Jews who refused to leave Egypt? Who, in their right mind, would want to remain in Egypt only to be subjected to back-breaking labor and brutal suffering? Perhaps there were those Jews who were exempted from the slavery and not subjected to the suffering that their brethren sustained. How could they remain indifferent to the suffering of their brothers? Apparently, they neither saw nor were sensitive to the pain of their fellow Jews. Such a person who does not empathize with the plight of his brethren does not deserve to be liberated with them.

This is the underlying meaning of the words, "No man could see his brother, nor could anyone rise from his place." Hashem punishes *middah k'neged middah*, measure for measure. If one wonders why they were punished in such a manner that they could not see one another, it is because they did not "see" and get up to help when they saw a Jew suffering.

In an alternative explanation, the wicked Jews were punished because they followed the pattern of centuries. Those who did not want to leave were not satisfied by simply staying back themselves; they had to make sure that others stayed with them. This attitude has plagued us for millennia. Those Jews that do not want to join in the quest for spiritual development want to arrange that those who are observant are similarly hampered. The adage of "live and let live" does not apply to them. That is why they were left with the Egyptians. Their attitude toward their brethren was inherently Egyptian in nature.

✳ ✳ ✳ ✳ ✳ ✳

ולכל בני ישראל לא יחרץ כלב לשנו

Against all Bnei Yisrael, no dog shall whet its tongue. (11:7)

Rashi (22:30) cites the *Mechilta* that teaches us that the dogs became the beneficiaries of *treifah* meat, in the event an animal is deemed not kosher as the result of a wound. This is all due to their keeping still during the deaths of the Egyptian firstborn. Another animal, the donkey, also received a reward for its role in the Egyptian exodus. The *Torah* instructs us (*Shemos* 13:13), "Every firstborn donkey you shall redeem with a lamb." *Rashi* tells us that this law applies only to the firstborn donkey, not to any other non-kosher animal. This is because the donkeys carried the Egyptian spoils that the Jews took with them out of Egypt.

The question is evident. Two unclean animals both played a role in the Exodus. Both were rewarded; one with being fed unkosher, defiled meat; the other with the exalted status of *kedushah*, sanctity, which applies to *bechorah*, the firstborn. Why did the donkey achieve *kedushas bechor,* while the dog became the repository for defiled meat?

Horav Yosef Chaim Sonnenfeld, zl, gives a practical explanation that conveys a compelling lesson. The donkeys acted in a proactive manner. Their good deeds consisted of exertion in carrying the heavy burdens that were placed upon them. They provided necessary assistance to the Jews. For helping another fellow to carry his burden, one earns the merit of being rewarded with added sanctity. The dog also assisted, but, by contrast, it was in a passive manner. For refraining from barking it deserved a reward, but since no exertion was expended on its part, the reward is not very impressive. Perhaps we can say it is fit for a dog.

I question the above thesis because the dog went against its nature and refrained from barking, but the donkey did what it usually does — it carried a load. One would think that the dog should receive a greater reward than the donkey. Apparently, active performance of a *chesed* is of greater significance than unnatural, passive accomplishment.

✹ ✹ ✹ ✹ ✹ ✹

ושמרתם את המצות כי בעצם היום הזה הוצאתי את צבאותיכם מארץ
מצרים

*"You shall guard the matzos, for on this very day I will have taken your
legions out of the land of Egypt." (12:17)*

*R*ashi cites the famous dictum of Rabbi Yoshiah, "Do not read the
word only as '*matzos*,' but rather, also, as '*mitzvos*,'
commandments. In this sense the *pasuk* is teaching us that just as
people do not permit the *matzos* to become leavened, so should they not
allow the *mitzvos* to become leavened, by leaving opportunities for their
fulfillment unattended. Rather, "if the opportunity to fulfill a *mitzvah* comes
to your hand, do it immediately." A noteworthy statement, but how does it fit
into the textual flow of the *pasuk*? What does meticulous observance of
mitzvos have to do with the fact that on *that very day* the Jewish People were
redeemed from Egypt?

The *Kesav Sofer* explains that it is a well-known axiom that, prior to
the *geulah*, Exodus, *Klal Yisrael* were at a precarious point. Had they
remained any longer in Egypt, they would have descended to the nadir of
depravity and reached the fiftieth level of spiritual impurity. If this occurred,
they could not have arisen from defeat and would have been relegated to a
posterity of servitude in Egypt. The Exodus teaches us the overwhelming
significance of seizing the moment. That fleeting moment made the
difference in their redemption. Had they waited another minute we would
still be there, enslaved to the Egyptian culture and mindset. Likewise, when
the opportunity for performing a *mitzvah* materializes, one should not waste
it and immediately react to perform the *mitzvah*.

Otzros HaTorah derives this same lesson from the blessings that
Yitzchak *Avinu* gave to Yaakov *Avinu*. The *Torah* relates (*Bereishis* 27:30),
"And it was, when Yitzchak had finished blessing Yaakov, and Yaakov had
scarcely left from the presence of Yitzchak his father, that Eisav his brother
came back from the hunt." *Rashi* adds, "This one left, and the other one
arrived." The *Midrash* delves into how they missed each other. But after all

is said and done, we are talking about mere moments, when Yaakov preceded Eisav in receiving the blessings, that made the difference in the lot of his descendants for all time. Another minute — had Eisav returned a moment earlier or had Yaakov tarried a moment longer — our history would have been forever altered!

When the wellsprings of spiritual bounty open in Heaven, we have to be prepared and waiting to receive our share — or lose it forever. The value of a moment is incredible. For some, it is the opportunity for tremendous spiritual or material benefit, while for others, it could mean the difference between success and failure. The *Gedolei Yisrael, Torah* leaders, knew how to value every minute of their lives. The following short vignettes, cited by *Otzros HaTorah*, lend us insight into their lives.

Horav Elchanan Wasserman, zl, the legendary *Rosh HaYeshivah* of Baranowitz and one of the preeminent *Torah* leaders of pre-World War II Europe, was known for his piety and intensity in *Torah* study. His diligence was so outstanding that, as a student in the *Telshe Yeshivah* in Lithuania, he would study for eighteen hours a day. Time was of the essence and it could not be wasted. As *Rosh HaYeshivah*, he refused to take a salary from the *yeshivah,* leaving him quite poor — but satisfied. It is related that his shoes were so worn-out that the students took up a collection in the *yeshivah* to purchase a new pair of shoes for their venerable *rebbe.* He accepted the gift, but after a while lamented receiving the new shoes. It seems that it took him an extra two minutes every day to lace up his new shoes, while his old, torn shoes no longer had laces. The amount of time he wasted from *Torah* study disturbed him greatly!

On the last *Yom Kippur* of his life, the great *tzaddik Horav Yehudah Leib Chasman, zl, Mashgiach* of *Yeshivas Chevron, davened Neilah* at his home, surrounded by his closest students. In his weakened state after fasting the entire day, the *Mashgiach* sat down and waited for the *zman,* time, to begin *Maariv.* He looked at his students and said, "In the *Haftorah* of *Minchah,* we read that *Yonah HaNavi* tells the captain and crew of the boat that was rocking precariously in the turbulent sea, 'Lift me up and throw me into the water!' Why did he say 'Lift me up'? He should have simply said, 'Throw me into the water.' He said this because he wanted to gain another moment of life! We must do the same. We have a few minutes left. Let us not waste these precious moments."

At times, one can delay a positive undertaking, and it can make the difference between success and failure. *Horav Sholom Schwadron, zl,* related the following story: A member of a distinguished *Yerushalmi* family once had occasion to spend *Shabbos* in a hotel. Shortly after the *Shabbos* meal, he noticed an Israeli soldier writing. When the soldier became aware of the man staring at him, he said, "You are surprised that I am writing on *Shabbos?* Well, let me tell you what led to this."

The soldier began, "I would like you to know that I believe in Hashem just as you do. Let me explain to you why I do not observe *Shabbos.* My parents were not observant. As a result, I grew up with no knowledge of Judaism. My sole exposure to Judaism was being called 'dirty Jew' by the Polish peasants. I was drafted into the army at the beginning of World War I and sent to the front. During an exceptionally heavy military attack, I noticed a group of Jewish soldiers taking out a *Sefer Tehillim* from their pockets and praying fervently to Hashem. I was heartbroken that I, also a Jew, had nothing. I was not accepted by the gentiles, but neither did I know how to act as a Jew.

"At that moment, I looked up at Heaven and said to Hashem, 'You know that I have no way of knowing of Your existence. I entreat You to demonstrate Your existence to me by having a piece of shrapnel puncture my finger, so that I will no longer be able to shoot.' The moment I finished speaking, a piece of shrapnel hit my finger and wounded me to the point that till this very day I cannot bend that finger. I was released from the army and decided that I would enter the *bais ha'medrash* on that very day and begin to study about my religion.

"Regrettably, I pushed off my visit to the *bais ha'medrash* until after the war. Then, I was already enrolled in school with three months left to graduation. One thing led to another, and by the time I found my way to the *bais ha'medrash,* my heart that had originally been so turned on, had turned to stone. Nothing could penetrate it. The motivation and enthusiasm that had reigned months earlier had cooled. I had waited too long. The mind understood, but the emotion was no longer there."

If the opportunity for *mitzvah* performance appears, do not waste it. Act immediately. A split second decision to act correctly, to follow up on a positive experience, can spell the difference between success or failure. In an incredible story cited by Rabbi Yechiel Spero in his book, *"Touched by a Story,"* we see how the saintly *Chafetz Chaim* exemplified this idea. The cold, harsh winters in Radin, Poland, home of the *Chafetz Chaim,* were a challenge for the poor Jews due to inadequate heating. As bad as it was at home, it was much worse outdoors. Consequently, they would remain at home, unless they had to take an occasional trip to the market.

Warm clothes were a scarce commodity. Gloves, especially were a sought-after item. Once a wealthy man came to visit the *Chafetz Chaim* and, after spending some time with the sage, left him a precious gift: an expensive pair of fur-lined gloves. The *Chafetz Chaim* was not one to accept gifts, nor was he inclined to wear such fancy gloves. However, when he saw how much it meant to the man, the *Chafetz Chaim* acquiesced and accepted the gift.

A few days later, the *Chafetz Chaim*, accompanied by a few of his closest students, traveled by train to a neighboring town to attend an important meeting. The compartment on the train in which they sat was small and compact. The trip was short, so the *Chafetz Chaim* sat in his coat with his new gloves stored in his pockets. After a short while, it became stuffy in the compartment, so one of the students opened the window to let in some fresh air. The *Chafetz Chaim* moved to another seat, and, in the process, his coat brushed against the open window, causing one of his gloves to fall out of his pocket and out the window. A student noticed this and, when he told his *rebbe*, the *Chafetz Chaim,* to the amazement of his students, took the second glove and immediately threw it out of the window as well.

Noticing the puzzled stare of his students, he explained, "Someone is going to be walking along the tracks one day and will find the beautiful glove, but since it is a single glove, it will have very little use for him. I asked myself, what benefit would I derive from a single glove. I might as well provide another person with a *pair* of gloves, so at least he will benefit from them."

The *Chafetz Chaim* was the paradigm of the *ish ha'chesed*, man of loving kindness. His thoughts before he acted were even more impressive. He saw an opportunity to perform *chesed,* and he acted immediately. Wasted opportunities are lost opportunities.

ויקח משה את עצמות יוסף עמו

Moshe took the bones of Yosef with him. (13:19)

*C*hazal emphasize Moshe *Rabbeinu's* great love for *mitzvos* in the *Talmud Sotah* 13a, "Come and see how beloved *mitzvos* were to Moshe." When all of *Klal Yisrael* were involved with gathering the Egyptian booty, Moshe occupied himself with the *mitzvah* of retrieving Yosef's coffin. He epitomized the *pasuk* in *Mishlei* 10:8, *Chacham lev yikach mitzvos*, "The wise of heart will seize *mitzvos*." The *Mechilta* adds, "Moshe's act of accessing Yosef's coffin demonstrated his wisdom and piety. When all of the Jews were busy with collecting the Egyptian spoils, Moshe was occupied with carrying out Yosef's bones." Why do both *Midrashim* place emphasis not only on Moshe's piety, but also on his wisdom? First of all, the people of *Klal Yisrael* were also involved in performing a *mitzvah*. Hashem instructed them to empty out Egypt. This was a command; even though it was enjoyable, it was no less a command. Moshe *Rabbeinu* was also involved in carrying out a command. Perhaps his command was not as *geshmack*, pleasant, as gathering the Egyptian wealth, but it does not indicate his great wisdom, rather it evidenced great piety and devotion. Furthermore, relinquishing great wealth in order to perform an act of *chesed shel emes*, true kindness, is an act of great piety, but one can hardly refer to it as wisdom. Indeed, one who is pious is not necessarily one who is "street smart." The two are not necessarily concomitant.

Horav Avraham Pam, zl, gives us a practical answer and teaches us an important lesson in life and its priorities. *Chazal* teach us that at first, when the sea saw the Jewish People coming towards it pursued by the Egyptians, it did not want to split. Hashem instructed Moshe to lift up his hand. The sea still did not split until it saw the *Arono shel Yosef*, the coffin of Yosef. Then it split. While the commentators offer a number of possibile explainations why the sea split in response to Yosef's coffin, one thing is clear: the coffin motivated the sea to split. If Moshe had occupied himself with the Egyptian booty in the same manner as his fellow co-religionists, then they would have spent all of their wealth at the bottom of the sea! It would not have split. It was Moshe's foresight, his act of piety, that represented incredible practical wisdom. The coffin of Yosef catalyzed the splitting of the Red Sea. Was Moshe a *tzaddik* or a *chacham*? Moshe's practical wisdom, coupled with his piety, made the difference that day, but he was no less wise than he was pious.

Rav Pam suggests that this concept has significant practical application. Let us take a moment to focus on that wonderful, sought after vocation — *Torah chinuch*, Jewish education. While many people agree that those who devote their lives to *Torah* dissemination — to assuring that our heritage is transmitted to our children in its pristine, unadulterated form, in an environment of sanctity and morality — exemplify piety, are they *chachamim*?

Does a career choice in Jewish education indicate one's wisdom, or inability to do anything else? After all, one who is talented, whose incisive mind can plumb the depths of the intricacies of *Talmud* and Jewish law is *certainly* capable of rising to the apex of the fields of medicine, law or commerce. Therefore, an individual who abdicates the opportunity for a financially lucrative career to become an educator, is to be viewed as pious. Is such a choice, however, to be viewed from a practical sense as sound? Does such a decision indicate practical wisdom, when one takes into account the modest financial remuneration?

Rav Pam emphatically responds in the affirmative. While it is certainly true that a professional secular career will reap greater financial gain, should this be the only barometer for determining success? There is more to life than making money. There is *sipuk ha'nefesh*, self-satisfaction, knowing that one is molding and shaping the future of *Klal Yisrael*, realizing that his toil will be recognized for generations to come. A *Torah* educator spends his workday in an atmosphere that is wholesome, unsullied, ethical and moral, among highly idealistic people with lofty spiritual goals in life. This reality cannot necessarily be asserted about any other profession. It goes without saying that the spiritual rewards for this endeavor far overshadow *anything* else that one may do.

I must add that this thesis in no way is meant to undermine the wonderful efforts and accomplishments of those who devote themselves to the service of humanity in such fields as medicine, sciences and social services. It is only meant to underscore the significance of the much-maligned field of *Torah chinuch*. A career in *Torah chinuch* is a career in the service of the Almighty. It is the ultimate implementation of practical wisdom and piety. It is not simply a career; it is a noble calling!

In way of a postscript, I must add that *chinuch* is not for everyone. Those who are not appropriate for it — or for whatever reason are unqualified — should stay away. They will do more harm than good. Not every *ben Torah* will make a suitable *rebbe*. However, many wonderful and talented *bnei Torah* shun the field due to reasons that are, at best, nonsensical. The loss to *Klal Yisrael* of this wonderful reservoir of talent is inestimable. Imagine, if *our rebbeim* would have felt this way, where would *we* be today?

❃ ❃ ❃ ❃ ❃ ❃

ואמר פרעה לבני ישראל נבכים הם בארץ סגר עליהם המדבר

Pharaoh will say of Bnei Yisrael, "They are confined in the land, the Wilderness has locked them in." (14:3)

T he prefix *"l"* before *Bnei Yisrael, l'Bnei Yisrael,* usually means *to Bnei Yisrael,* which, of course, is not textually correct. *Rashi,* therefore, interprets the prefix to mean *"al" about Bnei Yisrael.* The *Targum Yonasan,* however, contends that Pharaoh did speak to two members of *Bnei Yisrael,* Dassan and Aviram, Moshe *Rabbeinu's* nemeses throughout his reign as leader. It was to them that Pharaoh commented about the Jewish People's seeming inability to escape the wilderness. This evokes a glaring question. We are aware that during the three days of the plague of darkness, all of those Jews who were evil — those who refused to leave Egypt and be liberated from its bondage and decadent culture — died. Why did not these two rogues also perish? Why were they allowed to continue to remain with the nation throughout the wilderness? They did nothing but undermine Moshe at every juncture, disparage the Almighty, and sabotage every spiritual inspiration with their negativity and evil.

The *Marahil Diskin, zl,* explains that they had one great merit which protected them: they were *shotrim,* foremen, who oversaw the Jewish labor crews in Egypt. They were among those who saw to it that the workload was not overwhelming. When the quota was not met, they were the ones who were beaten by the Egyptian taskmasters. The beatings and consequent wounds caused their bodies to emit an offensive odor. No one can harm any Jewish person who suffers for another Jew and empathizes with his pain and anguish — not even the Angel of Death or the Red Sea! In Hashem's eyes one who suffers for another Jew will merit the greatest reward, even if he himself is an intrinsically evil person.

In the *hesped*, eulogy, rendered by *Horav Shmuel Auerbach, Shlita*, for his father, *Horav Shlomo Zalmen Auerbach, zl*, he emphasized his father's overwhelming compassion and empathy for his fellow man. He related that his father would often recount an incident concerning the saintly *Horav Baruch Frankel Teumim, zl*, the *Baruch Taam*, whose son entered into a *shidduch*, matrimonial match, with the daughter of a well-known wealthy man. It happened that during that time the town's water-carrier became ill. The *Baruch Taam* was distraught over the man's illness. He could not eat. He prayed incessantly for him to return to good health. He was so overcome with concern for this man's welfare that he personally became visibly transformed. His *mechutanim*, parents of his future daughter-in-law, came to town for a visit and were taken aback by his changed appearance. The first thing that came to their mind was that he had regrets regarding the *shidduch*. The parents of the girl asked, "Perhaps the *Rav* is unhappy with the *shidduch* and would like to retract?"

The family responded that this was not the case. The distress was the result of his concern for the water-carrier. When the girl's mother heard this, she approached the *Baruch Taam* and said, "I can understand that the *Rav* is concerned about the water-carrier, but is this not a bit too much? It is hurting the *Rav's* health."

When the *Baruch Taam* heard these words, he immediately nullified the *shidduch* saying, "If this woman has no compassion and does not empathize with another Jew's pain, then it is not a suitable family with which to make a *shidduch*."

Rav Shlomo Zalmen exemplified empathy for all Jews. He once heard that a young woman in the United States was widowed and left with six young orphans. Bereft of her husband, the woman was brokenhearted and left to fend for herself, to be mother and father to her children. *Rav* Shlomo Zalmen called her up, and after introducing himself, comforted her in her grief and then asked to speak to each of her children. Indeed, every *Erev Yom Tov*, he would call a number of widows and wish them *Gut Yom Tov*.

I recently read an incredible story about empathy for another Jew in Rabbi Yechiel Spero's book, *Touched by a Story*. *Horav Chaim Ozer Grodzenski, zl*, was the preeminent *Torah* leader of pre-World War II Europe. As *rav* of the prestigious city of Vilna, he had his hand on the pulse of European Jewry. His *shiurim*, lectures, which enthralled his students, were brilliant masterpieces covering the breadth and depth of the sea of *Talmud*. He would customarily walk home from the *yeshivah* accompanied by a throng of students, eager to hear his every word.

It was a bitter winter day and a blustery arctic wind intensified the already sub-zero temperatures. The old *Rosh HaYeshivah* was trudging along the streets of Vilna, accompanied by his students. A young man approached *Rav* Chaim Ozer and waited to ask a question. *Rav* Chaim Ozer turned to the young man, whom he did not recognize, and asked him, "How can I help you?"

The young man, not more than fifteen-years-old, answered with a terrible stutter that he sought a certain street. The young man's speech defect was magnified by nervousness in the presence of the *Rav*. Although *Rav* Chaim Ozer was practically home already, he turned around and, together with his students, walked the young man to his destination.

Twenty-five minutes later, frozen with cold, *Rav* Chaim Ozer and his students turned around and began the trek home. The students could not figure out their *rebbe*. This was a man who never wasted a moment. His poor health and advanced age did not permit him to be out in the cold longer than was absolutely necessary. Yet, he *walked* the young man to his destination when he could have simply given him verbal directions. Why? The worst that would have happened is that the young man would have had to ask someone else along the way to confirm the directions.

Sensing his students' query, the *Rosh HaYeshivah* looked at them and said, "This boy clearly had a stuttering problem. He was obviously embarrassed by his impediment. If I had simply given him directions, he would have had to ask others along the way to confirm the directions to the obscure street. I did not want to cause a Jew further humiliation. Therefore, I walked him to his destination to spare him the discomfort. Is that so bad?"

This is a paradigm of empathy for another Jew.

✹ ✹ ✹ ✹ ✹ ✹

ויבא עמלק וילחם עם ישראל ברפידם

Amalek came and battled Yisrael in Rephidim. (17:8)

R ashi cites a fascinating *Midrash* that behooves each of us to stop and ask ourselves whether we are guilty of this oversight. *Chazal* tell us that the *pasuk* which deals with Amalek's attacking *Klal Yisrael* is juxtaposed to the previous *pasuk* in which the Jews tested Hashem, asking, "Is Hashem in our midst or not?" Hashem responded, "I am always in your midst. I never leave your side. Yet, you ask such a question! I swear by your lives that as a lesson, the dog, Amalek, will come and bite you. Then you will cry out to Me and realize where I am."

Chazal (cited by *Rashi*) compare this to a man who placed his son upon his shoulders and set forth on a journey. Whenever the boy would see an object that caught his fancy, he would ask his father for it, and the father would oblige. This happened a number of times. They later encountered a man, at which point the son asked the man, "Have you seen my father?" Hearing this, the father said to his son, "Do you not know where I am?" He immediately cast his son off his shoulders, and a dog came and bit him.

The analogy is very apropos to us. Hashem is there for us <u>all</u> of the time. Whenever we ask, He responds. The answer may not always appeal to us, but there is always a response. Do we thank Him when we are happy with the response, or do we just complain when things do not go our way? Regrettably, some of us wait until the dog bites us before we look up to acknowledge Hashem.

✹ ✹ ✹ ✹ ✹ ✹

ויאמר משה אל יהושע בחר לנו אנשים וצא הלחם בעמלק

Moshe said to Yehoshua, "Choose men from us and go out, do battle with Amalek." (17:9)

W hy was Yehoshua selected to lead *Klal Yisrael* into battle against Amalek? The *Midrash* explains that Moshe told Yehoshua, "Your grandfather [Yosef *HaTzaddik*] said, [to Potiphar's wife], 'I fear G-d (*Bereishis* 42:48), and concerning this one

[Amalek] it is written (*Devarim* 25:18), 'And (he) did not fear G-d.' Let the grandson of he who said he fears Hashem come and punish the one about whom it is said that he does not fear Hashem." *Horav Aharon Kotler, zl,* derives a noteworthy lesson from *Chazal.* The agent that Hashem selects to bring about salvation must personally be undefiled and faultless, free of any taint of impropriety regarding the sin which catalyzed the punishment. During every generation, Hashem has prepared a *tzaddik,* righteous *Torah* leader, through whom the salvation will be realized. He has the power to battle against the Amalek of every generation, because he is not culpable and is free of any vestige of the sin that characterizes the enemy of *Torah* and the Jewish People. To triumph, one must know his enemy, recognize his shortcomings and understand who is best suited for vanquishing him.

מחר אנכי נצב על ראש הגבעה ומטה האלקים בידי
"Tomorrow I will stand on top of the hill with the staff of G-d in my hand."
(17:9)

*H*orav Yaakov Moshe Charlop, zl, explains that Amalek's objective in battling with *Klal Yisrael* was to undermine the concepts of *mitzvah,* command, and *chovah,* obligation. He sought to destroy the Jew's enthusiasm and passion to perform a *mitzvah,* transforming *mitzvah* and *chovah* into *reshus,* a discretionary endeavor. These three concepts are represented by the letters *mem, ches,* and *raish,* which spell *machar,* tomorrow. Moshe *Rabbeinu* was intimating to the people that *machar* he would stand on the top of the hill, meaning that he would address the incursion into the spiritual fabric of *Klal Yisrael* that Amalek was bent on destroying. He would save the *machar* and see to it that the people would maintain their obligatory allegiance to Hashem.

Pinchas was the antithesis of Amalek. The *Torah* tells us that he took a *romach,* spear — which also contains the letters *raish, mem,* and *ches* — and zealously defended Hashem's honor. He accomplished the opposite of Amalek by transforming the *reshus,* discretionary endeavor, into a *mitzvah* and the *mitzvah* into a *chovah,* obligation.

Parashas Yisro

וישמע יתרו... את כל אשר עשה אלקים למשה ולישראל עמו

And Yisro heard all that G-d did to Moshe and to Yisrael, His people.
(18:1)

Yisro was not the only one who heard about the miracles which Hashem wrought for His people. All the nations of the world heard. Yet, the *Torah* writes that only Yisro heard. Was his ability to hear different from that of the others? The commentators explain that everyone heard, but only Yisro applied what he heard.

To paraphrase *Horav Chaim Shmuelevitz, zl*, "Yisro did not simply hear; rather, he *derhered*, a *Yiddish* expression which denotes a specific quality of listening. We suggest another idea. More often than not, we attend a lecture, an ethical discourse, and are impressed with the message that has been expounded. We listened — we heard — we even accepted the idea, but, as far as we are concerned, it is a great idea — for someone else! It has nothing to do with us. There is no *personal* message. Yisro heard and understood the personal aspect of the miracles which Hashem had wrought.

❋ ❋ ❋ ❋ ❋ ❋

וישמע יתרו... את כל אשר עשה אלקים למשה ולישראל עמו

And Yisro heard all that G-d did to Moshe and to Yisrael, His people.
(18:1)

Rashi explains that Yisro heard two reports that had such a great effect on him that he left the comfort of his home and sought out *Klal Yisrael* in the wilderness. He heard about *Krias Yam Suf*, the splitting of the Red Sea, and the war with Amalek. The *Torah* seems to imply that in addition to impacting Yisro, these miracles are also interrelated with one another. We must endeavor to understand their significance, as well as their relationship.

In his *sefer Simchas HaTorah, Horav Simcha Hakohen Sheps, zl,* explains that with their victory over Amalek, *Klal Yisrael's* incredible power was revealed to the world. The question now arises: If *Klal Yisrael* was so powerful, why did they not simply battle the Egyptians also? Why was it necessary to split the Red Sea? They could have emerged triumphant from Egypt — not driven out as slaves.

Apparently, the Jews could not wage war with the Egyptians because they still maintained a spark of *hakoras ha'tov*, gratitude, to them for opening up their country to them many years earlier when Yosef was viceroy. Egypt had been their home away from home for many years. By right, they could not battle with them, because war is the antithesis of *hakoras ha'tov.* This is what inspired Yisro: the war with Amalek and the splitting of the Red Sea. The fact that they could vanquish Amalek, but they would not fight the Egyptians, precipitating the need for *Krias Yam Suf,* demonstrated the extraordinary character of this nation. This nation represented the ideal, a people whose character should serve as the exemplar of what a human being should strive to be. They were the people whom Yisro understood he should join.

✻ ✻ ✻ ✻ ✻ ✻

והודעת להם את הדרך ילכו בה

And you shall make known to them the path in which they should go.
(18:20)

In the *Talmud Bava Metzia* 30b, *Chazal* interpret the words, "the path," as a reference to performing acts of loving-kindness. In his *Shaarei Teshuvah* 3:13, *Rabbeinu Yonah* asserts that *tzedakah*, charity, is performed with one's money, while *gemillus chasadim*, acts of loving-kindness, are performed both with one's possessions and with one's body. A person should see to it that he provides assistance to his fellow man, regardless of his own personal financial standing. A smile, a nice word, a personal visit, serve this objective; it is not the monumental deeds that make the difference. Simple acts of caring can change a person's life. *Chesed* begins when we take notice of those around us in order to respond to their needs.

I recently read about a project initiated by a professor of clinical psychology. He encouraged his students to get involved in helping people. They asked, "What is there to do?" That is a typical question of those who are looking for a way to avoid responding to the needs of others. The professor took one of his students, whom we will call Joe, and brought him to a senior citizens center, so that he could do something for others. The following is what happened as a result of Joe's visit.

When Joe first came to the home, he noticed that there were a large number of elderly patients just lying around in bed wearing their old cotton gowns, doing nothing but staring up at the ceiling. These people were acting like they had become victims of senility, but this was not the case. Senility is not necessarily a natural consequence of old age. It often occurs when people do not feel loved or useful.

At first, Joe did not know what to do. Indeed, this was the first time he had been in such a home. The professor suggested that he approach a certain elderly woman and begin a conversation with her. Joe went over to the patient, and they began to talk. It was more of a monologue than a dialogue. Nobody had listened to the woman for so long that she had a lot to share. She talked about her life, the ups and downs, the successes and failures, the happy times and the sad ones. She even spoke about her impending death. She had made peace with the fact that she would not live forever. She had so much to say, but no one had cared to listen!

Joe was thoroughly moved by the experience. Therefore, he returned the following week. Soon he began to spend a day visiting many of the patients. It became known as "Joe's Day." He would come to the home, and all the patients would gather to speak and even to listen. Someone cared.

No longer did they sit around in their worn-out gowns, staring at the ceiling or at the clock on the wall. Some asked their children to bring them new clothes. They had their hair done; they wanted to look nice, because someone finally cared. Joe realized that kindness can be expressed through the little things we do. Look around, and you will find a lonely person who needs company; a hassled worker whom no one remembers to thank; a young student who seems forgotten by parents caught up in the maelstrom of life; a spouse who needs a smile; a child who needs an encouraging word. It is the little things that we do — or do not do — that make the difference. That is what *chesed* is all about.

One more story: *Horav Elazar M. Shach, zl,* was a giant in *Torah* scholarship. He was also a giant in *chesed.* He did not merely delegate others to perform acts of *chesed*; even at his advanced age, he personally went out of his way to help those in need. He exhibited a sense of caring for others that was unparalleled. An observant psychologist who lives in Yerushalayim related the following story. When he walked into *shul* on *Erev Pesach*, he was greeted by a number of *mispallelim*, worshippers, "You must have done something special to have merited a visit from *Rav* Shach."

"Who? What are you talking about?" he asked them.

"*Rav* Shach was walking around your courtyard last night for about an hour," they said.

"Impossible. You must be mistaken. Why would *Rav* Shach visit my courtyard?" the psychologist asked incredulously.

After awhile, it became clear to the psychologist that, indeed, *Rav* Shach had been at his house. He now became chagrined, exclaiming, "Woe is me. It is my fault. I told the *Rosh HaYeshivah* not to come up to the house. It is because of me that the *gadol ha'dor*, preeminent *Torah* leader of our generation, waited outside for an hour."

The worshippers looked at him, without a clue as to what he was talking about. The psychologist was miserable. On *Chol HaMoed*, one of the Intermediate Days of *Pesach*, he traveled to Bnei Brak to ask *mechilah*, beg forgiveness, from *Rav* Shach. The *Rosh HaYeshivah* joyfully welcomed him to his home, saying, "I should ask you for *mechilah*!"

Afterwards, *Rav* Shach explained what had occurred and what had precipitated his trip to Yerushalayim. On the night before *Pesach*, when everyone was occupied with *Bedikas Chametz*, searching their homes for *chametz*, a *bachur*, young man, came to speak to *Rav* Shach. The *Rosh HaYeshivah* perceived that something was clearly wrong emotionally with this *bachur*. He then telephoned the psychologist to ask if he would spend some time speaking with the young man. The psychologist was prepared to travel to Bnei Brak if that was what *Rav* Shach desired. *Rav* Shach told him that he would send the *bachur* over to him. Little did the psychologist know that *Rav* Shach, feeling that the *bachur* should not travel alone, would accompany him and wait outside for the duration of the visit.

Upon being asked why he did not send someone else with the *bachur*, *Rav* Shach responded, "I am an old man and, thus, have very little to do to prepare for the *Yom Tov* of *Pesach*. Why should I bother someone else who is busy? Furthermore, I had the opportunity to take a stroll and partake of the refreshing air of Yerushalayim while I thought of *divrei Torah*. What greater pleasure is there?" This story speaks for itself.

✹ ✹ ✹ ✹ ✹ ✹

כה תאמר לבית יעקב ותגיד לבני ישראל

"So shall you say to the house of Yaakov and relate to Bnei Yisrael." (19:3)

When was the last time someone got up and attributed his success in *Torah* study to his mother? It is certainly not a common scenario. *Horav Elazar M. Shach, zl*, is quoted as saying, "It is well worth it to work a lifetime, establishing seminaries for thousands of young women, in order that the result will be one good mother!" He substantiated this when he added, "Look at what one mother accomplished! *Rashi's* mother raised a son that illuminated the world. What would the *Torah* have been without *Rashi*? No *Rashi* on *Chumash* — no *Rashi* on *Navi* — no *Rashi* on *Talmud*. *Torah* would never have been the same. All because of one mother."

The commentators, each in his own manner, explain why Moshe *Rabbeinu* was instructed to convey the *Torah* first to *Bais Yaakov*, the women, and then to *Bnei Yisrael*, the men. The *Midrash* attributes it to the women's alacrity in *mitzvah* performance. *Pirkei D'Rabbi Eliezer* explains that men usually accede to their wive's advice. The *Moshav Zekeinim al HaTorah* from the *Baalei Tosfos* cites *Rabbeinu Moshe M'Narvona, zl*, who says that it was in Leah *Imeinu's* merit. She had a tablet made of gold, upon which was engraved the words, "*Torah tzivah lanu Moshe*," the *Torah* was commanded by Moshe. She would gaze at this tablet all day to the point that her eyes became tender as a result of the reflection from the gold. Therefore, her descendants/daughters, merited to hear the *Torah* first.

Rabbeinu Bachya asserts that women preceded men in hearing the

Torah because the success of a man's *Torah* study is based upon the women in his life. A mother sets the tone for a child's attitude toward *Torah* study. She inculcates a love for *Torah* in her child, a love that will continue to endure as he develops and matures. The *koach ha'chinuch*, power of education, that rests upon the mother is compelling. When the *Chafetz Chaim, zl*, would hold his mother's old, tattered *Sefer Tehillim* in his hands, he would become very emotional and say, "Do you have any idea how many tears my mother shed over this *Tehillim*, as she entreated Hashem to grant her that her son should be a *Yehudi kasheir*, proper Jew?"

The *Chafetz Chaim's* daughter once related the following story concerning her grandmother. She said, "My grandmother was not a miracle worker. I do remember that at the end of her life, after her son, my father, had become renown throughout the *Torah* world as the saintly *Chafetz Chaim*, a number of close friends approached her with the obvious question: 'How did you merit to have a son that illuminated the eyes of the world? What was your recipe for success?'

"She replied that she could not remember anything that she had done that would have catalyzed such success. After they pestered her some more, she added that there was one small thing that came to mind. Prior to her wedding, her mother had asked to speak to her. These were her words: 'My daughter, listen to what I have to say. We are commanded to raise our sons to study *Torah* and have *yiraas Shomayim*, fear of Heaven. Therefore, I ask of you that every free moment that you have, take your *Siddur* in hand and pray to Hashem that you merit to raise your children to be G-d-fearing and observant Jews who will devote themselves to *Torah* study. Do not forget to shed tears when you pray.' She gave her daughter a *Siddur* in which *Sefer Tehillim* was included.

"My grandmother ended by saying, 'That is all I did. Whenever I had a free moment, I would take out the *Siddur* and recite *Tehillim*, crying out my heart to Hashem that my *Yisrael'ke* would develop into a *talmid chacham, Torah* scholar, and a *yarei Shomayim*.'"

Upon relating this story, *Horav Eliezer M. Shach, zl*, would add, "*Rashi's rebbe* was *Rabbeinu Gershom Me'or Ha'golah*. He was greater than *Rashi*. Yet, *Rashi* merited to become the *Rabbon Shel Kol Yisrael*, quintessential *Torah* teacher of the Jewish People. Why? Because of his mother, the *tzadekes*, who was the sister of *Rabbeinu Shimon HaZakein m'Magence* and because of his saintly father."

It is related that *Rashi's* father possessed a valuable, precious stone that the priests needed for their idol. He, of course, was not about to grant them access to this stone. They cunningly convinced him to travel with them on a boat, with the intention of forcibly taking the stone from him. When *Rashi's* father realized what they were about to do, he threw the stone into the water, thereby forfeiting his own life. In return for this extraordinary act of *mesiras nefesh*, self-sacrifice, a *Bas Kol,* Voice from Heaven, came forth to announce that he would merit a son that would illuminate the world.

The *Gaon m'Vilna* said about *Horav Zalman, zl, m'Volozhin*, brother of *Horav Chaim, zl, m'Volozhin*, that he was above the human dimension. He was like a *Malach Elokim*, a Heavenly angel. This is attributed to his mother who, when she was in labor and about to give birth to him, refrained from any moaning whatsoever, because her husband was studying together with the *Shaagas Arye*. In her desire not to disturb these two giants of *Torah*, she contained her expression of pain until the final moment of birth. In this merit, the *Shaagas Arye* blessed her that her newly born son would be able to vanquish his *yetzer hara*, evil-inclination, and become similar to a Heavenly angel. This all demonstrates that when parents value *Torah* education, so do their children.

Children learn to respect what they see respected at home. When they are exposed to a double standard or hypocrisy, they react in kind. In concluding the impact that Jewish mothers have had on their children, we cite the mother of the *Rosh HaYeshivah* of *Yeshivas Chachmei Lublin* and founder of the *Daf HaYomi*, folio a day, *Horav Meir Shapiro, zl*. Rav Meir Shapiro would always relate two thoughts that his mother had shared with him as a young child. These ideas inspired him and, in turn, became the source of inspiration to so many others. His mother would say to him, "Meir'l, my child, see that you study well and learn *Torah*, because every day that goes by with no *Torah* learned is something precious lost that can never be retrieved. Who knows what the next day may bring?" She would also emphasize the greatness of *Torah* when she said, "Work harder and sacrifice more. For such a great and mighty *Torah*, this is too small a sacrifice."

When a child grows up hearing these two maxims as part of his daily lessons, it is no wonder that he achieved such distinction. Indeed, all of us are beneficiaries of *her* legacy.

✻ ✻ ✻ ✻ ✻ ✻

לא תחמד אשת רעך...וכל אשר לרעך

You shall not covet your fellow's wife…nor anything that belongs to your fellow. **(20:14)**

It seems that if one is not to covet anything that belongs to his friend, "anything" would include his house and his wife, etc. Why does the *Torah* make a point to emphasize certain possessions and then use the collective "anything" at the end of the *pasuk*? *Horav Shmuel Walkin, zl,* makes a practical suggestion. He says that the *Torah* is advising us how to not fall into the trap of envy and desire for what does not belong to us. When we see that our friend possesses an item of exceptional beauty or value, something we envy, we should think about everything else our friend has. This can be viewed from contrasting positions. On the one hand, our friend might have accumulated much "baggage": problems; challenging situations; major physical or financial losses. These might have catalyzed compensation for him in the form of his beautiful home. Alternatively, we should look at his many achievements, the wonderful acts of *chesed* that he has performed. The beautiful possessions which he now has might be his remuneration. When we look at our friend's possessions, we should view them in the context of "everything" that he has. It might change our mind regarding coveting what belongs to someone else.

✻ ✻ ✻ ✻ ✻ ✻

Parashas Mishpatim

כי תקנה עבד עברי שש שנים יעבד ובשבעת יצא לחפשי

If you buy a Jewish servant, he shall work for six years; and in the seventh, he shall go free. (21:2)

The *Ramban* explains why the *Torah's* civil laws begin with the laws of *eved Ivri*, the Hebrew servant. The freedom that the *Torah* demands for these servants after six years is a direct corollary to *Klal Yisrael's* liberation from Egypt. Indeed, this is the reason that in the *Haftorah* for *Parashas Mishpatim, Yirmiyahu HaNavi* emphasizes freedom of the *eved Ivri* after six years, warning that a lack of adherence to this law will catalyze *Klal Yisrael's* national exile. Furthermore, the *Yerushalmi* in *Meseches Rosh Hashanah* says that the laws of *eved Ivri* were presented as the Jews left Egypt and reiterated at *Har Sinai*. We ask: Was there no other time to command *Klal Yisrael* concerning the laws of the Jewish servant? Was the Egyptian exodus the only venue for these laws? Could they not have waited until they reached *Har Sinai*? *Horav Chaim Shmuelevitz, zl,* provides a practical answer to this question. It was at a time when they themselves had just been liberated from bondage, when they had finally experienced the joy of freedom, that they would gladly accept a *mitzvah* that limits how long a Jew could be subjected to servitude.

Otzros HaTorah cites an incredible story that gives pragmatic application to the concept that one gains deeper insight into a matter after he has personally experienced a corresponding situation. When the enemies of Nero Caesar of Rome were seeking him, he escaped from the capital and hid in the home of one of his trusted servants. Word got out that Nero was in the area, and an extensive search was conducted to find the monarch. Nero had no choice but to remain in the servant's home. When the rebels came and searched the house, Nero hid beneath a bed, pushing himself as far back as possible. The rebels entered the house and took it apart. They came to the bed, and instead of looking beneath it, they ran a sword back and forth. Apparently, they did not go far enough, because the sword missed Nero by a fraction of an inch. He held his breath and — if the concept of prayer can apply to such a despot — he prayed. After awhile, the rebels gave up their search and left.

The war finally ended, and Nero's forces had triumphed. Now came the opportunity to repay those who had been faithful him. He called to the palace the servant who had risked his and his family's lives for the king and asked what he wanted as a reward. He could have *anything* he desired. The servant responded that he wanted just one thing. He wanted to know what went through the king's mind as he lay beneath the bed while the rebels were searching for him. How did he feel at that time? Of all the things that the servant could have requested, he chose something that made no sense. At least we understand why he was a servant.

Upon hearing his request, the king immediately instructed his guards to shackle the servant and throw him into the dungeon. The nerve of the man! His insolence was outrageous. To throw away such an unprecedented opportunity was the epitome of *chutzpah*. Therefore, in three days, Nero himself would perform his execution. The day of the execution arrived, and the prisoner faced his final moments on earth. Nero climbed up the stairs of the gallows. He took the noose and placed it around the neck of his soon-to-be departed servant, pulling the rope slowly. The very last moment, as the servant was choking, Nero cut the rope, sparing him. At that moment, Nero whispered to the man, "Now you know how I felt under the bed!"

Nero explained his actions to the servant in the following manner: "I promised you anything that you wanted. Your request was impossible to convey orally. I could not explain to you my true emotions. The only way that you could actually understand how I felt was to experience a similar situation firsthand. I gave you the opportunity to experience what it felt like to be so close to death."

In order for *Klal Yisrael* to sense the inherent joy that a servant feels when he is liberated, so that they would accept the laws of *eved Ivri* correctly, it was essential that they hear the laws at a time when they were experiencing the joy of liberation.

וּרְצַע אֲדֹנָיו אֶת אָזְנוֹ בַּמַּרְצֵעַ

And his master shall bore through his ear the awl. (21:6)

*C*hazal explain that the ear is bored because it was the ear that heard that "*Bnei Yisrael* are My servants"(*Vayikra* 25:55). Yet, this *eved*, servant, felt so degraded that he chose to be a servant to a servant. He had the opportunity to be a free man, but he chose to remain subservient to a human master. This man had no self-esteem. His ear was bored so that he would have a constant reminder of what he had done to himself. Why wait six years to bore his ear? The beginning of his degradation was when he first became a servant. Why not bore his ear then?

In his response to this question, *Horav Yechezkel Levenstein, zl,* delves into the human psyche. He distinguishes between two individuals who are on the ladder of spiritual ascendancy, both on the same rung: one is ascending, while the other is descending — rapidly. One individual is basically doing well, but, as of late, he has manifested a tendency toward slacking off a bit. He has exhibited a slight decline in his spiritual affiliation, and he is gravitating gradually toward the blandishments of his *yetzer hara*, evil-inclination. This man is in trouble. He stands on the precipice about to fall into the nadir of depravity. Although to all appearances he presents himself as being spiritually healthy, his slight decline can rapidly transform into an uncontrollable downward spiral.

The other individual has already fallen to the bottom of the pit. He has destroyed his spiritual status quo, but a yearning, a tiny spark within his consciousness, has begun to ignite. Deep in the recesses of his soul, an awakening is beginning. If this person continues with his quest, his success is ensured.

There was an accepted maxim in the famed *Bais HaTalmud* of Kelm: A person who previously had not *davened*, prayed, with *kavanah*, proper concentration and devotion, but has now begun to recite some prayers with *kavanah*, is far better than he who has always *davened* with great *kavanah* but whose *kavanah* has recently begun to dwindle. The first individual is an *oleh* — he is ascending — while the latter is a *yoreid* — he is descending.

When a person is plummeting to the depths of depravity it is not an appropriate time to speak to him. While in the throes of descent, as he is plunging downward, he is not inclined to listen. The one who is ascending, however, is open to suggestion. While he may still be at the bottom of the ladder, he is facing upward. For him, there is hope.

At the point of his original sale, the servant is on a downward spiral. He has just stolen and been caught, but has no money to pay back his theft. He is willing to be sold into servitude. To bore his ear, to give him *mussar*, an ethical discourse, about what he is doing to his life will be to no avail — at this point. In contrast, the *eved* who has completed six years of labor, who has been a servant to another human being and has enjoyed it to the point that he wants to remain in a life of subservience, has reached the bottom. He can only go up. Now is the appropriate time to speak to him, to bore his ear and convey the *Torah's* lesson to him. For him, there is hope for success.

* * * * * *

חמשה בקר ישלם תחת השור וארבע צאן תחת השה
He shall pay five cattle in place of the ox, and four sheep in place of the sheep. (21:37)

One who steals livestock and either sells or slaughters it must pay five times the value of the ox and four times the value of the sheep. *Chazal* tell us that the *Torah* reduced the fine for a sheep, as a result of the embarrassment which the thief suffered when he carried the sheep on his shoulders. They add that if the humiliation of a common thief evokes Hashem's pity, how much more so should we be concerned with the feelings of innocent people. The *Torah* takes the feelings of a person very seriously. While no one would purposely hurt another person, all too often our thoughtlessness inadvertently causes unnecessary pain to another person. At times, our insatiable ego provokes us to act in a manner which, albeit unconscious, can have a detrimental effect on those around us. The following vignettes demonstrate how far some of our *gedolim*, *Torah* luminaries, went not to infringe upon another person's sensitivities.

Horav Sholom Schwadron, zl, the legendary *Maggid* of Yerushalayim, was a dynamic speaker. His words could penetrate the most obstinate heart and move the most intractable person. He related that he was once asked to substitute for a *mashgiach* in one of the *yeshivos*. The *mashgiach* had to go fundraising for an extended period of time. The students of the *yeshivah* asked *Rav* Sholom to give them *shmuessen*, ethical discourses, which was one of the functions of the *mashgiach*. *Rav* Sholom was in a quandary. He was asked to act as a *mashgiach* in the sense that he would speak with and motivate the *bachurim*, young men, of the *yeshivah*. Delivering *shmuessen* was a function that belonged solely to the *mashgiach*. If *Rav* Sholom's discourses would be impressive, then word would get back to the *mashgiach*, and it might make him feel bad. On the other hand, did he have the right to impede the students' spiritual development if he had the ability and the charisma to reach out to them? He decided to ask *Horav Yechezkel Levenstein, zl, mashgiach* of *Yeshivas Ponevezh*, for his opinion regarding the matter. *Rav* Chatzkel responded, "We have an accepted axiom that if the opportunity to build the *Bais HaMikdash* avails itself, but, simultaneously, this might cause someone to feel bad, it is better not to build!" *Rav* Sholom did not give the *shmuessen*.

In support of this, we see that Moshe *Rabbeinu* delayed going to Pharaoh for seven days, because he feared that his older brother, Aharon *HaKohen,* would be hurt. Imagine, Moshe knew that *Klal Yisrael's* liberation depended on him, yet he refrained from going because he did not want to hurt his brother. This is one more reason why he was worthy of the mantle of leadership.

It is not uncommon for principals and teachers to showcase a specific student. After all, a teacher looks good when he can display the fruits of his labor. The school administration takes great pride in their students who excel academically. Regrettably, this is a standard by which the common person measures success. They rarely notice the student who is diligent, but does not receive an A on his test; or the student who epitomizes ethical behavior and exemplary demeanor, but does not excel scholastically. This is human nature, and it probably will not change. *Horav Solumon Mutzafi, zl,* was as brilliant as he was pious. His virtue and saintliness were legendary. At the young age of six years old, he was the undisputed academic scholar of his school in Baghdad. One day the principal told him that the Chief Rabbi of Baghdad and a group of philanthropists from America were coming to visit the school. The principal had decided that young Solumon would be tested publicly to demonstrate to the visitors his brilliance and breadth of knowledge. This would certainly benefit the school.

Solumon refused to be part of the show. He felt it was wrong to benefit from his *Torah* knowledge. In addition, it would hurt his fellow classmates. The principal insisted; the young boy refused. When Solumon saw that it was a losing battle, he hid. For two hours he concealed himself in order not to hurt the other boys' feelings. Even as a young child, this great *tzaddik* showed signs of greatness.

❈ ❈ ❈ ❈ ❈ ❈

כל אלמנה ויתום לא תענון
You shall not cause pain to any widow or orphan. **(22:21)**

Only a very despicable person takes advantage of a widow or orphan. Regrettably, however, it happens. It is lamentable that those in power take advantage of those who are not. Those who are themselves insecure, frequently prey upon the weak and disadvantaged. They must exert their power over someone, so they choose to pick on those who are inherently vulnerable. Hashem will not tolerate the victimization of widows and orphans. He is the Father of orphans and the Judge of widows. They are not alone because they can turn to Hashem, Who will listen to their pleas.

Loneliness is a state which we all fear. It is not the loneliness of solitude that we fear. It is possible to be surrounded by a crowd and yet feel all alone. The number of people with whom we come in contact has nothing to do with our level of loneliness. The warmth of our hearts towards the people around us determines our level of loneliness. One can be in the midst of a crowd or in the comparative quiet of his home; it is a sense of self-worth — a feeling that others care about him and that he has friends who share common goals and aspirations — that drives away the feelings of loneliness. While at times it is good to be alone, it is never good to be lonely. A secular writer once defined city life as "millions of people being lonely together."

One who trusts in Hashem understands that he is never alone. Hashem is always with him. Moreover, a Jew has a past to which he can connect. He belongs to a tradition that is enduring and stable. The tragedy of so many of our alienated brethren is that they have severed their ties to the past. By uprooting themselves from our tradition, they have destroyed the bond of "belonging" to the Jewish family.

Hashem tells the widow and orphan that they are not alone. He is with them. This is the message for anyone who has experienced loneliness: Hashem is with you. There is no loneliness so great, so absolute, so utterly devastating than the loneliness of he who does not know to call upon Hashem in his time of need. He who cannot pray to Hashem with the inner confidence that he is being heard, that his entreaty is being acknowledged, is truly lonely. The ultimate answer to loneliness is faith in Hashem. The companionship of Hashem is the balm for all loneliness.

Lying in a hospital bed can catalyze this relationship. Hashem's *Shechinah* rests at the head of a sick person's bed. Finding oneself suddenly in a hospital bed can be a frightening experience. One day, we are movers and shakers, occupied with so many people and involved in many endeavors. Suddenly, it is all in the past. We are no longer occupied. We are passive respondents. We do not move; we are moved. We have become dependent upon the doctors, nurses, and our families. It is at this time of loneliness that we lay back and realize that we are not really alone. We are as alone as we want to be. The *Shechinah* is there to comfort and reassure us throughout our ordeal.

Parashas Terumah

דבר אל בני ישראל ויקחו לי תרומה

Speak to Bnei Yisrael and let them take for Me a portion. (25:2)

T he *Baal HaTurim* makes an interesting play on the word *terumah*. He says *terumah* consists of the same letters as *Torah/ mem*, which is a reference to the *Torah* that was given to us after Moshe *Rabbeinu*'s spending forty days and forty nights on *Har Sinai*. What does the *Baal HaTurim* mean, and what relationship exists between *terumah* and the forty days and nights that preceded the giving of the *Torah*?

The *Bais Yisrael* explains that when one contributes *terumah*, a donation, to a worthy cause, not only does he *give* but he also *takes*. Commensurate with how much he has given, he develops a partnership in the endeavor to which he has contributed. Clearly, he who gives a larger sum will assume a greater share in the partnership. This is alluded to with the words, "And let them *take* for Me a portion." By giving to the *Mishkan*, one actually takes for himself a portion in its construction.

This may be the case in regard to charity. When it comes to *Torah* study, however, the effort, diligence and dedication one applies to studying *Torah* seems secondary and extrinsic to the actual study. If anything, the effort expended supplements the actual *Torah* study. The *Baal HaTurim* addresses this misconception by comparing *terumah* to *Torah*. When one studies *Torah*, the effort and diligence is an intrinsic component of the learning, and thus, his portion in *Torah* is dependent upon the effort and dedication which he expends in this study. He earns his share in *Torah* in the manner that he studies it.

This idea is underscored by the comparison to *Torah,* which was given after Moshe spent forty days and forty nights on *Har Sinai*. It refers to those forty days about which Moshe *Rabbeinu* said, "I ate no bread, nor did I drink water." Moshe demonstrated how one develops a share in *Torah* — with extreme dedication and self-sacrifice.

דבר אל בני ישראל ויקחו לי תרומה

Speak to Bnei Yisrael and let them take for Me a portion. **(25:2)**

The *Midrash* expounds on the uniqueness of the *Mishkan* and *Klal Yisrael's* relationship to it, via their contribution towards its creation. The *Midrash* expresses a beautiful and noteworthy analogy. "Hashem says to *Klal Yisrael*, 'I sold you My *Torah*. I sold Myself with it, as it says: *Take for Me a portion.* This may be compared to a king who had an only daughter. A prince from a distant land came and asked for her hand in marriage. The king responded, 'I have one daughter. I will gladly give her to you in matrimony. It is difficult, however, for me to let her out of my sight. Yet, I know that she must leave with you when you return to your home. I ask only that you provide for me a room in your palace, so that I can be near my daughter.' Likewise, Hashem has given us His *Torah*. He cannot separate Himself from it. While He certainly wants us to have and use it, He seeks an opportunity whereby He can also be part of the equation. Consequently, He has asked us to make a *Mishkan* for Him, which will be 'His' room so that He can be near His *Torah*.

This *Midrash* conveys to us Hashem's unique relationship with the *Torah* and the character of His Presence in the *Mishkan*. There is a deeper message, however, that we are to derive from *Chazal. Horav Sholom Schwadron, zl,* gleans from *Chazal* the significance of a *makom Torah*, place where *Torah* is studied. Hashem says that He cannot separate Himself from His only child, the *Torah*. He, therefore, asks that we provide for Him a place where He can be close to His *Torah*. In other words, in a place where there is no *Torah* — there is also no place for Hashem! For the *Shechinah* to repose among us, we have to have the *Torah* close by. It must be an integral part of our daily lives if we want Hashem included. Incredible!

❋ ❋ ❋ ❋ ❋ ❋

ויקחו לי תרומה

And let them take for Me a portion. **(25:2)**

Horav Chaim Plagi, zl, cited by *Horav Yitzchak Zilberstein, Shlita,* notes that the word *terumah*, which is interpreted here as a contribution, has the same letters — *taf, raish, vav, mem, hay* —

as the word *ha'mosar*, that which is a luxury. He derives a noteworthy lesson from the similarity between these two words. When Hashem sees that a Jewish home is replete with luxuries, He "tells" its owner, "I see that you do not worry about how you spend your money. You are prepared to open up your wallet for all kinds of luxuries, items that are not essential, objects that reflect unnecessary indulgence on your part. Do you do the same for the poor man that comes to your door begging for alms? Do you manifest the same 'open door' policy for your *terumah* as you do for *mosar*?"

We do not realize that when we spend on ourselves, when we indulge ourselves in opulence, we open ourselves to criticism. Do we do the same for the poor, or do we assure them that suddenly we have no liquid assets available? If there is money for extravagances, we are obligated to have funds available to assist those who are in need.

❋ ❋ ❋ ❋ ❋ ❋

וְעָשִׂיתָ עָלָיו זֵר זָהָב סָבִיב

And you shall make on it a gold crown all around. **(25:11)**

In the *Talmud Yoma* 76b, *Chazal* say that the attachment of a golden rim/crown projecting upward and encircling the top of the *Aron* symbolized the crown of *Torah* which is available to whomever "wants it." What is the meaning of "wanting" the crown of *Torah*, and how does one demonstrate his desire to achieve this status? *Horav Elazar M. Shach, zl,* explains this concept with the following story, related to him by an elderly Jew, concerning one of the distinguished *rabbanim* of their generation. When this Jew was a young man, he studied in a small *yeshivah* in the city of Krason, which was situated in the outskirts of Kiev. Among the student population there was a young boy who strived very hard to achieve knowledge in *Torah*. His diligence was incredible. He had one problem, however — his mind was far from astute. His ability to grasp even the most simple *Talmudic* logic was extremely weak. He would go from student to student asking them, begging them, to assist him in understanding the *Talmud*. It was to no avail. As soon as he understood one *halachah* and he continued to the next, he forgot the first *halachah*. This went on and on until the students in the *bais ha'medrash* lost their patience with him.

The elderly Jew who was relating the story said that he continued to take pity on this boy and told him that he would always be available to answer questions and explain the *Talmud's* passages. This continued on a regular basis until he could no longer study for himself. He was always being pestered by the boy who, regrettably, did not retain what he was being taught. Finally, he lost it and said, "I also have to learn something!"

Hearing this, the boy walked away, dejected. After a short while, the young man wanted to see what had happened to the boy. Did he approach someone else, or did he just go study by himself? He looked around and there in the corner of the *bais ha'medrash* sat the boy, his head bent over a small *sefer*. Creeping up behind the boy, the young man saw it was a *Siddur*, and the young boy was reading from the *Tefillah* of *Ahavah Rabbah*, which precedes *Shma Yisrael*. He was praying to Hashem, *V'sein b'lebeinu l'havin*, "and instill in our hearts to understand." — "Hashem, please help me that I should no longer have to beg others to teach me the *Torah* lessons. Open my eyes to the light of *Torah*. Help me to understand. Please, Hashem!"

When the young man heard this brokenhearted entreaty, he sat down next to the boy and said, "Do not worry. I will study with you. I will always be there for you." The elderly gentleman concluded, "Look what became of that young boy. He is today one of the *gedolei ha'dor*, preeminent *Torah* scholars of the generation, and I am just an old man."

Rav Shach concluded, "That young boy demonstrated what it means to want the crown of *Torah*."

ועשית שלחן עצי שטים
You shall make a table of acacia wood. (25:23)

The *Kesav Sofer* cites his father, the *Chasam Sofer*, who related that he saw in the *sefer* of one of the *Rishonim* a reason that the *Torah* prioritizes the construction of the *Shulchan* before that of the *Menorah*. The *Shulchan* represents the *machazik Torah*, one who supports *Torah* study, while the *Menorah* symbolizes the *Torah* scholar, who actually studies the *Torah*. When Moshe *Rabbeinu* blessed *Klal Yisrael* prior to his demise, he spoke first to Zevulun, the tribe which is characterized as the

Torah supporter, prior to speaking to Yissachar, the *Torah* scholar. Without Zevulun's assistance, Yissachar would not be free to study *Torah*. If this is the case, however, why does the *Torah* prioritize the construction of the *Aron*, the symbol of the consummate *talmid chacham*, *Torah* scholar, before that of the *Shulchan*?

The *Kesav Sofer* explains that there are two types of *Torah* scholars. There is the righteous *talmid chacham* who does not need anyone's support. In fact, <u>he</u> is our source of sustenance. *Chazal* tell us that Rabbi Chanina ben Dosa was so great that the entire world was sustained in his merit. There are also *Torah* scholars who have not achieved this lofty spiritual plateau. They need the Zevuluns of every generation to support them.

The *Aron HaKodesh*, which contained the *Luchos* and was placed in the *Kodesh HaKodoshim*, Holy of Holies, symbolizes the "Rabbi Chanina ben Dosa" type of scholar, the quintessential *talmid chacham*, whose *Torah* study and piety take him above the realm of this physical world. It is in his merit that Zevulun is successful and is able to support *Torah* endeavor. This individual is sequestered in his four cubits of *Torah* law and does not benefit from the physical world around him. The *Menorah*, on the other hand, symbolizes the other type of *talmid chacham*, the one who must rely on Zevulun's support. Therefore, the *Shulchan* follows the *Aron*, but precedes the *Menorah*.

✱ ✱ ✱ ✱ ✱ ✱

ועשית את הקרשים למשכן עצי שטים עמדים
You shall make the beams of the Mishkan of acacia wood, standing erect.
(26:15)

*C*hazal in the *Talmud Yoma* 72a, interpret the term "standing erect" homiletically, as a guarantee that the Jewish nation will survive in the worst times. "Perhaps you will say that their hope of return is gone and their expectation is frustrated? But it is written, 'acacia wood, standing erect' — they will stand forever!" What is unique about acacia wood that *Chazal* saw in the term "standing erect" a portent for *Klal Yisrael's* endurance and steadfastness? Is it the nature of the wood, or is it the manner in which it was placed in the *Mishkan* that conveys the message?

This wood was special, and its uniqueness catalyzed the message and concomitantly the reason that *Klal Yisrael* has survived. According to the *Midrash Tanchuma*, there is a very special history regarding these planks. Yaakov *Avinu* anticipated the need for such lumber. Knowing that acacia trees do not grow in the wilderness, he planted these trees in Egypt and instructed his children that when they left their exile to take the trees with them. It was Yaakov *Avinu's* foresight that enabled his descendants to have the materials needed to erect the *Mishkan*. Throughout Jewish history, it was the foresight and planning of the previous generation that gave the next generation the opportunity and the foundation to persevere and triumph over the vicissitudes that have challenged us. Whether they were of a spiritual or a physical nature, be it internal conflict or external persecution, it was the lessons taught to us by our forebears, directly or by example, that have made the difference in our lives. We truly stand upon the shoulders of those who preceded us.

The ability to stand erect, resolute and with fortitude against the prevalent obstacles and forces that undermine and degrade the *Torah* way of life, is part of our national character. We have been fighting against the incursion of alien thought into our way of life throughout the millennia. The challenges brought on by the exile are not only spiritual, moral and philosophical. The component of suffering, persecution and anguish has had a detrimental effect on the Jewish psyche. Yet, in every generation, we have been blessed with giants of *Torah*, men of the spirit, whose piety, virtue, and faith comprise a spiritual force that has the compelling power to uplift, embolden and transform their followers into believing, committed, steadfastly observant Jews. One of the lowest periods for our People was only sixty odd years ago during the terrible years of the European Holocaust. Six million perished, while many who survived succumbed spiritually. Those who were saved were fortified by towering individuals whose mind and spirit triumphed over pain and torture and rallied others with their indomitable conviction. *The Klausenberger Rebbe, Horav Yekusiel Yehudah Halberstam, zl,* was such a giant. Clearly, he saved thousands from spiritual extinction by virtue of his love for all Jews that was manifest in his every endeavor.

Wherever the *Rebbe* went, he felt Hashem's Presence with him. When he arrived in Auschwitz, confronted by the heinous Nazi soldiers with their disparaging comments and brutal beatings, he would encourage his fellow Jews, "Do not fear them. *Hashem Yisborach* is with us. He preceded us here, and He is waiting to receive us. There is no place in the world that is devoid of His Presence."

This was the *Rebbe's* message to everyone. "Hashem is here with us." The *pasuk* in *Sefer Tehillim* 23:4, immortalized by so many of our People, was the *Rebbe's* catchphrase that he would recite constantly: "Though I walk in the valley of death I will fear no evil, for You are with me." No matter what happened to the *Rebbe*, he firmly believed in the Almighty's salvation.

Even during those terrible times, the *Rebbe* maintained his focus on *avodas Hashem*, serving the Almighty. Right beneath the searching eyes of the Nazis, he studied *Torah*, *davened* and observed *mitzvos*. Without regard to his personal safety, he would avoid even the most minor transgression. He refused to eat non-kosher food. He even managed to smuggle his *Tefillin* into camp, and he donned them every day. He avoided desecrating *Shabbos* and made sure that no one else did the work imposed on him.

The *kapos* could not tolerate the *Rebbe's* observance and would beat him viciously. He accepted these beatings as Hashem's judgment. He would often murmur, "This is because I did not serve You with joy." Slowly the *kapos* changed their attitude, as they began to recognize the *Rebbe's* unique character, principles and total devotion to Hashem. Looking at him with renewed respect, they began to treat him favorably.

When one remains resolute in adhering even to customs that have been transmitted through the generations, he has the foundation to maintain that fortitude for observing all the *mitzvos*. Those who have viewed our People's customs as a tradition that could be eliminated, soon had a similar attitude towards *mitzvah* observance in general. The *Klausenberger Rebbe* once related, "In Auschwitz, I wore only a torn, thin garment, even in the bitter cold. I preferred it to the other rags we were given, because the buttons were sewn on the left coinciding with the custom followed by my holy ancestors. Who knows? Perhaps I was permitted to continue living because I was careful about what I wore."

We now have an idea of the meaning of standing "erect." It was individuals of such indomitable spirit that have transmitted the legacy of *Torah* life to us.

ואתה תצוה את בני ישראל ויקחו אליך שמן זית זך

Now you shall command Bnei Yisrael that they shall take for you pure olive oil. (27:20)

Why are *Bnei Yisrael* commanded to bring the oil to Moshe *Rabbeinu*? What role did Moshe play in the lighting of the *Menorah*? Was this not the function of Aharon *HaKohen*? *Horav Chaim Shmuelevitz, zl*, explains that Moshe's relationship with Aharon was unique in the sense that they were like one person. Aharon reciprocated this feeling. Each one was filled with joy for the success of the other. Aharon was as happy when Moshe, his younger brother, became *Klal Yisrael's* leader, as if it were he that had ascended to this position. Likewise, Moshe was overjoyed to hear that Hashem had selected his brother to become the *Kohen Gadol*. The lighting of the *Menorah* was a form of appeasement to Aharon, since he was disturbed that neither he — nor any member of his tribe — had been involved in the *Chanukas HaMishkan*, Dedication of the *Mishkan*. Hashem told him, "Yours is greater than theirs, for you will light the *Menorah*." Aharon's anguish was Moshe's anguish. Consequently, when they brought the oil to Aharon for the lighting, it was as if they brought it also to Moshe. His involvement in the lighting of the *Menorah* was supportive. He was as excited about his brother's lighting as if he himself had been the one who lit the *Menorah*.

Aharon *HaKohen* was the quintessential *ohaiv Yisrael*, one who loved all Jews. His empathy was not only for his brother; it was for all Jews. This is why he merited to wear over his heart the *Choshen HaMishpat*, Breastplate, upon which were engraved the names of the Twelve Tribes, representing *Klal Yisrael*. The heart that was sensitive to all Jews should carry the *Choshen,* which served as an atonement for *Klal Yisrael*. Aharon's heart was pure, untainted by any vestige of jealousy. He was truly happy that Moshe had been chosen to lead *Klal Yisrael* — an unnatural character trait.

He was a unique individual, whose abounding love for others was characterized by a heart that was the pulse of the nation.

The true mark of a *gadol, Torah* leader, is his ability to be the pulse of the nation. The people's pain is his pain; their joy is his joy. There are those who "talk the talk," but the true *gedolim* live for their people throughout their lives — worrying, caring, sensitizing themselves to the needs of the wider *Klal Yisrael* — both spiritually and physically. Some go beyond the expected. Their sensitivity extends even to those whose emotions are not so strong, but are nonetheless, very fragile. Their sensitivities are just as important. The following story demonstrates this idea as it characterizes one of our greatest *Torah* leaders, *Horav Shlomo Zalman Auerbach, zl.* A *posek, halachic* arbiter, without peer, he was also a modern day Aharon *HaKohen* who loved all Jews with a love that was reciprocated.

A couple once arrived at his home to seek counsel regarding their son who was mentally challenged. They had the option of sending him to either of two fine institutions. Each one had pros and cons. They left the final decision up to *Rav* Shlomo Zalman.

The *Rav* asked, "What is the boy's preference? Where would he like to go?"

"*Rebbe,*" the father replied, somewhat taken aback, "did we not say that he is mentally disadvantaged? Regrettably, he is incapable of making even the most simple decision. Surely, he cannot have a say concerning which school he should attend."

Rav Shlomo Zalman looked at the parents in a manner which was not typical of his usual smiling countenance and said, "You are doing your child a grave injustice. Picture yourself in his position. To be suddenly evicted from the comfort of your home and placed in a strange place could be devastating. Even the most well-adjusted adult has a difficult time adapting to a new environment. This is especially true of a young child whose emotions are already very fragile. He needs more love and attention than the average child. You must include <u>him</u> in your decision."

While the parents did not disagree with *Rav* Shlomo Zalman, they had no idea how to implement his practical suggestions. Given their son's mental capacity, even normal communication was most difficult.

Realizing their dilemma, *Rav* Shlomo Zalman asked to see the child. "What is your name?" the *Rav* asked the boy affectionately when he came into the room.

"Akiva," the boy answered.

"You have a beautiful name," *Rav* Shlomo Zalman said. My name is *Rav* Shlomo Zalman Auerbach, and I am considered one of the great *Torah* scholars of our time. Many Jews throughout the world listen to what I have to say. I would like you, Akiva, also to listen to what I have to say. You will soon be going to a new school. I would like to ask a favor of you. Could you please be my helper to watch over the *kashrus* at the school? It means very much to me to have you do this."

The parents listened in total disbelief. They could not believe what they were hearing. To hear *Rav* Shlomo Zalman accord such accolades to himself was totally anomalous. This was a *gadol* who was the paragon of humility. How could he speak this way? It was not yet over. *Rav* Shlomo Zalman looked at Akiva and said, "By the power vested in me, I grant you *semichah*, ordination, and appoint you as my agent for all areas of *kashrus* coordination in your new school. Please carry out your duties courteously and responsibly."

When the parents looked at their Akiva, they understood what *Rav* Shlomo Zalman had done. The child's eyes glimmered with enthusiasm. His face exuded excitement. He could not wait to transfer to his new school. The transition went so smoothly that the boy never wanted to leave the school. He would often tell his parents, "I am the *mashgiach*, *kashrus* supervisor, for the *gadol ha'dor*, pre-eminent *Torah* leader of our generation. How can I leave my job?"

Once again, it is the little things that make a great person. In other words: when great people care about little people, they become greater.

וְעָשִׂיתָ בִגְדֵי קֹדֶשׁ לְאַהֲרֹן אָחִיךָ לְכָבוֹד וּלְתִפְאָרֶת

You shall make vestments of sanctity for Aharon your brother, for glory and splendor. **(28:2)**

G lory and splendor — *kavod* and *tiferes* seem synonymous. Wherein lies the difference between the concept of glory and splendor? The *Malbim* explains that *kavod*, glory, is a reference to the inherent spiritual potential with which one is endowed at conception due to the greatness of his *neshamah*, soul. *Tiferes*, splendor, is the realiazation of this potential, the achievement and fulfillment of the unique capabilities with which one is blessed. When Aharon *HaKohen* wore the *Bigdei Kehunah*, he represented these two facets of his unique spiritual character. He was bestowed with a *neshamah* that was destined for prominence. Second, the unique potential of his *neshamah* reached fulfillment and, thus, he became the progenitor of all future *Kohanim*.

Horav Avraham Pam, zl, asserts that this dual concept applies to *bnei Torah*. They are the modern-day wearers of *Bigdei Kehunah*. If we were to take into consideration the moral abyss that has become the standard of contemporary society — the permissiveness, licentiousness, violence and drug addiction that confronts us daily in the media and on the street — it is a wonder how in such a poisoned environment the level of *Torah* study manifest by *bnei Torah* is so incredibly high. Why do they not sink with the rest of society? How do they overcome the influence of moral degeneration? The answer is: the *kavod*, glory, the immense potential of the *neshamos* of these *bnei Torah*. The prodigious capabilities inherent in those who spend their lives in the pursuit of *Torah* knowledge, immersed in the holiness and purity of the *Torah* and *mitzvos,* are exceptional. They have removed themselves from the depravity to which our society has descended.

"What is the source of this spiritual endowment?" asks *Rav* Pam. He suggests that it quite probably is a bequest derived from a previous righteous ancestor who served the Almighty under extreme duress and *mesiras nefesh,* self-sacrifice. This total abnegation of one's self earned him the distinction of having his descendant display a similar dedication to *Torah* and *mitzvos*. As the *Rosh HaYeshivah* notes, with *kavod* comes the responsibility to obtain the mantle of *tiferes* and see to it that the enormous spiritual potential achieves fruition. It is not enough to just be better than those on the street. One must strive to set the standard and provide the beacon for others to follow.

✹ ✹ ✹ ✹ ✹ ✹

וְעָשִׂיתָ בִגְדֵי קֹדֶשׁ לְאַהֲרֹן אָחִיךָ לְכָבוֹד וּלְתִפְאָרֶת

You shall make vestments of sanctity for Aharon, your brother, for glory and splendor. **(28:2)**

The commentaries address the concepts of glory and splendor. *Ramban* asserts that the vestments were to honor the *Kohanim,* since these garments were similar to the clothes worn by royalty. *Sforno* says that the garments were for the glory of Hashem and to lend splendor to the *Kohen Gadol* as the pre-eminent teacher of the nation, so that he be held in the highest esteem by the *shevatim,* tribes, whose names he carried on the *Choshen HaMishpat.* Regardless of the purpose and function of the *Bigdei Kehunah,* they were exceptional garments that reflected dignity and beauty and raised the esteem of the *Kohanim* who wore them. Wearing these vestments was an integral component in the *Kohen's avodah,* service. Indeed, a *Kohen* who serves in the *Bais HaMikdash* without wearing the *Bigdei Kehunah* is liable for *kareis,* Heavenly excision.

In today's society we have a popular maxim that "clothes make the man." Regrettably, this is true, only in the sense that contemporary society perceives an individual by external appearances. Who a person is is based upon his internal essence, not by the way he dresses and the type of clothes he wears. Human values, however, attribute much to what they see externally. Thus, the *ben Torah* should reflect the dignity and regalness of the *Torah.* People look at us all the time: some with respect; others with envy and derision. We should raise the banner of the monarchy of *Torah* by the way we carry ourselves.

There is a fascinating story concerning this concept that occurred with *Horav Shimon Schwab, zl, Rav* of *Khal Adas Yeshurun,* in Washington Heights. On *Shushan Purim* in 1936, when *Rav Schwab* was a young rabbi in Germany, he was accused of publicly maligning the accursed Adolf Hitler. It seems that in the *Rav's Shabbos derashah,* sermon, on *Parashas Ki Sisa,* he discussed the sin of the Golden Calf. In his disparagement of the sin and the people's error in thinking that one needs a "middleman" to approach Hashem, he had said, "The Jews do not need a *vermittler*," German for "go between." A government spy, which was a common occurrence in *shul* during those times, misunderstood this and thought the *Rav* said, "Hitler," and that the German dictator was the focus of *Rav* Schwab's criticism.

Rav Schwab was brought before the Gestapo to explain himself. Making direct eye contact with the official, the *Rav* emphatically declared his innocence. This was not a sufficient defense for the Nazis. He was told that his case would be reviewed, and he would be advised of the verdict.

After that meeting, *Rav* Schwab feared for his life. He knew that he was not dealing with human beings. In his diary, he recorded that it took up until the middle of *Iyar* — two months — before the matter was cleared up and he was vindicated. During this period, he slept fitfully, if at all — with his clothes on. He feared that he would be arrested in the middle of the night, which was a common practice of those beasts, and taken to jail — or into the forest to be beaten or left to die.

In other cases, they would rouse their victim in the middle of the night and take him out to the town square for a public hanging. If this would be his fate, he would face it with dignity — and with his clothes on — as befits a *Torah* leader. He was not about to allow the Nazis to hang the *Rav* of the town in his nightclothes! *Chazal* view a *rav*, as well as any *Torah* leader, as *sheluchei d'Rachamana*, Hashem's emissaries, and, as such, he must maintain his semblance of dignity at all times. This is the meaning of *kavod* and *tiferes*.

✼ ✼ ✼ ✼ ✼ ✼

ועשית ציץ זהב טהור ופתחת עליו...קדש לד'...והיה על מצח אהרן

You shall make a forehead plate of pure gold and engrave upon it…"Holy to Hashem"…and it shall be on Aharon's brow. (28:36, 38)

The *Midrash* teaches that each of the *Kohen Gadol's begadim*, vestments, symbolized Divine atonement for various sins. The *Tzitz*, forehead plate, denoted Divine forgiveness for brazenness. The Hebrew words for brazenness are *azuz metzach*, literally a "bold brow," hence, the *Tzitz* is worn on the *metzach*, brow, of the *Kohen Gadol*.

Chutzpah, azus, brazenness, by any standard, is a character trait that demonstrates a person's lack of shame. It is a *middah,* character trait, that goes against the personality of a Jew, considering the fact that Jews are defined by three traits: *baishanim,* they have a sense of shame; *rachamanim,* they are compassionate; *gomlei chasadim,* they perform acts of loving kindness. Of course, if the brazenness is employed in a constructive manner, as when a person refuses to yield to the blandishments of contemporary moral standards or stands resolute in the face of overwhelming peer and social pressures, *chutzpah* is desirable.

In the period prior to *Moshiach's* advent, *chutzpah* will be one of the hallmarks of the generation. As mentioned, the true distinction of a *Torah* Jew is an inherent sense of shame, which prevents him from slipping into inappropriate behavior. Where does today's *chutzpah* manifest itself and from where does it originate? In the *frum,* observant, camp it is noticeable in the lack of *derech eretz,* respect/comportment, that is shown to our elders, our *rebbeim,* our parents. There used to be a time when a *gadol's, Torah* leader's, words were sacrosanct, when students had respect bordering on fear and awe, for their *rebbe.* A *yeshivah bachur* would *instinctively* show respect to his *rebbe.* Today, it is different. The student has to "hold" of the *rebbe;* the *rebbe* has to conform to the student's line of thinking. The days when a *rav* was held in the highest esteem are over. Today, he is an employee who often has to take a position commensurate with the future of his paycheck.

Where does this all originate? *Horav Moshe Aharon Stern, zl,* relates that he was once on a bus when an elderly gentleman boarded. *Rav* Stern said to a teenager sitting next to him, "Please stand up for him and give him your seat." The teenager replied insolently, "There are children on this bus that are younger than I. Let them get up for the old man."

Rav Stern looked at the young man incredulously and countered, "But they are not getting up." In the end, the teenager refused to give up his seat for the older gentleman. *Rav* Stern then got up and gave his seat to the man. The *rav* was now standing, the old man was sitting and so was the young man. Then *Rav* Stern looked at the teenager and said, "Will you at least get up for me?"

The teenager replied, rather smugly, "If you want to stand, that is your business."

This is the type of *chutzpah* that challenges us on a regular basis. *Chazal* foretold that this would occur, and it has.

Now, if you would like to know how this teenager became such a *mechutzaf*, *Rav* Stern cites another incident that occurred on the bus. This time, an elderly woman ascended the bus to find seating at a premium. Seated near the door, where the elderly woman stood with her packages, was a young woman and her young child. The people on the bus insistently told her, "Tell your son to stand up for this old woman!"

The mother turned to her son and said, "Do not get up; let her stand."

We teach our children *chutzpah* when they see us acting inappropriately to others. We intimate to them to ignore *mitzvos* in the *Torah*. As our children grow up, they perceive right and wrong consistent with what they see at home. The lessons we impart by our own demeanor can have a lasting effect. Hopefully, it will be of a positive nature.

ובלב כל חכם לב נתתי חכמה

"And I have endowed the heart of every wise-hearted person with wisdom."

(31:6)

*C*hazal in the *Talmud Berachos* 55a comment that Hashem grants wisdom only to those that are already endowed with wisdom. The commentators question this concept. If Hashem only gives wisdom to the individuals who are already wise, how did they get the original wisdom? Was that not also a gift from Hashem? In his *Nefesh HaChaim, Horav Chaim, zl, m'Volozhin*, explains that the original *chochmah*, wisdom, is a reference to *yiraas Shomayim*, fear of Heaven, as quoted in the *pasuk* in *Tehillim* 111:10, "The beginning of wisdom is the fear of Hashem." The rationale for this is that fear of Hashem is the *kli kibul*, vessel/container, which guards the wisdom, making certain that it is not wasted or lost.

In an alternative explanation, the *Gaon, zl, m'Vilna* explains that the original wisdom is what a person grasps as a result of his own toil. Commensurate with his effort, Hashem will inspire added wisdom to that which he has been able to achieve on his own. Hashem helps those who first help themselves.

Horav Chaim Shmuelevitz, zl, suggests that the original wisdom is a reference to one's aspiration, desire and devotion towards amassing wisdom. The greatest wisdom is the ability to discern the truth, to recognize what is truly *chochmah* and what is not.

Rav Chaim would relate that, as a young boy he studied in the Novardok *Yeshivah* under the guidance of his uncle, *Horav Avraham Yaffen, zl*. He once asked his uncle to point out to him the best student in the *yeshivah*. His uncle acquiesced and pointed to a certain young man and said, "He has the most penetrating mind in the *yeshivah*. He can fathom the profundities of the *Talmud* better than anyone." He pointed to another student and said, "He is the biggest *masmid*, most diligent student, in the *yeshivah*. He hardly ever leaves the *bais ha'medrash*." He continued, pointing to the student who was the most brilliant and to the student whose encyclopedic knowledge outshined everyone else.

Finally, the *Rosh HaYeshivah* led *Rav* Chaim to a corner of the *bais ha'medrash* and pointed to a student who was poring over his *seforim* and said, "He is the best student in the *yeshivah*."

Rav Chaim was amazed. "I do not understand. When you enumerated the virtues of the most exceptional students in the *yeshivah*, you never mentioned this *bachur*. Why not?"

Rav Avraham replied, "His attributes are different from the attributes of the other students. He is the *mevakesh*, the seeker, the student in the *yeshivah* who exemplifies the greatest desire to grow in *Torah* and *avodah*. He is the best *bachur*."

Rav Chaim concluded his story explaining, "That *bachur* spent days and nights studying *Torah*. Nothing stood in the way of his achieving *gadlus ba'Torah*, distinction in *Torah* learning. Do you know who he was? He was none other than the light of our generation, *Rav Yaakov Kanievesky*, the *Steipler Rav*."

✹ ✹ ✹ ✹ ✹ ✹

ועתה הניחה לי ויחר אפי בהם ואכלם...ועתה אם תשא חטאתם ואם אין מחני נא מספרך

And now, desist from Me. Let My anger flare up against them and I shall annihilate them..."And now if You would but forgive their sin! — but if not, erase me now from Your book." (32:10,32)

Moshe *Rabbeinu* took a powerful stand on behalf of *Klal Yisrael*. *Horav Yitzchak, zl, m'Volozhin*, comments that Moshe's stand was an act of pure *mesiras nefesh*, self-sacrifice, for the people he led. Veritably, they did not deserve it. *Chazal* tell us that *Satan* confused them and created pandemonium among the people. He asked them, "Where is Moshe, your teacher?" "He is in Heaven," the people replied. Immediately, *Satan* retorted, "He is dead!" At that moment, *Satan* projected an image of Moshe's bier being carried in Heaven. When the nation saw this, they arose the next morning and celebrated with the Golden Calf.

What a reaction to the death of their *rebbe* and leader! Yet, Moshe did not take their actions to heart. He knew what the people were. He understood their origins. Over two hundred years of back-breaking labor under the most degrading and brutal conditions will destroy even the most stalwart individual. Thus, they rebelled against Moshe and celebrated with idol worship at the news of his death. They did not appreciate him. Is that a reason to turn his back on them? Should he permit their obliteration in deference to his own honor? "No!" Moshe said. "A thousand like Moshe may die, but not one fingernail of a single Jew should be touched!" This is the capstone of *mesiras nefesh*.

Rav Itzele Volozhiner, as he was referred to affectionately and reverently, was such a leader. He would often be called upon to represent Russian Jewry at the Kremlin. It is related that upon those occasions when *Rav* Itzele went before the Czar, he would don his *tachrichim*, burial garments. He explained that when he went to the Czar, he was prepared for the worst scenario. He expected that he would be asked to make concessions, some of which would compromise his adherence to Jewish law. He was not prepared to accede to their demands. Since some of these demands might carry the *halachic* ruling of *Yehareig v'al yaavor*, "Be killed rather than transgress a command of the *Torah*," he was ready to die. He came "dressed" for the "occasion"! This was his *madreigah*, level, of *mesiras nefesh*. When he left his home, he left prepared to give up his life for *Klal Yisrael*. It was not something abstract that might occur. To *Rav* Itzele, it was something very real for which he was totally prepared.

✹ ✹ ✹ ✹ ✹ ✹

ויחל משה את פני ד' אלקיו
Moshe pleaded before Hashem, his G-d. (32:11)

During his tenure as *Klal Yisrael's* leader, Moshe *Rabbeinu* was called upon to entreat Hashem on their behalf on numerous occasions. Every time *Klal Yisrael* was in need, or they overstepped the bounds of respect and gratitude, Moshe was there to supplicate Hashem. Yet, we find that when Aharon *HaKohen* passed away,

Moshe eulogized him with the words, "Woe is to me for you, Aharon, my brother, were the pillar of prayer of *Klal Yisrael*." We see from this that Moshe characterizes Aharon as the *amuda d'tzelusa*, pillar of prayer, as if Aharon was the one who deserved the title — not Moshe. While it is clear that Aharon was the *ohaiv shalom v'rodef shalom*, he loved and pursued peace, and surely cared about the people, prayer seems to have been Moshe's domain.

The *Netziv, zl*, explains that Moshe and Aharon prayed and pleaded *Klal Yisrael's* case before the Almighty. The nature of the individual prayers of each was distinct one from the other. Moshe prayed for miracles. He undertook to entreat the Almighty to alter the course of nature for *Klal Yisrael*. Aharon, on the other hand, prayed for the "little" things: for the individual Jew who needed a livelihood; for the couple who were not yet blessed with a child; for the family that was besieged with illness or other anguish. When the individual needed a comforting prayer, he came to Aharon.

We might think that the power of prayer is needed for, and indicated through, the miracles that are catalyzed by one's entreaty. Moshe *Rabbeinu* taught us that the real power of prayer is demonstrated through daily supplication, through pleading our case to Hashem for the "little," natural events that often-times elude us. Aharon *HaKohen* performed that function. He was *Klal Yisrael's* pillar of prayer.

******

והלחת מעשה אלקים המה והמכתב מכתב אלקים היא חרות על הלחת... וירא את העגל ומחלת ויחר אף משה וישלך מידו את הלחת וישבר אתם תחת ההר

***The Luchos were G-d's handiwork, and the script was the script of G-d engraved on the Luchos... He saw the calf and the dances, and Moshe's anger flared up. He threw down the Luchos from his hands and shattered them at the foot of the mountain.* (32:16,19)**

The *Torah* describes the "craftsmanship" and physical makeup of the *Luchos*, continuing with a portrayal of Moshe *Rabbeinu's* shattering them when he saw the Golden Calf. Why does the *Torah* describe the *Luchos prior* to the act of the *chet ha'eigel*, sin of the Golden Calf, and not earlier when the *Torah* recounts how Hashem gave them to Moshe? It almost seems as if there is a connection between the structure of the *Luchos* and the sin of the Golden Calf. *Horav Sholom Schwadron, zl*, explains that one has to realize that just as the *Luchos* were not constructed in a natural manner, so, too, their shattering was equally miraculous. Thus, the *Torah* describes the unique character of the *Luchos* prior to giving us an account of their breakage.

To supplement this idea, *Rav* Sholom asks a compelling question: How did Moshe *physically* break the *Luchos*? They were not comprised of any breakable earthly matter. They were fashioned by Hashem, of a Heavenly element that was certainly stronger than any composite we have here on earth. Thus, when Moshe dropped them from his hands, they should not have shattered.

In response, *Rav* Sholom cites the *Ramban* who asks how Moshe could have broken the *Luchos,* given their source? How does man break what Hashem has fashioned? *Ramban* explains that as soon as Moshe came down from the mountain and came near the *tumah* — spiritual defilement — and sin of the Golden Calf, the letters that were miraculously engraved on the *Luchos* flew off, leaving just the stone. Moshe broke the stone upon which the *Luchos had been* engraved. The *Luchos* were no longer there — Hashem had taken them back to Heaven.

We now are able to elucidate our previous ambiguity. Indeed, there is something that has the power to shatter the *Luchos* that were Hashem's handiwork. *Tumah* and *cheit* — spiritual impurity and sin — can undermine the sanctity of the *Luchos*. The *tumah* causes the holy letters to fly off the stone, because *kedushah* and *tumah* cannot co-exist. Nothing can break Hashem's handiwork, but it cannot accompany sin and contamination. Sin and spiritual depravity can shatter Hashem's *Luchos*.

Rav Sholom expounds upon the idea that *kedushah* and *tumah* cannot co-exist. Imagine the sight of the engraved letters, Hashem's Divine handiwork, flying off the *Luchos*, because sanctity cannot be adulterated with impurity. They cannot work together. Certainly, they cannot endure together. When *Torah* is adulterated with secular impurity, whether it is transmitted via the material or its disseminator, it cannot last. Anything that is imbibed through sources, or in places, that intermingle *kodesh* with *chol* cannot have lasting value.

Moshe *Rabbeinu's* greatest display of *gevurah*, strength, was shattering the *Luchos*. This is his epitaph in the last *pasuk* in the *Torah*. *Horav Moshe Mordechai Epstein, zl*, comments that Moshe conveyed a powerful lesson to *Klal Yisrael* through his actions: Sin has the power to catalyze the shattering of a *Ma'aseh Elokim*, Hashem's handiwork. True, the lesson may be great, but how does Moshe's awesome strength come to the fore? The *Torah* is relating his incredible *gevurah*, not the significance of his message to the nation.

Rav Sholom explains that the key phrase is, *l'einei kol Yisrael*, "in front of the eyes of all *Yisrael*." Moshe feared no one. He taught his lesson in the presence of the entire nation. This demonstrated his remarkable *gevurah* — that when he had a message to convey nothing stood in his way: not people, not pressure, nothing. This is why he was the quintessential leader.

ומשרתו יהושע בן נון נער לא ימיש מתוך האהל
His servant, Yehoshua bin Nun, a lad, would not depart from within the tent. (33:11)

T he *Brisker Rav, zl*, cites a homiletic exposition of this *pasuk* which he heard from the *Maharil Diskin, zl*. *Rav* Yehoshua Leib said, "Yehoshua bin Nun would allow anyone who sought guidance to enter the tent — even a *naar*, young boy." Yehoshua was acutely aware of the significance of exposure to an individual such as Moshe *Rabbeinu*. Just to be in his presence for a short while availed one the opportunity to experience *kedushah*, holiness, and *taharah*, purity, at its zenith. This revelation could transform a person and steer him onto the correct path. Even a young child can benefit greatly from such an experience. This is especially true if the person who reaches out to him is someone who understands the indelible impression that he can make on the mind of a child and does not view it as being something beneath his dignity. In an incredible story, Rabbi Yechiel Spero, in his book, *Touched by a Story*, relates how the venerable *Mashgiach* of *Beth Medrash Govohah, Horav Matisyahu Solomon, Shlita*, reached out to a little boy and made the difference in his life.

Moshe Meir, or Mo, as his friends referred to him, was terribly alone. There are a number of things in life that no seven-year-old boy should have to face. Sitting *shivah*, the seven-day mourning period for the death of his father, truly was something with which this fragile child should not have had to contend. Unfortunately, this was his lot. One day, his father was alive, vibrant, enthusiastic, engaging and filled with life. The next moment, he was gone, felled by the *Malach Ha'maves*, Angel of Death, in the guise of a sudden illness. The house was filled with people, consoling his mother and older siblings. Yet, he was all alone. There is not much one can say to a seven-year-old boy, although he did hear all about his wonderful father, who was called back to *Shomayim*, to study *Torah* with Hashem.

There were many things that he did not understand. Apparently, his mother was also disturbed by his questions, because she was crying incessantly. People spoke to her and attempted to console her, but he was all alone. The people that did speak to him did not focus on his questions or his needs. He just sat there, immersed in a little cocoon, in his own sad, little world.

On the fifth day of *shivah*, *Rav* Mattisyahu Solomon came to be *menachem aveil*, offer condolences. Mo saw him enter the room, and he assumed it was another rabbi here to visit his uncles. He would not have been the first *rosh yeshivah* to come to the house. His uncles were distinguished leaders in the *Torah* community. We can imagine Mo's shock when instead of going over to them, the *Mashgiach* sat down opposite Mo. Suddenly, Mo wanted to be alone again. What would he say to this distinguished looking rabbi?

"So, young man, what is your name?" *Rav* Mattisyahu asked him in his deep English accent. "My name is Moshe Meir," the young boy replied.

"Do your friends call you Moshe Meir, or do you have another name?" *Rav* Mattisyahu queried, trying to find a springboard so the two of them could talk.

"My friends call me Mo." As Mo said this, he noticed that the crowd in the room was slowly moving closer, trying to listen in on the conversation between the *gadol* and the young boy.

"How old are you, Mo?" *Rav* Mattisyahu asked, noticing that the boy seemed to be perking up.

"Seven," Mo answered.

"Really? That is truly fascinating. Do you know that I was also young when my father passed away? I know how you feel. I can understand what you are going through," the *Mashgiach* said.

When Mo heard this, his eyes lit up. Imagine, he had something in common with this great rabbi. Indeed, the rabbi even understood how lonely and sad he was. The rest of the conversation seemed to spring forth, as Mo suddenly became comfortable talking with *Rav* Mattisyahu. After all, they had a common bond. They both had been orphaned at a young age.

As the *Mashgiach* was preparing to leave, he proposed an idea to Mo, "Perhaps, you and I can start a little club for boys who were young when they lost their father. You and I will be the founding members of the club." A smile began to spread across Mo's face as his eyes began to twinkle. The *Mashgiach* had struck pay dirt.

"Before I leave, we have to decide upon the rules," said the *Mashgiach*. "The rules of the club are that whenever one of us wants to call the other, we are allowed to do so — regardless of the situation. Whenever you want to call me and you are told that I am unavailable, just tell them to give me the following message: 'Tell him that Mo called.' I promise to call you right back."

Rav Mattisyahu arose, saying the traditional phrase wishing the young mourner that he be comforted among the other mourners of *Klal Yisrael*, and he left. A few moments, a few select words, a heart filled with understanding and sensitivity. Suddenly, the depression and loneliness of a young boy was transformed into hope and courage. The legacy that Yehoshua imparted continued to inspire yet another boy.

ובַיּוֹם הַשְּׁבִיעִי יִהְיֶה לָכֶם קֹדֶשׁ

"But the seventh day shall be holy for you." (35:2)

*S*hemiras Shabbos, observing *Shabbos Kodesh*, is not as difficult as it used to be. One can get a job and not be concerned that his *Shabbos* observance will be an obstacle. Indeed, Orthodoxy has become an accepted way of life in this country. It has not always been that way. *Shemiras Shabbos* often involved a great amount of *mesiras nefesh*, self-sacrifice. In this country, it was frequently a question of deciding between observing *Shabbos* and *parnassah*, earning a livelihood. In Europe, this dichotomy was the product of anti-Semitism. Yet, our forebears triumphed over adversity and overcame the challenges to their faith. The following is an incredible story of *mesiras nefesh* for *Shabbos Kodesh*, related by *Horav Shlomo Brevda, Shlita.*

The *Steipler Rav, Horav Yaakov Kanievsky, zl,* was a *gaon* and a *tzaddik.* His brilliance and encyclopedic knowledge of *Torah* was only overshadowed by his righteousness and total devotion to serving the Almighty. Prior to his engagement to the sister of the *Chazon Ish,* he shared an incident with her that happened to him in Siberia. He felt it was important that his intended be fully aware of his *mesiras nefesh* for *mitzvos.*

As a soldier conscripted into the Czar's army, the *Steipler* was forced to perform back-breaking labor in the frigid cold of the Siberian winter. Regardless of the overwhelming toil and below-freezing conditions, he performed the difficult work because he knew it was the only way that he could continue to serve the Almighty. The problem was that army dictates demanded that everyone work seven days a week. This obviously created a problem on *Shabbos.* The *Steipler* emphatically declared that by no means was he going to work on *Shabbos.* The Russian official did not need more than one insolent Jew who had the gall to refuse his orders. He predictably flew into a rage, typical of the anti-Semitic brute that he was. Suddenly, he stopped screaming, as a diabolical smile crossed his face.

Yes, he would grant the *Steipler's* request on the condition that the soldier pass a little test. If he could prove himself to be a strong warrior, he would be permitted to observe *Shabbos*. The test was "simple." The captain ordered his soldiers to form two rows opposite each other, arming themselves with truncheons. The *Steipler* was to "attempt" to make it from one end of the row to the other as the soldiers beat him mercilessly with their truncheons. If he survived the ordeal, he would be allowed to observe *Shabbos*.

The *Steipler* understood the situation. He was probably risking his life, but *Shabbos* was worth the ordeal. He put his hands over his head as protection, whispered a heartfelt prayer and forged ahead. The guards began to beat him with all they had: no mercy, no sensitivity, just pure brutal malevolence. The pain was intolerable, but the reward of keeping *Shabbos* was the pot of gold at the end. Inch by inch, he trudged forward, blinded by pain and covered with blood. He reached the end of the line and collapsed — with a faint smile on his lips. He had made it! The *Shabbos* that he cared about so much must have surely protected him. The captain reluctantly gave in to the *Steipler's* demand to observe *Shabbos*. The *Steipler* lay on the ground, bloodied and broken. Nobody bothered to pick him up, but he did not care. He had triumphed over the cruel officer. He had triumphed over the *yetzer hara*, evil-inclination. He had won *Shabbos Kodesh*.

The *Steipler* concluded the story, looked at his intended and asked, "Are you prepared to join me in a continuous quest of self-sacrifice for *Torah* and *mitzvos*? This is the life I plan to lead." The future *rebbetzin*, the mother of today's pre-eminent *gaon, Horav Chaim Kanievsky, Shlita*, replied in the affirmative, and they became *chassan* and *kallah*.

וכל הנשים אשר נשא לבן אתנה בחכמה
All the women whose hearts inspired them with wisdom. **(35:26)**

Shlomo *Ha'melech* says in *Mishlei* 1:8, "Hear, my child, the discipline of your father, and do not forsake the *Torah* teaching of your mother." The commentators wonder, what is the "*Torah*" of the mother? What is the unique lesson that the mother imparts? The *Admor m'Nadverna, Shlita,* cited by *Horav Yitzchok Zilberstein, Shlita,* explains that a father's role is to instruct his children to study *Torah.* He gives his children *mussar,* ethical lessons, and reprimands in order to keep them on the correct course of study and devotion. There is, however, another component to a child's *Torah* education without which a child cannot successfully climb the ladder of spiritual development: a *Torah* environment. The atmosphere in which a child grows — the surroundings that encompass his everyday endeavor — makes the difference in his attitude and demeanor with regard to his studies. This milieu is provided by the mother, the foundation of the home. This is the meaning of *Toras imecha,* the *Torah* of your mother. She sweetens the studies, enhances the lessons and gives excitement to their meaning. The child, in turn, loves *mitzvos* and seeks opportunities to serve Hashem with greater dedication and fervor.

Rav Zilberstein shares an incredible story about the enduring value of a mother's educational endeavor. A newly-married Russian immigrant was brought to him with the following question: He knows that he is a Jew, but is not aware whether he is a *Kohen, Levi* or *Yisrael.* How should the *rabbanim* view his status? After a lengthy discussion with the man about life in Russia, *Rav* Zilberstein asked him if there was anything about his home life, specifically something unique that his mother did, that came to mind.

Suddenly, the man's eyes twinkled as he smiled glowingly. "Yes, there was something my mother did every *Erev Yom Tov,*" he said. "She would buy a new pair of socks for my father. It became a big thing in my house, as all the children would wait enthusiastically for my father's *Yom Tov* gift."

The *rabbanim* immediately ascertained that the immigrant was a *Kohen.* Since his father would *Duchen,* bless the congregation on the Festival, standing before them in his stocking feet, his mother, out of her love and appreciation of the *mitzvah,* would purchase a new pair of socks for her husband. The immigrant remembered this detail of his early life, because it was a prime example of *Toras imecha*, his mother's *Torah*. Her ability to inspire him through action inculculated him with a love for the Festival. She set the tone in the home, an appreciation of *Yiddishkeit,* that her son remembered many years later.

✽ ✽ ✽ ✽ ✽ ✽

ויהיו הכרבים פרשי כנפים למעלה
The Keruvim were with wings spread upwards. (37:9)

The *Keruvim* resembled little children. Their wings spread upward/Heavenward may be an analogy to a young child's aspirations for spiritual greatness. Indeed, many young children have great aspirations for distinction in *Torah*. To the average observer, they appear to be innocent children, but, in reality, they are *Porsei kenafayim l'maaleh*, spreading their wings Heavenward. It is up to parents and educators to encourage their children's ambitions, providing them with various opportunities for spiritual advancement.

Horav Meir Shapiro, zl, the *Lubliner Rosh HaYeshivah*, and founder of the *Daf HaYomi* would relate that even as a young child, he thought about instituting the *Daf HaYomi* concept. Regrettably, those with whom he shared the notion viewed it as the unrealistic dream of a young child. Many years later, when that young child became the famous *Lubliner Rosh HaYeshivah* with the distinction that this title carried, he returned to the city of his youth and met those men who had mocked him as a youth. He reminded them, "Do you realize that your derision almost convinced me? I was about to give up on my idea and *Klal Yisrael* would have lost out on a wealth of *Torah* study."

Horav Yitzchak Zilberstein, Shlita, cites the *Chazon Ish* who asserts, "Every *ben Torah* in our generation should be considered as a possible future *gadol ha'dor*. Every child has the potential of achieving the apex of distinction in *Torah* erudition. It is up to the parents to encourage and enhance this spiritual growth."

Parashas Pekudei

אלה פקודי המשכן

These are the accountings of the Mishkan. (38:21)

*H*orav Moshe Feinstein, zl, derives a compelling lesson from the *pekudei*, accountings, of the *Mishkan*. A person has to make an accounting of everything that Hashem grants him: his life, his wealth, his abilities. There is a purpose in Hashem's gifts. The ways in which we use what He gives us determine whether we have fulfilled that purpose. We are granted life. Do we use it wisely? Do we use it for the right purpose? Do we take what Hashem has given us for granted, only to wake up when it is almost taken away?

How did we use the wealth which He has bestowed on us? Did we give *tzedakah*, charity, or did we live ostentatiously and give a few 'kopeks' to the poor? Hashem blessed us with abilities, with strengths, with acumen. How did we make use of these gifts? Did we use them to advance our knowledge of *Torah*, or did we employ them for trivial pursuits?

The *Torah* demands that one not waste even a penny of his material possessions. It is Hashem's gift, and if He did not want us to use it wisely, He would not have given it to us. The same idea applies to everything that He bestows on us. When Moshe *Rabbeinu* completed the *Mishkan,* he gave an accounting of everything that he used for its construction. One day, the Heavenly Tribunal will call upon us to give our accounting. Are we going to be prepared with the correct responses?

✻ ✻ ✻ ✻ ✻ ✻

אלה פקודי המשכן משכן העדת

These are the accountings of the Mishkan, the Mishkan of the Testimony.
(38:21)

*R*ashi notes that the word *Mishkan* is stated twice. He explains that it is "an allusion to the *Bais HaMikdash* which was *nismashkein*, taken as collateral — twice, during its two destructions, for the sins of *Klal Yisrael*." Furthermore, it is called *Mishkan HaEidus*, because it serves as "testimony for *Klal Yisrael* that Hashem overlooked the incident of the Golden Calf for them, since He rested His *Shechinah* among them in the *Mishkan*." What is *Rashi* telling us? Are we to view the destruction of the *Bais HaMikdash* as a way to collect collateral? Second, how is the *Mishkan* an indication that Hashem disregarded the sin of the Golden Calf?

Horav Yaakov Kamenetzky, zl, explains that if one were to become bankrupt, he would sell off those possessions that are luxuries, and those that he no longer needs. Those belongings that are essential, without which he cannot live, he would not sell; he would only give them up as collateral to be returned later when he has the funds to redeem them. When we take into account the gold and silver that the Jews possessed at the time that they were asked to contribute toward the *Mishkan*, it is noteworthy that they gave freely. One would think, in light of the upcoming wars with *Eretz Yisrael's* thirty-one kings, they would want to save their money for a "rainy" day. Could they not have made a *Mishkan* of copper where the *Shechinah* could repose? The mere fact that they readily gave of their gold and silver to the *Mishkan* suggests that *Klal Yisrael* viewed the *Mishkan* as essential to their spiritual survival.

We now understand why the *Bais HaMikdash* was taken as collateral. The Jews were acutely aware that they <u>must</u> have the *Bais HaMikdash* in their midst. To have it removed permanently was inconceivable. It could only be taken away on a temporary basis, a sort of collateral, to be returned when we were worthy.

This is also the idea behind the *vittur*, overlooking, of the sin of the Golden Calf. The primary cause of the sin was that they thought Moshe *Rabbeinu* had perished and that they had been left bereft of their beloved leader. This overwhelming fear catalyzed the sin. When they were able to demonstrate their extraordinary trust and conviction, Hashem disregarded, overlooked, their sin. The *Mishkan* attested to this fact.

✻ ✻ ✻ ✻ ✻ ✻

ביום החדש הראשון באחד לחדש תקים את משכן אהל מועד

***"On the day of the first month, on the first day of the month, you shall erect the Mishkan, the Ohel Moed."* (40:2)**

The *Midrash* relates that when Hashem commanded *Klal Yisrael* to make the *Mishkan*, they asked, "Will You remember the sin of the *Eigel*, Golden Calf?" Hashem replied, "No, I will forget that sin." They continued asking, "Will You also forget that we accepted the *Torah* at *Har Sinai* with a resounding *Na'aseh v'Nishma*!, We will do and we will listen?" Hashem answered, "No, I will remember that." The *Berditchever Rebbe, zl*, asks a compelling question about this *Midrash*. Certainly, Hashem does not forget. He remembers everything. Apparently, the concept of forgetting in relation to Hashem implies that Hashem has overlooked something by design. If this is the case, for what reason would Hashem consider "forgetting" such a momentous experience as our acceptance of the *Torah* with an overwhelming and determined acquiescence to perform its mandate without question and without rationale?

Rav Levi Yitzchak explains that with our fall to the nadir of depravity when we sinned with the Golden Calf, our previous acceptance of the *Torah* became greater and more crucial. Had we not sinned, one could venture to downplay our acceptance of the *Torah* by attributing it to the *emunah*, faith and conviction, which we inherited from our Patriarchs. It was not an indication of our own belief, but rather something that was integral to our national character. Once we sinned, however, we demonstrated retroactively that our initial response to the *Torah* was pure, and above all, our own sentiment. When we accepted the *Torah*, we did so with full faith and integrity. Regrettably, when we sinned with the Golden Calf, it was an indication of our spiritual descent.

We now understand the meaning of the *Midrash*. *Klal Yisrael* asks Hashem, "If You will forget the actual sin of the Golden Calf, will You concomitantly also forget the 'favorable' message that our malevolent actions imparted about our earlier acceptance of the *Torah*?" Hashem replied, "I will remember the good, but not the bad."

******

ספר ויקרא
SEFER VAYIKRA

To my Husband

Stephen McCain

my tower of strength and support

You have given me the confidence and ability to
realize my dreams, while never losing sight of reality.

You are the anchor who maintains the stability of our family.

The words of the Psalmist, King David,
express my hope and prayer for you –

ארך ימים אשביעהו ואראהו בישועתי

"With long life will I satisfy him and I will show him My salvation."
(Tehillim 91:16)

Dr. Marijah McCain

Parashas Vayikra

ויקרא אל משה וידבר ד' אליו

He called to Moshe, and Hashem said to him. (1:1)

R*ashi* explains that whenever Hashem commanded, instructed or spoke to Moshe, he always preceded his communication with a *kriah*, calling out, to him. *Kriah* is an expression of tenderness and affection. It is an expression used by the *Malachei HaShareis*, Ministering Angels, as it is written in *Yeshaya* 6:3, *V'kara zeh el zeh v'amar Kadosh, Kadosh, Kadosh...* "One [angel] *called* to another, saying 'Holy, Holy, Holy'..." *Rashi's* comment does not seem to be unique to this *pasuk*. His explanation that *kriah* is an expression of tenderness and affection could likewise have been written earlier when Hashem *called* to Moshe from the *s'neh*, Burning Bush, or prior to *Matan Torah,* the Giving of the *Torah*, when Hashem called to Moshe from *Har Sinai.* Why is the emphasis regarding tenderness and affection and the relationship to angels emphasized here, as we begin the laws of *korbanos*, ritual sacrifices?

The Piaczesner Rebbe, zl, explains that as it is written in regard to *Akeidas Yitzchak*, the Binding of Yitzchak, "Avraham went, took the ram, and sacrificed it as a burnt-offering in his son's place" (*Bereishis* 22:13) this is true of every animal sacrifice: it takes the place of a human. In this *parshah*, it is written, *Adam ki yakriv mikem korban,* "When a man *of you* brings a *korban*"(1:2). The emphasis is placed on the words "of you," because the animal is actually being sacrificed in place of the person. On Fast Days, we entreat Hashem that "the fat and blood that we lose as a result of the Fast should be accepted as a sacrifice upon the *Mizbayach*, Altar, to You, Hashem." Indeed, suffering per se cleanses away our sins, because it decreases our strength via loss of our fat and blood. *Klal Yisrael's* sufferings are a form of ritual sacrifice. Consequently, *Rashi* chooses the text which addresses animal sacrifices to emphasize this point: Any sacrifice that we make — whether it is animal sacrifices, delineated in the following text, in which an animal takes the place of a person, or it is a human being's own sufferings — constitutes Hashem "calling" to us. They are expressions of tenderness, of love from Hashem to us.

Despite the *Piaczesner Rebbe's* best efforts to provide hope, consolation and a degree of inner joy to his followers, in the end he was able to do little to alleviate their suffering. It had become critical for him to address the concept of suffering from a point of theological justification. Basically, what the *Rebbe* is saying here is that one can offer up his suffering as a form of *korban*, sacrifice, to Hashem. The call to sacrifice is a call to love. Hence, the suffering that a Jew endures for Hashem is an expression of profound love — which is reciprocated by the Almighty.

The *Rebbe* concludes his homily focusing on the concept of *dibuk chaveirim*, the bond between a Jew and his fellow Jew in fellowship and friendship — especially in times of hardship and distress. Suffering is an occasion for the sufferer to give to others, an opportunity for compassion and empathy. In return, the empathizer reciprocates with prayers and expressions of concern. This mutual interaction has cosmic significance in that it inspires the Ministering Angels to exchange greetings with each other, to call to one another, as evidenced by the *pasuk* in *Yeshaya* 6:3.

The *Rebbe* exhorts his followers to share with and help one another. "Even when one has no material resources, it is still possible to share. Mutual sharing and helping is not limited to giving charity or a loan. When one hears of the troubles sustained by other Jews and does all that he can to help them; if his heart is broken and his blood is frozen; if through his heart's motivation, he is inspired to pour out his broken heart to Hashem on behalf of other Jews, then this, too, is a wonderful gift which he gives to others. We receive the brokenheartedness and the repentance, and they, the subject of our prayers, receive the compassion and the good effects which we perform for them, as well as the prayer with which we supplicate Hashem on their behalf."

The *Rebbe* concludes with a powerful statement, "Although the angels call to one another just as humans do, the angels' words do not emerge from their own suffering. After all, an angel has never experienced a Jew's pain when he is being beaten; or his humiliation when he is being harassed and disparaged; or his terror, and his torment when he has no food."

Even if we can do nothing physical for our fellow Jew in need, we can still pray for him from our hearts. Caring, expressed in sincere, meaningful prayer — coupled with heartfelt concern — is a genuine contribution which goes a long way. It gives the benefactor a sense of worthiness. He no longer feels helpless. Regrettably, it is much easier to give up than to pray with sincerity and hope until the very last moment. This constitutes *tzedakah* at its zenith.

✹ ✹ ✹ ✹ ✹ ✹

אדם כי יקריב מכם קרבן לד'

When a man among you brings an offering to Hashem. (1:2)

We translate the word *korban* as sacrifice. This translation does not capture the full meaning of the word. *Horav S.R. Hirsch, zl,* explains that the word *korban* is derived from *karov*, coming near. One who offers a sacrifice is bringing himself closer to Hashem, elevating himself spiritually by his actions. *Horav Yitzchak Zilberstein, Shlita*, cites a homiletical rendering of this *pasuk* by the *Ohr HaChaim Hakadosh*, which is compelling and provides food for thought.

"When a man among you" chooses to bring closer the hearts of his estranged brethren to Hashem, such an individual is worthy of being called an *adam*, man. He does not have to offer any *korbanos*. He will never need to bring a sin-offering, since Hashem will protect him and ascertain that no sin will result from his activities. Hashem wants His children to be close to Him, and He will repay anyone who brings His children home.

Rav Zilberstein elaborates that there are many ways and circumstances in which we can effectively reach out to the alienated, the unacquainted and unaware. They are just waiting for an "invitation" to come closer. One of the most productive forms of outreach is for us to act in the manner in which a *frum*, observant, Jew should act. Our code of honor, integrity, decency and *menchlichkeit*, humanness, will win them over. Once they get to know us for who we are — not what they have been *misled* to believe — their hearts and minds will open up to us, and, consequently, to Hashem.

In his inimitable manner, *Rav* Zilberstein cites a fascinating story to support this idea. It was springtime, and a young *rebbe* was taking his third-grade class on a trip. As they were walking near an orange grove, a car came to a screeching stop next to them. The driver, clearly non-observant, jumped out and addressed the *rebbe*, "Could I ask you and your students for a favor? My brother is lying critically wounded in the hospital. The doctors do not know if he will make it. In fact, they are giving him very little chance for recovery. Could you *daven* with your students for my brother's recovery?"

As soon as the students heard his request, they all answered affirmatively. The man, tears welling up in his eyes, took out a wad of large bills from his wallet and gave it to the *rebbe*, "Here, take this for your time. Buy something for your nice students."

"*Chas v'shalom*, Heaven forbid! We do not take money for helping a fellow Jew. We will be happy to do whatever we can for him. May Hashem listen to our prayers on his behalf and grant him a speedy recovery."

The man took out a card from his pocket and wrote down his brother's name and his mother's name, so they could pray for his recovery. He also added their family name. When the *rebbe* noticed their last name, he realized that the brother was the head of a major crime family. In fact, he was in the hospital because one of his "competitors" had placed a bomb under his car. Nonetheless, the children prayed for him. He was a Jew. His name was written on the blackboard, and the children dedicated their learning in his merit.

A number of weeks went by and, once again, the *rebbe* took his young charges on a short trip. Lo and behold, once again the driver of the same car that had approached them last time pulled up, and the driver jumped out. He ran over and kissed the *rebbe*. "Do not ask what happened!" he exclaimed excitedly. "It was a miracle. My brother survived. It was surely because of the *tefillos*, prayers, of the young children. Thank you! Furthermore, when I told my brother that you refused to take money for your time, saying it was your responsibility to pray for another Jew in need, my brother said that he wants to arrange to study with a *chavrusa*, study partner, to learn more about the religion he has neglected to observe." Today, he is on the road to becoming a full-fledged *baal teshuvah*.

The lesson is simple. A man whose life revolved around money came to the realization that there are people who value something more than money, people who were happy to help another Jew. This message transformed a hardened criminal into a *ben Torah*. This is the meaning of a *korban* that brings *others* closer to Hashem.

זכר תמים יקריבנו

He shall offer an unblemished male. (1:3)

A *Korban Olah*, Elevation-Offering, must be brought from a <u>male</u> animal. *Horav S.R. Hirsch, zl*, explains that with regard to the *mitzvos* that we as Jews are to perform in life, Hashem expects "virile" independence from all of His children/subjects, male and female alike. The *mitzvos* for which we have to stand up, transform us into "men." This concept is analogous to manly strength, manly independence, which we are to dedicate to the service of Hashem. It is not the feminine aspect of man which is represented by endurance and tolerance, but rather the vigor and independence, the firm, resolute action that seeks closeness to the Almighty in the *Korban Olah*.

The *korban* must be *tamim*, whole, complete, without blemish. A blemished animal is not a sick animal. It can otherwise be completely healthy and vibrant, but if it has some minor permanent mutilation or abnormality, it is deemed unacceptable for the Altar. The *Navi Malachi* castigates those who offer blemished animals as degrading Hashem's Name. The Sanctuary — and everyone connected to it — represents the zenith of humanity, the best, most vigorous, and freshest of all that man has to offer. Pulsating life, active life filled with zest and joy — these words described the Sanctuary and those associated with it.

Those who dedicate their lives to the Jew's highest calling, studying Torah, are the most complete specimens of humanity. The "old days," when people would disparage those who went to *Kollel* as "cripples," lazy individuals who had no initiative or ability to succeed, are over. The spiritual renaissance we enjoy in this country is the product of some of the finest and most complete individuals who have ever given their lives for *Torah*. They are the *zachar tamim*, the independent and strong perfect examples of dedication and commitment to *Klal Yisrael*.

Tamim means perfect and whole. *Rav* Hirsch asserts that for each and every aspect of our relationship with Hashem, the first and most indispensable condition is that we apply the whole of ourselves: our whole heart; our whole soul; and our whole material possessions. Any aspect of our being that is lacking in devotion bespeaks a blemish in the relationship. *Achdus*, complete unity with the Almighty, demands that we do not hold back any aspect of ourselves from Him. Complete subservience is the result of the negation of any other state of existence. When a Jew comes close to Hashem, he should do so with every fibre of his being, with all of his faculties. One who dedicates all of himself to Hashem is promised a life, to paraphrase *Rav* Hirsch, "in which even pain and death lose their sting."

We must add that by no means is one who is physically challenged considered blemished. It is the dedication and wholesomeness of one's conviction and dedication that counts — not his physical aspect. "There is nothing so whole as a broken heart" is a wonderful and meaningful maxim — with an important lesson. I would like to cite a beautiful analogy, one that goes to the very core of handicaps and physical infirmities.

A water carrier in India would serve his master by toting water from the stream to his master's home. He carried the water in two pots, hung on either end of a long pole balanced across his shoulders. One of the pots had a small crack, whereas the other was perfect. Thus, when the servant reached his master's home, one pot was full while the other was half-empty.

This went on for two years. Every day the servant would arrive at his master's home with one full pot and one half-filled pot of water. Naturally, the whole pot felt very good; it was doing a complete job. The cracked pot, however, felt that its imperfection caused it to accomplish only part of its function.

One day, the cracked pot apologized to the water carrier. "I feel terrible," the pot said. "Every day you strain yourself to carry water for the master, but because of my defect, you do not receive full value for your effort."

The water carrier replied, "Do not worry. On our way home today, I would like you to look at the side of the road and notice the lovely flowers that are growing there."

As they returned, the cracked pot indeed noticed the pretty, winsome, wild flowers, the sun glistening off their bright petals. Yet, at the end of the road the pot was still disconcerted because once again half of its water had leaked out. Again, it apologized to its bearer for its failure.

The bearer said to the pot, "I told you to look at the lovely flowers that line your side of the path. Because I have always been aware of your 'flaw,' I planted flower seeds along your side of the path. Every day as we go to the master's home, *you* have inadvertently watered these seeds. Every day I am able to pick some of these beautiful flowers to adorn our master's table. Were you not just the way you are, our master would not have this beauty to grace his home."

A powerful analogy. Every creation has a purpose — one that is determined by its Creator. *Tamim*, perfect and whole, is not an external feature. It is an internal characteristic of an individual, reflecting his attitude and devotion to his Creator.

✳ ✳ ✳ ✳ ✳ ✳

דבר אל בני ישראל לאמר נפש כי תחטא בשגגה מכל מצות ד׳ אשר לא
תעשינה ועשה מאחת מהנה

Speak to Bnei Yisrael, saying: When a person will sin unintentionally from among all the commandments of Hashem that may not be done, and he commits one of them. (4:2)

C hazal, in *Toras Kohanim* derive from the words, "to *Bnei Yisrael*," that only a *Yisrael* brings a *Korban Chatas*, Sin-Offering, for an inadvertent sin. Gentiles do not bring a *Korban Chatas*. The *Bais HaLevi* explains that when one sins against Hashem, it is significant whether the transgression is committed *b'meizid*, purposely, or *b'shogeg*, inadvertently. When one sins against his fellowman, however, there is no difference. *Adam muad l'olam*, a man is always responsible for his actions against his fellowman.

When a gentile sins, his sin is only against Hashem. Therefore, if it is inadvertent, he is innocent and not liable for punishment. When a Jew sins against Hashem, he is also committing a grave injustice against his fellow Jew, since *Kol Yisrael areivim zeh lazeh*, all Jews are responsible one for another. Thus, any sin against Hashem is considered a sin against a Jew, because the national character of *Klal Yisrael* has been impugned by his sin against Hashem. Concerning a sin against a fellow Jew, there is no distinction between *shogeg* and *maizid*. Therefore, a Jew who sins inadvertently against Hashem is still obligated to bring a *Korban Chatas*.

Parashas Tzav

והאש על המזבח תוקד בו

The fire on the Altar shall be kept burning on it. (6:5)

What is the meaning of the word, *bo*, on it? It should simply have said, "The fire should be kept burning." It is obvious that this is a reference to the Altar. This question was asked by the *Gerer Rebbe, zl*, the *Imrei Emes*, as a young boy, of his grandfather, the *Sefas Emes*. The *Sefas Emes'* response was to challenge his brilliant grandson to answer the question himself. The *Imrei Emes* replied that, quite possibly, the Torah was telling us that the *Kohen* himself has to be filled with a fiery passion. The fire representing the *korban* should burn fiercely *within him* to the point that, as the flame rises, so should the flame burn concurrently *bo*, within him.

Horav Yitzchak Zilberstein, Shlita, relates that a *Yerushalmi* Jew, *Reb* Shimon Kohen, was such a person. In fact, as he lay mortally wounded, a victim of an Arab suicide bomber in the *Machaneh Yehudah* market, he recounted with a fiery passion how Hashem *brought him* to the fire that consumed his life.

He explained that, typically, he had no reason whatsoever to frequent the *Machaneh Yehuda Shuk*. For a number of years he had owned a fruit stand in the *Shuk*. Five years earlier, he had closed down the stand and decided to spend his newly-found time studying *Torah* in a nearby *Kollel*. He maintained a ritual to visit the market every *Erev Shabbos* to wish *Gut Shabbos* to the other vendors. On that fateful Thursday — not Friday — he said to his wife, "I want to go to the market *today* to wish my friends *Gut Shabbos*."

"Why are you going to the market today?" asked his wife. "It is only Thursday. You never go on Thursday."

He had no answer for her. He just went because he felt compelled to go that day. Under normal circumstances, he would have to wait between twenty and thirty minutes for the bus to arrive. This had gone on for thirty years! The bus had never come on time. For some "strange" reason, today, the bus arrived moments after he came to the bus stop. For thirty years, it had taken forty-five minutes for the bus to travel the distance from *Reb* Shimon's apartment to the market. Today, it took only seventeen minutes. For thirty years, whenever *Reb* Shimon came to the market, he had gone to his right, because that was where all the fruit vendors were situated. Today, he was thirsty, and he went to the left, so that he could first quench his thirst. Moments after he purchased his drink, the bomb exploded right near the place he should never have visited — under usual circumstances.

Apparently, today was not a typical day. *Reb* Shimon lay there in the emergency room, mere moments before he was to take leave of this world, recounting to his wife how everything that had transpired that day was for one purpose — so that he should become a sacrifice to Hashem. As he lay dying, Reb Shimon accepted Hashem's decree, realizing that Hashem's reasoning was beyond his ability to grasp. This was a person in whom Hashem's fire burnt brightly.

❋ ❋ ❋ ❋ ❋ ❋

תפיני מנחת פתים תקריב ריח ניחח לד׳

A repeatedly baked meal offering, broken into pieces, you shall offer it as a satisfying aroma to Hashem. **(6:14)**

A *Korban Minchah* is a simple sacrifice which, due to the simplicity of its contents — flour, oil and frankincense — is usually brought by people that are on the lowest rung of the financial ladder. The *Korban Minchah* is broken into pieces, so that the pieces will be small enough for the *Kohen* to perform the *Kemitzah*. *Horav Aharon Bakst, zl,* adds that the *pittim,* small pieces, help to create an image of more than is really there, so that the pan appears to be fuller than it is. The purpose is to show compassion for the poor man. The same idea applies with a *korban ha'of,* fowl-offering. The *Kohen* is instructed to split the bird with his bare hands. One does not remove the feathers prior to burning the entire bird. Why are the feathers left on the bird? *Rashi* explains that if the feathers were removed, the poor man, who is usually the individual bringing a fowl-offering, would be humiliated by its puny size. After all, once the feathers are removed, very little bird is left. It is better to endure the foul smell of burning feathers than to hurt the feelings of a poor Jew.

A powerful lesson can be derived from here. The *mitzvah* of *chesed* demands that one not only perform kindness to others, but also makes sure that he finds a way to do so in such a manner that he maintains the individual's self-esteem. Even if the benefactor is subject to humiliation and adversity, it is better that he suffers than hurts the feelings of another Jew — even if it is while performing an act of *chesed*. If we do not perform the act correctly, it is not *chesed*. To help someone in such a manner that he consequently experiences a humiliating incident is to distort the entire concept of *chesed*. Unquestionably, while the poor man's fowl is burning on the Altar, the stench that permeates the entire area is overpowering — but that is what *chesed* is all about. No one ever asserted that an act of loving-kindness has to be tailor-made to fit the mood and personality of the benefactor. It is supposed to help the beneficiary. He is the only one for whom we are obligated to show concern.

There is a powerful story that occurred concerning a *gabbai tzedakah*, charity collector, and the *Sanzer Rav, Horav Chaim Halberstam, zl*, that should be related. *Rav* Chaim once came to a small town. As he was walking through the community, he felt himself gravitating to one of the homes. "The scent of *Gan Eden* emanates from this house," *Rav* Chaim declared. "I must enter to discover what is producing this unique fragrance."

It happened to be the home of *Reb* Pesach, the town's *tzedakah* collector. *Rav* Chaim knocked. He was welcomed with the greatest look of shock and reverence. "I must find the source of the unique aroma that permeates your home," *Rav* Chaim said, as he walked around the small home. "I have found it!" he exclaimed, as he pointed to a large box. They immediately opened the box to discover nothing more than some old clothes, most of them unusable. On the bottom of the box, beneath the rags, they discovered a priest's garb.

"What is this?" *Rav* Chaim queried. "What did you do with this priest's vestments that earned it the aroma of *Gan Eden*?"

Reb Pesach sighed and related the following story: "As a *tzedakah* collector, my day never ends. As soon as I finish raising funds for one person in need, another situation arises that needs my attention. Awhile ago, I came home after an unusually difficult day to find a poor man at my door, crying bitterly that he had no money for food. He was deeply in debt, and his lenders had lost patience with him. I told him that I commiserated with his pain, but what could I do? I had already made my rounds for the day. I could not return to the same people again.

"'Woe is to me,' the poor man cried. I have no good fortune at all. Is it my lot to see my wife and children starve to death before my eyes? *Please* help me!' What could I do? I went out again and begged the local community to open up their hearts to this destitute Jew. No sooner had I returned, then another man came to my house with a similar request. How could I turn a deaf ear to his pleas? On the other hand, how could I return a third time to my supporters? That would be the height of *chutzpah*. These people had been kind and benevolent, but I could not take advantage of them. Then I thought of an idea, a strange idea. If it were to work, it would be worth everything.

"I went to the town bar where I usually would go to ask its owner for a contribution. I had already been there twice that day. Now, I returned for a different purpose. I was going to solicit the patrons, people who were far from caring, people who were frivolous and had no respect for anyone. They did, however, have money, and I would ask them for it. With the help of Hashem, I would succeed. It was my last hope.

"I went inside with feelings of trepidation. The spokesman for the rowdy group was a spoiled, young, rich boy. He called me over and began ridiculing me, 'You're back again, old man? Why waste your time?' I replied, 'I do not think it is a waste of time. I have come to solicit <u>you</u> on behalf of a man who is poverty-stricken and has no way of extricating himself from his overwhelming debts. In order to ease his life and give him some peace of mind, I am asking *you* to contribute to this most worthy cause. I am prepared to do almost anything to obtain your donation.

"'I have an idea,' the man replied. 'We used to have a priest in town, who recently passed away. I have his vestments. I want you to put them on and walk through town dressed like the priest. If you do that, I will give you the necessary funds that you seek.'

"I said to myself," *Reb* Pesach continued, "The worst that people will say is that *Reb* Pesach has lost his mind. But it is worth it, if it will generate the funds that I seek for this poor man.' So I donned the priest's vestments and walked all over town, hounded by laughter and shame. When I returned, the man took out his wallet and gave me the money I needed.

"When I removed the vestments, I thought to myself, 'These garments were used to perform a *mitzvah*; I am going to save them.' That is why they have been laying at the bottom of this box."

Tears began to course down *Rav* Chaim's face as he heard the end of the story, "Take these vestments and put them away in place of your *tachrichim*, burial shrouds. They will accompany you to *Gan Eden*. No prosecuting angel will be able to harm you while you are wearing these vestments. They exemplify the zenith of loving-kindness."

So it came to pass, many years later, when the Polish government sought to make a road through the Jewish cemetery, they disinterred a number of graves. *Reb* Pesach's was one of them. The *Chevra Kadisha*, Jewish sacred burial society, noticed that when they removed his remains from his grave, his entire body — with the exception of one leg — was completely intact. Nothing had decomposed, except for part of one leg — which was not covered by the priest's vestments, because it had been torn.

Chesed means a willingness to suffer abuse and humiliation to help another Jew. *Reb* Pesach did, and he was rewarded in kind.

✸ ✸ ✸ ✸ ✸ ✸

אם על תודה יקריבנו

If he shall offer it for a thanksgiving- offering. (7:12)

*I*bn Ezra explains that one must bring a thanksgiving offering when he has been saved from a *tzarah*, misfortune, trouble. *Horav Elazar M. Shach, zl*, gives a penetrating insight into the concept of *todah*, gratitude, from which we should all learn. A young man whose wife had just given birth to a baby girl a year after their *chasunah*, wedding, came to the *Rosh HaYeshivah* and asked if he should make a *kiddush*, festive reception, in honor and appreciation of the event. *Rav* Shach replied, "If your little girl had been born after eight years of marriage, would you still feel compelled to ask this question? Certainly not! You would have realized the importance of showing gratitude and giving praise to the Almighty. Now that Hashem has been benevolent and spared you the anguish of running to doctors to pursue every opportunity to have a child, should the display of gratitude be decreased?"

What a powerful statement! How many of us thank Hashem only when something or someone we value is almost taken from us, but fail to recognize His sustaining powers and His every day, every moment benefits? We say every day in the *Tefillah* of *Modim*, "For our lives, which are committed to Your power, and for our souls that are entrusted to You; for Your miracles that are with us every day; and for Your wonders and favors in every season — evening, morning and afternoon." Many of us say this *Tefillah* by rote, without concentrating on its meaning, until Hashem subtly gives us reason to understand its message.

אם על תודה יקריבנו והקריב על זבח התודה
If he shall offer it for a thanksgiving, he shall offer with the thanksgiving sacrifice. (7:12)

In *Parashas Vayikra*, Moshe *Rabbeinu* was instructed regarding the various *korbanos*, specifically to convey the laws to *Klal Yisrael,* so that they would know what sacrifices to offer on various occasions. In *Parashas Tzav,* the Torah addresses the *Kohanim,* instructing them in the intricacies of these *korbanos*. The question that confronts us is: Why is the *Korban Todah*, thanksgiving-offering, placed in *Parashas Tzav* and totally omitted from *Parashas Vayikra*? It seems from its placement that the *Korban Todah* is focused with greater intensity on the *Kohanim* than on the rest of *Klal Yisrael*. Why?

The *Korban Todah* was brought by an individual, "in recognition of a miraculous deliverance from harm, such as: those who travel at sea, or through the desert; who are released from prison, or who recover from illness." *Horav Yosef Chaim Sonnenfeld, zl,* explains that these conditions are occasions when he becomes acutely aware of Hashem's guiding hand, directing events in his life. These occurrences convey a profound message to a person: miracles occur. Hashem directs the universe in such a manner that, for the most part, the miracles remain subtle and covert. Every once in a while, however, a person recognizes that the miracles that have happened in his life are a sampling of the larger picture of miraculous events. The average person is not privy to overt miracles.

The *Kohanim* however, were witness to Hashem's Divine intervention into what we are used to referring to as "nature," on a daily basis. They felt Hashem's Imminent Presence in this world — constantly. In *Pirkei Avos* 5:5, *Chazal* tell us that there were regularly ten visible miracles in the *Bais HaMikdash*. Thus, the idea of expressing our gratitude to Hashem for His beneficence has greater application to the *Kohanim* who routinely experienced Divine intervention through visible miracles. The *Torah,* therefore, places the *Korban Todah* in *Parashas Tzav.*

We might add another reason for placing the *Korban Todah* in the *parsha* that addresses the *Kohanim.* Using *Rav* Yosef Chaim's thesis that the *Kohanim* experienced miracles on a regular basis, rendering them more attuned to miracles, we may suggest another reason for impressing upon them the significance of the *Korban Todah.* One who experiences miracles on a regular basis not only develops a profound awareness of Hashem's Divine intervention, but also the fear that he might become accustomed to miracles, almost to the point that he expects them, forgetting that they are an incredible gift. Sometimes we need reminders to "motivate" our sense of appreciation, to realize that it is all a gift.

This is likewise true of anyone who has been the beneficiary of Hashem's special favor. We become accustomed to it. We forget that it was a gift that can be abrogated at any time. While we certainly appreciate Hashem's gifts, all too often our gratitude is short-lived. We must remember that the actual gift might be limited in time.

It is appropriate to cite a compelling statement from the *Kav HaYashar.* Taking note of the fact that we no longer have the *Bais HaMikdash* and the ability to offer a *Korban Todah,* we must do something to demonstrate our *hakoras ha'tov,* appreciation, to Hashem. Therefore, "one who has been the beneficiary of Hashem's compassion and kindness — if he was saved from thieves, from a fire, from the clutches of death; or if he was gravely ill and healed — it is incumbent upon him to do something good or perform an act of kindness, where *it will be noticeable* that this is in lieu of a *korban* to Hashem." The *Kav HaYashar* adds that this applies to everyone, because which Jew can say he has never been saved from something terrible? Perhaps it might serve us all well to analyze our life's occurrences and pay tribute to the Almighty for shielding us in the past, as well as, hopefully, safeguarding us in the future.

٭ ٭ ٭ ٭ ٭

Parashas Shemini

ותצא אש מלפני ד' ותאכל אותם וימתו לפני ד'

*A fire came forth from before Hashem and consumed them, and they died
before Hashem. (10:2)*

In the *Talmud Sanhedrin* 52a *Chazal* cite the following conversation
that took place between Nadav and Avihu. They were walking in a
procession behind Moshe and Aharon, with *Klal Yisrael* following
behind them. Nadav said to Avihu, "When will these two old men die, so that
you and I will lead the generation?" Hashem replied to them, "We will see
who will bury whom." Although the question is clearly inappropriate, is it
sufficient reason for Hashem to cut both of their lives short? Does a single
statement carry so much weight that two people must be cut down in such a
tragic manner during the prime of their lives?

In his *Sefer Simchas HaTorah, Horav Simcha HaKohen Sheps, zl,*
offers the following explanation: He cites the *Midrash* in *Vayikra* in which
Rabbi Akiva explains why *Klal Yisrael* has been compared to an *ofe*, fowl.
Just as a fowl cannot fly without wings, so, too, *Klal Yisrael* is unable to
achieve anything without the help of their *zekeinim*, elders. *Rav* Sheps
explains that *Chazal* are not necessarily referring to actual elders, but, rather,
to the concept of *ziknah*, age/experience. Interestingly, *Chazal* does not say
that we need *talmidei chachamim*, Torah scholars. The requirement is one of
age. The reason for this is that with age one not only accumulates vast
scholarship in Torah knowledge, but he also develops experience in life. The
everyday challenges that we confront in our life's endeavor provide us with
an incredible educational experience. With every experience, we develop a
greater and more penetrating perception of life and how best to live. This
knowledge born of experience is invaluable.

This was the error of Nadav and Avihu. They did not recognize the
enormous advantage of *ziknah* and the wealth of life experience that it offers.
In the *Talmud Megillah* 31b, *Chazal* say, *Binyan ne'arim setirah, u'setiras*

zekeinim binyan, "The building of youth is demolishing, while the demolishing of old age is really building." In other words, old age it is constructive, while the building of youth is really demolishing — it has a detrimental effect. When Nadav and Avihu were speaking, they demonstrated a lack of respect for the concept of *ziknah*. This is *setiras ne'arim*, demolishing done by youth. It indicates an impulsivity that can have a detrimental effect. Hence, their "talk" was deeper than words. It manifest an attitude that has the ultimate potential to undermine the stability and continuity of *Klal Yisrael*.

✻ ✻ ✻ ✻ ✻ ✻

בקרבי אקדש ועל פני כל העם אכבד וידם אהרן
"I will be sanctified through those who are close to Me, and I will be honored before the entire People;" and Aharon was silent. (10:3)

The death of Aharon *Hakohen's* two sons and his reaction to the tragedy set the standard for *missas tzaddikim*, the death of the righteous, and our reaction to tragedy. *Horav Nachum, zl, m'Horodna* was struck again and again by the Divine Hand of punishment. Although his prayers had saved the lives of many, he was not able to save the lives of his own sons. His wife complained bitterly. Yet, he remained silent, never uttering a word of bitterness. After the *Shivah*, seven-days of mourning, was over, he soothed her with these words of *nechamah*, consolation, "Am I better than Rabbi Yochanan who lost ten sons? Hashem sanctifies His Name through those close to Him. May His Name be blessed forever."

The *Chafetz Chaim, zl*, lost a son. *Rav Avraham, zl*, was an outstanding genius whose brilliance and profundity were recognized by the great leaders of that generation. His acuity and encyclopedic knowledge were especially notable when dealing with the most complex *Talmudic* subjects, which he illuminated to all who had the privilege to study with him. He passed away on *Shabbos,* the twentieth of *Kislev*, at the age of twenty-three.

His saintly father was not at home when tragedy struck. After *Shabbos*, the *Chafetz Chaim* received a telegram urging him to return home immediately. When he returned home the next day, he saw a crowd of mourners returning from the local cemetery. He immediately understood what had occurred. He entered his home in a controlled, restrained manner and sat down on the floor to sit *Shivah*. He neither cried, nor emitted a sigh of pain.

"In truth," he said, "a great *illuy*, genius, has perished. When *Rav* Avraham was sixteen, he would innovate *chidushim*, novellae, like one of the *gedolim*, Torah leaders. Hashem has given, and Hashem has taken away. May Hashem's Name be blessed forever. Now I know that I am a Jew" (now I know what it takes to be a complete Jew).

He explained his comment by relating an episode that occurred during the Spanish Inquisition: "A mother had just stood by as the vicious murderer slaughtered her children right before her eyes. This *eishes chayil*, woman of valor, raised her eyes Heavenward and said, 'Hashem *Yisborach*, I have always loved *You*, but as long as I had my children, my love was divided in two. Now that I no longer have my children, my whole heart has become a torch of flaring love for You. I can now fulfill the *mitzvah* of *b'chol levavecha*, with *all* your heart.'"

The *Chafetz Chaim* concluded his words, saying, "Hashem, all the love I used to feel for my son, I now transfer to *You*!"

Rav Leib, the *Chafetz Chaim's* eldest son, related that his father later told him, "My sins caused it. When the severity of his condition became known to me in Warsaw, I rushed home. Regrettably, through *ma'aseh Satan*, an act of Satan, I missed the express train and was compelled to take the local. My journey was delayed from Above. Conceivably, had I returned in time, I would have prayed for him, and, possibly, with what few merits I possess, I might have interceded on his behalf. Hashem, however, Who knows everything, sent his *neshamah*, soul, to this world for a purpose. It is quite possible that during his brief stay in this world, he fulfilled that purpose."

There is no question that the *Chafetz Chaim* and other *gedolei Yisrael* who sustained personal tragedies felt the same pain and suffering as the common Jew. Their anguish at the loss of a child was overwhelming. Yet, they were able to transcend their personal emotions because they saw the total context. They understood that Hashem directs and guides world events, so that everything which occurs is a manifestation of His Divine will. We accept His will. If you think about it, how could a person live without believing in Hashem? Are we to think that tragedy is something that "just happens," that there is no rhyme or reason for the suffering that we collectively and individually sustain? When we believe in the Almighty, our conviction and faith will continue to guide us along the path that He forges for us.

Accepting Divine will is not easy, but people do it all of the time. Accepting it with love and retaining the ability to offer praise and song takes this virtue to an entirely different plateau. *Horav Yitzchak Zilberstein, Shlita,* cites a powerful story concerning the *Bamberger Rav, zl,* which took place after his young son was killed for refusing to bow down to an idol. Right after his son was killed, the *Rav* had his body taken into the *bais ha'medrash* and placed in front of the *Aron HaKodesh.* The *Rav* opened the *Aron* and with great weeping cried out, *Al ha'kol yisgadal v'yiskadash...* "For all this, let the Name of the King of Kings, the Holy One, Blessed is He, grow exalted, sanctified, praised, glorified, and extolled in the worlds that He has created." This *Tefillah* is said on *Shabbos* as the *Sefer Torah* is being carried through the *shul* on its way to the *bimah.* Regrettably, not everyone gives much thought to the message of these words. Perhaps this story will change that perspective.

✴ ✴ ✴ ✴ ✴ ✴

ואת החזיר כי מפריס פרסה הוא
And the pig, for its hoof is split. (11:7)

T he *chazir*, pig, is used as the symbol of an animal that is unkosher. Interestingly, it is specifically the *chazir* that has a *siman tahor*, one kosher sign: its hooves are split. Apparently, this unkosher animal has something to teach us. *Aron Eidus* explains that we can derive from the *chazir's* nature a significant lesson in regard to *avodas Hashem*, serving Hashem.

There are times when a person finds it difficult to maintain his spiritual level. He feels as if Heaven is distancing him, literally pushing him away from *kedushah*, sanctity, implying that, "You are not wanted." This can clearly have an overpowering effect upon a person. It can catalyze depression, engendering feelings of hopelessness. There is nothing worse than feeling unneeded and unwanted. Specifically at a time such as this, one must strengthen his conviction, encourage greater resolution, and ignore the emotions that are wreaking havoc on his mind. This is nothing more than a test from the Almighty to determine one's ability to withstand adversity and challenge.

We derive this approach from the *chazir*, whose name is similar to *chazarah*, to return. The pig typifies the nature of an animal that keeps returning. Regardless of the many times it is rejected, it keeps coming back. This is why it has a *siman taharah*, pure sign, on its hooves. Although its entire body is *tamei*, spiritually unclean; its hooves teach us an important lesson: do not give up. Even if you have sinned and fallen from your spiritual plateau, you are obligated to return to your original position and work your way back up. Do not run away, deferring to your emotions. Do not give in to your *yetzer hara*, evil inclination, that tells you to "throw in the towel." Never give up in your spiritual quest.

There is another good quality to be derived from the *chazir's* behavior. The *Midrash Lekach Tov* says that the *chazir* is given its name as a result of its unique mannerism. When it is "addressed" from behind, it does not simply turn its head around; it turns its entire body around to face the individual who is addressing it. It gives the addressor the respect of facing him fully. When one gives full recognition to the individual who is addressing him, he indicates his respect for that person.

The *chazir* is an unclean animal. Yet, he manifests certain character traits from which we could learn to better ourselves. This proves that one can learn from everything.

וְאֶת אֵלֶּה תְּשַׁקְּצוּ מִן הָעוֹף לֹא יֵאָכְלוּ שֶׁקֶץ הֵם

These shall you abominate from among the birds; they may not be eaten for they are an abomination. (11:13)

T he Torah enumerates twenty-four species of fowl which are not to be eaten. Interestingly, the Torah does not give the identifying characteristics of the non-kosher fowl, as it does for animals and fish. The *Mishnah* in *Chullin* 5:9 explains that a non-kosher fowl exhibits the character trait of cruelty, since when it eats it seizes its prey with its claws and lifts it off the ground. This idea is echoed by the *Ramban* in his commentary to the above *pasuk*: The common trait among all non-kosher species is a cruel nature. One who eats the flesh of these birds absorbs a part of their cruel nature into his psyche, adversely affecting him.

Horav Avraham Pam, zl, notes that as Jews we have a different perspective on the concept of cruelty than non-Jews do. Our definition is based upon the Torah's interpretation, while theirs is founded in their own concept of morality. When non-Jews speak of cruelty, they refer to an act of extreme violence perpetrated in a brutal and inhumane manner. We, on the other hand, do not think that one must wield a knife or shoot a gun to be considered cruel. In the *Talmud Bava Metzia* 58b, *Chazal* teach us that if one were to humiliate another person publicly, it is considered as if he had killed him. Indeed, words inflict a pain that is sharper and more lasting than the pain of a piercing sword. Verbal abuse, quite often, leaves scars that endure long after physical pain has subsided.

The energy that one's body receives as the result of ingesting non-kosher food is blemished energy. The body of a Jew has specific functions to perform — Torah study, *mitzvah* performance and acts of loving-kindness. When the body is sustained with food that is spiritually contaminated, the energy that is produced will do more harm than good. Thus, the Jew's desire to act appropriately is impeded as a result of ingesting this non-kosher food.

The destructive force is magnified when the contaminant enters his mind more deeply than his body. If a person sees, thinks, or reads material that is spiritually antithetical to Jewish belief and value, it creates untold havoc on his impressionable mind. Imagine pouring crystal clear fine wine into a filthy container. Likewise, if one's mind is sullied with inappropriate thoughts, he cannot understand the profundities and underlying meanings of Torah. Moreover, what his mind ingests leaves its imprimatur on his memory bank. His whole perspective on matters are shaped by what is stored in his mind.

Rav Pam concludes with a powerful analogy of the famous pianist who took out a one million dollar insurance policy on his *fingers*. When asked why he did something so strange, he replied, "My fingers are everything. My ability to play piano is dependent on the highly dexterous sensitivity of my fingers. If I lose this unique ability as a result of damage to my fingers, I am no longer different than any other pianist. Therefore, I must insure my fingers, because they define who I am."

The pianist understood that he possessed a valuable attribute that needed to be protected. We also have a unique attribute that deserves protection — our *neshamah*, soul. If one's mind becomes polluted with improper thoughts, so that what exits his mouth becomes inappropriate, how can he then expect to use these organs for Torah and *Tefillah*? When the pristine is kept in a soiled container, it will lose its purity. This is all the more reason to protect our minds and mouths from matters that will undermine their virtue.

✼ ✼ ✼ ✼ ✼ ✼

ואת החסידה
And the chasidah. (11:19)

*R*ashi explains that this fowl is called *chasidah* because it displays *chesed*, kindness, towards other members of its species by sharing food with them. If so, the obvious question arises: Why is it listed among the non-kosher fowl? One would think that such a noble attribute would warrant that this bird be considered kosher. The *Chidushei HaRim* replies that since this bird directs its kindness *only* toward members of its own species, but will not help others, it deviates from the Torah's idea of *chesed*. There is no such thing as selective *chesed*. We are to help all people, regardless of our personal feelings toward them. When one picks and chooses whom he wants to help, he is performing *chesed* only for one person — himself.

Horav Avraham Mordecai, zl, m'Gur, cites the *Yerushalmi* that refers to *achbarim*, rats, as *reshaim*, wicked, because when one of them sees a large quantity of food, it will call others to join in the meal. Why is the rat considered wicked? The rat is acting like the *chasidah*. It goes out of its way to share its discovery with other rats. Why is the *chasidah* given a complimentary name, while the *achbar* is considered wicked? Are they not both doing the same thing?

Imrei Shamai explains that when the *chasidah* displays kindness towards members of its species, it is not doing so at the expense of others. It is not stealing food. In contrast, the rat performs its kindness at the expense of the people from whom it steals. To give someone the shirt off one's own back is *chesed*; to give someone the shirt off someone else's back, is *rishus*, evil.

Parashas Tazria

ובמלאת ימי טהרה לבן או לבת תביא כבש בן שנתו לעלה ובן יונה או תר
לחטאת

*Upon the completion of the days of her purity for a son or for a daughter,
she shall bring a sheep within its first year for an elevation-offering, and a
young dove or a turtledove for a sin-offering.* (12:6)

Ayoledes, woman who has given birth, brings two *korbanos*: a
sheep, as a *Korban Olah;* and a fowl, as a *Korban Chatas. Chazal*
explain that the *Chatas*, sin-offering, is brought because a woman
who goes through childbirth suffers so much pain that she vows not to have
more children. Such a vow is sinful. Breaking it, which is likely to occur, is
more sinful. The reason for the *Korban Olah*, elevation-offering, however,
eludes us. The usual reasons that catalyze this *korban* do not apply to the
yoledes.

Abarbanel explains that the *Korban Olah* is a form of gratitude to
Hashem for granting her a child and for sparing her life through the ordeal of
childbirth. This reasoning is supported by a number of *Midrashim* that
obligate the woman to acknowledge Hashem's beneficence during her
involvement in the motherhood process. While all this is true, a *Korban
Todah*, thanksgiving-offering, seems more appropriate than an *Olah. Horav
Avigdor HaLevi Nebentzhal, Shlita,* addresses this question and suggests two
approaches. He explains that either the criteria for bringing a *Korban Todah*
do not apply to a *Yoledes,* or the demands of *Halachah* which apply to the
Jewish woman do not correspond with the *halachic* application of a *Korban
Todah.*

The first approach is based upon the *halachah* that one must
consume a *Korban Todah* in one day and one night, while one has two days
and one night to consume the usual *Korban Shelamim*, peace-offering. The
reason for this is that gratitude must be spontaneous. One must express
gratitude amidst joy and enthusiasm with a heart filled with song. Once one

waits and allows his obligation to be delayed, a significant component of the appreciation is diminished. Thus, as the time for consuming the *Todah* passes, the level of *simchah*, joy, is decreased. Therefore, the Torah shortened the time span allotted for its consumption, so that it would be eaten at the time of heightened joy.

This *halachah* concerning the *Korban Todah* creates a problem for the *yoledes,* who cannot bring a *korban* for forty days for a male birth and eighty days for a female birth. After such a lengthy time passes, the emotion that permeated the *yoledes* at the time the miracle of birth took place might have waned. Without a doubt, if she desires to bring a *Todah*, she may, but to say that every *yoledes* should be obligated to bring a *todah* does not seem consistent with the *halachos* that apply to that *korban*.

Second, another *halachah* which pertains to the *Korban Todah* does not coincide with the manner in which a *bas Yisrael*, Jewish woman, should act publicly. Together with the *korban Todah*, one must bring forty loaves, of which four are given to the *Kohen*. The *Netziv, zl*, explains why this *korban* necessitates so many breads. He says that since everything must be eaten in a short period of time, it behooves him to invite friends and relatives to share in the celebration of his good fortune. The greater number of participants involved in the celebration, the more magnified is the *Kiddush Hashem*, sanctification of Hashem's Name, which is the underlying purpose of *Todah* — thanking Hashem.

This *halachah*, however, does not concur with the *halachos* of *tznius*, modesty, that are the hallmark of the Jewish woman. It is inappropriate for a woman to call attention to herself in front of a crowd. The impropriety becomes more grievous when it is a married woman, which is the case with a *yoledes*. *Kol kevudah bas melech penimah*, "The entire glory of the daughter of the king lies on the inside" (*Tehillim* 45:14). This *pasuk*, which underscores much of the Torah's attitude toward the role of a woman, has been used by *Chazal* as a statement describing the private nature of the female role, as well as an elaborate praise of the private nature of the religious experience in general. Indeed, the private sphere should be the dominant area of a woman's life. Implicit in the woman's creation was the idea that she focus on a specific trait of the human personality — *tznius*.

While a woman may certainly offer a *Korban Todah*, to oblige her to do so after childbirth would not be consistent with the parameters of *hilchos tznius*. This statement will surely be cause for considerable discussion, especially in light of the influence of western civilization on contemporary Jewish society. *Rav* Nebentzhal cites two *mitzvos* that women do not usually perform, specifically because of constraints on them made by the laws of *tznius*.

Women do not light the *Chanukah* lights unless there is no man in the house. Why? The *Chasam Sofer* explains that because of the criteria of *pirsumei nissa*, publicizing the miracle, one should light the candles outside, in public. It is not the manner of a woman to stand outside of her house and publicly light the candles. It is not *tznius*. How far we are removed from the *Chasam Sofer's* perspective on Jewish life!

Kiddush Levanah, sanctifying and blessing the New Moon, is a time-bound *mitzvah*. Yet, while women do recite a *brachah* upon performing a *mitzvas asei shehazman grama*, time-bound *mitzvah*, they do not recite the *Kiddush Levanah* service. A number of reasons are cited. The *Rama* says that since this *mitzvah* should be performed publicly beneath the sky, preferably on the street, it is not consistent with the laws of *tznius*.

We have only to return to the sources to realize that to reverse a G-d-given role is to invite censure, both Divine and human. Regrettably, the effect of the society in which we live has somewhat distorted our perspective on what really is the G-d-given role of woman. Adam *Ha'rishon* gave Chavah a name which he saw *b'Ruach HaKodesh*, with Divine Inspiration, that would reflect her fundamental — though not necessarily exclusive — role in life: *eim kol chai*, mother of all life. Perhaps, if more people would accept this truth, there would be many fewer issues concerning our children's educational development.

וטמא טמא יקרא

He is to call out: "Contaminated, contaminated!" (13:45)

ashi explains that the *metzora* must warn people to distance themselves from him lest his *tumah*, spiritual defilement, contaminate them. The following narrative indicates how far we are removed from reality and the definition of sin. *Horav Elazar M. Shach, zl,* related that his uncle *Horav Isser Zalman Meltzer, zl,* the venerable *Rosh HaYeshivah* of *Eitz Chaim,* would give a *shmuess,* ethical discourse, on *Motzoei Shabbos,* during the month of *Elul.* The words that came from his heart entered the hearts of his students and deeply inspired them. The emotion that was felt in that room was overwhelming.

One time, the *Rosh HaYeshivah* stood at the lectern. He looked at the crowd and declared, "When a *Sefer Torah* is found to be *pasul,* invalid, we take a *gartel,* sash, and wrap and tie it around the outside of the *Sefer.* This way people will be aware that it is *pasul,* and they will not use it."

Suddenly, the *Rosh HaYeshivah* burst out in heartrending tears and screamed, "If so, how many *gartlech,* sashes, should we be wrapped with, so that people will realize how *pasul* we are? Yet, we still do not learn from our actions!"

As soon as these words left *Rav* Isser Zalman's mouth, the entire assemblage broke down in bitter weeping. *Rav* Isser Zalman was a *tzaddik.* His students were *talmidim* of their revered *rebbe.* He was their religious role model. Yet, they all wept *sincerely.* What should *we* say?

זאת תהיה תורת המצרע ביום טהרתו

This shall be the law of the metzora on the day of his purification. (14:2)

Living outside the camp of the rest of society, the *metzora* has the opportunity to reflect upon the effect of his disparaging words. He learns to realize how much evil he has generated. Words can hurt. They can also soothe. They can ameliorate one's grief. They can also cause untold pain. They can lift one's spirit. They can also cause crushing despair. They can bolster one's confidence. They can also rob one of his dignity. It all depends on one's thoughtfulness in speech — or his malevolence. And what about words spoken in anger, with no aforethought? How many families have such harshly spoken words divided? How many friendships have they destroyed? How many marriages have they soured? Words used thoughtfully can enhance relationships, elevate reputations, make people feel good — about themselves and others.

Words are not cheap; the old adage, "names will never harm me," is not true. Names do cause harm. Just ask any adult who had been called a name as a child. Ask him if he still remembers the name, and if it still bothers him. Then there are the words which we have not said, the compliment we did not give, the apology we did not express. This is especially true of parents and teachers. That little compliment, the few words of encouragement, the smile that comes with a job well done, goes a long way. Everybody thrives on a compliment; some hunger for it. It goes without saying that the derogatory or thoughtless remarks we make to our children and students can come back to haunt us later in life.

The following story demonstrates the devastating effect of a parent's scornful comment. It is a story about a woman who survived the Holocaust, moved to *Eretz Yisrael* and became an intelligent and articulate member of the community. She would often reminisce about her childhood in pre-World War II Europe. Once, during her musings, she declared that one of the happiest recollections of her life was the day in which she was forcibly taken by the Nazis from her home and transferred to an extermination camp.

Those listening to her story were understandably taken aback. Responding to their shocked expressions, she explained that her family situation was far from ideal. Apparently, her older sister had been the favored, *frum*, observant daughter, while she was the rebellious one. If there was one pat of butter and one pat of margarine, her sister would get the butter, while she would get the margarine. "After all," her mother would explain, "your older sister is exhausted from *davening* with such great *kavanah*, concentration, while you probably skipped a few pages. You can do with less."

The derision would increase and become more spiteful when she did something to anger her parents — which, regrettably, occurred more often than not. In anger, her mother would complain, "You probably are not even my biological daughter! Your sister was born at home, whereas you were born in a public clinic. The doctors probably exchanged my real daughter with you." This was certainly not her mother's usual refrain, but the painful effect of a derisive comment endures.

In 1942, the Nazis came to her hometown and rounded up the children. Only she and her parents were home at the time. Her father immediately wrote a *kvittel* to the *Gerrer Rebbe*. Her mother threw herself at the feet of the Nazi beasts, begging that they spare her child, "Please, I beg you. Let my child stay. I will do anything. I cannot live without her!" But her entreaties fell upon deaf ears.

The young girl, now turned adult, remembered that moment with great joy. "I felt no pain; I had no fear," she said. "I was overjoyed to finally hear that my mother truly loved me as a child." The affirmation that she was, indeed, her mother's own and beloved daughter, accepted and not rejected, overshadowed the fear of being taken away to her death.

Imagine, all these years later, this woman looked back on a devastating experience as being her greatest source of joy. After all, it was this experience that erased the pain in her heart that had been caused by words.

✳ ✳ ✳ ✳ ✳ ✳

ורחץ במים וטהר ואחר יבוא אל המחנה

And immerse himself in the water and become pure. Thereafter, he may
enter the camp. (14:8)

The punishment for speaking *lashon hara* is meant to teach the
slanderer a lesson. He now has some idea regarding the effect of
his words. As a result of his slanderous tongue, he caused a break
in relationships between people. Let him live alone, far from the center of the
community, so that he will begin to realize the harmful consequences of his
vile mouth. Furthermore, when he is alone, he has time to introspect and
focus on his life. He now has the opportunity to change his overall demeanor
and work on improving his character. Last, as *Horav Avigdor Halevi
Nebentzhal, Shlita*, explains, the *metzora*, having been distanced from the
three *machanos*, encampments, now realizes that Hashem views him as being
on a very low spiritual plateau. This is because a person's position relative to
the center of *kedushah*, sanctity, is an indicator of his spiritual level.

There is a direct corollary between the two positions. This is to be
noted from the fact that the *Kohen Gadol* walks into the *Kodshei
HaKodoshim*, Holy of Holies, on *Yom Kippur*, the holiest day of the year,
only after having been away from his home for seven days prior to *Yom
Kippur*. During his separation period, he lives on the *Har HaBayis*, Temple
Mount, in preparation for his awesome experience. Residing in this elevated
Makom, place, of *kedushah*, has a powerful effect on the *Kohen Gadol* —
one which now gives him access to the Holy of Holies. Thus, the *metzora*,
who is sent away from his original home, now understands that his spiritual
position has been changed; he has been distanced from his original standing.

Once we understand the depth of the punishment, we then have an
idea of the incredible reward in store for he who speaks positively of *Klal
Yisrael* collectively, as well as each Jew individually. The *Toesfta* in
Meseches Sotah 4:1 says that Hashem's reward is five hundred times greater
than His punishment. This is all the more reason to look for the positive
aspect in every person's behavior. At times, it might take a bit of imagination
to see the positive, as the following story demonstrates.

Two friends worked together, side by side, for an institution in *Eretz
Yisrael* for many years. After awhile, one of them suddenly passed away. The
funeral was attended by many of Yerushalayim's elite, among them *Horav*

Aryeh Levine, zl. It happened that *Rav* Aryeh was walking in the funeral procession together with the surviving friend, when the man left the procession and ran into a flower shop. A few minutes later, he rejoined the procession, this time carrying a flowerpot with him. The man's action shocked *Rav* Aryeh, who was fully aware of his lifelong relationship with the deceased. It continued to bother him until he decided that he must give the man *mussar*, reproach, for his lack of respect for his friend. He began by asking, "Can you please enlighten me why you felt it necessary to leave your friend's funeral procession to buy a potted plant?"

"*Rebbe*, let me explain my actions," the man replied. "Yesterday, a man who was being treated for leprosy passed away in the hospital. My friend, the deceased, was very close to this leper and would visit him often. When the leper died, the hospital staff was about to burn all of his effects due to contamination. The problem was that among his few possessions were his *Tefillin*. My friend had been negotiating with the hospital administration concerning the *Tefillin*. At the end, the hospital deferred and agreed to have the *Tefillin* stored in a flowerpot and then removed and buried in the ground. There was one condition: They had to have the flowerpot in the hospital by 12:00PM — today. Regrettably, my friend died suddenly and the risk of the *Tefillin* being destroyed was considerable. This is why I left the procession to purchase a flowerpot, and I am going immediately to the hospital to bury the *Tefillin*.

Rav Aryeh concluded the story by emphasizing to what length one must go to judge another person favorably.

לכפר על בני ישראל מכל חטאתם אחת בשנה

To bring atonement upon Bnei Yisrael for all their sins once a year.
(16:34)

*Y*om Kippur is not the only Festival that occurs once a year. Yet, the Torah emphasizes its singular annual occurrence. Why? *Horav Eliyahu Lopian, zl,* the venerable *Mashgiach* of *Kfar Chasidim,* asked this question in his *shmuess,* ethical discourse, on *Yom Kippur* 1960 shortly before *Neilah,* the Final Prayer of the day. In his reply, he cited the *Talmud* in *Moed Katan* 28 in which *Chazal* explain the juxtaposition of the death of Miriam to the *Parah Adumah,* Red Heifer. Just as the *Parah Adumah* atones, so, too, does *missas tzaddikim,* the passing of the righteous, achieve atonement for *Klal Yisrael.*

By implication, *Chazal* are teaching us that it is possible to have more than one *Yom Kippur* during the course of the year. The passing of a *tzaddik* atones for his immediate family. If he is a great *tzaddik,* the effect of the atonement will be more widespread, and even his community will achieve atonement. If the *gadol ha'dor,* preeminent Torah leader of the generation, passes away, it atones for the sins of the entire generation. This is the explanation of the words, "once a year." The Torah implies to us that *Yom Kippur,* with its concomitant atonement effect, should only occur once a year. In other words, we should not need the additional effect of a *tzaddik's* passing to remove the taint caused by our sins.

It so happened that shortly after *Kol Nidrei,* the opening prayer of *Yom Kippur,* was chanted, the *gadol ha'dor,* the *Brisker Rav, zl,* passed away in Yerushalayim. No one outside of Yerushalayim knew of his passing until after *Yom Kippur.* How *Rav* Elya Lopian knew remains a puzzle. Furthermore, the *Brisker Rav's* son, *Horav* Yosef Dov, related that shortly before his father's passing, the *Brisker Rav* had said, "This year we will have two *Yom Kippurim;* one will go, and the other will come."

✻ ✻ ✻ ✻ ✻ ✻

ושמרתם את חקתי ואת משפטי אשר יעשה אתם האדם וחי בהם

You shall observe My decrees and My laws, which man shall carry out and by which he shall live. (18:5)

I n his later years, The *Brisker Rav, zl,* was weak and infirm. Indeed, his close disciples sensed that every moment of his life was a struggle to fulfill the *mitzvah* of *V'chai bohem,* "And by which he shall live." When he took his various medicines, he would do so as if he was performing the greatest *mitzvah.* Every breath that he took was a *mitzvah* of "staying alive," simply to live as a Jew, because Hashem has given us this *mitzvah. Horav Ezriel Tauber, Shlita,* recollects that when his father became old, he was relegated to spending his days in a wheelchair. He could do nothing for himself. Everything was done for him. This was in stark contrast to his younger days, when — as a vibrant powerhouse of energy — he was able to raise *kavod Shomayim,* the honor of Heaven, by reaching out to thousands of Jews. Obviously, his present, sorry state catalyzed much depression. His children were always seeking ways to comfort and encourage him.

Once *Rav* Ezriel said to his father, "You know Hashem really did a great justice for you." His father looked back at him incredulously. "Let me explain," *Rav* Ezriel continued. "Tell me, Father, which *mitzvah* in the Torah have you never fulfilled *lishmah,* for the sake of the *mitzvah*?" His father's shock became even greater. Was there a *mitzvah* that had eluded his appropriate performance? He had tried to perform each and every *mitzvah* meticulously, following the precise letter of the law. To what was his son alluding?

"Yes, Father, there is one *mitzvah* that you did not perform for the sake of the *mitzvah*: the *mitzvah* of *V'chai bohem,* "And by which he shall live." The Torah admonishes us to live as Jews, just for that purpose — to live as Jews. You, Father, have always lived to fulfill *mitzvos,* to perform acts of loving-kindness. Every breath that you have taken was to do something to elevate *kavod Shomayim.* You have never lived, however, just for the purpose of living. Have you ever taken a breath and said, 'I am breathing solely for the purpose of fulfilling the *mitzvah* of *V'chai bohem,* so that there will be another living Jew in the world?'

"What did Hashem do for you? He provided you with the opportunity to serve Him *fully.* Seeing that every minute of your day was devoted to carrying out *mitzvos*, He saw to it that you could no longer do anything else but *live for Him*."

What a beautiful and powerful thought! Whoever would think that when Hashem removes our faculties, He is simultaneously providing us with an opportunity to just live for Him and not for any other reason? Unquestionably, one must be on a very elevated plateau of spiritual conviction to understand what it means to live — just for the purpose of living as a Jew.

It happened that as I was reading this thought concerning the *Brisker Rav,* I also came across a poignant article about another Jewish hero, one who recently passed away. He literally inspired thousands with his awesome faith and conviction. He exemplified existing for the purpose of living as a Jew, since his physical condition did not allow him to carry out many activities. His name was Mikey Butler, *zl*, a giant of *middos* and *emunah* who spent more than half of his twenty-four years of life in hospitals.

I never met Mikey, but when he passed away, a friend of his called me just to talk. Mikey was sick all of his life, yet he lived every minute fully, for the purpose of living. He lived on the threshold of death with a powerful belief in the meaning and value of life. His life story is a tale of courage, faith and triumph. Every minute of life that Hashem granted him was used to live as a Jew should live. He never complained. Two months before Mikey passed away — at a time when he could no longer see, hear, breathe, walk or talk — Mikey said, "G-d is good." Indeed, Mikey coined a phrase, a motto by which we should all live: "Day by glorious day." He sought every opportunity to perform acts of *chesed* and to inspire others, which he successfully accomplished. He wanted so badly to live one day as a healthy person, without the multitudes of medicine that had become his daily staple. He never got his wish. He did, however, live his life to its fullest potential, using every minute that was allotted to him just to continue living as a Jew. His life was a source of inspiration to thousands. His story will continue to serve as a blessing for him and a source of encouragement and hope to the many who will look to Mikey as the symbol of *V'chai bohem.*

✻ ✻ ✻ ✻ ✻ ✻

ומזרעך לא תתן להעביר למלך ולא תחלל את שם אלקיך

You shall not present any of your children to pass through for molech, and do not profane the Name of your G-d. (18:21)

*S*forno gives a powerful explanation for the sin of giving one's child to the *molech*, which has practical application in our lives. One who brings animal sacrifices to Hashem — but offers his children as sacrifices to the *molech* — demonstrates his priorities. He indicates his true allegiance. He gives his most precious possessions, his children, to the idol, while he gives his material possessions to Hashem. He thereby demonstrates his true loyalties.

Horav Shmuel Walkin, zl, notes that this occurs in our own times. We see fine, upstanding, observant Jews who contribute large sums of money to *yeshivos* to support Torah study. Yet, they send their most precious possessions, their children, elsewhere. The *yeshivah* is not adequate for their children. One can demonstrate no greater support of a *yeshivah* than to send his own children to study there. Writing a check is not as great a commitment to an institution as "contributing" one's own son. Regrettably, there are no plaques for that type of contribution.

✳ ✳ ✳ ✳ ✳ ✳

איש אמו ואביו תיראו

Every man, your mother and father shall you revere. (19:3)

T he *Torah* enjoins us to accord the proper reverence to our parents. While this *mitzvah* is imposed upon the child, it does not give a parent license to take unnecessary advantage of his child's *mitzvah*. *Horav Yitzchak Zilberstein, Shlita,* cites numerous instances in which parents take advantage of their children, asking them to perform menial tasks and errands that for the most part can and should be done themselves. "Bring me, take me, do for me" are common requests that parents make of their children that impose needless obligations upon a child. Surely, it does not enhance a relationship, especially if the parent does this out of laziness or an overactive ego. *Rav* Zilberstein writes that in the home of his father-in-law, *Horav Yosef Eliyashov, Shlita,* such words were not heard. Never did he ask his children to do for him something that he could do for himself. Children are not slaves. They are people who also have to rest.

One must give respect if he wants to receive respect. Parents <u>also</u> have to respect their children. Taking unnecessary advantage is not a way to earn respect. Some parents feel that by asking their children to serve them, they are giving them the opportunity to perform the *mitzvah* of *Kibbud av v'eim,* "Honor your father and mother." The proper way to do so is for the father to ask the child to "bring a glass of water/tea for your mother." When parents direct their request to the child, so that he serves the other parent, they encourage the aspect of honor without taking personal advantage for themselves.

לא תגנבו
You shall not steal. (19:11)

*H*orav Chaim Soloveitzhik, zl, was wont to say that a thief is not only a *rasha*, a wicked man, but he is also a *shoteh*, fool. Hashem decrees at the beginning of each year the amount of money one will earn during the course of that year. He will not have more — or less — than what is apportioned for him. If he is going to have the same amount regardless of what he does, why should he attempt to procure that money through avenues that are illegal and dangerous, if he can have it legitimately?

In the *bais ha'medresh* of *Novardok,* the following analogy was told to emphasize this point. There was a villager who lived in abject poverty all year. Every year, before *Pesach*, he would receive a check in the mail from a wealthy relative overseas. He waited for this envelope like a fish needs water. In fact, waiting daily for the mailman to make his delivery became an obsession with him. He would go down the road and follow the mailman from house to house until he realized that he was not stopping at his house. He would then become depressed until the next day when his hopes for mail began anew. It was becoming increasingly difficult to control his impatience. He was in dire need of funds for *Pesach,* as well as the rest of the year.

One day, he saw the mailman coming from afar and began his usual ritual of following him. This time, however, he noted a large manila envelope sticking out of the mailbag. Surely, this envelope contained a large sum of money, enough to sustain his family for the entire year. He could no longer contain himself, and he grabbed the envelope from the mailbag and ran away to a secluded corner in the forest. He opened the envelope and was pleasantly surprised to see that it was addressed to him. Regrettably, he could not enjoy the "stolen" money, which was rightfully his, because the constable had just caught up with him. No explaining would deter the police officer. The man was a thief and must be taken to jail to pay for his crime. Nothing the poor man said made a difference. He was a criminal.

From here the *Baalei Mussar*, ethicists, derive that even a thief will not "earn" more than what is decreed for him. Therefore, he might as well earn it in a legal and honorable manner.

⚹ ⚹ ⚹ ⚹ ⚹ ⚹

ולפני עור לא תתן מכשל

And you shall not place a stumbling block before the blind. **(19:14)**

*R*ashi explains that the Torah is teaching us that one should not render bad advice to an unsuspecting person. The advice one gives should be appropriately suited for the individual who is asking. To give wrong advice to an unsuspecting person is like placing an obstacle before a blind man. *Rashi* uses the words *eitzah hogenes lo*, "advice that is suited <u>for him</u>." The *Brisker Rav* suggests that implicit in these words is the enjoinment that the advice be suited specifically for the one who is asking. Even if, for many reasons, the one who is being asked should render different advice, he must direct his response specifically to the needs of the individual who is asking.

Once, the director of an institution came to consult with the *Brisker Rav* concerning accepting a certain individual to be the principal in his institution. The *Brisker Rav* felt it was a good choice, and the individual should be hired. When the person in question came to the *Rav* to ask his opinion about the position, the *Rav* instructed him not to take the position. When the director of the institution returned to the *Brisker Rav* and sought an explanation for the apparent paradoxical advice, the *Rav* explained, "Indeed, it would be a very smart choice for the institution to hire that individual as a principal. For the individual himself, however, I feel that he should not take the position because of the added pressure on his limited time." The advice must coincide with the one who is asking. Hence, while it may have been good for the school, it was not a good opportunity for the principal.

ואהבת לרעך כמוך

You shall love your fellow as yourself. **(19:18)**

*R*abbi Akiva refers to this *mitzvah* as the fundamental rule of the Torah. It is the ultimate maxim that summarizes the Jews' perspective of social behavior — in feelings, words and actions. We are to love everything that pertains *l'reiacha*, *to* the person, but not necessarily the person himself. The Torah does not expect the impossible of us. Such complete harmony of two diverse natures is seldom found. It is the

Jewish way to demand that we care for everything *about* the person. We are to assist in everything that furthers his well-being as if it were our own. Everyone is to seek and recognize his fellow as a *reia* — friend. Never should we view our friend's success as a hindrance to our own, but rather, we should rejoice in his well-being.

The *Kopitchnitzer Rebbe, zl,* would say that the *mitzvah* does not apply solely to loving the *frum,* observant, affiliated Jew. It is impossible not to love saintly and pious people. Rather, Hashem instructs us to love even those whom we would normally find it hard to love, those who differ from us in outlook, observance, in thought and deed. *Horav Yosef Chaim Sonnenfeld, zl,* loved *all* Jews, regardless of their lack of faith and worthiness. He worried about their welfare and did not entertain the slightest vestige of animus even toward the most wicked offenders. He would often comment, "If you see a Jew who has become a sinner, do not hate him, but pity him as you would anyone who is physically challenged. Most Jews who have abandoned their religion are captives of alien cultures, victims of improper and insufficient education. It is only because of the long and bitter *galus,* exile, that they have not yet discovered the path to return to their faith and origins."

He never failed to censure those who profaned Hashem's Name. Yet, he would not hesitate to criticize those who referred to them in inappropriate terms. When someone added the imprecation *yemach shemo,* may his name be obliterated, to the mention of a certain Jew who was probably the religious community's most virulent enemy, *Rav* Yosef Chaim protested, saying, "I am not in the habit of saying *yemach shemo* about any Jew." He explained that he derived this from the laws of *Yibum,* levirate marriage. According to Jewish law, if such a Jew were to die childless, his widow would not be allowed to remarry unless she either underwent *Yibum* or *Chalitzah,* release from her *Yibum* requirement. Since the Torah's stated rationale for *Yibum* is that the deceased's "name not be obliterated from *Yisrael,*" regardless of his religious beliefs, how can we say *yemach shemo* about any Jew?

Parashas Emor

אמר אל הכהנים בני אהרן ואמרת אלהם

Say to the Kohanim, the sons of Aharon, and tell them. (21:1)

*R*ashi explains that the redundancy of the words, *Emor, v'omarta,* "Say to the *Kohanim* and tell them," is teaching us an important lesson. *Emor v'omarta — l'hazhir gedolim al ha'ketanim,* "to caution the adults about the children." Basically, the *Torah* is expressing the significance of teaching the next generation. This concept applies not only to parents, but also to all of those charged with disseminating Torah. *L'hazhir,* to caution, may be derived from the word *zohar,* to shine/illuminate. It is imperative that the student notices the teacher's joy and enthusiasm about everything holy: Torah; *mitzvah* observance; acts of loving-kindness. Only when exhibiting these traits is he truly able to convey the beauty of being an observant Jew. It is not enough to merely teach; one must light up the students' eyes. This occurs when the student sees the *rebbe's* elation, his thrill and excitement at being able to impart his Torah knowledge to another Jew. When the teacher is enthusiastic about his work, the student senses its significance.

Horav Yitzchak Zilberstein, Shlita, relates the following story that occurred with *Horav Binyamin Finkel, Shlita.* In one of the developments outside of Yerushalayim, a lecture for *baalei teshuvah,* recent returnees to Jewish observance, was planned. Fifty people were to attend this *shiur.* As it would happen, the lecturer had a last-minute conflict that prevented him from attending. The organizers of the lecture called upon *Rav* Binyamin to give the *shiur* instead. Realizing the importance of maintaining credibility and continuity, he accepted the invitation. It took him considerable time using public transportation to reach the home of the sponsor. At first, he thought he had the wrong address; nobody seemed to be home. As he was about to leave, the door opened. A young man greeted him apologetically. Apparently, he had forgotten to organize the lecture and, therefore, no one had come.

Rav Binyamin had taken a lot of time to travel to the *shiur* and he was not going to waste it. "Let us learn together," he said to the young man, whose name was Moshe. The man was excited about the opportunity for a "one on one" *chavrusa*, study partner, with the *Mashgiach*. He even included his young son. The *seder ha'limud*, order of study, was to study *Mishnayos* for thirty minutes, followed by thirty minutes of *Talmud*. Prior to the *shiur*, Moshe asked *Rav* Binyamin, "When we finish studying the *Mishnayos,* can you please let me know?" "Surely," *Rav* Binyamin replied, not understanding why it was crucial for Moshe to know when they started studying the *Talmud* portion of the *Shiur*.

Thirty minutes had elapsed, and *Rav* Binyamin notified Moshe that they were about to begin the *Gemara*. Moshe arose from his chair. With great enthusiasm, he recited the *Bircas Shehechiyanu*. Moshe explained, "I have never studied *Gemara* before. This is my first time, and I wanted to thank Hashem for granting me the opportunity to study the *Talmud*."

Twenty years later, *Rav* Binyamin was walking down one of the streets in Yerushalayim when he was approached by a middle-aged man. To all outward appearances, he seemed to be a *rav* or *rosh yeshivah*. "*Rav* Finkel, do you recognize me?" the man asked. "Forgive me, but I do not," replied *Rav* Binyamin.

"I am Moshe, with whom you learned *Gemara* twenty years ago." "What brings you to Yerushalayim?" *Rav* Binyamin asked, visibly taken aback by the contrast between his present appearance and that of twenty years earlier.

"I have just taken a position as *rosh kollel* in one of the *kollelim* here in Yerushalayim. The *Shiur* that you gave me that night was the beginning of my total return to the Torah way of life."

Emor v'omarta: When the teacher demonstrates indifference to the subject and to the student, the lesson has a commensurate endurance. In contrast, when he displays excitement, joy and enthusiasm, he produces students of the caliber of Moshe, who follow in his path and continue his work.

Students are *machshiv*, appreciate and value, the Torah in the manner that the *rebbe* values it. In the following story cited by Rabbi Yechiel Spero, we see how a *gadol*, Torah luminary, valued the *Torah*. Horav Michel

Forshlager, zl, was a brilliant *talmid chacham*, Torah scholar, whose volumes of commentary on Torah and *Halachah* indicate his encyclopedic knowledge and utter brilliance. His *hasmadah*, diligence, in Torah study overshadowed even his erudition, so attached was he to *Torah* every waking minute of the day. *Horav Yaakov Y. Ruderman, zl, Rosh HaYeshivah* of *Ner Israel* in Baltimore would send the premier students of his nascent *yeshivah* on Friday afternoons to "speak in learning", discourse on various topics in the *Talmud*, with him.

Rav Michel did not care about his material surroundings. His life's essence was nothing but *Torah*. Understandably, the American students who visited with him were somewhat taken aback with the sparseness of his living conditions. To put it simply: *Rav* Michel lived in abject poverty. His home had one focus — Torah study — and nothing else. When his guests would arrive, *Rav* Michel would greet them with a big smile. His table was piled high with open *sefarim,* as he researched and plumbed the depths of Torah and its commentaries.

Before he began to speak in learning, he would excuse himself, leave the room and return a few minutes later. His behavior seemed strange to the young *yeshivah* students: He went out to exchange his old worn-out sweater for one that was slightly less tattered. *Rav* Michel felt the need to explain his actions: "There is a reason for changing sweaters before I speak in learning with you. I own two sweaters — one is for weekdays and one is reserved for *Shabbos*. Before you walked in I was wearing the weekday one, but before I speak *divrei Torah* with two such distinguished *yeshivah* students, I feel compelled to put on my *Shabbos* sweater as a token of *kavod haTorah*, honor for the *Torah*, which you embody."

This is Torah study at its zenith. When one is *machshiv Torah*, he also values and reveres those who study and disseminate Torah. Regrettably, he who does not respect those who study the Torah is not demonstrating respect for the Torah either. This is to be noted especially by parents. Parents convey a critical message to their children by their every action. The esteem in which they hold their children's *rebbeim* foreshadows the respect the children will show to these same *rebbeim*. It always begins at home: *Emor v'omarta*, "the adults are cautioned regarding the children."

אמר אל הכהנים בני אהרן
Say to the Kohanim, the sons of Aharon. (21:1)

The *Midrash* tells us that Hashem showed Moshe *Rabbeinu* an outline of the future, the various Torah leaders of every generation. He showed him Shaul *Ha'melech*, the first king of the Jewish People, and the manner in which he died tragically by the sword. When Moshe saw this, he asked, "Is it proper that the first king to reign over Your children should perish by the sword?" Hashem replied, "You say this to Me. *Emor el haKohanim*, say this to the *Kohanim*, whom he killed in the city of *Nov*. They serve as an indictment against him." Apparently, Moshe agreed with the *Kohanim's* incrimination of Shaul. His only question was in regard to Shaul being the first king. What is the significance of being first?

Horav Nosson Wachtfogel, zl, notes that throughout the *Torah* we find primacy and precedence given to the *rishon*, first. *Terumah* and *Maaser* have *kedushah*, sanctity, because they are first. Adam *HaRishon's* sin was overwhelming because he was the first man, thus attributing greater significance to his sin. Reuven would have been the *Kohen* and king over *Klal Yisrael* had he not erred. Even the gentile nations acknowledge the relevance and distinction to be accorded to the first, to the one who inaugurates a position. During the Polish Revolution, Marshal Wosilski, Poland's first marshal, came to the president and demanded that he abdicate his position. The president was guarded by two powerful soldiers who moved forward to kill the seditious marshal. As they moved toward him, the marshal opened his tunic and declared, "Are you prepared to kill the first Polish marshal?" Upon hearing this, they immediately moved back, a move that heralded the beginning of the end for the Polish president.

Likewise, Moshe claimed that Shaul was the first king and should, therefore, not have died such a humiliating death by the sword. Hashem replied by citing the *pasuk, Emor el haKohanim*, "Say to the *Kohanim:*" While it is true that being the first of anything engenders great distinction, how will you respond to the accusation brought by the *Kohanim* of *Nov*? They are also *rishon*, first. The *Kehunah*, priesthood, is honored first in every endeavor. Indeed, all of *Shevet Levi* receives distinction because they were the first ones to stand up for the honor of Heaven during the sin of the Golden Calf. After Levi was criticized by Yaakov *Avinu*, he repented and became the first *Rosh HaYeshivah* of the *Shivtei Kah*, Tribes. Yes, the fact that Shaul was the first king is of great significance. He reduced that significance, however, by killing the *Kohanim* who also had the advantage of being first. As with every honor, it is beneficial only if the individual values it. The favored position can only assist one who acknowledges the advantage that it generates. Apparently, Shaul did not respect the position of the *Kohanim*. Thus, his inaugural position of monarchy was similarly not honored.

✻ ✻ ✻ ✻ ✻ ✻

אמר אל הכהנים בני אהרן ואמרת אלהם
Say to the Kohanim, the sons of Aharon, and tell them. (21:1)

*R*ashi explains that the apparent redundancy of the words *Emor, v'omarta*, <u>Say</u> to the *Kohanim* and <u>tell</u> them, is a reference to the important role the adult *Kohanim* play in teaching the laws to their children. I recently read how the *Brisker Rav, zl*, raised his children and the critical significance he gave to supervising their educational development <u>personally</u>. While some of contemporary society's enlightened parents might feel his approach was a bit to the right of center, he succeeded in laying the foundation for generations of offspring dedicated to *emes*, spiritual integrity, and the *Torah* way. The *Brisker Rav* said later on in his life, that when he was young, he was personally aware of where his children were and what they were doing twenty-four hours a day, seven-days a week. Furthermore, his children were acutely aware of his supervision and impact upon every aspect of their lives. This probably would not be comfortable for some of today's children or their parents. They are not, however, *gedolei Yisrael*.

The *Brisker Rav* was a firm believer that a child have a <u>sense</u> of freedom, but nonetheless the parent should monitor everything. Granting total freedom to a child is courting disaster. A parent should combine discipline with love, taking a deep interest in his life, regardless of his age. Yet, the parent should be strict with regard to granting him total independence.

The *Brisker Rav* did not waste money on frivolities or materialistic notions. On the other hand, when the demands were spiritual, he always found the money. Even if an old *Chumash* or *Siddur* was not worn or torn, if a child wanted a new one, the *Brisker Rav* purchased it. The greatest respect was accorded to his children's *rebbeim*. Consequently, the children learned to emulate these values in their own homes.

While there is much to be written about the *Brisker Rav's* approach to *chinuch ha'banim*, the following vignette summarizes it, teaching us what we should do in order to achieve success in raising our children. The *Brisker Rav* was once taking a stroll in Yerushalayim, when a man came up to him and said, "I am very envious of the *Brisker Rav*. All of his children go in the *richtigen vehg*, proper way, *b'derech ha'Torah*, in the path of the Torah, even though they were raised during turbulent times. Many other families, even some of the most distinguished *rabbinic* families in Lithuania, did not fare so well. Many of the young people were swept up in the revolutionary movements and the like."

The *Brisker Rav* did not respond. He simply listened and nodded his head in acknowledgment. Approximately one half hour later, he turned to his son, *Rav* Rephael, who was with him at the time, and said, "Ah, they do not know how many tears I shed as I *shokeled*, rocked, each baby in the carriage; how I prayed; and how many *kapitlach*, chapters, of *Tehillim*, I recited for them that they should follow in the path of Torah."

Rav Rephael followed in his father's footsteps. A master *mechanech*, educator, he raised his only child, a daughter, in the *Brisker* way of integrity and simplicity. He understood the crucial value of the home, especially when it came to a girl's educational development. He would say, "Whereas a son's domain is in the *yeshivah*, the daughter absorbs her *Yiddishkeit* primarily in the home. Parental example and life experience are her primary texts — even in contemporary times."

His daughter recalled an incident that demonstrated her father's approach to infusing his perspective of *pashtus*, simplicity, in her education at home: "I remember when I was young and about to enter the first grade. I was an only daughter, which would normally grant my parents license to spoil me. The situation was far from that. I was given a simple, homemade briefcase with the straps stitched on by hand. My maternal grandmother came over and declared, "I am buying her a nice new leather book bag with a matching lunch bag — a special set." My father said, "Wait a moment. She will not go to school the first day with both pieces of the set. If she does, it will cause jealousy. First, she will bring the book bag, then, a few weeks later, she can bring the matching lunch bag."

This orientation is quite different from that to which our children are accustomed today. Interestingly, many years later, *Rav* Rephael's daughter recalled the incident with pride as having a seminal influence on her life.

✼ ✼ ✼ ✼ ✼ ✼

ובת איש כהן כי תחל לזנות את אביה היא מחללת

If the daughter of a man who is a Kohen will be defiled through having illicit relationships, she desecrates her father. (21:9)

One would think that her sin is serious enough. Why does the Torah add that she desecrates her father? In the *Derashos HaRan* the question is raised why Avraham *Avinu* was prepared to allow Yitzchak to marry into a family from Charan, yet he rejected anyone from Canaan? The people of Charan were idol worshippers, while the Canaanites were steeped in licentiousness and moral depravity. Is one form of malevolence less evil than the other? The *Ran* explains that both activities are reprehensible. The sin of idol worship is a philosophic distortion that a parent does not necessarily transmit from parent to child. A character flaw, however, such as moral degeneracy, is transmitted from parent to child. This is why the Torah adds that the daughter of a *Kohen* who debases herself demonstrates that her perversion and wanton behavior are part of her family legacy. Her perverse actions degrade her father, because they indicate a genetic flaw in her moral makeup.

In his *Shoeil u'Meishiv, Horav Yosef Shaul Natanson, zl,* applies this thesis *halachically. Halachah* states that a *Kohen* whose daughter renounces her faith may still *duchen,* bless the people. The *Magen Avraham* questions this law. Idol worship is a grave sin. Should the father not be held in contempt for his daughter's actions?

The *Shoeil u'Meishiv* contends that a father is discredited only when the child's transgression is such that it reflects the parent's moral turpitude. If the sin, however, is one that bespeaks a child's cognitive perversity, an imperfection in his philosophic perspective, the onus of guilt is not attributed to the parent.

✼ ✼ ✼ ✼ ✼ ✼

וינחחו במשמר לפרש להם על פי ד'

They placed him under guard to clarify for themselves through Hashem.
(24:12)

R ashi explains that the blasphemer was incarcerated because Moshe Rabbeinu was not sure if he was to be punished with the death penalty or not. The commentators question this. What reason could there possibly be for not executing him? Is he any better than an individual who curses his parents, a sin that is punishable by death? Certainly, one who blasphemes the Almighty is guilty of a treasonous offense that should carry with it the death penalty. *Horav Tzvi Hersh Ferber, zl,* explains that the Heavenly Tribunal adjudicates in a manner similar to that of earthly judgment. Let us approach this transgression from an earthly perspective.

Imagine a person of ill repute, a drunkard and ne'er-do-well, a depressed, poor man for whom life's many opportunities have passed by. If he were to stand in the street and publicly curse the king, would anybody listen? Would anybody make a public outcry? No! Because he is a nothing. True, he would be punished, but he would not be executed, because to do so would be to validate his very existence. If a powerful, distinguished, nobleman were to commit the same transgression, he would surely be put to death, because the sin is weighed relative to the sinner. A nobleman who humiliates the king commits a public act of treason. He must be executed as a demonstration of the king's power and authority. When a man of no standing insults the king, it is not considered to be much of an insult.

The same idea applies to the incident of the blasphemer. He was a person of questionable lineage, descending from the union of an Egyptian father and a Jewish mother whose moral behavior was reprehensible. Such a person certainly was not held in high regard by the community. Thus, conceivably he should not receive a serious punishment. Nonetheless, the verdict issued against him was death, since it is important to destroy the few thorns in the vineyard before they have an effect upon the grapes.

Parashas Behar

וכי ימוך אחיך ומטה ידו עמך והחזקת בו

If your brother becomes impoverished that his means falter in your
proximity, you shall strengthen him. **(25:35)**

We have an obligation toward our fellow Jew that is both moral and filial. In order to help him get back on his feet, it is essential that we *feel* his pain and *experience* his hurt and humiliation. The *Ben Ish Chai* gives an incredible *mashal*, analogy, that underscores this point. A king wanted his only son to become proficient in all branches of learning, so that when the time came, he would be able to assume the position of monarch. He also wanted him to become knowledgeable in all areas pertaining to running the country. The king chose a wise man who was a master teacher to perform the task of educating the prince. After a number of years, the teacher sent the prince home to the king to be tested in all areas of knowledge. After successfully passing the various tests, the king acknowledged the teacher's singular ability to teach the prince, rewarding the wise man with one hundred thousand gold coins.

A short while later, the wise man approached the king with a request, " If it pleases the king, I would like to take the prince for a short course to teach him something that he has not yet learned. It will take only about an hour." The king acquiesced to the wise man's request, immediately sending the prince to the wise man's house for his lesson. The prince entered the man's home, and the teacher locked the door, pulled out a rubber truncheon and began beating the prince mercilessly on his legs. Fifty times he struck him until blood began to ooze from the welts. The prince cried out in pain, but no one heard his pleas for help. When the "lesson" was concluded, the teacher sent the wounded prince home to his father.

We can only imagine the king's anger upon seeing his blood-spattered, injured son. He immediately sent his guards to pick up the teacher and prepare him for the gallows. Yet, the king could not bring himself to go through with the execution until he received some kind of explanation for the teacher's inexplicable behavior.

"Before I carry out the death sentence against you, explain to me why a person in his right mind would throw everything away — the wealth, the glory, the honor! Why?" asked the king.

"I will explain my actions, my dear king," replied the teacher. "My intentions were totally noble, consistent with your mandate to me that I teach the prince the dynamics of monarchy. A leader must mete out punishment that is commensurate with the degree of the transgression. Imagine if a person would steal a cow valued at two hundred dollars, and the prince would sentence the thief to one thousand lashes. As a prince, he has not experienced pain and injury to his body because he has never sustained any punishment. Therefore, it was necessary for the prince to *feel* firsthand what pain is like. Otherwise, when he issued a sentence, he would conceivably overdo it."

When the king heard the logic behind the teacher's actions, he immediately freed him and added to his reward.

The same idea applies to those who are asked to assist those who have fallen on hard times. How should the wealthy man know what it means to go hungry? Hashem, therefore, provided them with one day a year — *Yom Kippur* — when we all fast and sense what the poor man feels on many-a-day. When the poor man stands at your door seeking alms, put yourself in his shoes, so that your assistance to him will be meaningful as well as beneficial.

וכי ימוך אחיך ומטה ידו עמך והחזקת בו

If your brother becomes impoverished that his means falter in your proximity, you shall strengthen him. **(25:35)**

T he *mitzvah* of *Vehechezakta*, "And you shall strengthen him," remains in force regardless of how many times one is called upon to help his fellow. Moreover, the obligation to lend financial assistance to a fellow Jew in need applies — no matter how the person uses the money — even if it is used inappropriately. That is precisely what the *yetzer hara*, evil inclination, tells us: "Do not help him, for he only squanders the money that you give him. Do not waste your valuable time from *Torah* study on charitable acts of loving-kindness. Leaving the house at night to help a Jew in need taxes your *shalom bayis*, marital harmony." The list goes on. The *yetzer hara* will always present you with an alternative to the *chesed* you are about to perform. In reality, some of these *taanos*, claims, have merit. So how should one respond to the *yetzer hara*?

The *Chafetz Chaim* gave the following response. When he attended the *Knessiah Gedolah* in Vienna in 1923, he was a guest in the home of *Rav* Akiva Schreiber. Many people came to the house to obtain an audience — or even a glimpse of the *Chafetz Chaim*. The answer to most people was — no. The *Chafetz Chaim* was not a young man, and his time was limited. A wealthy *Torah askan*, mover and shaker, from England came to *Rav* Schreiber and said that he must speak to the *Chafetz Chaim* for a few moments. Indeed, his entire future depended upon the result of his meeting with the *Chafetz Chaim*. Apparently, the man's toil and involvement on behalf of *Klal Yisrael* made a difference, and he was invited to the *Chafetz Chaim's* table.

The man waited for the *Chafetz Chaim* to *bentch*, say the *Bircas HaMazon*, Grace after the meal, to present his dilemma. It did not take that long. During the meal, the *Chafetz Chaim* recited the twenty-third Psalm of *Tehillim, Mizmor leDavid, Hashem ro'ie lo echzar*, "Hashem is my Shepherd, I shall not lack." As he concluded the last *pasuk*, "May only goodness and kindness pursue me all the days of my life," he turned to the guest from England and asked, "What does David *Ha'melech* mean when he requests that goodness and kindness be his pursuers? To be pursued is to be harassed. Why would David want to be badgered by *tov* and *chesed*?

"The answer is," explained the *Chafetz Chaim*, "that there are times when one's involvement in many acts of loving-kindness can actually haunt him as they rob him of his every free moment. He has neither night nor day. The acts of *chesed* get in the way of his business. They disrupt his home life. He literally becomes a prisoner to the many demands on his time and good nature. The *yetzer hara* sees this situation as an auspicious time for him to sneak in and use his wiles to put a halt to these wonderful activities. David *Ha'melech* admonishes us, 'Do not worry if your pursuers are *tov* and *chesed*. On the contrary, pray to Hashem that they should be your *only* pursuers and nothing else. From such lofty pursuers as *tov* and *chesed*, one has nothing to worry about.'"

When the guest heard these words from the *Chafetz Chaim*, he picked himself up and thanked his host. The host was bewildered, "Why are you leaving so soon?" he asked. " Didn't you came to seek the *Chafetz Chaim's* advice."

The visitor replied, "I came to ask the *Chafetz Chaim* a question which he has already answered for me. Let me explain. In my city, I have undertaken to support a school and also a *gemillas chesed*, charitable organization. These two endeavors are eminently successful, but they rob me of my time. I simply have no time whatsoever left for myself. My personal business ventures are suffering because I do not have the time to attend to them properly. My wife feels I should transfer the daily control of these organizations to someone else, so that I can return to my business. I personally would rather not defer control of these wonderful organizations to others. Thus, in the interest of *shalom bayis*, I came to the *Chafetz Chaim* to seek his advice. When I heard the saintly *Chafetz Chaim* explain the *pasuk* in *Tehillim* that David *Ha'melech asks* that good and kindness should always be his pursuers, I realized that the sage was referring to my query. He had given me the answer before I even asked the question. I am returning home to my wife to relay to her the *gadol ha'dor's* reply."

ושכבתם ואין מחריד

And you will lie down with none to frighten you. **(26:6)**

Jew who trusts in Hashem maintains the firm belief that regardless of the situation, Hashem is always there and can turn things around at any time. Indeed, *Chazal* have stated it best with their powerful maxim, "Even if a sharp sword lays on the neck of a person, he should not give up believing that Hashem's compassion will spare him." We have only to look at *Eretz Yisrael* and the way people live there to see this truth. Hashem protects us under the most precarious circumstances. *Horav Yaakov Galinsky, Shlita*, relates an incident that occurred during one of the more traumatic days of World War II, when he was prisoner in one of the concentration camps. On that day, the accursed Nazis had burnt all the inmates' *Tefillin* and — if that was not sufficiently devastating — they killed many of the Jewish prisoners. It was a day when hopelessness and despair reigned throughout the camp.

It was on that very day that an inmate, a simple Jew from a small village in Poland, came over to *Rav* Galinsky and said, "Even if a sharp sword lays on the neck of a person, he should not give up believing that Hashem's compassion will spare him."

The man continued by underscoring the various parts of this maxim. "First, what greater danger can one face than having a <u>sharp</u> <u>sword</u> on his <u>neck</u>. The sword is there; it is already sharpened; and it is already in place on the neck. Death is imminent! Yet, *Chazal* tell us to *continue* hoping, not to give up, to believe that even at this very last moment — he could still be spared — if Hashem wills it."

Rav Galinsky remembers how those poignant, but powerful, words left an enduring impression on him, infusing him with courage and faith to keep on hoping. Do not worry about tomorrow. Live today to its fullest. All too often, we waste today's gift of life wondering what tomorrow will bring. A Jew never gives up.

ואם לא תשמעו לי ...ונתתי פני בכם ונגפתם לפני איביכם ורדו בכם שנאיכם

But if you will not listen to Me… And I will turn My attention against you,
you will be struck down before your enemies; those who hate you will
subjugate you. **(26:14,17)**

nyone who has studied Jewish history knows that this curse has regrettably become true. Sixty-plus years ago, during the European Holocaust, the world saw how Hashem orchestrated events so that we were "struck down before enemies;" and "those who hate you will subjugate you." There were also those who survived those tragic years with their faith and conviction intact. Regrettably, there were those who survived in body, but their belief in the Almighty was impaired. While no one can question anyone who survived those atrocities, there is one question that keeps on being asked, a question that goes right to the core of our *emunah*, faith, in Hashem: "Where was Hashem during the Holocaust? How could He have allowed this to happen?"

While there are a number of possible explanations, the following analogy cited in *Otzros HaTorah* gives us a practical approach. A young boy was acting his age. At times, he was proper and his behavior was exemplary. Every once in a while, however, he would lose it and act up. Whenever this occurred, his father would take him to the window of their home and point to the forest. "My child, do you see that forest outside of our home?" the father would ask. "In that forest there is a fierce wolf. When you act inappropriately, the wolf will come out of the forest and hurt you." This form of discipline would probably not receive great accolades from any child psychologist, but it seemed to work for that father. After a few days, the child's fear of the wolf dissipated, and he was back to his old ways. The father warned his son once again, but the child's response to that did not last very long either.

Seeing that he had no recourse but to take action, the father went to the forest, sought out a hunter and purchased a wolf's skin. He dressed himself in the wolf's skin and went home. As soon as his son saw him masquerading as a wolf, he trembled with fear. He thought this was the real thing. The father went through the whole act, howling and baring his teeth. The child naturally became hysterical. For good measure, the father even scratched his son slightly with his "paws" and left the house.

The child cried bitterly, realizing that he was being punished for his misbehavior. A bit later, the father returned home to find his son crying. The child related to his father everything that had occurred and then asked, "Where were you when the wolf attacked me? Why were you not here to protect me?"

The message of this analogy is evident. One who studies the history of the Holocaust sees quite clearly that there was no mere concealment of Hashem's Presence. This was no simple chain of events. On the contrary, one can sense Hashem's Guiding Hand throughout the process. Hitler's rise to power is a historical anomaly. He was poor and unstable, totally incapable and unfit for any kind of employment. Yet, this man who lived on the fringe of society rose from the dung heap to reign over half of the civilized world. He ascended to the throne of German leadership directly from a jail cell. Is this to be regarded as a natural course of events?

The entire progression of the Second World War was atypical and unnatural. The German Army's ability to vanquish strong countries in a short span of time was unprecedented and unpredicted by the greatest military strategists. Hitler's pact with Soviet Russia, a pact which enabled him to quickly overrun Poland, was inexplicable. Stalin's refusal to respond to intelligence about an imminent German attack was unexplainable. The result was that two million more Jews became subservient to the Nazi empire. Indeed, the only thing more astounding than the Nazis' success was their sudden failure and ultimate defeat. Historians are hard-put to develop any sort of reasonable theory to explain these anomalies.

Thus, it seems clear that "Hashem was there." Indeed, He brought it about. We have to wonder, why? It was unquestionably the *Middas HaDin*, attribute of Strict Justice, that was visible throughout. While we cannot fathom Hashem's reasoning, we are obliged to deal with those matters that are in the realm of our understanding. To the extent that we can, we are mandated to define and clarify for ourselves the general paths of Divine Justice. This is neither the place nor the forum for this thesis. Nevertheless, our objective is to ponder — not to accuse; to derive a lesson — not to critique. The question which is catalyzed by the Holocaust is not the issue of Divine Justice, but rather the meaning and significance of the Holocaust, its message and future lessons. The question is not, "Where is G-d?" but rather, "Where was man?"

וכל מעשר בקר וצאן כל אשר יעבר תחת השבט העשירי יהיה קדש לד'

Any tithe of cattle or sheep, any that passes under the staff, the tenth one shall be holy to Hashem. **(27:32)**

C hazal describe the process of tithing animals as being a tedious process in which each group of ten animals are counted, with the tenth animal being marked as *Maaser* for Hashem. This procedure applies regardless of the number of animals one owns. One can have ten thousand head of cattle; he must count each one individually, with the tenth one being designated as *Maaser.* This seems quite inefficient. One would think that it is more efficacious to simply count all the animals and deduct ten percent.

Horav Eliezer Gordon, zl, was once on a fundraising trip for the *Telshe Yeshivah* in Lithuania, when he posed this question to a wealthy man who had balked at the *Rosh HaYeshivah's* request for a sizable contribution. *Rav* Leizer asked the businessman, "Why does the Torah demand such a roundabout, inefficient manner for counting one's assets?" The wealthy man was at a loss for an answer.

"Let me explain," said *Rav* Leizer. "If the Torah would enjoin a wealthy man to give up ten percent of his possessions, he would be hard-pressed to comply. Ten percent can amount to a considerable sum of money. Therefore, the Torah prescribes the method of individual counting of one's flock. Over and over, the wealthy man counts his flock, realizing that for every nine animals that he keeps for himself, he gives only one to Hashem. He might even feel a bit embarrassed when he sees how much he possesses and how little he is giving to Hashem. This will motivate him to give generously and joyfully. When a person realizes with how much he has been blessed, he will gladly part with the *Maaser.*"

"My friend," continued *Rav* Leizer, "look at how much you have and you will realize that, in proportion, I am not really asking for that much."

In citing the above, *Horav Avraham Pam, zl,* notes that people often refrain from being as charitable as they should be because they do not acknowledge all of Hashem's blessings to them. When a person takes the time to contemplate the many blessings that Hashem has granted him, he will more readily acquiesce to share some of it with those less fortunate than he.

Dedicated in loving memory of

Mr. David Salamon

ר' אלחר חיים דוד בן ר' מנחם שמואל ז"ל
נפטר כ"ח אייר תשס"ז

Husband, Father, Grandfather, Great-Grandfather....

The gleam in his eye, the glee in his smile, was there for his offspring as they were for a clever *vort*. His fluency and familiarity with all *Tanach*, with so much *Talmud*, and his ease and comfort in a half dozen languages, reflected an Old World standard: of love of learning, and that knowledge is its own reward.

He was a survivor who managed his memories and his losses by immersing himself in the history and geography of the Europe that he left. When so many chose to place money above the Sabbath, his *Shemiras Shabbos* taught his family where the true riches and values lay.

His loyalty and love for his family defined him, and only a *hachnasas Sefer Torah* could be a rival for such *nachas*. In his memory, may we live what he cherished: love of Torah, of tradition, of family.

With love and respect,

Ruthie and Sam Salamon
Rachel Sora and Aton Holzer and Family
Miram and Yosef Meir Salamon and Family
Yehuda Eliezer Salamon

זדים הליצוני עד מאד ומתורתך לא נטיתי
"Willful sinners taunted me exceedingly, but I did not swerve from Your Torah".
(*Tehillim 119:51*)

Parashas Bamidbar

וידבר ד' אל משה במדבר סיני באהל מועד

Hashem spoke to Moshe in the wilderness of Sinai, in the Ohel Moed. (1:1)

T he *Midrash* notes that great significance is accorded to the fact that *Klal Yisrael* received the Torah in the wilderness. The *midbar*, wilderness thus, becomes the setting for receiving the Torah, which is intrinsic to the Jewish national character. What characteristic of the *midbar* evokes such consideration? *Chazal* derive from here that one must make himself like a *midbar*, whereby he is *hefker*, ownerless, giving up his rights to possession, totally relying on Hashem without a care in the world for himself. *Horav Yaakov Neiman, zl*, in his *Darkei Mussar*, expounds upon this concept. He explains that one who is situated in a desolate wilderness is alone — without food and drink, prey to the animals that roam there. While there, he is without hope for salvation. Such a person realizes that he can rely on only one Being for salvation: Hashem. For Hashem is there for all, under all instances and circumstances.

This must be the perspective of one who seeks to acquire Torah — complete and unequivocal trust in the Almighty. Indeed, we say this every day in the *Ahavah Rabbah* prayer preceding *Krias Shma*, "For the sake of our forefathers who trusted in You and whom You taught the decrees of life, may You be equally gracious to us and teach us." It was our ancestors' *bitachon*, trust, that warranted the Torah for them.

One who worries about his sustenance cannot conceivably apply himself wholeheartedly to Torah study. On the other hand, one who trusts in Hashem and studies *Torah* has nothing to worry about; Hashem will sustain him. In his commentary to *Pirkei Avos* 3:5, the *Chasid Yaavetz*, cites an incredible thought from one of the distinguished leaders of his time. It says in *Tehillim* 1:2,3: "But his desire is in the Torah of Hashem, and in His Torah he meditates day and night. He shall be like a tree deeply rooted alongside brooks of water, that yields its fruit in due season, and whose leaf never withers, and everything that he does will succeed." What is the meaning of a tree planted alongside the river? Such a tree cannot bear fruit, because of the excessive moisture at the side of the river. Although it is true that its leaf never withers, it is extremely weak and wilting. What success can such a weak tree hope to enjoy? Why does David *Ha'melech* analogize the *talmid chacham*, Torah scholar, to such a tree? We must say to the individual who studies Torah day in and day out, night and day, without thinking about *parnassah*, a livelihood: Hashem will provide for him. He will be like a tree, which although it is firmly rooted on the banks of the river — a place not suitable for producing healthy fruit, Hashem — nevertheless, ensures that it bears fruit. So, too, will the Torah scholar be miraculously sustained by Hashem.

A *talmid chacham* living in Manchester, England, studied diligently for many years despite his abject poverty. Many times he was offered a position that would guarantee him a set income, yet he refused to accept. He would always give the same response, "Hashem is the One Who sustains; I have nothing to worry about." His family grew. With each child, his parents would insist that it was already enough; he must go to work. He responded in his usual calm manner, "Hashem is taking care of me." This happened after the birth of his tenth child, the birth of his eleventh child and again when his twelfth child was born. He did not worry, as he ignored everyone and continued his devotion to Torah study.

Shortly after the *Bris*, circumcision, of his thirteenth child, he received an express letter from a distinguished law firm requesting his presence at the reading of the will of a Mr. John Klabari. He could not understand the meaning of this. He neither had any idea who the deceased was, nor did he have any interest in wasting a day in a lawyer's office. He quickly sent a letter to the attorney notifying him of his error in inviting the wrong person to the reading of the will. The lawyer returned a note to him to the effect that there was no error, and by law he was required to attend the reading.

The court date arrived, and our hero left the *bais ha'medrash* to attend the reading. He was shocked to discover that John Klabari had been a very wealthy man who had died childless. Prior to his death, he had asked that his entire estate by given to the family in the city who had the most children. Apparently, when number thirteen was born, it brought this young man's family "over the top," granting him the status necessary for inheriting the entire estate, which was valued at millions of pounds. What did this *talmid chacham* respond when he heard the exciting news? "Hashem sustains everyone. There is nothing to worry about."

※ ※ ※ ※ ※ ※

פקדיהם למטה דן שנים וששים אלף ושבע מאות
Their count, for the tribe of Dan: sixty-two thousand, seven hundred.
(1:39)

The tribe of Dan was considerably larger than most of the other tribes. This phenomenon is all the more notable given the fact that Dan had only one child. *Horav Yechezkel Levenstein, zl*, takes this idea further. Binyamin had ten sons. One would assume that, allowing for the course of "nature," Binyamin's tribe should be fairly sizable. Dan, on the other hand, who had only one child, should probably have a much smaller number of descendants. Yet when we look at the final tally, Binyamin's tribe was half the size of the tribe of Dan. What happened? *Rav Chatzkel* derives from here that Hashem listens to the pleas of the weak and downtrodden who have no one upon whom to rely but Hashem. One who foolishly relies on his own talents and attributes quickly discovers that, without Hashem's Divine Assistance, his G-d-given gifts are of little use. One has only to look back at those in his generation/class who have succeeded. Were they the individuals whom everyone expected to succeed? Success in every endeavor is from Hashem, and the sooner one accepts this fact, the quicker envy and its ensuing consequences will be relegated to the past.

Hashem helps the weak. When life seems to push an individual up against a wall, with no place to turn, suddenly salvation occurs. One should never give up hope, for Hashem's salvation can come in a moment's notice. The *Chafetz Chaim, zl*, related the following story: It was the custom in Galicia that Jews would assemble in the *shul* on *Shabbos* shortly before *Maariv* to recite *Tehillim*. As the *kedushah*, holiness, of the day ebbed away, these people would entreat the Almighty with their heartrending pleas, employing the time-honored medium of *Tehillim*. One *Shabbos*, a Jew entered the *shul* and noticed that in one corner another Jew was reciting *Tehillim* with extreme devotion and intense fervor. One could sense the fiery passion and extreme emotion emanating from this person. This was no usual *Tehillim* recitation. To see another Jew pour out his heart to the Almighty with such zeal was truly inspiring. Thus, the second Jew decided to stand next to this person as he also began to recite *Tehillim*.

Soon, both Jews were crying out to Hashem, each supplicating Him for his own individual needs, each elevated by his deep concentration and expression of emotion. After *Maariv*, the second Jew turned to the first and asked, "I know it is not my business, but I see that you are obviously anguished. What is it that bothers you so? Perhaps I could be of some assistance."

The man responded with a deep sigh, "Yes, I have what to cry about. I have a daughter who is of marriageable age, and I have no dowry for her. She sits at home all day, depressed and dejected. During the week, I am not home to witness her sorrow. On *Shabbos*, however, I am home and when I look at my child, it breaks my heart that I can do nothing to help her. So I go to *shul* and cry out my heart to the Almighty. Perhaps He will listen to my entreaty."

When the second man heard this explanation, he said, "I have a son who excels in *middos tovos*, exemplary character traits, and *yiraas Shomayim*, fear of Heaven. Regrettably, I have no money. If you are willing to make a *shidduch*, matrimonial match, with me, I am ready and willing."

The wedding took place, and the young couple was blessed with incredible *nachas*, Jewish bliss. Among their descendants were four *gedolei Yisrael,* preeminent Torah leaders: *Horav* Yehudah Hakohen, author of the *Kuntros Ha'sfeikos*; *Horav* Chaim Hakohen; *Horav* Aryeh Leib Hakohen Heller, author of the *Ketzos Ha'choshen*; and *Horav* Mordechai Hakohen, who was *rav* in the city of Chodrov. From the depths of despair and hopelessness, a future of shining hope bloomed forth that illuminated *Klal Yisrael* for generations to come. One should *never* give up hope.

ונשיא לבני גד אליסף בן רעואל

And the leader of Bnei Gad is Eliyasaf ben Reuel. (2:14)

Interestingly, in 1:14 above, this same *Nasi* is called *ben* Deuel. *Rambam* comments that he actually had both names, both of which described his essence. Deuel is a contraction of *daas Keil*, knowledge of God. Both names reflect the *Nasi's* engrossment in understanding Hashem and in getting closer to Him. The *Chida* cites the *sefer Imrei Noam* who asserts that Moshe *Rabbeinu* was buried in Gad's portion because Gad displayed a remarkable attribute. When Dan was selected to be the leader of his *degel*, flag, Gad remained silent and did not dispute his selection. He could easily have contended that he was the firstborn of Zilpah, while Dan was the firstborn of Bilhah. Why should he not have been chosen as leader of the *degel*? For maintaining his silence, the *raish* of Reuel was added to denote that he had become a *reia Keil*, friend of G-d, which is a reference to Moshe, who was buried in his portion.

The lesson from here is powerful. Had Gad argued that *he* wanted to be head of the *degel*, what would he ultimately benefit from his dispute? He would have become the leader. What *kavod*, honor, however, would he ultimately have taken with him to the grave? Nothing! His silence, on the other hand, earned him an honor for posterity — the *Adon ha'Neviim*, master of Prophets, the quintessential leader of *Klal Yisrael* would be buried in his portion. This distinction outweighs anything he could have received had he *spoken up*. This is what *Chazal* mean when they say in *Pirkei Avos* (1:17), "I have found nothing better for oneself than silence."

The author of the *Sdei Chemed, Horav Chizkiyah Medini, zl,* was a renowned *Talmudic* genius. He was proficient in every area of Torah knowledge and *Talmudic* jurisprudence. His encyclopedic knowledge is manifest throughout the *seforim* that he authored. He writes that, as a young man, he excelled in neither brilliance nor acumen. It was only after an episode that occurred, coupled with his reaction to it, that Hashem blessed him by granting him his extraordinary abilities.

When he was a young man, he studied in a *kollel* together with a group of distinguished *bnei Torah*. One member of the group, regrettably, was deficient in his ethical character. For some reason, he was envious of *Rav* Chizkiyah. He bribed an Arab woman to assert that when she would come to clean the *bais ha'medrash* in the early morning, *Rav* Chizkiyah was there and would make inappropriate advances to her. Word spread, and *Rav* Chizkiyah was humiliated and scorned. His reputation was besmirched. The *Rosh Kollel*, knowing the impeccable character of *Rav* Chizkiyah, did not believe the girl, so he relieved her of her position.

After a while, the money that financed her lies ran out. The girl then went to *Rav* Chizkiyah and begged his forgiveness, pleading with him to understand that she badly needed the money. She was prepared to acknowledge her miscreancy publicly in order to clear *Rav* Chizkiyah's name. She concluded by asking *Rav* Chizkiyah if, after his name was cleared, it would be possible for him to intercede on her behalf with the *Rosh Kollel*, so that she could regain her position.

At that moment, *Rav* Chizkiyah was in a quandary. What should he do? On the one hand, he had the opportunity to vindicate himself. On the other hand, at what expense! To clear his name meant to condemn the other *kollel* fellow. A *chillul Hashem*, desecration of Hashem's Name, of epic proportion would result from this. It would be better for him to continue suffering in his humiliation than to catalyze a further *chillul Hashem*. *Rav* Chizkiyah replied to the Arab girl, "What you ask of me, I agree to do. I will speak in your behalf to the *Rosh Kollel*. I forbid you, however, to ever relate to anyone any information concerning the bribe that you accepted!"

Rav Chizkiyah concluded by saying that at that moment in which he accepted upon himself a vow of silence, he felt that the wellspring of wisdom opened up. From then on he absorbed a spiritual flow of wisdom that enabled him to achieve proficiency in all areas of Torah erudition. All this was granted to him as a reward for maintaining his silence.

אל תכריתו את שבט משפחת הקהתי... וזאת עשו להם וחיו... אהרן ובניו
יבאו ושמו אותם איש איש על עבדתו

"Do not allow the tribe of the family of Kehas to be cut off...This is what you shall do for them so that they shall live...Aharon and his sons shall come and assign them, each man to his work." (4:18,19)

The *Midrash* comments that the members of the family of Kehas were assigned to carry the *Mishkan* and its *keilim*, vessels. Recognizing that the *Aron HaKodesh* was the preeminent component, they neglected the *Shulchan*, *Menorah* and *Mizbachos* in order to run to carry the *Aron*. The result was contention, bickering and, eventually, a lack of respect. Hashem punished them, and members of that family died prematurely. Thus, Hashem issued the command that each family member of Kehas be assigned a specific task, thereby preventing any dispute over who had the privilege to carry each specific item of the *Mishkan*. The *Mesillas Yesharim* devotes a chapter of his magnum opus to the topic of *Mishkal ha'chassidus*. A *chasid* is defined as one who goes beyond the letter of the law, who truly loves Hashem and is not satisfied with merely getting by. He always endeavors to do more. *Mishkal ha'chassidus* focuses on weighing one's actions, especially those that are laudatory, to be sure that what appears to be a positive gesture is truly what it seems. The *yetzer hara*, evil-inclination, is crafty and has the ability to paint a sin as a *mitzvah*. What begins as a righteous deed can sometimes end as a tragedy. The classic case is the reaction of *Bnei Kehas* to transporting the *Mishkan*. What should have been noble, lofty and honorable was transformed into a *chillul Hashem*, desecration of Hashem's Name. Had they weighed their good intentions, it would be apparent that Hashem's will could not be fulfilled by bickering and in-fighting.

In his inimitable manner, *Horav Avraham Pam, zl*, dedicates a *shmuess*, ethical discourse, in *The Pleasant Way*, to this malady. He first cites a number of narratives in which the father of the *Mussar* movement, *Horav Yisrael Salanter, zl*, demonstrates the importance of thinking before one acts piously. In these instances, to act piously would have meant taking advantage of someone else. The *Rosh HaYeshivah* then concentrates on some practical issues to which, regrettably, many could relate.

Hachnosas orchim, welcoming guests to one's home, is one of the benchmarks of the Jewish People which we inherited from our Patriarch *Avraham Avinu*. Yet, the husband and father should take into consideration that he also has a wife and children at home. His wife also puts in a hard day, and his children would like his attention at the meal. The number of guests and their frequency should be considered. Another example is that when the *Chafetz Chaim* had guests at his home on Friday night, he would first recite *Kiddush*, make *Ha'motzi*, eat, and only then, after his guests had eaten, did he sing *Shalom Aleichem*. He felt that his guests, who were usually poor Jews who probably were hungry, should eat. The Heavenly Angels could wait for their *Shalom Aleichem*.

Reciting *Kaddish* for a parent is a *halachah*. It is a merit for both the parent and the son. To contend in *shul* about who and when one says *Kaddish* is not only demeaning for the son, it also detracts from the parent's merit. It is probably a greater *zchus*, merit, for the parent if his son is *mevater*, concedes, and does not compete for the *Kaddish*.

While rejoicing with a *chassan* and *kallah* at their wedding is a great *mitzvah*, those who have young children at home should not do so at the expense of the grandparents, who are usually the babysitters. Even when the babysitter is a teenager who can use the money, she still has to go to school the next day. In addition, *bachurim* who insist on dancing into the wee hours of the morning should consider the fact that the parents of the *chassan* and *kallah* are undoubtedly exhausted and would like to conclude the festivities.

Last, is *sholom bayis*, matrimonial harmony. *Rav* Pam describes a scenario in which a young wife prepares a special dinner for her husband. I might add that she, herself, has put in a full day at two different jobs, so that she can support him in *kollel*. Supper is called for 7:00PM. At 8:00PM, her husband comes home. He probably has forgotten about using his cell phone for something as "insignificant" as notifying his wife that he was occupied with a *mitzvah*, so that he would be late coming home. Is this a *mitzvah*, or is it a lack of sensitivity?

Shabbos Bamidbar is usually the *Shabbos* before *Shavuos*, the time that we received the Torah. As we prepare to embrace Hashem's gift to us, let us remember to properly implement the lessons the Torah teaches us.

והביא האיש את אשתו אל הכהן

The man shall bring his wife to the Kohen. (5:15)

ashi notes that the Torah presents the laws of *sotah,* whereby the man is compelled to bring his wayward wife to the *Kohen,* following the laws of *Matnos Kehunah,* gifts to the *Kohen.* This teaches us that one who refrains from giving the *Kohen* his due, will end up coming to him with his wife. To quote the words of the *Midrash,* "A door which is not open for charity is open for the doctor." One close student of *Horav Elazar M. Shach, zl* brought him five thousand dollars to be dispersed for charity. When *Rav* Shach queried him concerning the source of the funds, the man related the following story:

A certain *talmid chacham,* Torah scholar, was to undergo a surgical procedure. The surgeon's fee was five-thousand dollars. One of the friends of the *talmid chacham* was able to appeal to the *Kupas Cholim,* organization for the sick and needy, to underwrite the surgery. After the procedure, the *talmid chacham* gave his friend one hundred dollars to give to *Rav* Shach for the benefit of charity. After about an hour, he returned with another forty nine hundred dollars, explaining, "When I came home and related to my wife that I was giving one hundred dollars to charity, she felt I was wrong. In truth, I had saved five-thousand dollars. Therefore, I should contribute the <u>entire</u> amount of the surgery to *tzedakah.*"

When *Rav* Shach heard this, he said, "Please invite this couple to my home. If this is the way they act, I would like to bless them."

❋ ❋ ❋ ❋ ❋ ❋

"A man or woman who shall dissociate himself by taking a Nazirite vow of abstinence." (6:2)

Rashi explains the juxtaposition of the laws of *Nazir* to the laws of *sotah*, the wayward wife. This juxtaposition teaches us that one who sees a *sotah* in her degradation should take a vow to abstain from wine, since wine can stimulate immorality. There is a far cry between the *Nazir*, who signifies *kedushah*, sanctity, at its zenith, and the *sotah*, who reflects spiritual degeneracy at its nadir. Yet, one who sees this degradation should accept upon himself the vow of *Nezirus*. Is this not an extreme reaction? *Horav Baruch Sorotzkin, zl*, looks at this pragmatically. There is no absolute in regard to good or evil, no area that is strictly black or white. There is a lot of gray. Ever since the sin of Adam *HaRishon*, our perception of good and evil has been distorted. One's perception depends on one's objective. For example, wine can be, and is frequently, used as a symbol of *kedushah*. It is used for *Kiddush*, for any joyous occasion, and it was used extensively in the *Bais HaMikdash*. On the other hand, it is also associated with evil. It causes one to forget oneself and do things that he would never consider doing had he not been inebriated. It leads to debauchery and other sinful behavior. Where does one draw the line? Is wine good or evil?

The answer depends on how much, when, and for what purpose the wine is used. It can raise one's feelings of joy, so that he can thereby elevate himself spiritually. Alternatively, he can drink like a sot and act like one, too. Interestingly, when Yitzchak *Avinu* blessed his sons, both Yaakov and Eisav brought him tasty food. Yaakov included wine, while Eisav did not. Why? When Yitzchak blessed Yaakov, he added that his vineyards should be blessed. He did not share this blessing with Eisav. Why?

Yaakov was acutely aware of the spiritual benefits which he derived from wine. He sensed that when his father was about to bless him, he should bring wine, so that it would elevate his father's spirit and heighten his emotions. This would catalyze a sense of joy that would permeate his essence, bringing about greater blessing from the recesses of his *neshamah*, soul. Yitzchak, concomitantly blessed Yaakov with vineyards, because he understood their advantage for Yaakov. Eisav, on the other hand, had an exclusive perspective on wine and how it catalyzed sinful behavior. Yitzchak knew what wine would do to his errant son. He, therefore, did not bless him with vineyards.

One who sees a *sotah* in her degradation, who witnesses the negative effect of wine, should wonder whether it could happen to him. There must be a hidden message if Hashem has caused him to take notice. He should be concerned that the ugly consequences of wine could take him captive, as it did the *sotah*.

The *Nazir* is obligated to respond to the message. He should sense that he has a shortcoming within his psyche that must be addressed before he falls prey to his *yetzer hara*, evil-inclination. The *Rosh HaYeshivah* cites the *Sifri* that distinguishes between one who eats food on *Yom Kippur* and the *Nazir* who is prohibited from eating the skins and pips of the grapes. The individual who eats food on *Yom Kippur* does so in a manner that causes him pain. Alternatively, the food is of such a nature that he is pained by eating it. The *Nazir* also has an unnatural and painful eating experience when he eats the forbidden food. In the former case, the individual is not in violation of Torah law. In contrast, the Torah informs us that such a *Nazir* is in violation of his own *nezirus*, just as if he had eaten the main part of the grape. The *Nazir* realizes that he has a serious problem. He has no control over himself. Therefore, he frequently and easily submits to his *yetzer hara*. He must distance himself from anything that is even remotely derivative of grapes. Once he indulges, however slightly, he is unable to assert himself. He is a person who will believe that darkness is light and bitter is sweet. He cannot permit the *yetzer hara* to have any access to him whatsoever.

✼ ✼ ✼ ✼ ✼ ✼

איש או אשה כי יפלא לנדר נדר נזיר להזיר לד׳

"A man or a woman who shall dissociate himself by taking a Nazirite vow of abstinence for the sake of Hashem." (6:2)

*C*hazal teach us that one who witnesses the *sotah*, wayward wife, during her degradation, should take upon himself the vow of a *Nazir* and abstain from drinking wine. The *yetzer hara*, evil-inclination, takes hold of a person during his weak moments — a situation that can be brought about by drinking wine. The *yetzer hara* does not distinguish between victims. Immorality is only one of the many pitfalls to which he leads an unsuspecting victim. What about the *Nazir* who falls into the clutches of the *yetzer hara*? *Chazal* tell us about Shimon *HaTzaddik* who met a shepherd who was so impressed with the beautiful locks of his hair that he took a Nazirite vow so that he could cut them off *l'shem Shomayim*, for the sake of Heaven. This is a *Nazir* who controlled his *yetzer hara* that could lead him to *gaavah*, arrogance. In the *Talmud Sotah* 10b, *Chazal* tell us about another *Nazir*, one who fell into the abyss of arrogance. In the end, he was hung by his locks. We return to our original question: What do we do when we witness a *Nazir* in his degradation?

Horav Yitzchak Aizik Sher, zl, suggests that we follow the proven antidote for overcoming the blandishments of one's *yetzer hara* — Torah study. Therefore, we should go to the *bais ha'medrash*, take out a *Gemara* and learn! Yet, we find that even Torah study does not always protect us from haughtiness. David *Ha'melech's* son, Avshalom, was certainly a *talmid chacham*, Torah scholar, whose Torah did not protect him from falling into the nadir of sin. If Torah is the ultimate weapon to counteract the *yetzer hara*, why do *Chazal* not simply say that one who sees a *sotah* in her degradation should study Torah?

We derive from here, explains the *Mashgiach* of Slabodka, that at times, the *yetzer hara* masquerades itself as a *mitzvah*. In these situations, the *mitzvah* is being fulfilled at the behest of — and being sustained by — the *yetzer hara*. Therefore, *Chazal* have instructed us that one must study Torah with fear, trepidation and sweat, implying that casual study has no place in the Torah milieu. While Torah study certainly engenders *yiraas Shomayim*, fear of Heaven, this applies only if the student is serious about his learning. One who approaches Torah study for the wrong reason — for example, to derive honor from his scholarship — will only exacerbate his arrogance. He will not become a better person as a result of his learning. In this case, the *yetzer hara* becomes his *chavrusa*, study partner.

One can accept the Nazirite vow for a number of reasons. If he is doing it to overwhelm the *yetzer hara* within himself, he will succeed. If he seeks to elevate himself to become like a *Kohen*, but, in truth, in the recesses of his heart he simply wants to be superior to his peers, then the Nazirite vow will have a negative effect on him.

The *yetzer hara* has incredible powers. It can ensnare a person and convince him that he is performing a *mitzvah* when, in reality, he is descending to the depths of sin. Avshalom was great, so great that he had a strong and distinguished following. Yet, despite all of his Torah scholarship, he died a sinner, banished from his home and his People. One must always make sure that his intentions are noble and that he remains focused on his goal.

* * * * * *

איש או אשה כי יפלא לנדר נדר נזיר להזיר לד'

"A man or a woman who shall dissociate himself by taking a Nazirite vow of abstinence for the sake of Hashem." (6:2)

Rashi explains the juxtaposition of *Nazir* to the incident of *sotah* as teaching us a lesson that one who witnesses a *sotah* during her degradation should become a *Nazir*. First, by abstaining from wine, he will be distancing himself from one of the agents which catalyze a breakdown in one's defenses against immoral behavior. This advice is rendered to everyone, regardless of how removed <u>he</u> is from personally falling into a similar situation. This is a powerful demand. Second, it is not the sin that he sees; it is not even her miserable gut-wrenching death that he sees; it is the humiliation of her hair exposed and her clothes torn. Why is witnessing the punishment not a sufficient deterrent? Why does he have to become a *Nazir*? I suggest that after witnessing the painful death that the *sotah* suffers, one would be seriously moved.

Horav Elazar M. Shach, zl, derives from here that a person must protect himself by placing a barrier between himself and the opportunity for sin. Inspiration and various stimuli affect a person up to a point. When the *yetzer hara,* evil-inclination, takes hold of him, however, all of the stimuli become irrelevant. Inspiration becomes a thing of the past as one is engulfed by the fire and passion of the *yetzer hara.* The only protection is the fence that one has erected to guard himself from falling into the realm of sin. Therefore, *Chazal* say: Become a *Nazir*; abstain from wine, so that you will never fall into the clutches of the *yetzer hara.*

The *Alter, zl, m'Kelm* posits that nothing will halt a *baal taavah,* one who is lustful, from deferring to his desires. Even if he sees the ugly consequences of his submission to his heart's cravings, he will nonetheless carry out his infatuations. He relates the famous story about the wise man whose father was a drunkard. This caused much humiliation for the distinguished son. He often attempted to convince his father not to fall prey to the bottle, but to no avail.

They were once walking together when they chanced upon a man who was clearly inebriated, lying in the alley amid his own filth. The son turned to his father and asked, "Do you now see the horrible consequences of drink?"

Instead of the expected reply, the father bent over the drunk and whispered into his ear, "Tell me, my friend, where did you purchase such powerful whiskey?"

The *baal taavoh* is obsessed with his desires, and reason is not effective. He must erect fences around himself to protect himself from falling into the abyss of sinful desire.

✹ ✹ ✹ ✹ ✹ ✹

כה תברכו את בני ישראל
"So shall you bless Bnei Yisrael." (6:23)

The *Midrash* comments that *Klal Yisrael* complained to Hashem, "You instruct the *Kohanim* to bless us. We need nothing but Your blessing." Hashem responded, "Even though I instruct the *Kohanim* to bless you, I still stand over them and bless you." The statement, "We <u>need</u> nothing but Your blessing," is enigmatic. It implies that Hashem's blessing "suffices" and we need nothing else. Is this true? Our attitude should be that we desire no other blessing but Hashem's! The *Ksav Sofer* explains that Hashem's blessing is unlike that of mortal man. A human being's blessing invariably focuses on areas of a material nature, regardless of whether these blessings are inherently good for the person. Some people would be better off with less material abundance. For others, honor and distinction can produce a negative result. Do we really know what is good for us? How many people supplicate the Almighty for specific blessings which, in the long term, might not be favorable?

This is what *Klal Yisrael* meant when they implied that Hashem's blessing was "sufficient." If the *Kohanim* bless us, how will they know what is good for us and what is not? We only need Your *brachah*, because only what You consider to be a *brachah* for us is truly a *brachah*. Otherwise, it is not a blessing. We do not need blessings from human beings, since they do not know what is truly a blessing for us.

Hashem, therefore, instructed the *Kohanim* to give a general blessing with no specifics, a blessing that has a number of connotations. Hashem decides what is best for us. This is what is meant by Hashem's reply that He stands over the *Kohanim*. He determines each person's blessing. The *Kohanim* say, "Hashem should watch over you" — He decides what that means. Everyone is protected in accordance to what is best for him.

The *Shomer Emunim* cites the *Baal Shem Tov* who gives the following explanation for the *pasuk* in *Tehillim* (145:19), "The will of those who fear Him He will do; and their cry He will hear, and save them." Two questions come to mind upon reading this *pasuk*: First, once Hashem carries out the will of those who fear Him, what need is there to listen to their pleas again? Has He not already done what they ask? Second, should it not have been the other way around that first Hashem listens, and then He performs what they ask? The *Baal Shem Tov* explains that *initially* Hashem listens to the pleas of all who cry out to Him — regardless if it is for a positive or a negative purpose. Even a thief who cries out for assistance may receive an affirmative response. The difference is that once the thief is caught and he again makes his plea, Hashem will not listen. The *tzaddik*, righteous Jew, who has prayed for something which, unbeknownst to him, was to his detriment can once again beseech Hashem when he realizes his error. Hashem will listen to him. He performs the will of those who fear Him and demonstrates His compassion by listening again to their pleas when they realize that they were in error.

The *Chafetz Chaim* suggests that when a person entreats Hashem, he should not say, "Please grant me this," since a person does not know what is inherently good for him and what is not. Instead he should say, "Hashem, if this is good for me, please grant it to me — and if it is not good for me, I do not want it." A depressed man, who lived in abject poverty, once came to the *Chafetz Chaim* to pour out his heart to the sage. During the course of the conversation, the man revealed that for years, he had just eked out a living. Their lifestyle was not extravagant, but he provided for his family in such a manner that they managed from year to year, covering their basic necessities. The problem was that he was greedy, he wanted to be wealthy. He purchased a lottery ticket and prayed. He poured out his heart to Hashem, begging Him for this one big win. Hashem listened and the man won the jackpot, twenty thousand rubles. Not being much of a businessman, it did not take long before a few bad investments quickly depleted his winnings. He was now destitute with no means of supporting his family. What could he do?

The *Chafetz Chaim* sighed heavily and said, "I cannot help you. *Chazal* state that Hashem decrees about each person whether he will be wealthy or poor. The *Chesed L'Avraham* adds that He also decrees how much a person will earn each week. Now, since you were basically earning a living each week, why did you "bother" Hashem to allow you to win the lottery? Do you not realize that the winnings from the lottery was your livelihood for the next few years? Hashem just gave it to you earlier!"

We do not know what is best for us. Only Hashem knows. So why not "allow" Him to make the decision without our assistance? The *Chafetz Chaim* once asked a Jew about his well-being. The person answered with the typical response, "A little better would not hurt." The *Chafetz Chaim* immediately countered, "How do you know that? Hashem knows what is best for you. He is compassionate and merciful. Surely, He wants you to have the best — the very best — for you. If 'better' was 'best' for you — He would grant it. Apparently, it is not best for you, so do not complain."

Last, we cite a powerful thought from *Horav Shimshon Pinkus*, *zl*. He cites the *pasuk* in *Bereishis* (48:22) in which Yaakov *Avinu* gives Shechem to Yosef "which I took from the hand of the Emori with my sword and my bow." *Targum Onkelos* interprets "sword" and "bow" as prayer and supplication. This teaches us that prayer is a form of weaponry. If one shoots enough arrows, something should hit its mark. A prayer, if it is said often enough, resolutely, with fervor and passion, will have an effect. In fact, *Rav* Pinkus says that every time he was adamant in prayer, Hashem answered his request. He learned the hard way, however, that persistence may not always be the correct approach. At times, Heaven has other plans.

He once had to reclaim a car in Cyprus for a friend who was heavily involved in Jewish outreach. His vehicle was absolutely a major part of his work, since he would go to places off the beaten path in search of young people to bring closer to *Yiddishkeit*. When *Rav* Shimshon arrived at the tax office, he realized that he had forgotten to bring along the necessary documents. He decided to rely on his "weaponry," and he prayed to Hashem to help him retrieve the car for his friend. As he approached the official, he took out some official papers that were in English. When the official asked him what the papers were, *Rav* Shimshon looked at him incredulously and asked, "What do you mean? Do you not know what these papers represent?" The official, not wanting to concede that he could not read English, was taken aback, but quickly proceeded to release the car. With the help of the Almighty, *Rav* Shimshon's friend received the car and was now able to continue his work.

The very first time his friend took the car out, he was in an accident which tragically claimed his life. *Rav* Shimshon concluded by saying that this episode taught him a lesson: If Heaven delays you, if, for some reason, it seems that this is not the time, do not be stubborn, do not push on. It is just not yet the time.

פרשת בהעלותך
Parashas Beha'alosecha

בהעלתך את הנרת אל מול פני המנורה יאירו שבעת הנרות
*"When you kindle the lamps, toward the face of the Menorah shall the
seven lamps cast light." (8:1)*

Rashi cites *Chazal* who explain the use of the word *Beha'alosecha,*
which really means "when you bring up," as opposed to
beha'adlikcha, when you kindle. It is necessary for the *Kohen* to
keep the flame in place until *shalheves oleh m'eilehah*, the flame rises on its
own, from the oil in the wick and not from the *Kohen's* flame. This
explanation is seemingly superfluous, since it is obvious that the flame
should be burning on its own. Otherwise, as soon as the *Kohen* takes away
his light, the lamp on the *Menorah* will extinguish. Do we really need a
specific word to convey a *halachah* that is obvious?

Horav Avigdor Halevi Nebentzhal, Shlita, offers a homiletic
approach. The three *Klei Kodesh*, holy appurtenances, that stand in the
Heichal — the *Menorah, Mizbayach Ha'ketores*, and *Shulchan* — signify the
three pillars upon which the world rests. The *Menorah* denotes the Pillar of
Torah, since the *Menorah* is closely related to wisdom. The *Mizbayach
Ha'ketores*, Altar of Incense, signifies the Pillar of *Avodah*, prayer/service
and devotion to the Almighty. The *Shulchan*, Table, closely connected with
food and sustenance, connotes *gemillus chasadim*, acts of loving-kindness.
The *shoresh*, source, for these three *Keilim* which were outside in the *Heichal*
was the *Aron HaKodesh*, Holy Ark, which alludes to *emunah*, faith, in the
Almighty. This teaches us that the three pillars of the world, Torah, *Avodah*
and *Gemillus Chasadim*, must have their source in *emunah*. If they are not
the outgrowth of pure faith and conviction, they are missing the most
essential component of their existence.

When the Torah teaches us the laws that apply to the lighting of the
Menorah, its intention is to convey to us the manner in which we should
transmit *Torah* to our students. The *rebbe* should involve himself in the
teaching process until the student grasps the material on his own. When one

seeks to transfer the flame of Torah to his student, he must see to it that the flame burns brightly within the student — on its own. One who teaches and communicates Torah wisdom to his student is not assured of success until the student is able to understand the material to the point that he can be *mechadesh*, say/write original thoughts and novellae. One who simply repeats by rote, but cannot innovate his own original deductions based upon the *derech*, approach to Torah thought, taught him by his *rebbe*, has not really grasped the flame. It is not "rising on its own."

Horav Chaim Shmuelevitz, zl, was wont to say, "One who can simply 'say over' what his *rebbe* said on a specific topic is not considered a true disciple. He must be able to 'say over' on his own what his *rebbe would have said*." This indicates that he has absorbed his *rebbe's* approach to understanding the profundity of Torah. Every *Rosh HaYeshivah* had his own unique methodology and approach to the *nituach ha'sugya*, analysis and dialectic, of the subject matter. A true student should be able to distinguish between the approach of *Rav* Shimon Shkop and that of *Rav* Chaim Brisker. There was also the *derech* of the *Chasam Sofer* that was used primarily in the Hungarian *yeshivos*. To be able to perceive what one's *rebbe* would say indicates one's depth of understanding.

Rav Nebentzhal continues with the responsibilities imposed upon the *yeshivah* toward its students in transmitting the Torah lesson. He cites the *Gaon, zl, m'Vilna,* who posits that when one teaches, he should not complete his thesis, but rather leave over one point for the student to delve into and cogitate himself. This is applicable only if the student is capable of deducing the concept on his own. If he is, however, incapable, then the *rebbe* should teach it over and over, as the famous *Rav* Preida taught his student four hundred times until he understood <u>each</u> lesson.

Once, *Horav Eliyahu Eliezer Dessler, zl,* the *Michtav M'Eliyahu,* was giving a *shmuess,* ethical discourse, during which he explained two of *Chazal's* teachings that seemed to contradict one another. When the lecture was over, the students realized that he had not answered the original question. He wanted to see who would come over and ask him for the answer. This is the meaning of the flame rising on its own: The student is inspired to think on his own, to question, respond, compare and expound on the analysis presented to him.

Rav Nebentzhal suggests that the *yeshivah* has another function: to imbue the student with a love of Torah. Only a student who loves the Torah, who senses the "*v'haarev na*," sweetness of Torah, will be driven to plumb its profundities with enthusiasm and fervor. He must realize that the Torah is not merely another wisdom — it is his lifeline. The *bren*, fire/passion, that one invests into Torah study should burn fiercely. To study Torah with a *kaltkeit*, cold, distant feeling is to invite trouble. The flame surely cannot rise on its own if originally it had not been present. The initial break with Orthodoxy came about in this manner. Interestingly, the original founders of the *Haskalah* movement, which undermined and attempted to totally destroy the Torah, were themselves observant Jews. Their approach was to "cool off" one's *yiraas Shomayim*, fear of Heaven. They considered *mitzvos* to be nothing more than Jewish tradition and custom, relegating observance to a matter of culture. The result was that their own children became apostates and converted out of the faith. When the fire is extinguished, nothing remains but a cold heart.

The *Chazon Ish* related that a father once came to him complaining that his son was extreme in his observance. The *Chazon Ish* commented, "This father thinks that middle of the road refers to one who observes fifty percent of the *mitzvos*. He does not understand that the absolute minimum that a Jew must observe is all 613 *mitzvos*. One who refrains from performing thirty-eight of the thirty-nine types of labor on *Shabbos* is still a *mechallel Shabbos*, desecrator of the *Shabbos*." When we do not transmit the flame to the next generation in such a manner that it burns brightly on its own, the result is a Jew who is distant, cold and dispassionate in his observance. His observance is — at best — sterile and will not produce a second generation of Torah-observant Jews.

ויאמרו האנשים ההמה אליו אנחנו טמאים לנפש אדם למה נגרע לבלתי
הקריב את קרבן ד'

*Those men said to him, "We are contaminated through a human corpse;
why should we be diminished by not offering Hashem's offering?" (9:7)*

T he *Sifri* derives from the Torah's use of the word *anashim*, a term
reserved for distinguished men, that these individuals were
kesheirim v'charaidim l'mitzvos, proper men who were eager and
meticulous in *mitzvah* observance. There are people who observe whatever
they are told to observe. Yet, they will look for loopholes and *heteirim*,
halachic dispensations, to get around an obligation. Then there are those who
seek every opportunity to observe *mitzvos*, to carry out Hashem's will. One
who loves Hashem does not look for a way out. On the contrary, he will seize
every opportunity that brings him closer to Hashem. These men had been
deprived of a *mitzvah*. While it is true that they were involved in another
mitzvah, they did not look at it that way. They did not want to miss an
opportunity to offer the *Korban Pesach*.

Our *gedolei Yisrael*, Torah luminaries, of each generation were
characterized by this unique attitude toward *mitzvos*. The *Gaon, zl, m'Vilna*
was imprisoned during the Festival of *Succos*. He did everything within his
ability to stay awake, to the point of holding his eyes open, so that he should
not fall asleep outside of the *succah*.

A Russian Jew who was a student in Radin related that he once
stayed up all Thursday, *Mishmor* night, studying Torah. As he left in the wee
hours of the morning, the snow was beginning to descend and the wind's
fury was intensifying, as the temperature plummeted to below zero. He
rushed through the quiet streets to get home and catch a few hours of rest
before the sun rose. Suddenly, he noticed something moving surreptitiously
through the streets. Back and forth the figure moved, stopping every once in
a while, then continuing on. The student was nervous. Who could this be in
the middle of the night? Filled with fear, he decided to continue on to his
home. As he came closer, he was extremely surprised to see that it was none
other than the saintly *Chafetz Chaim*. "Why are you outside in the middle of
the night?" the *Chafetz Chaim* asked, clearly agitated, but concerned. "Go
right home to sleep."

The next day, the student discovered that this was the *third* night that the *Chafetz Chaim* had been circling the city, in the bitter cold and raging snow, waiting for the *levanah*, moon, to appear, so that he could fulfill the *mitzvah* of *Kiddush Levanah*.

A bit closer to our own time, we can learn about devotion to *mitzvos* from the *Klausenberger Rebbe, zl.* The *Rebbe* survived the Holocaust with his faith intact, making sure to observe whatever *mitzvos* he could, risking his life not to transgress any negative commandments. His dedication and commitment are legendary. Probably the most difficult time was during the eight days of *Pesach* when his body, already wracked with pain from the cruel labor to which he was subjected, had to be sustained without eating the smallest crumb of *chametz*. Together with a small group of fellow prisoners, he was able to gather a small store of potatoes, hiding them in the cracks of the barracks walls and between the bunks. One day, a Nazi guard found the "treasure" and confiscated it. The *Rebbe's* reaction was typical, "We have done our part; Hashem will do what is good in His eyes."

The *Rebbe's* words became a reality, as the day before *Pesach* the Nazis suddenly — and for no apparent reason — assigned an entire group of Jews to help the farmers whose fields bordered the camp. Their job was to open up the stores of potatoes which had been underground all winter. This work assignment provided them with the means to smuggle a large quantity of potatoes back to the camp.

By an overt miracle, they were able to procure some grain, which they crushed with their fingers and some rocks until it was fine enough to be flour. They baked tiny little *matzos* in secret and prepared for the *Seder*. Fifteen men gathered around the *Rebbe,* as he recited the entire *Hagaddah* from memory. His bitter weeping shook the entire assemblage, who listened with tears streaming down their faces. While they certainly did not have four cups of wine, and *marror*, bitter herbs, was a part of their daily routine, they did have *matzoh*. The *Rebbe* spoke words of encouragement to the men who sat enraptured by his words. They were amazed how he spoke of a future filled with hope. When others were filled with depression and devastation, the *Rebbe's* mind was replete with spiritual matters that transcended the realm of the average person's understanding. The experience may be summed up with the words of a non-observant Jew who had been invited to the *Seder*. He sat silently, watching, listening, absorbing everything that was taking place. He did not utter a sound, until he could no longer contain himself and he exclaimed, "Jewish brothers! If I did not personally experience this beautiful scene I would never have believed that such a thing was possible…that Jews should observe the commandment of eating *matzoh* right under the noses of the Nazi murderers, with death staring them in the face. I would never have believed it."

Surviving the week of *Pesach* took superhuman strength — both physically and emotionally. The *Rebbe* hardly ate anything. He refused to eat *chametz* of any sort. He left his daily portion of bread unclaimed for anyone who wanted it. He would eat nothing more than unpeeled potatoes that were occasionally obtained for him, baking them in an empty can that he *koshered* in boiling water before *Pesach.* On the last day of *Pesach*, the *Rebbe* was on a work detail outside of the campgrounds. He refused to eat a baked potato that someone had managed to obtain for him, because it was not prepared in a utensil that had been *koshered* for *Pesach.* As he was working, he came upon the head of a sugar beet. He felt this was his reward for not eating the potato. As he ate the beet, he remarked, "I have never eaten anything as sweet as this." This is commitment to *mitzvos.*

******

והאיש משה ענו מאד

***Now the man Moshe was exceedingly humble.* (12:3)**

The *Daas Zekeinim* notes that the word *anav*, humble, is written without a *yud.* This implies that Moshe *Rabbeinu's* humility extended to every organ in his body. The word *anav* without a *yud* is spelled *ayin,* which is spelled out — *ayin, yud, nun* = 130; *nun,* spelled out — *nun, vav, non* = 106; *vav,* spelled out — *vav, vav*= 12, total 248, which is the number of organs in the body. What is the meaning of humility throughout the entire body? *Horav Shmuel David Walkin*, *zl,* renders the following explanation based on an episode that occurred with the *Baal HaTanya.* The *Baal HaTanya* decided to leave Mezritch to return home. He felt that remaining in Mezritch in close proximity to the famous *Maggid* was harmful to his character. He saw himself becoming haughty about his spiritual ascendancy. It was better that he should return home and become a *baal agalah*, wagon driver, than become a *baal gaavah*, an arrogant and pompous man. He was traveling home just before Pesach when the roads, which had been affected by the spring thaw, were flooded and filled with deep potholes. It took a very experienced wagon driver to guide the coach along the way, and not fall into any of the holes in the road. The wagon driver turned to his passengers and asked, "Have you ever seen such a fine driver as I? No other driver could have guided you so brilliantly as I have!"

When the *Baal HaTanya* heard this, he realized that one who is arrogant will be so regardless of his position. The *baal agalah* who thinks highly of himself will be the same *baal gaavah* as the *talmid chacham*, Torah scholar, who allows his erudition to go to his head. A *baal gaavah* is a *baal gaavah*, regardless of his position. This is what is meant by referring to Moshe as humble in every one of his organs. Regardless of what he would do, with whichever part of his body, he viewed himself as insignificant and unworthy.

✻ ✻ ✻ ✻ ✻ ✻

ותסגר מרים מחוץ למחנה שבעת ימים והעם לא נסע עד האסף מרים

So Miriam was quarantined outside the camp for seven days, and the people did not journey until Miriam was brought in. **(12:15)**

*R*ashi says that the distinction of having the entire nation wait for her was accorded to Miriam as a reward for her waiting and watching the infant Moshe when he was left in a basket in the river. Miriam waited and watched over Moshe as a natural instinct, an expression of love for her baby brother. Of course, she would remain in the background to see what would take place. It was the natural, right thing to do. Indeed, if she would have had to pay a great amount of money for the opportunity to guard her little brother, she would have certainly done so. Her reward is incredible. For waiting a short while just to see what would happen to her brother, all of *Klal Yisrael* waited for her for seven days. This teaches us how crucial it is to empathize with another person. A few minutes were valued by Hashem as being so significant that an entire nation waited — for a considerable length of time for her to heal.

A son was born to *Horav Chaim Shmuelevitz, zl*, during the Israeli War of Independence. The *Bris Milah* took place in the hospital as the shells and bombs were exploding outside. As the walls of the building shook, everyone in attendance appreciated the emotional and spiritual respite from the devastation that was going on in the streets of the city. Returning to their home, the family had to run, dodging exploding shells and seeking refuge in any place that provided cover from the ravages of war. Running between houses, *Rav* Chaim sensed a presence in the doorway of one of the houses. It was a young wounded boy, his arms and legs bound in bandages. *Rav* Chaim stopped and began to cry. He was so emotionally overcome with the plight of the young child that he ignored the exploding shells, as well as the immediate danger to his own life. He just had to stop and cry — empathize with the young boy's pain.

Rav Chaim explained, "People think that empathy means to help another in need. What can you do for someone who is wounded, wrapped in bandages, and has been helped as much as possible? What more can be done for him? The answer is that while assistance may be ruled out, empathy is not! One can *share* in his pain, *feel* his anguish. When an individual carries a heavy load, everyone understands that we should help. What do you do, however, for the one that is carrying a load of 'pain'? We are obligated to try to 'feel' his pain and share his anguish."

✼ ✼ ✼ ✼ ✼ ✼

Parashas Shelach

שלח לך אנשים ויתרו את ארץ כנען
"Send for yourself people and they will spy the land" (13:2)

Rashi notes that the passage about the *meraglim*, spies, is juxtaposed to the previous passage which relates the incident of Miriam speaking against her brother, Moshe *Rabbeinu*. He explains that since Miriam was stricken over matters relating to speech, the spies should have had enough sense to take heed and learn a lesson from her debacle. *Horav Zalmen Sorotzkin, zl,* questions the comparison between Miriam's speaking against Moshe and the *meraglim's* speaking against the inanimate wood and stones of *Eretz Yisrael.* Obviously, there must be a differential between the two. *Horav Shmuel David Walkin, zl,* explains that Miriam speaking against Moshe created a mindset that should have taught the *meraglim* an important lesson: the critical impact of a *negiah,* personal prejudice/vested interest. He derives this from the following hypothesis.

Chazal teach us that the women of that generation were *tzidkaniyos,* righteous women. It was in their *zchus,* merit, that *Klal Yisrael* was liberated from Egypt. They refused to contribute their jewelry toward creating the *eigel,* Golden Calf. *Bnos Tzlafchad* were just a few of the many women who loved and yearned for *Eretz Yisrael.* At every juncture when the men disputed Moshe, the women had supported his leadership. This whole pattern of support ended during the episode of the *meraglim.* Suddenly, the women agreed with the men and contended with Moshe. *Chazal* tell us that they all cried on that fateful night. They all complained on that night. What catalyzed this change of heart? What brought about this sudden about-face? It was Miriam's words against Moshe. When she said that Moshe was not treating his wife the way other men treated their wives, this resulted in an uproar among the women: "What? Moshe, our revered leader, is not treating his wife properly? We should support her and rebel against him." Miriam's provocative statement had a tragic effect. It turned the women, who heretofore had been Moshe's greatest supporters, into his antagonists.

It was their *negios*, personal prejudices, that turned the tide. Moshe, who until now they considered as *kadosh*, holy and perfect, was quickly transformed into someone who was unfit to lead. The *meraglim* should have derived from Miriam's fiasco that *negios* sway a person's perspective and pervert his vision. He is no longer able to see reality in its clear light. This constitutes the parallel between Miriam and the *meraglim*. They should have learned from her error. They did not, and we still suffer from the consequences until this very day.

✻ ✻ ✻ ✻ ✻ ✻

ותשא כל העדה ויתנו את קולם ויבכו העם בלילה ההוא

The entire assembly raised up and issued its voice; the people wept that night. (14:1)

That fateful night became a night of weeping for our entire nation for posterity. It was *Tishah B'Av*, the national day of tragedy on which our *Batei Mikdash* were destroyed and other tragedies occurred. What precipitated this? Were they really that bad? In the *Yalkut Shimoni*, *Chazal* say that weeping is infectious. The spies returned and fanned out throughout their respective tribes. They called together their close families. In somber voices laden with emotion, each related his story. They wept as they spoke, and when they wept those who listened shared in their emotional outburst. Crying will do that. When someone stands in front of us and cries, we become emotionally moved and it leaves an impact on us. This response spread throughout the nation, until everyone began wailing and grieving over the terrible outlook for the future. The unwarranted weeping of *Klal Yisrael* rose up to Heaven and Hashem responded, saying, "You cried for no reason. I will give you a *b'chiah l'doros*, a reason to cry for generations." *Tishah B'Av* became our national day of mourning. Our greatest tragedies occurred on this day — all because of our unwarranted, needless weeping.

Let us analyze this. It is human nature to become emotional when someone in front of us begins to weep uncontrollably. Parents and educators are swayed when their child/student begins to cry. Imagine an entire nation crying uncontrollably. Can a person be held accountable for giving in to his emotions in the face of such public weeping? On this night the depression and hopelessness were overpowering. The fear was overwhelming. The people were totally unable to cope. Should they really have been blamed and punished so gravely?

We derive from here, posits *Horav Gershon Liebman, zl*, how much the Torah demands that a Jew be independent, that he not be controlled and easily swayed; that he stand resolute, uncoerced by falsity and deception. One who believes in, and recognizes, the truth will not be moved — regardless of how many others fall prey to emotion and misguided influence. The unwarranted weeping should not have reached such proportions, because there was no reason to fear a lack of success. Hashem had been with them up until this point. He promised to take them into the land without mishap. They should have maintained their conviction, despite the weeping. Indeed, as soon as they heard their punishment, they lamented their past weeping and were prepared to ascend to the land. This only demonstrates the shallowness of their weeping. When one *believes* in an ideal, when he *knows* that he is acting correctly and in good faith, he should not fear what others have to say. The truth should fortify his conviction and give him the fortitude to withstand whatever criticism insecure individuals may level at him.

******

ויתאבלו העם מאד. וישכמו בבקר ויעלו אל ראש ההר לאמר הננו ועלינו...כי חטאנו. ויאמר משה למה זה אתם עברים את פי ד׳ והיא לא תצלח.

And the people mourned exceedingly. They awoke early in the morning and ascended toward the mountaintop saying, "We are ready and we shall ascend... for we have sinned." Moshe said, "Why do you transgress the word of Hashem? It will not succeed." **(14:39-41)**

An incredible transformation seems to be taking place before our very eyes. The same people who wept *b'chinam*, for no reason — who earlier that evening had eschewed Moshe *Rabbeinu* and *Eretz Yisrael* — were now prepared to eat their words and push on to the Holy Land. Is there a greater indication of *teshuvah*, repentance? Immediately after Moshe conveyed to them the consequence of their rebellion — that *only* their children would enter *Eretz Yisrael* — they repented according to the *halachic* process. They regretted their rebellion by morning. They abandoned their sinful behavior, and they confessed to their sin. We do not find a parallel in Jewish history where immediately after the nation sinned, they repented.

Yet, Hashem does not accept their *teshuvah*. In fact, they were considered *reshaim*, wicked, for attempting to ascend to *Eretz Yisrael*. Why? *Horav Avigdor Halevi Nebentzhal, Shlita*, explains that while their intentions were possibly noble, their timing was faulty. Hashem had already declared that they were to wander in the wilderness for forty-years. To ascend to *Eretz Yisrael* at this juncture — after Hashem said no — was rebellious. Hashem had issued His edict. All they could do now was to accept it. *Teshuvah* is certainly a process by which the sin is expunged, but it takes time and effort. Apparently, their *teshuvah* was insufficient.

Rav Nebentzhal adds that quite possibly their *teshuvah* was an improper and incorrect form of repentance. Since their initial regret and ensuing confession were misplaced, their *teshuvah* was of no value. Only yesterday the people had fallen under the influence of the *meraglim*, spies, who slandered *Eretz Yisrael* and *Klal Yisrael's* ability to triumph against its inhabitants. They were clearly aware that Hashem had said that they would conquer the land. Their mistake was in assuming that Hashem had no control over the giants who inhabited *Eretz Yisrael*. They acceded to Hashem's awesome power, but they thought that His powers had limitations. When Moshe told them that they were not going to enter the land as a result of their misgivings, they accepted that they had erred. Their error, however, went deeper than they thought. They thought that they had underestimated *Eretz Yisrael*. Their real sin was in underestimating Hashem! The next day, they decided to storm the mountain and ascend to the land, because they now realized the critical significance of *Eretz Yisrael*. What about Hashem? He had said that now was not the time to ascend. Once again, they failed to reckon with Hashem's decree. They did not understand that just as *Eretz Yisrael's* giants were meaningless before Hashem, so, too, was *Eretz Yisrael* without meaning if Hashem *Yisborach* did not want them to go there. The only thing that matters is Hashem's will, and, at the current time, it was not supportive of their endeavor. Indeed, if we consider it, not only did their action not represent *teshuvah*, in reality it was a continuation of their original sin of not acknowledging Hashem.

There are people who, albeit observant, fail to correlate the *mitzvos* with Hashem. As far as they are concerned, there are *mitzvos* — and there is the will of Hashem. For example, we will make the statement regarding an individual, "He is observant *and* he is also a great *ohaiv Yisrael*; he loves Jews, and he loves *Eretz Yisrael*." This sort of statement can cause one to think that there is a dichotomy between an observant Jew and one who is an *ohaiv Yisrael,* or *ohaiv Eretz Yisrael*. These are both aspects of Jewish observance and, thus, included in the Torah. Everything we do must be viewed as the *ratzon Hashem*, will of G-d. It is all part of one large package. We do not cut and paste *mitzvos*.

This form of equanimity towards the will of Hashem exemplified the European Jew, who never looked for ways to cut corners in *mitzvah* observance. Hashem gave us 613 *mitzvos*. They are all equally His will and, therefore, we are enjoined to observe them. The same attitude applied to transgression. If an activity or endeavor was not in accordance with the will of Hashem, they did not look for loopholes to get around the sin. What was wrong remained wrong. *Heiteirim, halachic* dispensations, were not sought as a means to circumvent various inconveniences. The following story is one of the first stories I heard from my revered *rebbe, Horav Tzvi Hirsch Meisels, zl,* the *Veitzener Rav.*

It was *Erev Rosh Hashanah,* when the Nazi guards of Auschwitz rounded up 1600 youngsters under the age of eighteen for a *Selektzia,* Selection, to see who was healthy enough to be kept alive. They put a pole with a cross bar in place and the children had to pass beneath the bar. If their heads reached the bar, they lived. If not, they were condemned to die. In the end, 1400 youngsters were condemned to die on *Rosh Hashanah.* Horrified parents and relatives went through the motions of attempting to bribe the guards and *kapos* on behalf of their sons. There were, of course, men of great reason who refused to redeem their sons at the cost of another child, which was the inevitable consequence of their dealing. If 1400 youngsters had been counted, there had to be that exact number — if not others had to take the place of the missing children. On that fateful *Rosh Hashanah,* a simple, unassuming Jew approached *Rav* Meisels with a *halachic* query. "*Rebbe,*" he said in a shaking voice, "my only son, my beloved child, is in that barracks doomed to die. I have money to redeem him, but it will be at the expense of another child. I have already lost everything. My son is all I have left. May I redeem him? Please answer me, and I will submit to whatever you decide."

Rav Meisels turned to the father and with great trepidation replied, "How can you expect me to give a ruling in such circumstances and under such duress? I have no *seforim, halachic* responsa, to research. I have no one with whom to confer. This is a most difficult question for me to decide."

Reflecting on the query, a number of thoughts went through *Rav* Meisel's mind. There were pros and cons, but the bottom line was that it was a difficult *shaaleh*, with very little logic to permit redeeming the boy. The father kept on begging, crying bitterly, *"Rebbe,"* he pleaded, "You must decide this question while I still have the chance to save my only son."

Rav Meisels implored the man to desist from pressing the question, "I cannot render a proper decision without my *seforim*."

The Jew persisted, *"Rebbe*, does that mean that you do not permit me to save my only child? If so, I will willingly accept, with love, your ruling."

"No, my dear friend," *Rav* Meisels countered. "I did not say that it is not permitted. I only said that I cannot reasonably rule either way. Do whatever you feel you should do, as if you had never asked me at all."

When the brokenhearted father realized that *Rav* Meisels could not be swayed into rendering a decision, he cried out passionately, *"Ribono Shel Olam*, I did what the Torah demands of me. I asked a *shaileh* of the *rav*, the only *rav* who was available. If he cannot give me an outright *heter,* then that implies that a question in *Halachah* remains regarding granting me permission to redeem my child. If that is the case, then I abide by this "non"-ruling, even though this means that my child will die tomorrow. I will do nothing to override what the Torah ordains."

Rav Meisels could do nothing to dissuade the father who walked around for the rest of the day with a subtle smile on his face. He felt he was about to sacrifice his only child to Hashem in the manner of the *Akeidas Yitzchak*. This man's righteousness was exemplary and indicative of a complete *temimus*, wholesomeness and perfection in his *avodas Hashem*, service to Hashem: *Mi k'amcha Yisrael?* "Who is like Your nation *Yisrael?"*

כי דבר ד' בזה ואת מצותו הפר הכרת תכרת הנפש ההיא עונה בה

For he scorned the word of Hashem and broke His commandment; that
person will surely be cut off, his sin is upon him. (15:31)

One who humiliates a *talmid chacham*, Torah scholar, is included in
the transgression of *dvar Hashem bazah*, "For he scorned the
word of Hashem." In the *Shulchan Aruch*, it is cited as a *halachah*
prohibiting embarrassing a Torah scholar, a sin which cuts the sinner off
from *Olam Haba*, the World to Come. The *Chafetz Chaim, zl*, writes in his
Hilchos Lashon Hara that although people understand the gravity of
humiliating a Torah scholar, it does not serve as a deterrent. They fall prey to
their *yetzer hara*, evil-inclination, which tells them that the concept of *talmid
chacham* applies only to the days of yore when the leading Torah scholars
were the authors of the *Talmud*. This is categorically untrue. In every
generation a standard exists that is appropriate to that generation. A scholar
who meets the criteria of that generation is a *talmid chacham* who must be
respected. One who denigrates a *talmid chacham* commits a grave sin. I
would be so bold as to suggest that this idea applies equally to any scholar in
a position of authority, who disseminates Torah to the masses. All too often
we view those individuals who teach Torah to our children as employees
with whom we deal according to our whims. It is essentially such an attitude
that undermines Torah authority and cheapens the entire fabric of our Torah
standards. When children perceive their parents' attitude and lack of respect,
what should they do? The apple does not fall far from the tree.

The story is related about a man in Yerushalayim, who shortly after
the passing of *Horav Moshe Feinstein, zl,* became very ill with excruciating
headaches. He sought the counsel of the greatest specialists, to no avail.
Finally, he went to one of the distinguished *rabbanim* of *Eretz Yisrael* to ask
for his blessing. After the *rav* discovered that the headaches began during
Rav Moshe's *levayah*, funeral, which was held in Yerushalayim, he
immediately asked the man if he had ever negated the *kavod*, honor, of the
venerable sage. The man replied in the negative. He would never have
impugned the dignity of *Rav* Moshe. The *rav* said that he should execute the
goral ha'Gra, the *Gaon M'Vilna's* lot, which would hopefully reveal the
source of his illness. This method, which ultimately falls on a *pasuk* in the
Torah that alludes to the answer to one's question, indicated the *pasuk* in
Bamidbar 12:8, "Why did you not fear to speak against My servant, Moshe?"

Clearly, this man must have said or done something to impugn the honor of *Rav* Moshe.

At first, the man could not remember anything negative that he had done. Suddenly, an incident came to mind that caused him to shudder. "I remember now what happened. It was *Shushan Purim,* and *Rav* Moshe's *levayah* was dragging on and on. The streets of Yerushalayim were filled with thousands of people who had thronged to the funeral of the *gadol ha'dor,* preeminent Torah leader of the generation. It bothered me that everyone's *simchas Purim* was delayed as a result of the funeral. Indeed, I conveyed my feelings to those around me. I now realize that this was insensitive and insolent."

The *rav* listened to the man and said, "There is a process cited in the *Shulchan Aruch* which must be carried out in the event the individual who was shamed is deceased. You must go to the *kever,* grave, of *Rav* Moshe and assemble a *minyan* of ten men, and ask *mechilah,* beg forgiveness, of his *neshamah,* soul." The man followed the *rav's* instructions. Soon after, he was healed of his headaches.

פרשת קרח
Parashas Korach

ויקח קרח
And Korach separated / took himself. (16:1)

orach's rebellion, first against Moshe *Rabbeinu* and Aharon, and afterwards against Hashem, serves as the paradigm of a *machlokes shelo l'shem Shomayim*, controversy not for the sake of Heaven. In *Pirkei Avos*, *Chazal* teach us that a *machlokes shehee l'shem Shomayim sofah l'hiskayem*, a controversy that is for the sake of Heaven will endure.

Regrettably, many people often delude themselves into thinking that they are entering a dispute for a noble purpose, but are actually being misled by their own *yetzer hara*, evil-inclination. How is one to determine if one's dispute is for the sake of Heaven? How is one to discern between what is noble and holy and what is for purposes of self-esteem in order to carry out a personal agenda? Actually, *Chazal* teach us the answer when they say, "What is a *machlokes l'shem Shomayim*? This is the *machlokes* between Hillel and Shamai."

Horav Yonasan Eibeshitz, zl, in his *Yaaros Devash* explains that if the two antagonists see eye to eye in everything else other than the subject of their dispute; if they are close *friends b'lev v'nefesh*, in heart and soul, and their only discord is in regard to this one area, then they are like Hillel and Shamai, who loved each other and whose family members married one another. If the dispute, however, extends beyond the subject matter and the two parties do not talk but rather attack each other — disparaging, slandering, demeaning one another — then it is **not** a *machlokes l'shem Shomayim*.

This is a simple — but practical — criterion, one that is often ignored in the fiery passion of a *machlokes*. Another practical test is to question one's motives. Does he seek to win, or does he seek the truth? What if the other side is proven correct? Can he handle losing — or will he be content to see that the truth wins out? Will he be happy for his friend if he wins? Alternatively, will he be happy if his friend loses the dispute? If his friend's loss brings him joy, or if he just fights to win and cannot tolerate losing, his motives are not for the sake of Heaven. They are for himself. Heaven is his excuse — not his purpose.

✽ ✽ ✽ ✽ ✽ ✽

ויקח קרח...ודתן ואבירם... ואון בן פלת בני ראובן

And Korach separated / took himself... and Dasan and Aviram... and On ben Peles sons of Reuven. (16:1)

The *Rebbe* of a group of *chassidim,* who were also followers of *Horav Chaim Soloveitchik, zl,* passed away. His son, who was the designated heir, was not able to assume the mantel of leadership. It was just too much for him, both physically and emotionally. There were two grandsons who were prepared to take the position, but their personalities were different from one another. One of the grandsons was particularly extreme in one area. Although the majority of the *Rebbe's* followers were inclined to accept him, some of the *chassidim* were not prepared to accept his extreme nature. They were in a quandary as to whom to accept as the new *Rebbe.* Being close to *Rav* Chaim, they turned to him for advice. The question was: Do they accept the grandson, who — for the most part — seemed agreeable to everyone, except for his one area of extremism, or do they follow the other grandson?

Rav Chaim listened to their query, went over to his bookcase and removed a *Chumash.* He turned to *Parashas Korach* and asked, "The *parshah* begins by mentioning On *ben* Peles at the outset of the rebellion and then, suddenly, his name disappears. What happened to him? *Chazal* tell us that On's wife saved him with some practical advice. She said, 'What difference does it make if Moshe is the leader or Korach is the leader? You are still nothing more than the student, a nondescript insignificant aide.'"

Now, let us analyze this assertion. Korach and Moshe *Rabbeinu* were not in a dispute over who would be *Klal Yisrael's* leader. There was a much deeper question. Korach claimed that Hashem listened to Moshe because of his righteousness: *Tzaddik gozer v'Hakadosh Baruch Hu mekayem*, "The righteous decree and Hashem fulfills their demand." He asserted that Moshe was leading the nation according to his vested interests. Moshe countered that this claim was ludicrous and could not be further from the truth. Everything that he did was consistent with the *dvar*, word, of Hashem. He was merely Hashem's agent. A controversy of such a critical nature cannot and should not be discredited with a mere statement, however practical, from On's wife. This was no simple dispute.

Rav Chaim explained that On's wife made a very compelling declaration. She countered, "How do you know that if Moshe was deposed and Korach became the *Kohen Gadol*, that this new leader would not have *his* own agenda? You forget that when one sits in the seat of power, he sees things differently. His perspective is not the same as that of the fellow on the street. You might be surprised to discover that Moshe actually knew what he was doing!" When people do not see the entire picture, they cannot develop a clear plan of action. It is always easy to decide world events from the vantage point of the kitchen table. On's wife understood that it is easy to question a leader's decision as long as one does not look at the larger picture — the perspective as viewed from behind his desk.

Rav Chaim turned to the *chassidim* and said, "You are not totally in favor of one grandson because you do not agree with the way he acts in a certain area, while the other grandson does not seem to have this extremism. How do you know, however, that once the second grandson becomes *Rebbe,* he will not change his position? I suggest that you desist from the controversy and allow the majority to rule."

❋ ❋ ❋ ❋ ❋ ❋

ויקח קרח בן יצהר בן קהת בן לוי

Korach ben Yitzhar ben Kehas ben Levi separated / took himself. **(16:1)**

*R*ashi explains that Korach's genealogy stops with Levi and does not list Yaakov *Avinu* as the Patriarch of the family, because Yaakov prayed on his deathbed that his name be omitted, so as not to be associated with Korach's assembly. Actually, what difference does it make if Yaakov's name is mentioned or not? Is it really a taint on his honor to be listed together with a descendant who became corrupt? Are we to believe that

Yaakov was so concerned with his honor? *Horav Elazar M. Shach, zl,* derives from here that the Heavenly Tribunal has a much different way of reckoning than we do in the earthly domain. We will have to answer for areas of neglect that under normal circumstances we would otherwise overlook.

The *Rambam* in *Hilchos Teshuvah* 3:2 asserts that we do not necessarily understand the balance of sins and merits. In Heaven, the total is adjudicated and deciphered in a manner that does not coincide with the earthly domain. Thus, we should be meticulous to apply ourselves to <u>every</u> detail in our life's endeavor. What we might view as miniscule might be viewed in the Heavenly domain as significant, having great bearing on our ultimate judgment. Hashem might judge one individual for his grandson's negative activity because had he been more circumspect with his own son's education, his grandson might have demonstrated a more positive attitude to Torah and *mitzvos*. If the grandfather neglects his son's *Torah* education, what can we truly expect from the third generation?

Yaakov *Avinu* was concerned that history might hold him responsible for his grandson's rebellion. He, therefore, requested that his name be omitted from Korach's genealogy as a way of declaring that he had nothing whatsoever to do with Korach's dastardly act. His *chinuch* was pure and untainted. Whatever character flaws contributed to Korach's malevolence originated in the subsequent generation.

✹ ✹ ✹ ✹ ✹ ✹

ויקמו לפני משה
They arose before Moshe. (16:2)

One would think that they arose with *derech eretz*, respect. The *Targum Yonasan* says *kamu b'chuzpah*, they arose with audacity, calling attention to the fact that they were getting up for Moshe. *Horav Elazar M. Shach, zl,* relates that once the two *geonei ha'dor*, preeminent *Torah* leaders of their generation, *Horav Akiva Eiger, zl,* and *Horav Yaakov, zl, m'Lisa,* the *Nesivos HaMishpat,* were taking a stroll. They walked by a group of uncouth ruffians who were sitting on a bench. The young delinquents demonstrated their lack of respect by not rising when the two *gedolim* walked by. *Rav* Yaakov turned to *Rav* Akiva Eiger and said, "It seems that we have reached the *Ikvesa D'Moshicha*, the period preceding the advent of *Moshiach*, about which *Chazal* say, *chutzpah yasgi*, "the people will be filled with audacity." *Rav* Akiva Eiger countered, "They are still far removed from the type of *chutzpah* which will plague the generations preceding *Moshiach*. Now we walk by, and those derelicts do not get up. During the period prior to *Moshiach, we* will be sitting on stools, they will go by and if we do not rise for them, *they* will say about us that *we* have *chutzpah*!"

We must take into consideration that *Rav* Akiva Eiger said this quite some time ago — and his perspective was apparently very realistic, seeing into the future what unfortunately seems to have become true. Regrettably, there are those who think that *chutzpah yasgi* is a *mitzvah* that has to be fulfilled with all the *hidurim*. They forget it is only a condition which mirrors the society in which we live.

✳ ✳ ✳ ✳ ✳ ✳

לא חמור אחד מהם נשאתי ולא הרעתי את אחד מהם

"I have not taken even a single donkey of theirs, nor have I wronged even one of them." (16:15)

*M*aaseh avos siman l'banim, "the actions of the fathers are a portent for the children." This axiom applies to *machlokes*, controversy, as well. Korach may well have been the first to undermine and rebel against a Jewish leader. He certainly was not the last. The *Bostoner Rebbe, Shlita*, notes that Shmuel *HaNavi*, as he turned over the kingdom to Shaul *Ha'melech*, used the same words that Moshe used: "Bear witness against me...whose ox have I taken? Whose donkey have I taken? Who have I defrauded and oppressed?" (*Shmuel* I 12:3). The people replied that Shmuel had not deprived or oppressed them.

Imagine after a lifetime of service to *Klal Yisrael*, the best Shmuel *HaNavi* could ask for was not gratitude, not praise, but, "Yes — you were not a thief. Yes — you did not oppress us." With this in mind, communal leaders come to the fore, perform their function, whether it is teaching, leading, advising or guiding, knowing fully well that gratitude is something they can only hope for from a unique minority. They do not expect much in the way of praise. Instead, they become quite accustomed to the complaints, high expectations and subtle abuse. It is worse when the perpetrator is someone whom they have really helped. That is life and this attitude goes with the territory. Why should we expect to be different than Moshe *Rabbeinu*?

What really is the cause of dissent? Why is it that the same people who benefit the most from his leadership are the very individuals who go out of their way to sabotage everything that leader does? The answer is they cannot tolerate the fact that they had been helped by someone, that they were weak and had to turn to someone else for assistance. For some people, gratitude is an overwhelming debt. One who is weak is not hated. One who is poor is not vilified. It is the powerful and mighty that are disparaged. Those who are in a position of supremacy — who are popular because of the wonderful things they do for others — they are slandered. Why? What did they do to deserve such a malignant reaction? Why did Moshe *Rabbeinu*, the *Adon HaNeviim*, master of prophets, *Klal Yisrael's* quintessential leader, a person whose every moment was devoted to his flock, deserve to have a Korach impugn his leadership?

The answer is that he did not deserve it, but, regrettably, it was a natural reaction of *simple* people. Their disagreement with Moshe was perhaps genuine by a small percentage, but mostly it was a matter of envy and insecurity. No one can forgive his protector. There is no loathing that any man harbors more intensely than that toward his benefactor. It may sound cynical, but one only has to peruse history to note a constant hatred towards one's sponsor. No one likes to be on the receiving end, but then, they are not waiting in line to dispense aid to others, either.

זאת התורה אדם כי ימות באהל

This is the teaching regarding a man if he will die in a tent. (19:14)

I n the *Talmud Berachos* 63b, *Chazal* interpret this *pasuk* homiletically. "*Reish Lakish* says the words of *Torah* endure only for one who kills himself for it, as it says, 'This is the Torah/teaching (regarding) a man if he would die in a tent.'" The commentators suggest varied explanations for the meaning of *Chazal's* statement. The *Chafetz Chaim, zl,* explains that *Chazal* are intimating that one must be meticulous about his time and how he spends it. Every free moment should be dedicated to Torah study. He gives the following analogy: A wealthy businessman, who would spend the greater part of his waking hours immersed in business activity, finally came to the realization that he was literally wasting his time. His *davening* was no longer a spiritual experience. He ran into *shul* and then ran out — during those days that he even *made time* to attend. Torah study was a thing of the past. The years passed, and he now realized that before long he would have to give a reckoning to the Heavenly Tribunal about how he had spent his days in this world. He decided that from now on, he would change his *seder ha'yom*, daily schedule.

The next day, he did not rush through his *davening*. Afterwards, he sat and learned for two hours. When he arrived at the business three hours late, his wife questioned his tardiness. He made up an excuse, because he was not yet ready for an altercation. This continued for a number of weeks. He was running out of excuses, and his wife was tiring of being alone in the store. One day, her patience ran out, and she decided to search the city to find out what he was doing with his precious time. When she discovered her husband in the *bais ha'medrash,* immersed in the sea of *Talmud*, she became upset.

"Why are you studying Torah at a time when the store is filled with customers? Where is your sense of *achrayos*, responsibility, to the community?" she asked, quite upset.

The husband calmly looked into his wife's eyes and replied, "My dear, what would you do if one day the angel of death paid me a visit and took me from this world? Would you tell him that the store is filled with customers? You know you cannot argue with death. You would 'give *zich an eitzah*,' you would find a way around the problem. Therefore, make believe that every day I die for a few hours and will be resurrected after I complete my daily *seder*, schedule, of learning."

The *Chafetz Chaim* explains that every individual should view himself as "dead" and, thus, whatever excuses he might have had not to study Torah will no longer be available to him. *Horav Chaim Soloveitzhik, zl,* supplements this thought. Imagine, says *Rav* Chaim, that one day Hashem would allow all those who have passed away from this world to leave their graves for one hour and during that hour they would be allowed to do whatever they want. Once word would get out in this world, everybody would rush to the cemetery to greet their long-lost relatives and friends to spend that special hour with them. We can imagine the surprise and shock on everyone's faces when, as soon as the graves opened up, the deceased all ran to the *bais ha'medrash* to study Torah for an hour. They would not have time for anything else! This is the meaning of what *Chazal* are telling us. The *Torah* endures only for he who views the time allotted to him in this world as a special gift, as if he was rising from the dead for a short while, and he has to make effective use of every second.

The *gedolei Yisrael*, Torah leaders of each generation, viewed "killing oneself for the study of Torah" as an imperative to study Torah under hardship and without the usual comforts that so many of us seek. The enjoyment should be derived from the Torah study itself, not the embellishments that one creates, so that the learning will conform to his comfort zone. In the preface to the *Biur HaGra* on *Shulchan Aruch*, the *Gaon m'Vilna's* sons relate the incredible level of *perishus* — abstinence from the pleasures of this world — and piety that their father achieved. From the moment he reached the age of *Bar-Mitzvah*, he never looked outside his four cubits. He ate a piece of stale bread soaked in water twice-a-day as his meals. Furthermore, he did not chew this bread, instead he swallowed it whole. He never slept more than two hours in the course of a 24-hour day. This was divided into four half-hour segments. During the half-hour "nap" his mouth would constantly be reviewing passages from the *Talmud* or *Midrash*. Three half-hours at night and one-half hour during the day was the extent of his daily sleep.

Horav Mendel Kaplan, zl, would say that Hashem counts the pain we suffer on His computer. The *Midrash* says that if someone toils in Torah until he needs his last bit of strength to drop onto his bed and fall asleep, then, when saliva begins to drip from his mouth, Hashem cherishes it like the incense offering in the *Bais HaMikdash.*

There is another form of killing oneself for Torah: overcoming difficulties in learning. There are students who have to struggle to understand the subject matter. For some, this causes humiliation and precludes success in learning. *Rav* Mendel would extol the qualities of one who was not discouraged by failure nor afraid to make mistakes. The humiliation should not be a deterrent in his quest for achievement in Torah knowledge. He would say that one who is injured in battle — or, in contemporary society, in a sporting event — will wear his bandage as a badge of honor. Similarly, when someone falls while trying to learn, it is to his credit. He would encourage his *talmidim,* students, "Do not be afraid to make mistakes. One does not succeed from getting honors — only from humiliation. You should act in *shiur* like you do on the basketball court. Do not be afraid to shoot the ball because you might miss. You have to accept embarrassment for Torah. By nature, honor feels good and it might even make you feel stronger, but it is a *segulah,* talisman, to humiliate yourself for Torah."

זאת התורה אדם כי ימות באהל

This is the teaching/Torah regarding a man if he will die in a tent. **(19:14)**

T he *Chida* cites the *Panim Meiros* who gives the following interpretation for this *pasuk.* "This is the Torah" — this is one of the unique qualities of the Torah; "a man if he will die" — even if a person were to die; "in a tent" — he still remains in the tent of Torah." Since his Torah thoughts are being related to others, it is considered as if his lips are speaking from the grave. The *Chida* adds that this applies to everyone whose name is mentioned; even if a number of citations are made from one who heard from another, who heard from the original source, they all receive the merit of having their lips speak from the grave. The *Ben Ish Chai* cites the *Maharsha* who posits that one can be *mechayeh meisim*, resurrect the dead, even in contemporary times. How? When one cites *divrei Torah*, words of Torah, from the deceased, he causes his lips to speak from the grave, thereby creating a vehicle through which the deceased momentarily lives on. *Horav Chaim Palagi, zl,* writes that if the *Torah* thoughts of a deceased are cited in his name, his *neshamah*, soul, is transported from its Heavenly abode to the place where his Torah thoughts are being cited.

A Heavenly angel once appeared to the *Bais Yosef* and said, "Last night you analyzed and correctly interpreted the words of the *Rambam*. The *Rambam* was so pleased that he said that when you pass from this world, he will come to greet and escort you to your place in *Gan Eden*."

The *Maginei Shlomo* was written for the purpose of resolving the difficult passages in *Rashi* which the *Baalei Tosfos* dispute and question. In the preface to the *sefer,* written by his grandson it is related that the author once commented to his students that *Rashi* had appeared to him in a dream and said, "Because you trouble yourself to save me from the powerful and brilliant lions of Torah, the *Baalei Tosfos*, I, together with my students, will come greet you in *Olam Haba*, the World To Come." On the day of the *Maginei Shlomo's petirah*, passing, approximately one half-hour before his soul left its earthly abode, he lay in bed surrounded by a group of Torah scholars. He looked up and said, "Make room for the light of *Yisrael*, *Rabbeinu* Shlomo Yitzchaki, *Rashi*, who has arrived with his entourage to accompany me on my journey to the next world. I stood by his side throughout the years to elucidate his commentary and resolve the challenges posed by the *Baalei Tosfos,* so now he is compensating me."

In his preface to the *Mekor Baruch*, *Horav Nachum Ginzberg, zl,* writes that he had once met *Horav Meir Simchah, zl, m'Dvinsk*, the *Ohr Sameiach,* who appeared overjoyed, his face shining. *Rav* Meir Simchah related that earlier that day he had the *zchus*, merit, to develop a brilliant novellae which he felt was *l'amitah shel Torah*, coincided with the truthful essence of the Torah. Shortly thereafter, he dozed off and dreamt that he was witness to an assembly in Heaven attended by the greatest Torah luminaries.

They were lamenting the fact that in the material world there was no one who was writing Torah thoughts and novellae that correlated with the Divine Truth. Suddenly, the *Rashba* arose and declared that in the city of Dvinsk, there is a *rav* who is more successful than he had been in concurring his novellae with the Divine Truth. The *Rashba* was referring to a question he had on a passage in the *Talmud* which led him subsequently to posit that the text was in error and should be erased. The *Ohr Sameiach*, however, was able to explicate the passage brilliantly.

Horav Chaim Palagi, zl, writes that one who contributes toward the publishing of a *sefer* will eventually sit next to the author in *Gan Eden*. It was his contribution that enabled the lips of the author to speak from the grave. He, therefore, shares in the reward.

✳ ✳ ✳ ✳ ✳ ✳

וירב העם עם משה...ולו גוענו בגוע אחינו לפני ד'...קח את המטה והקהל את
העדה...ודברתם אל הסלע לעיניהם ונתן מימיו

The people quarreled with Moshe..."If only we had perished as our brethren perished before Hashem..." "Take the staff and gather together the assembly...and speak to the rock before their eyes and it shall give its waters." (20:3,8)

The commentators have varied approaches for explaining Moshe *Rabbeinu's* "sin." They seem to ignore the genesis of this sin — what led up to it and what was the spiritual climate at the time. *Horav S.R. Hirsch, zl,* focuses upon the background, so that we have a better perspective of what occurred and why. Actually, this was not the first time the people complained about a lack of water. They did so earlier in their sojourn. At that time, Hashem instructed Moshe to take the *mateh*, staff, and *strike* the stone, so that water would emerge. He did. It gave forth water, and everybody was happy. What happened this time? Why was Moshe told to *speak* to the stone rather than strike it? Furthermore, what did they mean when they said, "If only we had perished, as our brethren perished before Hashem?"

Rav Hirsch notes that after the victory over Amalek, we do not find the staff in Moshe's hands again. The staff of G-d in Moshe's hands signifies that he is being sent by Hashem to perform an act that is a direct intervention of Hashem. Moshe is *following* orders and *carrying out* the will of the Almighty. The people felt that by bringing them to this waterless place, Moshe and Aharon were betraying their mission from Hashem. It was not in accordance with His will that they ended up in this place. Hashem would never have led them to a place where they would die of thirst.

Hearing this, Hashem instructed Moshe to "take the staff" — show the people that you represent Me and that they are here as a result of My will. "Gather together the assembly" refers to the assembly of the future, those who would be the future of *Klal Yisrael*: Let them see how you *speak* to the rock. A blow with the staff, as had occurred many years earlier, would give the impression that the water was the result of a fresh intervention by Hashem in response to the people's complaint. This was not to be. It was necessary for the people to realize that it was Hashem who led them to this place — not Moshe and Aharon. They also had to be taught that it was not their uproar that catalyzed Hashem's intervention. No! The water had already been provided for them by Hashem *before* they came. It only required a few words from Moshe to make it flow freely to the people. It was not a fresh miracle, but rather a few well-placed words from Moshe was all that was necessary to bring forth their undeniable present requirements.

This manner of obtaining water from the rock — speaking — would have convinced the people of the profound error they had committed in maligning Moshe and Aharon by accusing them of leading them to this waterless place against the will of G-d. Whereas the water gushing forth only as a result of the blow with the staff could still leave room for one to err. They would say that their having been led to this place was originally a willful, arbitrary act of Moshe and Aharon, and that only their subsequent revolt brought about a merciful miracle from Hashem.

The message was clear: Moshe was instructed to take the staff, the same staff that he had not used for forty years. He was to show the people that the staff still existed; he was still Hashem's messenger. As they stood at the threshold of *Eretz Yisrael,* however, with a new future awaiting them, they had to become aware of a new form of "staff," the **word** of Moshe — and the Moshes of every generation — was to be the symbol of Hashem's constant supervision over the nation. The period of *nissim geluim*, overt miracles, was coming to an end. Henceforth, they would be under the guidance of *nissim nistarim*, covert, but no less miraculous miracles. The *dvar Torah*, word of Torah, would replace the staff, as it would bring forth sweet water from a stone. Regrettably, the lesson was not learned.

❋ ❋ ❋ ❋ ❋ ❋

לכן לא תביאו את הקהל הזה אל הארץ

"Therefore, you will not bring this congregation to the land." (20:12)

The opportunity to enter *Eretz Yisrael* together with the nation was taken away from Moshe *Rabbeinu*. What a tragic punishment for a man who had reached the zenith of spirituality, the quintessential leader of *Klal Yisrael*, whose great hope and desire was to enter the land. Why? What did Moshe do that sealed his fate? True, the Torah details his sin which is discussed and explained by the commentators. There must have been something else, however, something that he could have, and should have, done that might have catalyzed a last minute reprieve. What was it?

In the *Midrash* to *Sefer Devarim*, *Chazal* say that when Hashem saw Moshe "weighing" the decree for a moment and did not *immediately* respond with prayer, Hashem then made an oath that Moshe would never enter the land. *Horav Eliyahu Lopian, zl*, derives a compelling lesson from here. If Moshe *Rabbeinu* would have supplicated Hashem *immediately* upon hearing the decree against him, he would have succeeded in averting the decree. It is only because he relied on his ability to pray *later* that all of his five hundred and fifteen prayers were not accepted.

Those few moments changed the course of Jewish history. Had Moshe prayed immediately, he would have received permission to enter *Eretz Yisrael*. *Chazal* teach us that had Moshe entered *Eretz Yisrael* and succeeded in building the *Bais HaMikdash*, it never would have been destroyed. History would have been altered forever! No exile; no Inquisition; no Holocaust! All because of a few moments that demonstrated a lack of alacrity.

Zerizus, alacrity, indicates love. It displays that a person cares. He cannot wait to perform Hashem's will. Avraham *Avinu* was told to sacrifice his beloved Yitzchak. He did not tarry or dawdle. He went to do it with alacrity, with enthusiasm, with love. Those few minutes made the difference.

This idea applies equally to all of us. We can go to *davening* just making it in time to put on *Tallis* and *Tefillin* before *Barchu*, or, alternatively, we can come to *shul* early and prepare ourselves to greet Hashem through prayer. If we want our *davening* to reach its potential, we must demonstrate what it really means to us.

Regrettably, when we arrive late, consider the thinking that we manifest.

וירא בלק בן צפור

Balak ben Tzipor saw. **(22:2)**

T he *Midrash* relates that Hashem foresaw that the gentile nations
might claim that they adopted their lifestyle because they were
lacking leadership. He, therefore, provided them with leadership
that was both powerful and brilliant. When he established Shlomo *Ha'melech*
as monarch, he provided the pagans with Nevuchadnezer. Shlomo built the
Bais HaMikdash, while his counterpart destroyed it. He gave great wealth to
David *Ha'melech*, who used it to build the *Bais HaMikdash*. Hashem also
provided Haman with great wealth, which he used in an attempt to destroy
the Jewish nation. Hashem provided the Jewish People with a great *navi*,
prophet, Moshe *Rabbeinu*. The pagans were also afforded a distinguished
prophet, Bilaam, who did everything possible to catalyze the downfall of
Klal Yisrael. This all demonstrates that, despite what Hashem did for the
nations, they were not able to sustain it. In fact, they extirpated whatever
opportunities Hashem granted them. Yet, when we consider the situation,
they still have a legitimate reason to gripe about their circumstances. They
could postulate that while Hashem provided the Jewish nation with righteous
and noble leadership, He furnished the other nations with leadership that was
wicked, evil and immoral. How could the pagans be expected to repent under
the leadership of a man with the character of Bilaam, who redefined
hedonism and took evil to a new low?

Otzros HaTorah cites the *Lev Aharon* who explains that prior to
giving the Torah to *Klal Yisrael*, Hashem first went to every other nation and
offered it to them. They flatly refused to accept it for various reasons,
basically because the values of Torah were not consistent with their
weltenshauung, world perspective, and national character. Nonetheless, they
still demanded a prophet of the caliber of Moshe. They received what they
had requested — a prophet without *Torah*. Bilaam probably had some
incredible qualities, but, without Torah, they were meaningless. Hashem's
response to the nations of the world is simple, "You want to repent and

change your ways without the Torah? Impossible!" No prophet or any leader can create a lasting spiritual metamorphosis unless it is based on Torah.

❊ ❊ ❊ ❊ ❊ ❊

ויאמר אליהם לינו פה הלילה והשבתי אתכם דבר כאשר דבר ד' אלי

He (Bilaam) said to them, "Spend the night here and I will give you a response, as Hashem will speak to me." (22:8)

Bilaam, the consummate liar, presents himself as a saint. He will do nothing without the express permission of G-d. Typical of his sinful demeanor, he continues reiterating his total deference to the Almighty. Indeed, his bogus personality, his ersatz character, is his greatest mark of evil. It is one thing to carry out evil, but to dress it up as an act of piety and virtuosity is the nadir of shamelessness. At least Bilaam was following the legacy bestowed upon him by his ancestor Lavan *HoArami*, the virtuosic swindler who transformed evil into an art. Bilaam had no qualms about cursing *Klal Yisrael*. His intense hatred for Hashem's People burned within him. Yet, he would never go against Hashem. He had to find a way to demonstrate his iniquity while preserving his sense of righteousness. It was necessary for him to find a *heter*, dispensation, to destroy our nation.

Bilaam thought that he could get away with his swindling. In the end, however, whom did he really succeed in fooling? Only one person — himself. When one lies enough, he begins to believe his own lies. When one attempts to fool those around him, by presenting himself as a righteous person — when, in reality, he is nothing more than a chameleon — he fools himself. He begins to believe that he is righteous! Bilaam asked to die as a righteous and just person. That is hypocrisy at its lowest point! He actually believed that he was worthy of sainthood!

Horav Avigdor Halevi Nebentzhal, Shlita, posits that the reason the Torah relates the episode about Bilaam is that a little bit of Bilaam lurks within the recesses of each one of us. Each of us has to contend with his own hypocritical nature and inconsistencies. The "Bilaam factor" is alive and well within all of us. The only question is: How much? We fool ourselves — for what purpose? It is related that an *Admor, chassidic Rebbe,* once asked one of his *chassidim* who had sinned and attempted to gloss over his iniquity,

"Whom do you think you are fooling? You cannot fool Hashem. You also cannot fool all of the people around you. Apparently the only person whom you might succeed in fooling is yourself. What do you gain by fooling a fool?" This idea is regrettably true concerning each one of us.

The people of Sodom exemplified this form of evil. *Chazal* tell us that the Sodomites were very clever. They invited poor people to their community. They even gave freely of their money to the poor, making sure to mark each one of the coins that they gave to the poor. There was, however, one clause in their charity policy: No one was allowed to sell food to a poor man. Consequently, when people perished from starvation, they would retrieve their coins. Then there is the story of the bed that was set aside for guests. If the traveler was too tall for the bed, his legs were shortened. If he was too short, they would stretch him. *Rav* Nebentzhal contends that some of us use the Sodom bed as an analogy to the Torah. The Torah has to fit into our lifestyle. When its *mitzvos* are too much, we shorten the Torah. We make it fit into our purview, consistent with our needs and values. In the end, we are only fooling ourselves.

✱ ✱ ✱ ✱ ✱ ✱

הן עם כלביא יקום וכארי יתנשא לא ישכב עד יאכל טרף

"Behold! A people who will rise like a lion cub and raise itself like a lion; it will not lie down until it consumes prey." (23:24)

The Holocaust transformed the proud Jewish nation into homeless wanderers. Throughout his powerful homilies, The *Piazsesner Rebbe, zl,* attempts to console and sustain his brokenhearted *chassidim* with the idea that their present circumstance was already foreshadowed in the very manner that the Torah was given. Moreover, the opportunity to serve Hashem is available anywhere, even in the ghetto. Included in his *derashos,* homilies, are a number of themes to strengthen the inner resources of his people. He focuses on the nobility that the Jewish heritage confers on us. Our pedigree must remind us that we are princes and, even when the Nazi dogs beat and attempt to degrade us, we are still nobility and should act in a consistent manner. He writes that not only is the Jewish spirit holy, even the very body of a Jew is unique in its sanctity.

In his *derashah* to *Parashas Balak,* he posits that — unlike the rest of Creation, which was created by the Divine word — *Klal Yisrael* was created directly by the hands of Hashem. Therefore, a Jew's holiness extends to all levels of his existence, even the physical. Actually, in his commentary to *Bereishis* 1:27, "And G-d created man in His image," *Rashi* says, "Everything else was created by the Divine word, but man was created by the Divine hands." What does this mean? One would think that being created by Divine speech is a higher level than being created by the physical action of hands. How is it then that man who stands at the pinnacle of Creation was created by hand, while the rest of Creation was created by Divine speech?

The *Piazsesner* explains that for all other creations, the holiness did not extend from Above all the way to their very essence; it remained in the realm of words. For the Jew, however, holiness extended even into his lowest level, the level of physicality and action. He was created by the Divine hands, so that he is entirely holy.

This is also why *Klal Yisrael* is considered to be the eternal people. Everything was created by Divine speech, by means of a word that remains above and beyond them, which shines upon them only from afar. The light is not permanently available within them; it flashes like lightning, giving temporary illumination. *Klal Yisrael* however, was created with the Divine hands, so that the Divine sanctity penetrates to their level of physical action and to whatever place they may be found. Hence, as a nation, we are eternal and even the individual physical body of the Jew is eternal. When he expends his energies for Torah study and *mitzvah* observance, that physical energy becomes integrated with the Torah and Divine source. Thus, his body rises to the world of eternity and remains eternal. Only the foods which the individual ate throughout his life — and which were added to his body — are subject to decomposition and decay.

Thus, the Jew is able to strengthen himself during periods of travail, so that even when he lies down, he is not fallen. Even in his low state, he is still able to vanquish his enemies. He was created with the Divine hands which causes his holiness to extend to his Jewish essence. This is the underlying meaning of Bilaam's blessing. The Jew rises and strengthens himself like a lion. He does not fall down completely; he just crouches. Despite this position, he can triumph over his enemies. He rises like a lion, even during the most difficult troubles; under the most compelling duress, he leaps up like the king of beasts.

At a time when the Jew's body was both attacked and maligned, the *Rebbe* emphasizes the solid affirmation of the corporeal holiness of the Jew. In both his physical and spiritual essence, the Jew is holy and eternal; he represents the Divine light hidden in all reality. It is specifically for this reason that he is despised, such that attempts are constantly made to destroy him. It is precisely for this same reason, however, that the Jew's dignity is inviolable, his nobility is sacrosanct, and his survival and ultimate triumph is assured: *Mi k'amcha Yisrael,* "Who is like Your Nation — Yisrael?"

Jewish resilience is a character trait endemic to *Klal Yisrael.* The ability to pick oneself up, shake off the dirt and go on, is something inherently Jewish. In *Moed Katan* 9b the *Talmud* cites the following story: Rabbi Shimon *bar* Yochai told his son to approach two of his disciples and ask them for a blessing. His son was baffled by with the blessings he received. They began with what seemed to be an ambiguous blessing, such as, "May you plant and not harvest," which was interpreted as, "May you have children, and may they not die." In the *Sefer HaChaim,* the brother of the *Maharal m'Prague* wonders why these wise men gave a blessing which sounded like a curse. Why did they not give an unambiguous blessing? He explains that this world is the world of hardship and *yissurim,* anguish. It is normal for every individual to experience the vicissitudes of life. When the wise men said, "May it be the will," they were not referring to Hashem's will, but rather, "May this be *your* will." They meant that you should desire these problems and prepare yourself for any eventuality that may arise, because that is the way of the world.

Horav Gedalya Eiseman, Shlita, comments that most of the damage caused by hardship results from not anticipating it. If people would prepare themselves for possible hardship, accepting the fact that life is tough and that trials and tribulations are to be expected as part of normal living — realizing that everyone suffers in one way or another — they would have an easier time coping with adversity.

Intellectual awareness of the truth is not enough. It is necessary that one live his life *feeling* this awareness in his psyche. This requires self-discipline and practice. Indeed, the *Alter, zl, m'Kelm* listed among his goals for character perfection the resolution to train himself not to expect everything to go his way.

✱✱✱✱✱✱

יזל מים מדליו

"Water will flow from his buckets / wells." (24:7)

I n the *Talmud Nedarim* 81a, *Chazal* say, "Take heed with the sons of the poor, for from them Torah will go forth, as it is stated, "Water shall flow *midalyo,* 'from his wells,' which can alternatively be read *mi dalav,* 'from his poor.' Thus the *pasuk* means: Torah, which is compared to water, shall flow from *Klal Yisrael's* poor. *Horav Eliezer M. Shach, zl,* would relate the story concerning a very wealthy and powerful man from a town near Kovno who sought a husband for his daughter. He was prepared to offer complete support, so that the young man could become a *posek, halachic* arbitrator, of such a caliber that he would ascend to a distinguished pulpit.

He was presented with two young men, both brilliant and erudite, but from diverse backgrounds. One was descended from an illustrious lineage of famous rabbinic scholars. The other young scholar came from a simple home, simple pedigree and simple surroundings. Not knowing what to do, he went to the preeminent Torah scholar and *Rav* of Kovno, *Horav Yitzchak Elchanan Spektor,* asking for guidance in this dilemma. He described both young men, adding that his personal choice was the one whose background was most impressive, despite the fact that this young man's parents insisted on receiving a very hefty dowry.

Rav Yitzchak Elchanan told him, "If you ask my opinion, I suggest that you select the young man who hails from a simple background. Why? Because the young man who descends from Torah elite grew up in a home where Torah reigned paramount and its study and erudition was a way of life. His parents devoted their lives to raising him from day one to grow in Torah. It is no wonder that he is a Torah scholar. He simply followed in the manner of his breeding. If he were to be torn away from his parents' influence and would have to assume the yoke of family support on his *own* shoulders, would he be able to withstand the pressure? I do not know. The other young man, however, had to fight his entire life to overcome one obstacle after another, triumphing over life's challenges, in order to study Torah with proficiency and diligence. Such a young man is assured of a position."

פרשת פנחס
Parashas Pinchas

תנה לנו אחזה בתוך אחי אבינו

"Give us a possession (in Eretz Yisrael) among our father's brothers."
(27:4)

T he five daughters of Tzlafchad came to Moshe *Rabbeinu* with a *taanah*, complaint. They understood from the law that *Eretz Yisrael* was being divided up among the males of each family. Since their father had died without leaving any male offspring, they were concerned lest they be deprived of securing a portion of *Eretz Yisrael*. *Rashi* explains that their request was not motivated by a desire for financial gain, but rather by a passionate love for the Holy Land. This is why the *pasuk* traces their lineage back to Yosef *HaTzaddik*, whose love for *Eretz Yisrael* was boundless. The *meraglim*, spies, stand in contrast to *Bnos* Tzlafchad; they slandered the land because they lacked that intrinsic love for the country.

When someone cares deeply about an object, a person, a mission, or an organization, he will move heaven and earth to assure its success. His love forms the basis for his perspective and, concomitantly, his reaction. The *meraglim* described *Eretz Yisrael* as they saw it. They saw a country that was heavily fortified, cities that were inhabited by powerful giants and fruit that was unusual in its size. Wherever they went, they noticed that funerals were taking place. Everything *seemed* to be against them. They also forgot that Hashem, Who took them out of Egypt amidst the greatest miracles and wonders, had promised them that they would conquer the land. Had their *emunah* in Hashem been on an appropriate level, it would have overwhelmed whatever doubts regarding the land they might have harbored. Yehoshua and Calev, the two members of the spying mission who clung steadfastly to their conviction, had no problem believing in the successful result of their quest to inhabit the land.

The result depends upon one's attitude. When one views the land with love, when he believes that it is good — as *Bnos* Tzlafchad did — then any challenge that surfaces can, and will, be dealt with successfully. If the love for the land is apathetic, however, then any challenge that arises will generate a sense of hopelessness. The *meraglim's* lackluster feelings *towards Eretz Yisrael* reflected a deficiency in their spiritual character that lay at the foundation of their sin.

Love conquers whatever ambiguities one might have in regard to an endeavor. *Horav Avraham Pam, zl,* applies this concept to encourage *bnei Torah* to *shteig,* excel, and become great *talmidei chachamim,* Torah scholars. Many *bnei Torah* have the desire to achieve distinction in Torah erudition, whether it is in the area of *harbotzas Torah,* dissemination, or in *psak, halachic* arbitration. Regrettably, for many, these dreams remain nothing more than fantasies. What happens?

A young man assesses his capabilities and potential, realizing that he does not have what it takes to achieve greatness in Torah. He is confronted with uncertainties. He strives to teach and imbue others with a love of Torah, but, alas, he does not know if he has the necessary skills to perform this function. Will he find a decent position? Will he make a living, or will he have to scrounge from paycheck to paycheck? These and many other doubts enter the mind of a young person about to embark on the path that leads to greatness in Torah. These ambiguities can depress him to the point that he may give up before he even starts. He might choose a more secure and comfortable vocation. Of course, he would love to devote himself to a life of Torah, but so much uncertainty stands in his way.

Rav Pam posits that the source of this attitude is rooted in a lack of true *ahavas Torah,* love of Torah. One who *truly* desires distinction in Torah, whose love and passion for Torah is unequivocal, will not be bothered by doubts. Even for one whose level of intellectual acuity is limited, his desire and commitment will merit him great *Siyata d'Shmaya,* Divine assistance, to realize his goal. Hashem grants wisdom to he who desires and strives for it.

Love of Torah conquers questions of *parnassah,* livelihood. This does not suggest that one who dedicates himself to Torah will prosper materially. It only implies that the usual issues of material sustenance will not plague him. Hashem takes care of His own, of those whose love for His Torah transcend their material needs.

Last, *Rav* Pam comments that this principle is not reserved only for

Torah study. It applies to every area of spiritual endeavor. How often are we inspired to act on behalf of the community, in a spiritual endeavor, a *tzedakah* campaign, a neglected *mitzvah* awareness program, a *chesed* project, a *kiruv*, outreach, affair, only to be left with the inspiration and nothing else? We often perceive the need, and we have the tools and ability to carry out the task, but we withdraw at the last minute due to self-doubting. Will I succeed? Why has no one else undertaken this project? Will I receive community support? These and other doubts cross one's mind, and soon the self-doubting develops into a negative attitude, so that he rejects the plan. The fire of idealism has been extinguished by the feelings of ambiguity and uncertainty. *Bnos* Tzlafchad teach us a valuable lesson: When one loves something — nothing stands in the way. When someone cares about Torah, about *Klal Yisrael*, about the *Ribono Shel Olam*, he doesn't just talk — he acts.

✴ ✴ ✴ ✴ ✴ ✴

יפקד ד'... איש על העדה
"May Hashem… appoint a man over the assembly." (27:16)

It is related that when the *rav* of Slutzk, Poland, *Horav Yaakov David Ridvaz, zl,* was nearing death, the leaders of the community came to him to discuss the issue of a successor for the position of *rav*. After they left, his *rebbetzin* entered and implored him, "My dear husband, you are surely aware that our financial straits are, at best, terrible. Please ask the leaders of the community to see to it that we receive a greater stipend. There is no way we can go on like this."

Rav Yaakov David looked up at his wife and said, "Should I be different from Moshe, whose primary concern prior to his death was for the community of *Klal Yisrael* — not for his family? We do not find Moshe supplicating Hashem for his personal needs — only for the needs of his flock."

His *rebbetzin*, who was a wise and learned woman, responded "Perhaps, that is why his grandson, Shevuel *ben* Gershom, ended up as a priest for idols." (This is a reference to Yonasan *ben* Gershom, who was later called Shevuel after he "returned to Hashem.") Prior to his repentance, however, he served as a priest, since he refused to accept charity and was willing to do anything to satisfy his desire for money (*Bava Basra* 110a). When the *Ridvaz* heard this, he agreed with his wife and implored the lay leadership on behalf of his family.

This is not the place to discuss the propriety of her claim. Rather, this story is meant to point out that our spiritual leadership also has needs. A *rav* has a family, a *rosh yeshivah* has a wife and children. All too often, we think only of ourselves and the spiritual leader's obligation to serve *us*. Do we ever think about *his* family and his needs? We turn to them for advice regarding family situations, *shidduchim*, livelihood issues, problems with our children. Yet, do we ever stop to think that they also might have issues on their mind? To whom do *they* turn for advice, solace or a shoulder on which to cry? Do we ever take into consideration that the *rebbe* who teaches our children also has a family, and perhaps he has a situation at home that is taking its toll on him? The answer to all these questions is probably no. The reason is that we think that our spiritual leadership is here to serve us, and their circumstances are not our concern. While this is regrettable, it is probably true.

On second thought, getting back to the *Ridvaz*, he really should not have had to turn to his lay leadership for assistance. Had they been proper leaders, they would have cared enough about their *rav* to offer help on their own. I guess things have not changed much over the years.

✻ ✻ ✻ ✻ ✻ ✻

אשר יצא לפניהם ואשר יבא לפניהם ואשר יוציאם ואשר יביאם ולא תהיה
עדת ד' כצאן אשר אין להם רעה

"Who shall go out before them and come in before them, who shall take them out and bring them in; and let the assembly of Hashem not be like sheep that have no shepherd." (27:17)

The *Kesav Sofer* explains the distinction between a shepherd who shepherds sheep and a spiritual leader whose only focus is the welfare of his human flock. A shepherd has one goal — himself. Everything he does is to ensure that his flock retains its current value. His flock is nothing more than a means, a vehicle, to increase the shepherd's material wealth. The *roeh Yisrael's*, Jewish spiritual leader's, mindset is focused only on his people, their physical and spiritual welfare, their families and their concerns, both personal and general. The Torah leader is prepared to sacrifice his life for his people. He goes out before them, as he leads in times of danger. Unlike the shepherd — who, upon seeing a wolf runs for his life, leaving his flock open to danger — the Torah leader stands resolute and fearless in the face any problem or challenge which confronts his people. He goes *before* them and *remains* with them throughout their ordeal.

Horav Elchanan Wasserman, zl, the venerable *Rosh HaYeshivah* of Pre-World War II Baranovitz, exemplified this caliber of leadership. His devotion to *Klal Yisrael* in general, and his *yeshivah* community in particular, was legend. *Rav* Elchanan spent a good part of 1938 in America on behalf of his *yeshivah*. During this time, he crisscrossed the country reaching out to Jews, inspiring and encouraging them to strengthen their ties with *Hashem Yisborach*. The political situation in Europe was rapidly deteriorating. As *Rav* Elchanan packed his bags to return to Europe, the black clouds of war were ominously approaching. Given this dangerous situation, friends approached *Rav* Elchanan and implored him to stay in America. They suggested that perhaps he should even bring over his two sons who remained in Europe. *Rav* Elchanan rejected their plea, countering, "I do not have only two sons. I have four-hundred; all of the *yeshivah bachurim* are my sons. How can I leave them?" The *Rosh HaYeshivah* had decided that it was his moral obligation and duty to return to Poland, despite the imminent danger — even at the expense of his life. He would not listen to the many arguments that encouraged him to stay — for America's sake.

His rejoinder was simple, "I am a soldier; I have to go to the front." He changed planes in England, where the great sage *Horav Eliyahu Lopian, zl*, futilely attempted to convince him to stay in England. Even as he was boarding the plane, *Rav* Elyah begged *Rav* Elchanan to stay. *Rav* Elchanan answered with resolve, "We shall all have to endure *chibut ha'kever*, buffeting the grave. I want to suffer this together with my students."

The account of *Rav* Elchanan's last moments and that of the Baranovitch community have become the paradigm for *mesiras nefesh*, self-sacrifice. The Lithuanian terrorists entered the house where *Rav* Elchanan was hiding, searching for the rabbis who were "collaborating with the communists." *Rav* Elchanan was engrossed in learning together with his *chavrusa*, study partner. The terrorists then searched and humiliated him.

Rav Elchanan was fully aware of what was in store for him. Instead of fear and anxiety, his face brightened, exhibiting what could best be described as an angelic expression. The Jews who saw him then later described his countenance and demeanor as that of a great Torah leader preparing to give up his life *Al Kiddush Hashem*, to sanctify Hashem's Name.

Even the two savage Lithuanians who were his guards were struck by his visage and were filled with dread and awe. One of them was prepared to release the *Rosh HaYeshivah*. His partner, regrettably, refused, insisting that he be taken to the seventh fort together with the others.

While he was being led away, *Rav* Elchanan told his fellow captives, "Apparently they consider us *tzaddikim*, righteous people, in Heaven, for we have been selected to atone for *Klal Yisrael* with our lives. If so, we must repent completely, here and now. We must realize that our sacrifices will be more pleasing if accompanied by *teshuvah*, repentance, and we shall thereby save the lives of our brothers and sisters in America."

Rav Elchanan then exhorted them that martyrs must, in their last moments, expunge any impure thoughts from their minds, lest their sacrifice becomes invalidated. Hence, he focused on repentance and total devotion to Hashem.

Twenty-four hours later, the entire group was machine-gunned to death. It was a holy brotherhood — a community with its *yeshivah* — led by their beloved *Rosh HaYeshivah*, who would not leave them. As he lived with them so did he die with them, exemplifying a leader who goes out before them and comes in before them. As he cared for them in this world, *Rav* Elchanan accompanied his community to the World to Come.

"You shall place some of your majesty upon him." (27:20)

I n the *Talmud Bava Basra* 75a, *Chazal* derive from the word *meihodcha*, *some* of your majesty, that only a portion of Moshe *Rabbeinu's* majesty was being transferred to Yehoshua, but not all of it. They relate that when the *zekeinim*, elders, of that generation contemplated the difference between Moshe and Yehoshua, they would say that the face of Moshe was like the sun, while Yehoshua's face was like the moon. *Chazal* conclude with the statement, "Woe, for that shame! Woe for that disgrace!" What is the meaning of "that" shame and "that" disgrace? To what are *Chazal* referring?

The *Chida, zl*, gives a practical and timely answer to this question. Yehoshua merited to become Moshe's heir apparent and the next leader of *Klal Yisrael*, because he would arise early every morning and organize the benches in the *bais ha'medrash*. He would place the mats in their proper place in the morning and do this once again at the end of the day. He was the first to arrive and the last to leave, making sure that the menial labor involved in presenting a clean, organized *bais ha'medrash* was carried out personally by him. The elders, who probably were not prepared to do this menial labor at the time because it was not dignified, now regretted their earlier decision. What they previously thought was humiliating, they presently realized was a source of distinction. They now regretted "that" shame and "that" disgrace which they had refused to exhibit.

The *Tanna* in *Pirkei Avos* 4:8 says: "Whoever honors the Torah, will himself be honored by people." *Otzros HaTorah* infers from here that one who disgraces his honor, who is willing to humiliate himself for the sake of the Torah, will, in turn, achieve honor and esteem in the eyes of his fellow man. Indeed, *Chazal* teach us that King Achav merited to reign over *Klal Yisrael* for twenty- two years, because he accorded honor to the Torah which was given to *Klal Yisrael* through the medium of the twenty-two letters of the Hebrew alphabet.

It is related that *Rashi's* grandfather merited to have such a grandson that would light up the world with his commentary on Torah, because he used his beard to wipe off the dust in front of the *Aron HaKodesh*, Holy Ark. The *Tashbatz* would always make a point to dust off the *seforim* in the *bais ha'medrash*. It is related that it was revealed to him from Heaven that the *seforim* which he himself had authored, would never decay. Indeed, *Horav Chaim Kanievski, Shlita*, attested that he once found an original copy of the *Tashbatz*, and it was in perfect condition.

Horav Michel Yehudah Lefkowitz, Shlita, relates that he once went to be *menachem aveil*, comfort the bereaved, at a home where an elderly father had passed away and left over a family of sons who all were great *talmidei chachamin*, Torah scholars. He asked the sons to what they attributed their father's incredible *zchus*, merit, to have such distinguished offspring? They replied that their father was a simple carpenter, who would go to the *bais ha'medrash* and fix whatever benches or furniture needed repair, during his free time. Apparently, this man was no simple craftsman. His appreciation of Torah earned him the ultimate *Torah nachas*.

Parashas Matos

החלצו מאתכם אנשים לצבא ויהיו על מדין לתת נקמת ד' במדין... וישלח
אתם משה... ואת פינחס בן אלעזר הכהן לצבא

*"Arm men from among yourselves for the army that they be against
Midyan to inflict Hashem's vengeance against Midyan…" And Moshe sent
them… and Pinchas ben Elazar HaKohen, to the army.* (31:3,6)

ashi comments that Pinchas went along, so that he could avenge
Yosef, his mother's ancestor. This is a reference to the time when
the Midyanites sold Yosef. This statement demands clarification.
The Torah clearly states that the battle with Midyan was to be fought
exclusively *l'shem Shomayim*, for the sake of Heaven. No vestige of personal
interest was to play a role in any segment of the battle. Yet, Pinchas did
possess a personal interest aside from the national cause. The Midyanites had
participated in the sale of his maternal ancestor, Yosef. As *Rashi* indicates,
Pinchas was selected specifically because he had an issue to settle with
Midyan. It is intriguing that Moshe *Rabbeinu* would send Pinchas on a
mission that was to be carried out solely *l'shem Shomayim*, when, in fact, due
to his personal agenda, Pinchas would be lacking in his total devotion to
l'shem Shomayim.

Horav Mordechai Rogov, zl, derives from here that Pinchas was a
person whose focus was directed entirely toward Hashem. While,
undoubtedly, Pinchas had personal considerations for destroying Midyan, his
intentions were noble as he expunged any personal benefits which were to be
gained by his actions. This might be difficult for us to grasp, because, to the
average person, a division of allegiances is overwhelming. Pinchas, however,
was not an average person.

Rav Rogov adds that even when Pinchas fought in order to avenge
the honor and dignity of his ancestor, Yosef, he did not view the battle as
some form of personal vendetta, but, rather, as one fought for the national
honor of the Jewish People. Hence, avenging his honor was a step forward in

advancing the interests of the entire Jewish People. Pinchas' distinction was that he functioned on a plane in which his every intention was solely for the sake of Hashem.

Horav Yisrael Salanter, zl, once noted that there are two *mitzvos* which relate to the *Yom Kippur* fast. There is a *mitzvah* to eat on *Erev Yom Kippur* as well as to fast on *Yom Kippur.* It is definitely more difficult to eat on *Erev Yom Kippur l'shem Shomayim* than it is to fast on *Yom Kippur.* Eating on *Erev Yom Kippur* is a *mitzvah* that has a side-benefit: one is eating. Thus, to fulfill the *mitzvah* correctly, one must be oblivious to the benefits of the food that he is ingesting. To fast on *Yom Kippur,* however, is obviously *l'shem Shomayim,* because what other motive could one have for fasting?

When Pinchas prepared for battle with Midyan, his objective was clear and unequivocally *l'shem Shomayim.* He could have had other motives, but *Rashi* tells us that he did not. This was the character of the person whom Hashem refers to as *b'kano es kinaasi,* "when he zealously avenged *Me* [My vengeance]" (*Bamidbar* 25:11).

✴ ✴ ✴ ✴ ✴ ✴

והייתם נקים מד' ומישראל
"And you will be vindicated from Hashem and from Yisrael." (32:22)

We are exhorted not to give the appearance that we are sinning in any way. In the *Talmud Yoma* 38a, *Chazal* praise the Garmo family, who were the bakers of the *Lechem HaPanim,* Showbread, because there never was found among the members of their family any high-quality bread. This was done so that no one would ever suspect them of helping themselves to the Showbread. Their concern regarding what some jealous person might assert caused them to be extra-meticulous in their personal lifestyle.

Horav Yosef Chaim Sonnenfeld, zl, was known for exemplifying this trait. Never did he take advantage — nor did he permit any member of his family to benefit — of the numerous charity funds that went through his hands. This money was to be used to support the poor and needy of Yerushalayim. Even though he certainly came under the purview of the charity funds criteria, he would never personally benefit from it so as not to give anyone the opportunity to talk.

Indeed, once his own granddaughter, who had been orphaned at a young age, came to him and asked for support. She was about to marry a budding young *talmid chacham*, Torah scholar, who was penniless. She asked, "Of all the money that goes through your hands to sustain Yerushalayim's poor, can you not find something for your own granddaughter? Why should I be less entitled to receive assistance than anyone else?"

Rav Yosef Chaim was visibly moved by her tearful request, and replied in turn, "Please do not press me further. Would you want me to break the strict rules of conduct that I have imposed upon myself? For my entire life, I have never personally gained from the funds that I administer. These funds were entrusted to me to share with others — not with myself. Our Torah demands that one remain vindicated from Hashem and *Yisrael*. I am prepared to sell my bed and all my personal belongings to help you in your time of need, but I will not personally take advantage of the *tzedakah* money entrusted to me. I know how much you have suffered in your life, and you truly deserve Hashem's mercy. Go in peace, and may Hashem shine His countenance upon you and grant you much joy in life, so that the wealthiest girls in town will be envious of you."

Rav Yosef Chaim's blessing came to fruition. His granddaughter went on to become the matriarch of a noble and beautiful family, whose sons were included among the most illustrious Torah scholars in Yerushalayim. This source of pride and comfort was more valuable than anything money could buy.

Parashas Masei

את שלש הערים תתנו מעבר לירדן ואת שלש הערים תתנו בארץ כנען ערי
מקלט תהיינה

The three cities shall you designate on the [other] side of the Yarden, and three cities shall you designate in the Land of Canaan; they shall be cities of refuge. (35:14)

Rashi cites *Chazal* in the *Talmud Makos* 9a, who note that the number of Cities of Refuge in *Ever haYarden* was disproportionate to the number of residents. On the other side of the *Yarden* there were only two and one-half tribes, in contrast to the nine tribes that lived in *Eretz Yisrael*. *Chazal* explain that in Gilaad, which was in *Ever haYarden*, there were many killers. *Ramban* adds that although the Cities of Refuge were specifically for unintentional murderers, nonetheless, since there was a high incidence of intentional murder, it stands to reason that these murderers would attempt to conceal their malevolence by making their actions appear to be inadvertent. Alternatively, the *Maharal* explains that the mere fact that there were many intentional murderers in Gilaad indicates that there was a low regard for the value of human life. It, therefore, follows that those who were not murderers, simply tended to be negligent. Thus, there were many preventable, unintentionable killings in the area of *Ever haYarden*.

The environment in which one finds himself plays a compelling role in his spiritual progress. A good environment creates positive spiritual circumstances in which one can grow in his relationship with Hashem. In contrast, an atmosphere that is spiritually decadent will harm one's *neshamah*, soul. One would think that the effect of the environment is commensurate with one's *direct* involvement with its members and relative to his firsthand exposure to its endeavors. We derive from the *Maharal's* explanation that the influence of the environment goes much deeper and is much more infectious and far-reaching than we assume. The mere fact that killers live in a city diminishes the value of human life. One becomes aware that murder is not frowned upon as much in this community, since murderers are included among its citizenry. The individual slowly becomes desensitized to the sanctity and primacy of human life. Hence, an act of unintentional murder is something that does not affect him as much as it should. This catalyzes an increase in bloodshed.

We live in a society where integrity is a medieval value, in which morality is archaic and where secular leadership, both communal and political, has redefined the meaning of ethicality and virtue. Does this not in some way impact our own thought process? The only way to counteract this influence is through awareness and insulation. Prevention is the best antidote for the influence of the environment.

✴ ✴ ✴ ✴ ✴ ✴

וישב בה עד מות הכהן הגדל

He shall dwell in it until the death of the Kohen Gadol. (35:25)

The *Kohen Gadol* carries some of the onus regarding the fatal accidents that occur during his watch, since he should have prayed that these accidents not occur during his tenure. *Sforno* explains that since there were varied forms of unintentional killings, it was almost impossible for the earthly court to determine the length of time for each individual killer's sentence of exile. Thus, it is left up to Hashem to render His judgment through the medium of an event ordained only by Him.

The responsibility of the *gedolei Yisrael*, Torah leaders, of each generation to pray for the members of their generation is awesome. *Horav Elazar M. Shach, zl*, took this responsibility very seriously, as evidenced in the following narrative: One of the young men in Ponevezh, himself a child of Holocaust survivors, had a son. It did not take long before it was discovered that the infant suffered from a serious disease that plagued one of his internal organs. The parents practically lived in doctors' offices, as they went from specialist to specialist seeking whatever medical advice they could. It was during 1970 that the child went through his most difficult period. The child had to undergo a serious surgical procedure in America. The entire Ponevezh *Yeshivah*, including the *Rosh HaYeshivah, Rav* Shach, recited *Tehillim* in his *zchus*, merit.

Indeed, the joy was palpable throughout the *yeshivah* when the good news of a successful surgery arrived. *Rav* Shach was among those who were overjoyed for the family. He added that he would continue to recite *Tehillim* for the child.

"Why?" the parents asked. "*Baruch Hashem,* the result is positive."

"Yes, I know," he replied. "I still would like to be the *shomer,* watchman, that everything continues to be fine."

A number of years later, the child had grown up and was now in the *parshah* of *Shidduchim,* looking for a mate with whom to share the rest of his life. The parents spoke to the intended girl's parents and encouraged them to check out the surgery that their son had undergone years earlier, so that everything would be clearly revealed. They suggested that besides the medical records, the parents should seek the advice of a *gadol,* Torah leader.

They went to *Rav* Shach, who, after inquiring about the young man's health, wished them all the best, *Mazel Tov,* and that the young couple should merit to build a beautiful home in *Yisrael* amid much joy and success.

Nonetheless, the young man was not always in the best of health. As *Rav* Shach had blessed them, they had a wonderful marriage, raising children who were bright and accomplished. The people of the neighborhood could see that this family was the beneficiary of an exceptional blessing. The young man's father, who was *Rav* Shach's *talmid,* student, was concerned about his son's health, but nevertheless he did not worry obsessively, because of his deep abiding faith in Hashem.

Everything was fine until *Mar Cheshvon* 16, 2002, when the venerable *Rosh HaYeshivah, Rav* Shach, passed away. The father was acutely aware that *Rav* Shach's passing would affect his son. He knew that ever since that fateful day of his surgery, the *Rosh HaYeshivah* had recited *Tehillim daily* for his son. After all, he said he would be his *shomer.* Now, he was gone. Shortly thereafter, the father's terrible fear was realized, as his son suddenly took ill and passed away. The *shomer ne'eman,* faithful watchman, the *Rosh HaYeshivah* who was so devoted to *Klal Yisrael,* was no longer there to intercede in his behalf.

While this thesis is about *gedolei Yisrael* and their responsibility to pray for the community, as parents we cannot forget our own obligation to pray for our children — and, as we age, for our grandchildren. A parent certainly prays for their child's health and success, both spiritually and materially. I feel that to the degree a parent values his child's success in the spiritual arena, to that end he will supplicate the Almighty. The *Tehillim* recited and the *treren*, tears, shed by a parent, make the difference. Above all, the child senses that the value system in his home is unique. *Ruchniyus*, spirituality, plays a starring role in the character of the home. The following incredible story, cited by Rabbi Yechiel Spero in *Touched by a Story 2*, demonstrates a mother's prayer and the enduring effect it had on her illustrious son.

Rabbi Moshe Sherer, zl, was the Torah *askan*, communal worker, par excellence. As president of Agudath Israel, he was the major spokesman for Orthodox Jewry for over fifty years. His total subservience to the *gedolei Yisrael* was legendary. It did not happen overnight. He hailed from a home whose hallmarks were Torah commitment; trust in *gedolei Yisrael;* and *emunah peshutah*, unequivocal faith in Hashem. Whenever one of the Sherer children was ill, Mrs. Sherer would immediately visit the *Stoliner Rebbe, zl,* to ask for his blessing. His response was that she should light another *Shabbos* candle. She had a large family, and the ailments were typical. One can only imagine that her *Shabbos* candle-lighting was a major endeavor.

There was another aspect of Mrs. Sherer's candle-lighting that was special. Young Moshe Sherer would silently observe his mother stand there and weep softly, as she entreated Hashem on behalf of her family. What did she say, he would wonder? Why did the candle-lighting take so long? One Friday evening, determined to find an answer to his pressing questions, he hid beneath the table on which the candles were placed. Once and for all, he was going to know what his mother was saying.

What he heard is something that remained with him — and serves as a lesson for each of us.

Since Moshe could not fit his entire body within the cramped space beneath the table, his hands were left sticking out. His mother did not notice his hands as she approached the table to begin her weekly ritual. She recited the *brachah*, blessing, and accompanying prayer. She then added her own *Tefillah*: *Ribbono Shel Olam, Baleichten zolst du di oigen fun meina kinderlach in Dein heiliga Torah*, "Please, Hashem, light up my children's eyes through the precious words of Your holy Torah. Please allow them to perceive the light of Your holy Torah."

These words were spoken over and over, as she wept with total devotion. Moshe was mesmerized by what he heard. His reverie broke as one of his mother's warm tears landed in the palm of his outstretched hand. He never forgot the feeling or the impact of that warm teardrop. The teardrop wove its way into his heart and mind, as that moment left an indelible impression on him for life.

The *Kohen Gadol* feels a kinship to all Jews. Parents certainly feel an abiding love for their children. Perhaps, if we all would begin to pray for others, Hashem would listen to us when we pray for ourselves.

ספר דברים
SEFER DEVARIM

To my Eishes Chayil

Dr. Marijah McCain

an incomparable "accomplished woman"

פיה פתחה בחכמה ותורת חסד על לשונה

*"She opens her mouth with wisdom and
a lesson of kindness is on her tongue." (Mishlei 31:26)*

Her love and commitment to her family and to helping
others is the paradigm of *chesed*, loving kindness.

Personally and professionally she conducts herself
with devotion, sensitivity and caring.

Her faith in Hashem is unwavering
– He guides her every action –

Stephen McCain

אמר לד׳ מחסי ומצודתי, אלקי אבטח בו

*"I will say of Hashem 'He is my refuge and my fortress, my G-d,
I will trust in Him. (Tehillim 91:2)*

אלה הדברים אשר דבר משה... בין פארן ובין תפל ולבן

These are the words which Moshe spoke... between Paran and Tofel and Lavan. (1:1)

Rashi explains that Moshe *Rabbeinu's* words were an admonishment to the people, and the places that he mentioned are allusions to various sins that occurred. "Paran" is a reference to the sin of the *meraglim*, spies, who were sent from the wilderness of Paran, and "Tofel" and "Lavan" refer to the Jews' complaints concerning the *manna*. Upon studying the text, two questions present themselves. First, the word "between" (*between Paran and Tofel and Lavan*) suggests a connection between the two aforementioned incidents. Yet, this is hardly possible, since the two sins occurred thirty-eight years apart. The *meraglim* sinned right at the beginning of their forty-year sojourn, while the complaint about the *manna* occurred near the end.

Second, the names Tofel and Lavan are enigmatic. The word "*tofel*" in Hebrew means to attach, and "*lavan*" means white. These definitions imply that the people attached one word to another to formulate their complaint about the *manna,* which happened to be white. What aspect of the Torah's allusion to the *manna* underscores its color?

In addressing these questions, *Horav David Feinstein, Shlita,* suggests that the connection between the two sins was the Jews' complaining. In the incident of the spies, they complained about *Eretz Yisrael*; concerning the *manna*, they referred to it as *lechem haklokeil*, the light bread. The common thread that runs between them is that in both cases they were tired of living under Hashem's constant observation. *Chazal* teach us that the *manna* was white because it whitened, cleansed, *Klal Yisrael's* sins.

The *manna* communicated a compelling lesson to each individual when he gathered it. Each day, they were able to gather only one measure of *manna* per family member. This measure was edible for only that day. If they would attempt to gather extra, it was useless, since it would disappear by the time they arrived home. Also, any leftover *manna* became wormy at the end of the day. Thus, it was essential that *Klal Yisrael* maintain its utmost faith that Hashem would provide their gift of *manna* on the next day. Every day, each Jew would examine his actions: Was he worthy of *manna* for another day — or not? He knew that if he was not worthy, he would not receive Hashem's gift. Consequently, the daily *manna* catalyzed a powerful *teshuvah*, repentance movement, by which daily introspection became a common and natural occurrence.

During the episode of the spies, the Jews were concerned that once they arrived in *Eretz Yisrael,* their every action would once again be under constant Heavenly scrutiny. Does not Moshe later tell the Jews that *Eretz Yisrael* is a land "where the eyes of Hashem are on it from the beginning of the year until the end of the year"? (*Devarim* 11:12). They knew that they were leaving the scrutiny engendered by the daily *manna* to live under the scrutiny of *Eretz Yisrael*. This was very likely why the spies' negative report made them want to go back to Egypt. They were not interested in living under such close inspection.

During both incidents, the spies and the *manna*, the people had a parallel complaint: Hashem was watching them too closely. It was more than they were willing to confront. When one is insecure about himself and diffident about his actions, if he questions the integrity of his service to Hashem, it would make sense that he could not deal with scrutiny from Above. He has two choices: either he cleans up his act and changes his ways; or he learns to live with scrutiny.

❋ ❋ ❋ ❋ ❋ ❋

בין פארן ובין תפל ולבן וחצרת ודי זהב
Between Paran and Tofel and Lavan, and Chatzeiros and Di Zahav. (1:1)

*R*ashi explains that these names are all allusions to a variety of sins committed by the people. Paran is a reference to the wilderness of Paran from where the *meraglim*, spies, were sent out on their mission. In an alternative explanation, *Rashi* says that Chatzeiros also refers to the sin of the spies, since Chatzeiros is where Miriam was punished for speaking ill of Moshe *Rabbeinu*. Moshe said to them, "You should have learned a lesson about *lashon hara*, defamatory speech, from what Hashem did to Miriam at Chatzeiros. Yet, you went ahead and spoke against Hashem and *Eretz Yisrael*." We wonder why it was necessary to rebuke them twice for the same sin.

The *Maharal m'Prague* explains that the first rebuke was for the actual sin of speaking disparagingly. The second reproach was specifically for not learning a lesson from the incident of Miriam. Exclusive of the actual sin is another indiscretion — that of failing to derive a deterrent from what happened to Miriam as a result of her strong criticism of Moshe. One who sees the effect of a sin and does not take note to correct his own ways is committing a sin by the omission itself.

❊ ❊ ❊ ❊ ❊ ❊

לא תגורו מפני איש
You shall not fear in the face of man. (1:17)

The *Torah* exhorts the judges not to adjudicate out of fear, lest it color their attitude toward the case.

When the *Brisker Rav*, zl, was *Rav* in Brisk, there was a young man from a wealthy family who was a *moser*, government informer, and the cause of much pain and anguish in the community. When his mother died, she left in her will the directive that when her son married, the *Rav* of Brisk should officiate at the wedding ceremony. A short while later, the young man became engaged, and he requested that the *Brisker Rav* officiate at his wedding. The *Rav* refused emphatically, saying that it was forbidden to officiate at the wedding of an informer.

The groom offered the *Rav* a substantial amount of money to change his mind, to no avail. The *Brisker Rav* was not swayed by material benefits. The young man threatened to go to the authorities and inform on the *Rav*, as he had done before to another *rav*. The *Brisker Rav* was not moved by his threats. The community was in an uproar. They were acutely aware of the groom's threats and the dire consequences. The leaders of the community, together with the *Rav's* closest students, entreated him to rescind his decision.

On *Motzoei Shabbos*, the *Rav* raised his cup to recite *Havdalah*, and at that moment another one of the *Rav's* close students entered the house. The *Rav*, knowing fully-well the purpose of his visit, became so agitated that he spilled the wine from the cup.

After he calmed down, the *Rav* told him, "I know why you have come here. You should know that only one thing determines my actions — *Halachah*, Jewish law. If you will prove to me that *Halachah* permits me to officiate at the wedding of an informer — I will do so. If, however, you cannot, and the *Halachah* is as I arbitrated it, then there is no alternative but to refuse to go through with this travesty."

Once *Horav Yechezkel Abramsky*, *zl*, was asked to arbitrate a monetary dispute. His response to the questioner was that he had nothing to worry about. The questioner was concerned lest people circulate rumors regarding his integrity in business, asserting that he was not acting in accordance with *Halachah*. *Rav* Chatzkel replied, "What will people say? This is a common malady. What did people say when they walked behind Boaz's coffin at his funeral? Surely, the slanderers were saying, 'He died the day after he married Rus, the Moavite. For transgressing a Biblical ordinance, Hashem immediately punished him.' This is what *some* people were saying. They were certainly not aware of *Chazal's* interpretation of '*Movi v'lo Moavis*,' a (male) member of Moav, but not a female member. Rus was totally permitted to Boaz, yet people talk. Who says we must concern ourselves with those who are unschooled and not proficient in Jewish law?

"Furthermore, not only was this absolutely not a punishment for Boaz, on the contrary, it was a blessing. Hashem, the *Mesabev sibos*, cause of all causes, catalyzed a chain of events that Boaz should merit one more *mitzvah*, one more unprecedented opportunity — to sow the seeds of *Moshiach Tzidkeinu*, one day before he was to leave this world."

As usual, there are always those who will see things in the negative, because they look through a distorted spectrum. Then there are those who look with *emes*, with veracity, and see the positive aspect of an occurrence. It all depends on the lens through which one gazes.

ולא שמע ד' בקלכם ולא האזין אליכם. ותשבו בקדש ימים רבים כימים אשר
ישבתם.

But Hashem did not listen to your voice and He did not give ear to you.
You stayed in Kadesh many days, [as many] as the days that you dwelt.
(1:45,46)

*R*ashi tells us that they remained in Kadesh for nineteen years, half
of the thirty-eight remaining years they were to spend in the
wilderness. In the *Midrash, Chazal* say that *Tefillah oseh
mechtzah*, "Prayer makes/accomplishes one-half." The *Netziv, zl,* explains
that when *Klal Yisrael* heard the terrible decree that befell them — that they
would now have to spend thirty-eight more years in the wilderness — they
cried bitterly and supplicated Hashem to rescind His devastating decree.
While their prayer did not *fully* succeed in eradicating Hashem's decree, it
did achieve partial success in that they were allowed to remain in one place
for an extended period of time, cutting back on their wandering. The *Netziv*
teaches us a compelling lesson. One should never despair, even if he does not
notice an apparent response to his prayers. No prayer is wasted. The response
may be negative, but there certainly is a positive consequence as a result of
one's prayer.

Our *gedolei Yisrael, Torah* leaders, exemplified the three pillars
which sustain the world. *Torah, Avodah* and *Gemillus chasadim* — the study
of Torah, service to G-d (i.e. prayer), and acts of loving-kindness. Yet, there
were individuals who, besides exemplifying distinction in Torah knowledge,
their *avodas ha'lev,* service of the heart, was quintessential. The *Steipler Rav,*
himself an individual whose prayers were known for their wondrous efficacy,
said about the Manchester *Rosh Yeshivah, Horav Yehudah Zev Segal, zl,* that
he was the *Amud ha'Tefillah,* pillar of prayer, of our generation. Anyone who
saw the *Rosh Yeshivah daven* witnessed *avodah sh'blev* at its zenith. When
the *Rosh Yeshivah* prayed, he felt himself in the presence of the Almighty in
every sense of the word. I once had the privilege of seeing him recite the
Birkas Asher Yotzar; it was an experience I will always remember.

On a return flight from *Eretz Yisrael,* the *Rosh Yeshivah* was in the
midst of *Shemoneh Esrai,* when the plane was struck by lightening. The
passengers were understandably shaken and remained so, until the pilot
announced the all-clear. A secular Jew who observed the *Rosh Yeshivah*

continue his *Shemoneh Esrai* throughout the ordeal as if nothing had occurred, seemingly oblivious to the anxiety shared by all the passengers, said, "It was surely in the rabbi's merit that we were saved."

As an aid to proper *kavanah*, concentration, during his prayers, the *Rosh Yeshivah* recited every *Tefillah* from a text. His *Asher Yotzar* was recited from a *Siddur* with the intensity and concentration of a person saying *Neilah*, the closing prayer on *Yom Kippur*.

The *Rosh Yeshivah* saw nothing belittling in *davening* from a *Siddur* with a translation. In fact, he felt that this improved one's concentration. On *Hoshanah Rabah* one year, someone offered him a card on which were printed the *Hoshanos* to facilitate encircling the *Bimah* with a *Lulav* and *Esrog*. The *Rosh Yeshivah* thanked the person, but declined to use the card saying that he preferred to *daven* from his large *Siddur*, even though it was somewhat cumbersome, because it contained a translation.

Kavanah was something he would always emphasize concerning *davening*. He advised his *talmidim*, students, to be mindful of the axiom in *Orach Chaim* 1:4: "Better a little with *kavanah* than a lot without *kavanah*."

The *Rosh Yeshivah* felt that spiritual refinement was the result of proper *Tefillah*. He felt that the term *avodas ha'lev*, service of the heart, had a deeper connotation. Prayer, when approached properly, is a service that refines the heart, as it draws the supplicant closer to the Almighty and deepens his understanding of his purpose in life.

His efforts in *Tefillah* were based to a large degree on his firm faith in prayer's power to help in the most devastating situations, even when everything seemed hopeless. Once, an x-ray indicated that a certain individual was stricken with a dreaded disease. A subsequent x-ray showed no sign of illness. The *Rosh Yeshivah* explained the apparent contradiction between the x-rays in the following manner. "The first x-ray was not wrong. Your disease was there, but the power of prayer rescinded the decree."

When a *yeshivah* student was diagnosed with a dreaded disease, the doctors attempted to save his life through surgery. Regrettably, the surgery was not successful in reversing the course of the disease, and the doctors soon despaired for his life. The boy's father approached the *Rosh Yeshivah* for a *brachah*, blessing, for his son's life. Following the *Chafetz Chaim's* suggestion, the *Rosh Yeshivah* told the father that if he would dedicate his son's life to Torah, he would have a complete recovery. Although the father had been planning for his son to pursue a secular career, he readily agreed to the *Rosh Yeshivah's* suggestion. That night as the *Rosh Yeshivah davened* the *Shemoneh Esrai* of *Maariv*, he was heard saying, *Tatte! Ich hob em tzugezagt,* "Father! I promised him." He felt that his *Tefillah* achieved success — a feeling that was soon substantiated when the family sought a second opinion. The second doctor felt that the patient's alarming weakness was attributed to having been given the wrong medication. As soon as a new prescription was administered, the boy's condition improved. Today, he is a healthy, outstanding *talmid chacham*, Torah scholar, and has raised a beautiful family.

Due to his total devotion to *Tefillah*, the *Rosh Yeshivah* became an individual that people would turn to from far and wide to receive his blessing. Even gentiles sought his blessing. A surgeon who operated upon the *Rosh Yeshivah* asked that he be blessed with steady hands, so that he could continue his work for many years to come. The *Rosh Yeshivah* was once hospitalized and was attended to by a *talmid*, student. The *talmid* happened to be in the corridor and noticed a gentile woman pacing nervously up and down the corridor. He asked her what was the matter. She replied that her four-year-old son had fallen from a tree and lay in a coma. When the *talmid* related this later to the *Rosh Yeshivah*, he appeared pained and said, "And so what if he is a gentile? — Does it not say, *V'rachamav al kol maasov,* 'And His mercy is on All His works.' And this is a child untainted by sin." He instructed the *talmid* to ask the woman for her son's name and then mentioned the name and repeated the phrase, *V'rachamav al kol maasov.*

A few days later, the woman joyfully informed the *talmid* that her son had regained consciousness, and the doctors were hopeful for a complete recovery. "It is all due to the Rabbi's prayers," she declared.

Upon being told the news, the *Rosh HaYeshivah* in his inimitable manner responded, *V'rachamov al kol maasov.*

Parashas Va'eschanan

ואתחנן אל ד' בעת ההיא לאמר

And I pleaded to Hashem at that time, saying. (3:23)

Moshe *Rabbeinu* relates how he entreated Hashem to permit him to enter *Eretz Yisrael*. *Chazal* underscore the power of *Tefillah.* Because no one exemplified the performance of *maasim tovim*, good deeds, more than Moshe, Hashem listened to his pleas and allowed him to ascend to the top of the cliff and gaze at *Eretz Yisrael*. His prayers catalyzed the fulfillment of part of his request. What is there about prayer that is so effective? In his *Nesivos Olam*, the *Maharal* writes that when one prays to the Almighty, he indicates that he is totally dependent, unable to exist without Him. This is the attitude one should manifest when he prays.

Horav Shraga Feivel Mendlowitz, zl, taught that an essential component of the prayer service is the prior preparation. While one's external behavior demonstrates who is an earnest *Torah* scholar, this is not necessarily the case when it comes to *Tefillah*. The length of his prayer service is no indication that the petitioner takes his prayer any more seriously than one who prays quickly. It is all in the preparation. *Rav* Shraga Feivel would compare one who is praying to a mountain climber, who exerts great effort to make it to the summit. Once he is there, however, he strolls around with ease. So, too, with prayer. When a person prepares diligently for his encounter with the Almighty, his prayer will then spring forth unimpeded from his heart. No foreign thoughts will enter his mind. Indeed, one's alacrity in prayer might even be an indication of his devotion.

Horav Moshe Aharon Stern, zl, was well known for his impassioned prayer. From deep within the recesses of his heart, he would supplicate the Almighty like a humble servant looking up to his master for salvation. He meticulously enunciated every word. When he would recite those sections of the prayer that praised Hashem, his enthusiasm was palpable. His focus was consummate; his worship was sincere and fervent.

He was scrupulous about *davening* with a *minyan*. If he could not find a *minyan*, he still felt that one should pray in a *shul*, rather than pray at home. The synagogue is a place specifically designated for prayer, and its ambience is conducive to prayer. This environment stimulates greater devotion and concentration. *Rav* Moshe Aharon would cite the following incident which he heard from the *Chazon Ish, zl*. A young couple, who were about to be married in a week, met for the last time prior to the customary seven-day separation before the wedding. They met before *shkiah*, sunset, and did not part until late into the night. Before taking leave, the bride reminded the groom to remember to *daven Maariv*. He responded that he had already *davened*. This struck the girl as odd, since they had been together for the entire evening, and it is improper to *daven* before sunset. Disturbed, she told her father about the incident when she came home that night. Her father decided to consult the *Chazon Ish* in regard to the matter. The *Chazon Ish* advised him to break the engagement. This was no simple matter, especially in light of the fact that it was a week before the wedding, but how can one marry someone who does not pray?

When it was pointed out to *Rav* Moshe Aharon that one cannot compare not praying with simply not praying with a *minyan*, his response was unequivocal, "You are right. If my daughter was engaged to a boy, and we discovered one week before the wedding that he does not *daven* with a *minyan*, I would not break the engagement. Would I have known ahead of time that such was the case, however, I would never have agreed to the match in the first place. A boy who does not *daven* with a *minyan* is not serious about *davening*!"

Horav Elya Lopian, zl, frequently urged his students to pray with devotion. "Heartfelt prayer," he said, "can rend the Heavens, especially if accompanied by tears." He would quote the *Sefer Chassidim* who writes, "The Almighty answers the requests of some individuals solely due to the intensity of their entreaties and the copious tears they shed. Even though they might possess neither merit nor good deeds, Hashem accepts their prayers and fulfills their desires."

We often think that prayer is connected to a specific time and place. Undoubtedly, it is more propitious to pray the specific prayers outlined by *Chazal* and to do so in a proper *shul*. Yet, *Tefillah* is not bound by time or place. One may pour out his heart to Hashem with devotion and fervor whenever he chooses, wherever he is. *Horav Simchah Bunim, zl,* *m'Peshischa* writes that one is mistaken if he thinks that in order to pray one must wrap himself in a *Tallis* and seclude himself. It is not so. Wherever a person might find himself, providing it is a clean place, he may pour out his heart to Hashem, because He is always there and He always listens.

I recently saw a poignant story on *Tefillah* in Rabbi Yechiel Spero's *Touched by a Story,* which is well worth reading. It is about a survivor of World War II's ravages. Hitler, Stalin, the persecution in the camps, and the loneliness and bitterness, depravation and pain had all taken their toll. His name was Siberiate, and he was speaking to a group of survivors who, like himself, had suffered and were now prepared to go on. He began his short speech in the following manner:

"I always thought that the most valuable commodity was money, until I came to Siberia and worked eighteen hours a day mining gold. I figured that I could always smuggle a little bit into my pocket, and in a short while I would be rich. What a fool I was to think that my gold had value in Siberia. In the cold misery of the slave labor camp, money was worthless. It was food that we needed. What good was gold if there was nothing to buy!

"As the hunger pangs gnawed within me, my focus turned to food. No longer did gold hold any significance. I needed food if I were to survive. The bitter hunger overwhelmed me until, one day, a passing guard walked by smoking a cigarette. The aroma of the cigarette filled the air and captivated me. Suddenly, my hunger pains became secondary to my cravings for a cigarette. The feeling of calm and relaxation that permeated my body after a cigarette lasted much longer than whatever food I would be able to scrounge.

"A cigarette was extremely difficult to procure. While tobacco was not an elusive commodity, the paper in which it needed to be wrapped was very scarce. Even the guards were hard-pressed to find paper in which to wrap their tobacco. Now, it was no longer gold, food, or cigarettes that were of great value. Plain paper became my focus.

"I would yearn for days for that elusive cigarette, and the pleasure that I derived from it which lasted me for the next few days until I could obtain my next cigarette. One day, my fortune changed. An elderly peasant approached me and asked me if I knew how to read. His son was a soldier in the Soviet Union's Army, stationed hundreds of kilometers away. He would periodically write a letter conveying his personal news to his father. The father, an itinerant peasant, could not read, so he made a deal with me: I would read him his son's letter and, in return, he would give me the envelope to use as a wrapper for my cigarettes.

"I was overjoyed. This envelope had enough paper to roll at least three cigarettes! As I was preparing the envelope, however, I noticed that there was some lettering on the envelope. After closer examination, I realized that it was Hebrew lettering! Reading the letters carefully, I saw that the writing was from *davening*. It had been years since I had *davened*, but I knew what I was reading. I picked up the envelope, folded it and put it in my pocket.

"One of the men in our labor group was learned. When I showed him my discovery, he exclaimed excitedly that this was a page from a *Siddur*. He was overjoyed. Hashem had not forgotten about us! How could we forget about Him? So we started a *Minyan*. Three times a day, the *shliach tzibbur*, reader, stood up and read from the envelope. Our one-page *Siddur* served as the primer for a group of depressed inmates to find solace and strength through the medium of *Tefillah*.

"This prayer meeting created a transformation that was incredible. The wretched souls who previously had nothing left for which to live, now had hope. Their lives now had meaning and purpose as they looked forward longingly to *daven* together every day. It suddenly dawned on me that I had now discovered the most valuable thing in the world. It was not gold, nor was it food or cigarettes. It was prayer. The ability to connect with Hashem, to reach out and speak to Him, gave us hope. Without hope, we had nothing. With hope, we had everything.

"There was another aspect of this discovery, however, that was mind-boggling. The page of the *Siddur* contained a message that was both compelling and timely. The page began with the declaration in *Az Yashir*, *Hashem yimloch l'olam v'aed*, "Hashem will rule forever!" With the small lettering on the page was the heartfelt plea of *Ahavah rabah, Avinu Av HaRachamon ha'meracheim racheim aleinu*, "Our Father, our Compassionate Father, Who is merciful, have mercy on us!"

✼ ✼ ✼ ✼ ✼ ✼

לא תספו על הדבר אשר אנכי מצוה אתכם ולא תגרעו ממנו

Do not add to the word which I command you and do no subtract from it.

(4:2)

The sequence of these commands is enigmatic. One would think that the admonition against subtraction should precede the one against adding to the Torah. First, we should be taught not to remove anything from the Torah that Hashem has given us. Then, we should be exhorted against attempting to be more pious than the Creator by adding *mitzvos* to His Torah. *Horav David Feinstein, Shlita,* explains that the command against subtracting from the Torah is actually an explanation of why we are not permitted to add to the Torah. Whenever one attempts to add to the Torah, he is really subtracting from it, because, in effect, he is disputing the Torah's completeness. He indicates that it needs more. By taking the liberty to add, one is detracting from the Torah's perfection.

It is not uncommon for members of the Torah community to be questioned concerning their ability to compromise. We are called intractable and inflexible, because we are not willing to concede our position on Torah and *mitzvos*. There is a famous incident that occurred with the *Bais HaLevi* that is compelling. It took place during a rabbinical assembly in Russia when a number of Torah's greatest leaders were gathered to discuss the pressing issues of the day. One of the free-thinking, wealthy, lay people posed a suggestion: "Rabbis! Gathered here some of Judaism's greatest leaders. It would be only proper that you convene to discuss the possibility of "easing" the load of *mitzvos* on contemporary society. As you know fully well, many of the *mitzvos* of the *Torah* are outdated and not in tune with modern society."

The *Bais HaLevi* rose, responding to this contemptuous individual with the following *mashal*, analogy. "There was once a businessman who succeeded in only one thing — amassing large debts. He purchased great amounts of merchandise on credit and then could not pay his bills. Understandably, his reputation waned as his debts rose. One night, shortly after midnight, he knocked on the door of one of his biggest creditors, someone whom he owed 100,000 ruble. He told the creditor that inasmuch as it had been a number of years since he had last given him any payment on his debt, he wanted to make an exact accounting of the debt.

"The creditor was not really interested in meeting with the man at that time of the night, but the hope of collecting his debt motivated him to pull out his ledgers and go through the entire bill. They haggled back and forth, examining every bill, every detail, until the debtor was able to adjust the debt to 50,000 ruble. The creditor was understandably upset, but he realized that even at fifty cents on the dollar, he was doing better than nothing at all. So he agreed to the compromise, expecting to receive a check immediately for the balance. We can only imagine his dejection and disgust when the debtor bid him good-night as he sauntered towards the door."

"You are not paying me?" the creditor exclaimed.

"No, of course not," the debtor replied, "you know I have no money."

"So why did you bother to go through the entire bill, inferring that you were going to do something about it?" the creditor screamed.

"You do not seem to understand," the debtor responded. "Every time I borrowed money, I felt bad that I was taking someone else's money, when I knew I would not be able to repay. This feeling lay like a stone on my heart. I knew I had to do something about it. That is why I came here tonight to go over the bills. At least now I feel better. I no longer owe you 100,000 ruble. I only owe you 50,000 ruble. This brings joy to my heart, since I feel that I have at least placated you somewhat."

The *Bais HaLevi* concluded the analogy, as he looked with piercing eyes at the arrogant skeptic, "You do not seek compromise for the purpose of strengthening your service to Hashem. Even if you only had the Ten Commandments to observe, you would find a way out of it. For people like you, no compromise will suffice. You seek one thing and only one thing: to abolish the Torah — totally and unequivocally. You have no desire to pay your debt. You only want to alleviate your conscience. The Torah is immutable and unalterable. It is perfect and complete. Accept it in its totality, with devotion and self-sacrifice, as your ancestors have done. You will never receive from us a dispensation to diminish your holy debt to Hashem."

וְשִׁנַּנְתָּם לְבָנֶיךָ וְדִבַּרְתָּ בָּם בְּשִׁבְתְּךָ בְּבֵיתֶךָ וּבְלֶכְתְּךָ בַּדֶּרֶךְ וּבְשָׁכְבְּךָ וּבְקוּמֶךָ

You shall teach them thoroughly to your children and you shall speak of them while you sit in your home and while you walk on the way, when you lie down and when you rise. **(6:7)**

R*ashi* explains that the word *v'shinantom* is a *lashon chidud*, a word which expresses sharpness, implying that the words of Torah should be sharp in one's mouth. This way, if a person was to question you in a matter of Torah, you will not hesitate, but rather respond immediately. The *Boyaner Rebbe*, *zl*, *Rav* Avraham Yaakov, rendered the *pasuk* in the following manner: Once a wealthy businessman approached the *Rebbe* with regard to his son. It seems that as the man was climbing the ladder of success in the world of commerce, he became slightly delinquent in his relationship with the Torah and *mitzvos*. As he was becoming more modern and distant from the traditions of his forebears, his attitude towards his son's Torah education became equally alienated. The *yeshivah* was replaced by the secular school. His friends were free-thinking and free-spirited, and slowly the son regarded Torah, *mitzvos* and *Yiddishkeit* in general as archaic and foreign. What was the father to do?

The *Rebbe* invited the man to attend the *Tisch*, festive meal, together with his son that Friday night, at which time he would offer his reply. The man came to the *Tisch* that night together with his son. The *Rebbe* greeted him and assigned him a prominent seat at the *Rebbe's* side. The *Rebbe* commenced to deliver his *divrei Torah* on the *parshah* on the *pasuk*, *V'shinantom l'vanecha v'dibarta bam*. Focusing on the sequence of the text, he questioned the Torah's placing the exhortation," And you shall speak of them," directly following the enjoinment, "You shall teach them to your children." Should not one first become personally proficient in Torah and then teach his sons Torah? Moreover, "when you lie down, etc." is part of one's own Torah study. First, one should address his own Torah lessons in whichever place or position he may find himself and then concentrate on his son's Torah study.

The *Rebbe* explained that the Torah is teaching us a practical lesson. When one teaches his son Torah, if he fulfills the *"V'shinantom,"* then he will have no problem with the *"V'dibarta bam."* He will then be able to speak *divrei Torah* with his son. If, however, he has neglected to teach his son Torah, if he has indicated that there are other more important areas of intellectual endeavor to which to devote one's time, then they will not have Torah to speak about. Regrettably, they will have very little in common — spiritually. The son does not fathom his father's language, because their vernacular is no longer the same. This is underscored by the continuation of the *pasuk*, "While you sit at home, and while you walk on the way, etc." Everywhere you go, under all circumstances, you will have the same ideology as your son, and, thus, you have something with which to converse with him. If you send your son to places that teach material that is antithetical to Torah perspective, then you can expect the scope of your relationship with your son to be extremely limited.

Parashas Eikev

ועתה ישראל מה ד' אלקיך שאל מעמך כי אם ליראה את ד' אלקיך

And now, Yisrael, what does Hashem, your G-d, ask of you but to fear Hashem, your G-d. (10:12)

I n the *Talmud Menachos* 43b, *Chazal* derive from the words *mah Hashem,* "What does Hashem", as alluding to the word *meiah,* one hundred; that a Jew should recite one hundred *berachos,* blessings, daily. What is the relationship between the recitation of *berachos* and *yiraas Shomayim,* fear of Heaven? *Horav Yaakov Beifus, Shlita,* in his *sefer Chaim Shel Torah,* gives the following analogy: A small town in Europe had an idyllic lifestyle; quiet, pleasant, away from the tumult of the large cities. There was a road that passed through the town, which was originally used by the peddlers in the community for their horses and buggies. With the introduction of the automobile, lifestyles changed. The little road soon became a busy highway, dividing the town in half. The quick pace of the speeding cars back and forth on the highway became a danger for the citizens of the town and their families. People feared for the safety of their children. Suggestions poured in, but nothing practical enough to address the danger posed by the highway. One day, someone came up with a functional idea to solve the problem: speed bumps, every few feet. Consequently, along the road that traversed the town, speed bumps were placed to slow down the cars. Life soon reverted to its original slow-paced, idyllic state.

This same idea applies to *yiraas Shomayim.* The *Rema* in the beginning of *Orach Chaim,* writes that *Shivisi Hashem l'negdi tamid,* "I place Hashem before me constantly," is an important rule of the Torah and a crucial step for those who follow in Hashem's ways. A person's day involves many different circumstances, many of which remove him from the perfect environment for *mitzvah* observance. Thus, he needs reminders to keep him on track to remember that he is always in Hashem's Presence. The hundred *brachos* that one is to recite daily are one hundred meetings with Hashem. A *berachah* recited with the proper *kavanah,* intention/concentration, enunciated correctly, is a rendezvous with the Almighty during which one becomes acutely aware that he is in the Presence of Hashem. This catalyzes a heightened sense of *yiraas Shomayim*.

If one only takes the time to think about the meaning of the words *Baruch Atah Hashem*, "Blessed are You, Hashem," he would realize that he is speaking to the Almighty. This alone should generate a feeling of fear and awe.

A *talmid chacham*, Torah scholar, who was critically ill came to *Horav Shlomo Zalman Auerbach, zl,* asking for advice concerning what he could do to merit a speedy recovery. *Rav* Shlomo Zalman replied, "I do not think that I am the appropriate person to ask, but I know what I would do if I was in your situation. I would be meticulous in reciting the one hundred *brachos* we are to recite daily."

✱ ✱ ✱ ✱ ✱ ✱

עשה משפט יתום ואלמנה
He carries out the judgment of the orphan and widow. (10:18)

The attitude of our *gedolei Yisrael*, Torah leaders, towards widows and orphans was exemplary. While they empathized and were sensitive to the needs of all Jews, they were especially circumspect with those individuals who were alone. *Horav Elazar M. Shach, zl,* would go out of his way to ease the plight and loneliness of a widow. He would say, "Any widow, regardless of her strong nature, experiences a feeling of loneliness. It is difficult for her to acclimate herself to her new circumstances. After a while, the reality of her husband's demise seems to settle and she begins to find comfort and the strength to go on. Everything that one can do to assist such a woman in need achieves a great *mitzvah*."

One of *Rav* Shach's close students recounts how he was walking down one of the streets of Yerushalayim when he saw his venerable *rebbe* going into an apartment building. He followed him up a few flights, to the home of a widow whose husband had passed away a few years earlier. Her husband had been a student of *Rav* Shach and the *Rosh Yeshivah* felt a strong obligation to see to the needs of his widow. *Rav* Shach at the time was over

100-years-old. He sat with the widow for about half-an-hour and talked. He then played with her young children. One can only imagine what such a visit did for the mood in her home.

The *Bais HaLevi* remarried later on in life after his wife passed away. His second wife was a widow with a family of her own. The *Bais HaLevi* took her children into his home and treated them as if they were his own. Indeed, if he felt that his own children were mistreating his wife's children, he would exclaim, "An orphan!" and he would then punish his children. This, despite the fact that his own children were orphans. The *Bais HaLevi* spared no expense in caring for his wife's children, to the extent that when he passed away his own children were in dire financial straits.

This legacy of caring for widows and orphans was transmitted to the next generation. Once *Horav Chaim Soloveitchik, zl,* was presiding over an important meeting of *rabbanim* when a widow came to the door and asked to speak with him. He immediately left the room and spoke to her for about half-an-hour. Those in attendance were reasonably impressed until the widow later said, "That is nothing. His father (the *Bais HaLevi*) would spend hours talking with me."

The *Brisker Rav, zl,* was once approached by a student in *Yeshivas Chevron* and asked for advice concerning a *shidduch,* matrimonial match. The *Rav* replied that he does not advise on these issues. The young man then said, "I have no father with whom to discuss my issues, thus, I came to the *Rav.*" The *Brisker Rav* replied, "If that is the case, you may come to me at any time with any sort of question, and I will see to it that you receive the necessary advice."

The Manchester *Rosh HaYeshivah, Rav Yehudah Zev Segal, zl,* was known for his sensitive and caring heart. This was especially true with regard to widows and orphans. He showered orphans with love and concern and provided emotional support and guidance, and, at times, financial assistance to widows. When no one called, he would call them to reiterate his offer. Once, while paying a *shivah* call, comforting the bereaved, to a student upon the loss of his mother, *Rav* Segal confided that from the time the student's father had died more than twenty years earlier, his mother had visited him weekly to pour out her troubles and discuss her situation.

When visiting *rabbanim* in various communities in England, he made it a point to also visit the widows of the *rabbanim* he had previously visited. He explained that it was extremely painful to a widow when she no longer could play hostess to those who used to come to pay their respects to her husband. He made every effort to attend the wedding of an orphan. When one of his students, a *baal teshuvah*, who was raised in a secular home devoid of Torah, was forced to leave the *yeshivah* and return home upon the death of his father, the *Rosh Yeshivah* told him, "From now on, I will be your father."

Shortly after the *Rosh HaYeshivah's* passing, the family received the following letter. I include an excerpt from it because of its message to all of us:

"I have been a widow for twenty-one years. Many people do not realize that what is missing most for a person who is alone, is the warmth and caring of another human being. This is where the *Rosh HaYeshivah* excelled. His genuine warmth and concern was comforting. His initial "How are you?" and his inquiring about my health, livelihood, and all other pertinent matters, always gave me the feeling that someone cared for me. It also gave me the strength I needed to continue carrying my burden. His readiness to listen to my problems at any time and to give them his utmost attention was quite unique...

"I do not know how I could have managed without his emotional support and guidance all these difficult years. May he be a *meilitz yosher*, intercessor, for us all."

As a postscript, I would like to add a point and be so bold as to draw focus on another type of "orphan" — those boys or girls whose parents either do not care, or are incapable of caring for their children's emotional, spiritual and even physical needs. Every community has its dysfunctional families who need our assistance. Are these children to be viewed in a different light? They also have no one to turn to, or in some cases, the one's they turn to are detrimental to them. We must open our hearts, homes and minds to them as well, because they also need our love.

לאהבה את ד׳ אלקיכם ולעבדו בכל לבבכם ובכל נפשכם

*To love Hashem, your G-d, and to serve Him with all your heart and with
all your soul.* (11:13)

I n the first passage of *Shema*, the Torah adds *u'b'chol me'odecha*, "and
with all your money." What is the meaning of this term? Let me share
with you two examples of this quality. The *Satmar Rebbe, zl*, was a
towering figure in a spiritual and inspirational sense. His encyclopedic
knowledge was only surpassed by his love for his fellow Jew. His devotion
to *mitzvos* was an inspiration to all who came in contact with him. When he
came to these shores, a remnant of the fires of the Holocaust, he rallied the
other survivors not to lose hope, not to fall prey to apathy, but instead to
embrace the Torah and *mitzvos* with fervor and love, and serve the Almighty
as they did before the tragic Holocaust. Slowly, he succeeded in establishing
yeshivos, *chadorim*, schools for girls, *chesed* organizations and just about
everything that was needed for a vibrant Jewish community. He did not end
his mission in the Williamsburg section of Brooklyn, New York. Next he set
his sights on Chicago, to give encouragement and succor to the survivors of
that community. The *Rebbe* gathered his strength and with great resolve
traveled there with the hope that his presence would inspire a renaissance of
European *Yiddishkeit* in the Midwest.

The *Rebbe* spent seven days in Chicago, during which time people
from all walks of life thronged to see him. Some came for blessings, others
came to imbibe his Torah, and still others came just to listen, to see, to
remember what it used to be like in Europe. People gave him money. With
every *berachah* there was a *pidyon*, money for redemption, and over the
week the *Rebbe* amassed a small fortune. Four thousand dollars was an
incredible amount of money in those days — enough money to support his
many charitable endeavors in New York. Yes, the trip was very successful in
many ways.

Prior to leaving town, the *Rebbe* made it a point to check the
condition of the community *mikveh*, ritualarium. After speaking with a
number of lay leaders, he discovered that the *mikveh* was in dire need of
repair. "Why is it not being fixed?" asked the *Rebbe* incredulously. "We have
no money," they replied. "No money for a *mikveh*! How is it possible that
there is money for everything else and for *taharas mishpachah*, family

purity, there is no money?" the *Rebbe* asked.

The *Rebbe* began explaining to them the significance of a kosher *mikveh* in a community until they all agreed that something must be done immediately to repair the *mikveh*. "How much money is needed?" asked the *Rebbe*.

"Approximately $5,000 dollars," they replied.

The *Rebbe* did not waver for a moment as he took out from his briefcase the $4,000 dollars that he had raised in Chicago, and said, "Here, take this money and I will personally sign a note for the remaining one thousand dollars, but, there will be a *mikveh* in Chicago."

The *Rebbe* returned to New York with empty pockets and another thousand dollars in debt, but his heart was overflowing with joy. He had been able to express his unequivocal love to Hashem with "all his money."

Horav Nachum, zl, m'Chernobel was told that a nearby community was in need of a *mikveh*. He turned to one of the great philanthropists of that time and said, "I will sell you my portion in *Gan Eden* for your contribution to build the *mikveh* in that community." The man jumped at the offer. What an unparalleled opportunity! The Chernobler's *Gan Eden* was certainly impressive. To be able to acquire it for mere money was truly a once-in-a-lifetime opportunity.

When the Chernobler was later asked what motivated him to sell his *Gan Eden* for a *mikveh*, he responded, "The Torah instructs us to love Hashem *b'chol me'odecha*, "with all your money." I have not been blessed with material abundance. I do not have anything of monetary value that I can give up for Hashem. The only item of value that I possess is my portion in the World to Come. I am thus compelled to sell it in order to fulfill the *mitzvah* of serving the Almighty "with all my money." Otherwise, my *Krias Shema* which I recite daily is meaningless."

We now have a glimpse of what it means to serve Hashem with all that we possess.

❋ ❋ ❋ ❋ ❋ ❋

לאהבה את ד׳ אלקיכם ולעבדו בכל לבבכם
To love Hashem, your G-d, and to serve Him with all your heart. (11:13)

ashi explains that one must serve Hashem for no other reason than because of deep, abiding love for Him. We are to serve Him with all our heart, and *Chazal* interpret this as a reference to *tefillah*, prayer, which should emanate from the heart. Perhaps, we might add, that when one prays, it should be indicative that his prayer is out of love for Hashem, not for personal motive. Everything we do should be a reflection of our unequivocal love for the Almighty and not for ourselves.

I recently read a beautiful analogy in *Touched by a Story I*, by Rabbi Yechiel Spero, which can be applied here. The story took place in Yerushalayim during the second World War as Rommel and his Afrika Corps were getting closer to the Holy Land. The mood in the country was one of fear and anxiety. Tensions rose as the people prepared for the worst. The *Shomer Emunim Shul*, in the heart of the *Meah Shearim* district was the place to be on *Simchas Torah*. The dancing and singing would attain such fervor that one felt a spiritual ascendancy like no other time of the year. That year, regrettably, the impending doom took its toll on the worshippers and the *davening* was listless, without the usual heart and passion. After a few minutes, the *rav* of the *shul*, Horav Aharon Roth, ordered the dancing to come to a halt as he addressed the crowd.

"My dear friends, I would like to share a story with you that I feel has great meaning for us. There was once a king who decided to make for himself a very festive and unique birthday party. He sent out letters throughout the land inviting the most graceful dancers, the finest musicians, and the most creative choreographers. They were all to assemble dressed in their most lavish outfits for the grand event.

"All was arranged and the special day arrived. Everything proceeded as meticulously planned. What a sight — the music, the dancers, the outfits — everything blended together in a most unique harmony as truly befits a king's party. Suddenly, out of the corner of his eye, the king noticed a slight commotion in the back as an elderly, crippled man struggled to make his way to the dance floor. Not only was he crippled, he was also blind and, thus, kept bumping into the tables and chairs.

"After much exertion, the man finally made it to the dance floor and began to hobble around in a makeshift dance using his crutches as means of support. The king was mesmerized as he ignored the rest of the show and focused on the poor, wretched man who was doing his best to maintain his balance.

"One of the king's servants was taken aback with this sight and asked for an explanation. 'My king, we have assembled here tonight the finest choreographed dances, yet, you ignore everyone but that poor cripple who is hobbling around on his crutches.'

"The king smiled and explained, 'You are right. All those who have gathered here tonight are truly talented and their performance is certainly exemplary. But, let me ask you, are they not also deriving personal enjoyment from their performance? Are they dancing solely for me, or are they also satisfying a personal desire? The cripple, however, has nothing personal to gain from his dancing. He cannot see, he cannot dance. Yet, he does so because I requested it. He is acting solely for *me*! Look at his face, how contorted it is with pain. But, he continues to dance, because he wants to please me. That is why his dancing is so precious to me — because it is for me.'

"My dear friends," *Rav* Aharon concluded, "In past years our dancing was different. We danced for Hashem, but we *also* danced for ourselves. We derived personal joy and benefit from the dancing. This year, however, with Hitler's forces almost at our doorstep and the fate of the Jewish People on our minds, we have the unique opportunity to dance *solely* for Hashem. Let us dance tonight — for Him!"

Many of us pray with great concentration and devotion — but, we pray for ourselves. We should aspire to elevate our prayer so that we pray to please Hashem. When we will pray for <u>Him</u>, he will listen to <u>us</u>.

כי מנסה ד' אלקיכם אתכם לדעת הישכם אהבים את ד' אלקיכם

"For Hashem, your G-d, is testing you to know whether you love Hashem, your G-d." (13:4)

A *navi sheker*, false prophet, appears and attempts to dissuade us from serving Hashem. We are not to listen to him, even if he exhibits miraculous abilities. The Torah adds that this is all a test to determine if we truly love Hashem. The use of the word 'love' seems questionable. The test involves our commitment towards serving Hashem — not our love of Him. *Horav Yosef Shaul Natanson, zl*, the *baal Shoel u'Meishiv*, explains this with the following analogy: A teacher has a class of students comprised of two groups — those who truly want to learn, and those who come to class because their parents coerce them. How does he distinguish one group from the other? On a day that is either a vacation day or a "snow" day, he sees which students are happy to be free of school and which students regret not being able to spend the day engrossed in their studies.

Likewise, when the false prophet attempts to convince us to veer from our commitment to Torah and *mitzvos*, the reaction should not be, "Oh great! We can now worship idols." This response indicates a lack of love in the manner in which we served Hashem. We served Him simply out of fear of punishment; now that we are availed an alternative, we will seize the opportunity. The *navi sheker* is Hashem's way of testing us to determine who worships Him out of love and who does not.

✶ ✶ ✶ ✶ ✶ ✶

לא תאבה לו ולא תשמע אליו ולא תחום עינך עליו ולא תחמל ולא תכסה עליו

You shall not accede to him and not hearken to him; your eye shall not take pity on him, you shall not be compassionate nor conceal for him.

(13:9)

The Torah emphasizes that the *meisis*, enticer, has forfeited all claim to receiving any compassion from the *Bais Din*, the Jewish court system. He is an exception to the rule that all Jews love one another and seek out one another's positive traits. The court is normally enjoined to find any reason to extend mercy to a transgressor. Not so with the enticer. We are to do everything possible to deny him absolution for his sin. If one were to delve into the *halachos*, laws, we see that every avenue for saving another transgressor is closed to the enticer. In fact, we are exhorted not to have any mercy on him, a response that is contrary to the Jewish tendency towards mercy. Why is this?

Horav Aharon Kotler, zl, posits that the laws which apply to the enticer may be relevant only if he entices someone to worship idols. The enormity of the transgression and the magnitude of the evil, however, are evident when anyone entices another Jew to sin — regardless of the transgression. Whenever someone convinces another person to veer from the Torah way, we are not to extend mercy to him.

Chazal teach us that one who causes another Jew to sin is worse than he who kills him. If one shoots an arrow at someone and misses, he is not punished. If the enticer makes an attempt to convince another Jew to leave the faith and does not succeed, he is still culpable.

Rav Aharon makes a powerful inference from here. We are taught that the reward Hashem gives for a positive action is five hundred times greater than the punishment He metes out for a sinful deed. If so, then let us reflect upon the enormity of the punishment to which an enticer is subject and derive some faint inkling of the benefit that will be showered upon he who brings another Jew closer to Hashem! If every bit of mercy is rejected for a *meisis*, then how much more so, will one who guides and inspires another Jew be privileged to be the beneficiary of Hashem's boundless compassion. Regarding the enticer, the Torah emphasizes that five forms of mercy are to be withheld from him. Can we imagine what it would mean if these five forms of mercy were multiplied five hundred times and showered on us?

✳ ✳ ✳ ✳ ✳ ✳

טמא הוא לכם מבשרם לא תאכלו

It is unclean to you; from their flesh you shall not eat. (14:8)

One day a group of close students entered the study of *Horav Zelig Reuven Bengis*, *zl*, the *Av Beis Din* of Yerushalayim, to find him bent over his *seforim*, weeping uncontrollably. They immediately asked the *rav* what was wrong. He pointed to an article in an Israeli newspaper that reported that a shipment of non-kosher meat had arrived at the Israeli seaport. He then looked up at them with tear-filled eyes, saying, "I know that no observant Jew will even come in contact with this meat, but the mere thought that descendants of our *Avos*, Patriarchs — Avraham, Yitzchak and Yaakov — will fall prey to this meat is too much for me to handle."

One wonders how distant each of us is from such an emotional response and why?

✳ ✳ ✳ ✳ ✳ ✳

כי יהיה בך אביון... לא תאמץ את לבבך... כי פתח תפתח את ידך לו

If there shall be a destitute person among you... you shall not harden your heart... Rather, you shall open your hand to him. (15:7,8)

The *Mishnah* in *Pirkei Avos* 5:13 teaches us: "There are four character types among people: A) The individual who says, "My (property) is mine, and yours is yours" reflects an average character type, but some say this is characteristic of Sodom; B) The one who says, "Mine is yours, and yours is mine" is an unlearned person; C) The individual who says, "Mine is yours, and yours is yours" is scrupulously pious; D) The one who says, "Yours is mine, and mine is mine" is wicked. *Chazal* are teaching us that everybody finds himself included in one of these four character types. Let us attempt to analyze these four types.

The individual who says, "Mine is yours, and yours is mine," has no sense of direction. He is a fool. He is basically asserting that nothing belongs to anybody! He denies Divine Providence which grants people their possessions. Perhaps his foolishness is a result of illiteracy and ignorance.

The one who says, "Mine is mine, and yours is mine," is certainly wicked. He believes that every possession has an address — his! Everything belongs to him. The pious man who believes that "mine is yours and yours is yours" understands that whatever Hashem has granted him is for a higher purpose — to share with others. Whatever he owns, he seeks to enable others access to it.

The anomaly is the fourth character type, which seems to be the cause for dispute. One who says, "Mine is mine, and yours is yours," is either average or as evil as Sodom. In other words, if this is Sodom, the alternative is the pious man who says, "Mine is yours, and yours is yours!" One is either as evil as Sodom or as pious as a *chasid* — nothing in between. Incredible!

Horav Baruch Mordechai Ezrachi, Shlita, makes a powerful implication. If one views himself in context of the *Mishnah*, he is left with only one choice if, in fact, he is not evil, pious, or mixed up. He is a member of that debased form of humanity — Sodom! This teaches us a compelling lesson. A person exists in this world for one purpose — for others: he is not here to serve himself or his needs. We also must realize that being a *chasid*, a pious man, is not a luxury or an added accolade. It is the *minimal* character type that a person can be in order to fulfill the reason for his creation and continued existence. The mere fact that he understands the need to be pious and is not, is in itself an indication that he is of the Sodom character type.

The prevalent attitude of Sodom was, "Mine is mine, and yours is yours." No theft, no robbery, no cheating — at least not blatantly, but its origins were there. The line of demarcation between what is mine and what is yours is very fine. After a while, it even becomes indiscernible for some.

Chazal teach us that Yerushalayim was destroyed because the people of that generation decided cases according to Torah law. This means that they limited their decisions to the letter of the law of the Torah and did not perform actions that would have gone *lifnim meshuras ha'din*, "beyond the letter of the law." We wonder if this is a reason to destroy Yerushalayim? Certainly, adhering strictly to the letter of the law may indicate a flaw in their ethical character, but is this an indication of evil? *Rav* Ezrachi derives from here that the person who makes claim to his little world, his spot, his home, his car, his seat, reflects a Sodomite character. "What is mine is mine, and I refuse to relinquish it to you," reflects *middas* Sodom. Such a person demonstrates an attitude that is reprehensible. He will not go beyond the letter of the law to share with anybody. What is his is his, and he looks to the letter of the law to support his position. One must strive to distance himself from this position, or — in other words — to seek piety, which is the only alternative.

✳ ✳ ✳ ✳ ✳ ✳

כי פתח תפתח את ידך לו והעבט תעביטנו די מחסרו אשר יחסר לו
Rather, you shall open your hand to him; you shall lend him his requirement, whatever is lacking to him. (15:8)

We are enjoined to take care of the needs of those who are in dire financial straits. *Horav Moshe Leib Sassover, zl,* once gave all of his money away to a poor man of dubious background. In fact, rumor had it that the individual was evil. Yet, this did not prevent *Rav* Moshe Leib from giving him charity. When asked how he could give away all of his money to a wicked man, *Rav* Moshe Leib replied, "I am also not a *tzaddik,* righteous man. I figured that if I went beyond the letter of the law and sustained one who acts inappropriately, Hashem will do the same for me."

The rule is clear: when someone comes to us for charity, we should not check him out to see if his *tzitzis* are the correct *shiur,* measurement, or if he acts appropriately. We give to a Jew because he is in need. It is not up to us to determine his integrity. Some of us demand five letters of approbation before we give a man a simple dollar. One would think that if a Jew is willing to humiliate himself going from door to door seeking alms, that would be sufficient evidence of need. Regrettably, some of us feel that for their "dollar," they have license to destroy another Jew's self-esteem. Are they also prepared to withstand a similar scrutiny from Hashem when they need His favor?

The Jewish People are a charitable people. Indeed, we contribute in much greater proportions than our population numbers would suggest.

Tzedakah/charity is a primary component of the Jewish DNA. It is the *mitzvah* through which we identify the first Jew, Avraham *Avinu*, the *amud ha'chesed*, pillar of loving-kindness. All too often, however, we equate the Hebrew word *tzedakah* with the English word "charity." I recently read that these two words are so different from each other that the word charity does not do justice to the word *tzedakah*, actually distorting the Jewish concept of helping others. The word charity is derived from the Latin *caritas*, which means love. Similarly, the word philanthropy is a derivative of the Greek word, *philo* — which means love — and *throp* — which means man. Thus, charity and philanthropy are equated with the love of man. The non-Jewish foundation for charity is love and compassion for others. I feel for the unfortunate; therefore, I contribute to them.

The term *tzedakah*, however, is derived from *tzedek*, which means righteousness and justice. The Jew <u>must</u> give, because it is the right thing to do. It is of no concern whether I like the person in need or if I feel compassion or love for him. I give because the Torah obligates me to give. It, therefore, is the righteous and just thing to do. Even if the beggar curses and humiliates me, I must give *tzedakah*. Love does not play a role in Jewish charity; righteousness and justice are the determining factors.

Why is this? Why do I not have a say regarding who I want to support, to which organization I want to contribute? The answer is that everything belongs to Hashem and is on loan to us to distribute as Hashem decides. Thus, when we give *tzedakah*, we are really giving back to Hashem, so that we can have access to the *remainder* of our earnings. Veritably, we are just brokers handling someone else's money. Hashem gives us the money and instructs us in its use and disbursement. Those who have material wealth have been blessed for a purpose. They are there to help those who turn to them — regardless of their appearance and personality. The choice has been made for us.

There are various forms of *tzedakah*. One does not necessarily have to give money. He can contribute his time, energy, or wisdom. For some people in need, an hour of someone's time is more valuable than his check. They need advice; they need an ear that will listen. Dispensing a check might be easier, but it is impersonal and, at times, not what the person needs.

We must remember that what we do for others does not go to waste.

We may not immediately see the returns, but, in due time, our efforts produce fruit, and, at times, it might even be personal. Shlomo *Ha'melech* says in *Koheles* 11:1, "Send your bread upon the waters, for after many days you will find it." Our efforts on behalf of others will come back to help us in the future. I recently heard the following compelling story from Rabbi Yechiel Spero:

A young soldier was walking down a side street in Chevron, when suddenly — out of nowhere — an Arab pounced on him and stabbed him! The young man fell to the ground, bleeding profusely from an internal wound. He was quickly bleeding to death when another Israeli soldier came running and immediately attempted to seal the wound, called emergency rescue and stayed with the victim. He did all this despite the apparent danger to his own life from the attacker's compatriots who seemed to appear from everywhere. With the help of Hashem, the wounded soldier was soon in surgery and on the road to recovery.

The question that plagued the family of the wounded soldier was: Who was Hashem's messenger? Who was the soldier who had risked his life to save their son/brother? They put up signs in public places asking for the man's identity. After all, they wanted to thank him. No one came forward. No one had any idea as to the other soldier's identity.

One day, eighteen months later, a woman walked into the grocery store owned by the wounded soldier's parents and said, "You are searching for my son. He was the soldier who saved your son's life. He does not seek accolades. He performed a *mitzvah,* and that is his greatest reward."

The father was visibly impressed and could not stop showering the woman with praise for her son's brave and decisive actions. After he concluded speaking, the woman said, "I would like to share a story with you that sheds light on my son's actions. Twenty years ago, I came into this store. I was in the early stages of pregnancy, despondent and miserable. I had no money and very little hope for any success in life. My future appeared very bleak, and I wanted to terminate my pregnancy. While I realize now the folly of what I was thinking, at that time I had no guidance and no one to whom to turn.

"For some reason, I poured out my heart to you, and you listened. You gave me the courage and fortitude to carry my child to full term. I gave birth to a son. It was this son, the one whom you encouraged me to give birth to, that saved your son. Thank you for everything. I now feel that I have repaid my debt."

What an incredible story. Nothing we do for others goes to waste; rather, it is placed on deposit until that day when *we* can make use of it.

✵ ✵ ✵ ✵ ✵ ✵

ולקחת את המרצע ונתתה באזנו ובדלת
Then you shall take the awl and put it through his ear and the door.
(15:17)

The *eved Ivri*, Jewish bondsman, is sold into slavery because he cannot repay his theft. He is to go free after six years. If he chooses to stay on as a slave, he must have his ear bored. *Chazal* explain that the individual whose ear heard at *Har Sinai*, *Lo tignov*, "Do not steal," and went ahead and stole, let his ear be pierced. Why is the ear not pierced *immediately* when he is sold into slavery as a result of his act of theft? The injunction against stealing occurred six years earlier and that is when he should have been punished. Why now?

Horav Aryeh Levin, zl, explains that one who steals demonstrates a failing. He indicates that he has experienced a shortcoming in his spiritual standing. He has deferred to his *yetzer hara*, evil-inclination, something that can happen to anyone. Therefore, his ear is not pierced simply due to the act of stealing. When a person gives up hope, when he expresses his lack of *bitachon*, trust, in Hashem, by refusing to return to the outside world where he will have to fend for himself — he demonstrates a lack of faith and trust in Hashem. When the *eved* says that he loves his master and relies solely on his master for sustenance and support, he shows that he does not rely on Hashem. For this, his ear is pierced. A person who has a momentary lapse is not held in contempt. One who gives up hope is punished.

✵ ✵ ✵ ✵ ✵ ✵

ושפטו את העם משפט צדק

And they shall judge the people with righteous judgment. (16:18)

C hazal derive from here the importance of always seeking the positive in a person, of judging everyone in a favorable light. They cite an incident that teaches us a powerful lesson. In days of old, it was not uncommon for men to leave their families for an extended period of time in order to search for a livelihood. One such individual left his family. For three years, he worked for someone. At the conclusion of his service, he counted the days longingly, with great anticipation, until he could finally return home to his wife and children. As he was about to leave, he approached his master and asked to be paid. The master replied, "I have no money." Astounded, the worker countered, "If you do not have cash, at least give me fruit." Once again the master replied in the negative, "I have no fruit." Undaunted, the worker said, "Give me some land." "I have no land," was the reply. "How about a few animals?" the worker queried. The response was again negative, "I have no animals. I have nothing."

Depressed and dejected, the worker returned home. Brokenhearted and poor, he had to face his family after three years away from home. It was right before *Succos*, and he did not want to mar the joy of the Festival. He decided to let things be for a few days and then see what he could do.

Immediately after *Yom Tov*, the master appeared at his home with the full salary that he was owed. In addition, he brought a donkey laden with food and gifts for the entire family. The worker was overjoyed with this wonderful surprise.

The master then asked the worker, "When I responded negatively to all of your requests, what did you think?"

"I never thought you were lying," the worker replied. "Each time you said, 'No,' I assumed you had a good reason. I conjectured that you had no money, because it was all invested. Proabaly, your animals and your land were leased to various people. Your fruit was likely not tithed, and your possessions were quite possibly consecrated to the *Beis HaMikdash*."

"You are absolutely right. I had made a vow to give all of my possessions away, and I just received a *heter*, annulment, for my vow. My investments were recently returned to me with a healthy profit, which I share with you. As you judged me favorably, so should Hashem judge you favorably."

A powerful lesson is to be derived from here. We think that judging favorably applies when there is no monetary loss. How about when one loses a considerable amount of money? Should he just suffer his losses in silence? Apparently, the injunction to judge people favorably applies under **all** circumstances — even when one's gut feeling tells him that someone is taking advantage of him. *Horav Aharon, zl, m'Belz*, would say, "Just as when one is confronted with a difficult *Rambam*, he will toil and labor to find some way to understand the meaning, so, too, must we endeavor to understand the actions of our co-religionists. There is a *shverer*, difficult *Rambam*, so, too, is there a *shverer 'Yid.'*"

The *Maharal* attributes the quality of viewing people and situations in a positive light to a *lev tov*, good heart. One whose heart is intrinsically good will always seek the best for his friend. One who has an evil heart views people through a jaundiced perspective.

We find a *pasuk* in the Torah that can only be understood if we apply the concept of *limud z'chus*, judging favorably. In *Devarim* 22:27, the Torah tells us about a *naarah ha'me'orasah*, betrothed virgin girl, who was attacked and violated in the field away from anyone who could have come to her aid. The Torah writes that nothing should be done to the girl, because she certainly must have cried out for help to no avail. How do we assert that she surely cried out? There is no proof of this fact. *Horav Yitzchak, zl, m'Boyan*, derives from here that we judge this girl favorably, assuming that she was not a willing party to this sin.

The *Tiferes Shlomo* questions this. What is to be gained by giving her the benefit of the doubt? Does this ameliorate her sin? Does she become righteous simply because we judge her favorably? Hashem certainly knows the truth, and that is all that matters. Or is there an added factor which Hashem takes into consideration?

The *Tiferes Shlomo* explains that, indeed, the attitude Hashem takes to human sin is related to the manner in which people view the sin. When man judges favorably and looks at his fellow's actions from a positive viewpoint, Hashem does the same, even though He surely knows the truth. Nonetheless, He bases His decision on man's perspective. Hashem will not pass a negative judgment unless the human dimension has done so — already. If we are *melamed zchus* on our fellow's actions, Hashem will concur with our judgment.

✳ ✳ ✳ ✳ ✳ ✳

לא תטה משפט לא תכיר פנים

You shall not pervert judgment, you shall not recognize someone's presence. (16:19)

The *pasuk* addresses the judge who must render judgment without permitting the stature of either one of the litigants to influence his ruling. This idea applies to one who is called upon to uphold the law of the Torah. He should neither fear man nor be swayed from supporting the truth, because his adversary is a man of means — both materially and physically. The Torah personality must be prepared to battle for Torah against any incursion, regardless with whom he must contend. Yet, at the same time, he must be gentle and loving, reaching out to all segments of the Jewish community who seek his guidance and help.

The *Chazon Ish, zl,* exemplified this dual personality. In his *hesped,* eulogy, for the *Chazon Ish, Horav Eliyahu Meir Bloch, zl,* said that the *Chazon Ish* embodied these two seemingly incongruous qualities. On the one hand, as David *Ha'melech* lamented about Shaul *Ha'melech* and his son Yonasan, *Eich naflu giborim, vayovdu klei milchamah,* "How the mighty have fallen and the weapons of war have been lost" (*Shmuel* II, 1:27). A true *gadol* is a fighter in the battle for Torah supremacy. His passing means that the weapons in the war of Torah against perfidy have been laid to rest. The *gadol,* Torah giant, is the champion in the province of protecting *kavod Shomayim,* the honor of Heaven, and preserving the veracity of Torah from those who would distort and impugn it.

On the other hand, David *Ha'melech* was known for his gentle and caring nature. When he studied Torah or dealt with people, his personality shone forth as he reflected the epitome of refinement and affability. His compassion was unsurpassed in dealing with others. Does this mean that he was inconsistent, that his personality was an anomaly? No! He exemplified the concept of a Torah personality.

So, too, was the *Chazon Ish* acutely aware of the difference between the *bais ha'medrash* and the battleground, between the foe who sought to pervert and undermine Torah values and the friend who needed instruction and encouragement. The *Chazon Ish* was, therefore, able to be the general in the battle to preserve the authentic values of Torah, to subvert those whose singular purpose it was to destroy the teachings of the Torah as transmitted in their pristine, unalterable nature throughout the generations. At the same time, he was a kind and loving father to <u>all</u> of those who turned to him.

❋ ❋ ❋ ❋ ❋ ❋

לא תטה משפט לא תכיר פנים ולא תקח שחד כי השחד יעור עיני חכמים

You shall not pervert judgment, you shall not recognize someone's presence and you shall not accept a bribe, for the bribe will blind the eyes of the wise. **(16:19)**

When we establish a Jewish court system, it must be focused on justice and truth. Integrity is a value-laden word, which, regrettably, has different meanings to a variety of people. The Torah sets the standard for absolute truth and justice, concepts that are not simply great political idioms, but are intrinsic to the survival of a Torah nation. Everyone is treated equally in a Jewish court of law. There cannot be a show of favoritism towards one plaintiff over another.

A judge who accepts any form of bribe must withdraw himself from presiding over the case, because he can no longer be objective in rendering judgment. A bribe consists of any favor, even a non-monetary service. *Chazal* cite a number of examples of the minutest favors in cases that might seem trivial and insignificant to us. This does not mean that *Chazal* were so fickle that their judgment would be impaired as a result of an insignificant benefit they derived from someone. As *Horav Avraham Pam, zl,* explains, our *Chazal* had an acute understanding of the meaning of *hakoras ha'tov,* gratitude. They felt *totally* indebted to any benefactor from whom they received a favor.

We do not relate to this concept of *hakoras ha'tov* because we live in a world in which many people feel that they deserve everything that they receive. The great Jews of yesterday understood that there was no limit to the feelings of gratitude they must have to those who did even a minor favor for them.

In his inimitable manner, the *Rosh Yeshivah* explains how every person is the recipient of kindness and favors from those around him. One must demonstrate his gratitude to anyone who does him a service, regardless of his religious affiliation. Even if someone pays for a service, it does not absolve him from his obligation towards his benefactor. Many of the problems that contribute to the crises facing the American family would never surface if gratitude and appreciation for one's spouse would be recognized as a critical component in a marriage. Indeed, the many daily chores which are viewed as routine are rarely acknowledged. If people would only live by the credo of *hakoras ha'tov*, the world would truly be a better place.

Yeshivos would have a much easier time dealing with their financial burdens if former students, who are now alumni, would recognize and acknowledge their debt of gratitude. Regrettably, this problem is not new and it is not going to recede, especially in a generation that blames all its problems on the "school."

The problem has its genesis in the way we raise our children. *Rav* Pam points out that even young children must be taught to say, "Thank you," when they receive something — anything. While they may not yet understand what they are saying, in time, they will be trained that a debt of gratitude exists, and they are obligated to acknowledge and repay it. As the young child matures into adulthood, this character trait will become an innate quality that is integral to their Jewish psyche.

תמים תהיה עם ד׳ אלקיך

You shall be wholehearted with Hashem, your G-d. (18:13)

Faith means to believe unequivocally, without first asking questions. We are instructed to be wholehearted with Hashem, to place our trust in Him — first and foremost. We go through life, enduring many trials and tribulations. In every situation, we are to view these challenges as events orchestrated by Hashem for a Divine purpose. We recite a prayer at the end of the *Shabbos Mussaf, Ein Keilokeinu,* "There is none like our G-d" (the Sephardic and universal custom in *Eretz Yisrael* is to recite this *Tefillah* daily), that begs elucidation. Immediately after the first stanza, when we declare that there is none like Hashem, we say, "*Mi Keilokeinu,* "Who is like our G-d?" Why ask a question after it has already been answered? I would think that the order should be reversed, with the stanza, "Who is like our G-d?" first, followed by, "There is none like our G-d."

Horav Yosef Chaim Sonnenfeld, zl, applies a parable to respond to this question. A man has to enter a long, dark, winding cave. He has no lights to guide him. If he has a modicum of common sense, he will not go any further into the cave unless he is absolutely sure that he can retrace his steps to the entrance. If he thinks it through, he might prepare a way out by laying down a rope as he goes farther and deeper into the cave. As long as he holds onto the rope, he will be able to locate the entrance by following the course of the rope.

The same idea applies to the concept of philosophical speculation, which is no less perilous than a dark and winding cave. Prior to approaching the subject too deeply, one must see to it that he has established a secure way out of the "cave." Thus, one must first anchor himself firmly in his belief in Hashem with the declaration of, *Ein Keilokeinu,* "There is no one like our G-d." Once this position has been firmly stated, there is now room for dialectic with questions such as, "Who is like our G-d?" Before we delve into the question, the answer must first be rooted in our minds!

Our *gedolei Yisrael* embodied the principles of *emunah* and *bitachon,* faith and trust, in the Almighty. Their unshakable faith enabled them to confront the challenges and vicissitudes of life. The Manchester *Rosh Yeshivah, Horav Yehudah Zev Segal, zl,* was well-known for his faith and sanctity. He lived the words of the *Rabbeinu* Yonah, "The meaning of *bitachon*, trust, in Hashem, is that one knows in his heart that everything is through the hand of Hashem, and that it is in His power to deviate from the ways of nature." His rock-firm faith in Hashem gave him the fortitude to remain calm and relaxed when others were tense and anxious.

One who believes in Hashem is never anxious. The Manchester *Rosh Yeshivah* was meticulous to arrive at a wedding at the prescribed time, so as not to delay the wedding on his account. Once, he entered the wedding hall on time, only to find that the *chassan*, groom, had not arrived. The family of the *kallah*, bride, was understandably anxious and tense. The *Rosh Yeshivah* asked, "Why is everybody tense? Only because the wedding had to take place on time. They forget one thing: the meaning of "on time." The invitation reads, *b'shaah tovah u'mutzlachas*, "at a good and fortuitous time." If the *chassan* is delayed, it is an indication that it is not yet the good and fortuitous time. When this time arrives, he will be here." This healthy attitude was the result of a deep-rooted sense of faith.

כי ימצא חלל באדמה... נפל בשדה לא נודע מי הכהו
If a corpse will be found on the land... fallen in the field, it was not known who smote him. (21:1)

The *Baal HaTurim* notes that the laws of the *eglah arufah*, axed heifer, is written between two chapters that address *Klal Yisrael* going out to war. He explains that the Torah is subtly delivering a message to he who hates another Jew and feels that during wartime — when people are in a tumult and disorganized — no one will notice if he kills his adversary. They will probably blame it on the enemy. The Torah teaches us that the Elders must expunge this attitude from the community so that people do not feel free to spill innocent blood wantonly.

Horav Ze'ev Weinberger, Shlita, gives a practical explanation. The Torah is teaching us that during war, when the value of human life has greatly depreciated and death is all around us, we should not forget any Jew. Even during times of strife, we are enjoined to care for the Jew in need and not say, "There are more important things to worry about now." If a Jew is murdered, we are exhorted to bring an atonement, because we must care —

at all times, for all Jews.

This is what Yosef alluded to his father, Yaakov *Avinu*, when he sent *agalos*, wagons, which is the same word as *eglah* — a reference to the *eglah arufah*, the last *halachah* that they studied together before Yosef's untimely sale into slavery. He was conveying that, regardless of his exalted position, he still retained in his mind the infinite value of every *Yiddishe neshamah*, Jewish soul. This idea is especially significant in the aftermath of the Holocaust, when we refer to the tragic deaths of six-million Jews in one breath. Our sensitivity to life has, regrettably, been diminished.

Parashas Ki Seitzei

ותפשו בו אביו ואמו

Then his father and mother shall grasp him. (21:19)

The parents demonstrate that their love for, and commitment to, the Almighty transcends the love they have for their child, as they together take him to *Bais Din*, Jewish court, to be brought to trial. Society's values must supercede human emotion. Obviously, it must be extremely difficult to take one's child and bring him to a trial that will probably cost him his life. A young Torah scholar once visited *Horav Yechezkel Abramsky, zl.* During the course of the conversation, the young man remarked that he was currently studying the laws of the *ben sorrer u'moreh,* wayward and rebellious child. Immediately, *Rav* Abramsky said, "Let me share with you an incredible story that occurred when I was a *rav* in Russia."

As *Rav* in the city, it was not unusual to be besieged with more than just *sheilos,* questions, regarding Jewish law. Many times, people came to request a blessing, to supplicate Hashem on their behalf, or simply to discuss a problem. One day, a woman came over and begged, "*Rebbe,* I entreat you to pray to Hashem that my son should die!" When *Rav* Abramsky heard this shocking request, he was understandably taken aback. Why would a sane woman want to see her son dead?

The distraught mother began to explain her predicament. It seems that her son, who was an only child, had recently been conscripted into the Russian Army. Everybody was acutely aware of the magnitude of this spiritual tragedy. Rarely, did anyone leave the army as an observant Jew. Regardless of the Jewish soldier's status prior to entering the army, being confronted with challenges to the spirit on a regular basis — coupled with exposure to a harsh, base environment — destroyed whatever *Yiddishkeit* he had. Therefore, the mother said that it was preferable that her son leave this world as a committed, observant Jew, than grow to be an atheist who denigrated everything Judaism represented.

Rav Abramsky was both shocked and impressed by her request. This was no ordinary woman. Here was a woman who was prepared to see her only child die prematurely, as long as he died as an observant Jew. It was mind-boggling. If this boy died, she would be all alone in the world with no future: no *Kaddish*, no one to carry on her name. Yet, it was all worth it, as long as her son would not have to contend with the spiritual trials and challenges that were so ingrained in the army way of life.

They both began to cry: the mother for her son; *Rav* Abramsky for the mother and her son. At the end, the *Rav* said, "No, we will not pray for him to die. We will pray that he lives and withstands the challenges and emerges triumphant from the army wholly committed to *Yiddishkeit*." Their prayers were answered, and the young man completed his tour of duty as an observant Jew.

Rav Abramsky looked at the young scholar and said, "At that moment, I was able to visualize the type of individual and the strength of character parents must possess in order to be prepared to grasp their son and bring him to *Bais Din*. Such parents truly love their son. They know that if he is allowed to live he will desecrate the Torah and lose his portion in the Eternal world. They would rather he lose his life than forfeit eternity."

✻ ✻ ✻ ✻ ✻ ✻

הקם תקים עמו
You shall surely raise [it], with him. (22:4)

The *Midrash* states an interesting *halachah*. If the owner of the animal decides to sit beside his animal and say to his would-be benefactor, "Since you have a *mitzvah* to unload my animal, do it and I will watch," the *halachah* is clear: he is not obligated to do a thing. The Torah states, *Hakeim takim imo*, "You shall surely raise [it], *with* him." It must be performed with the owner sharing in the endeavor. The *Chafetz Chaim, zl*, suggests a practical application to this *halachah*. We may ask Hashem to assist us in our endeavor to ascend the ladder of spiritual success *only* if *we* share in the activity. If we ask Hashem to protect us from speaking *lashon hara,* slanderous speech, and we do everything within our power to watch what we say, then we can expect Hashem's Divine assistance. If we sit back, however, and expect Hashem to act for us, then we are demonstrating gross *chutzpah.* Hashem will assist us in <u>our</u> endeavor. The first step, however, must be made by us.

The *Chafetz Chaim* gives the following analogy: A poor man meets one of the wealthier citizens of the town and pours out his sorrows. The wealthy man listens intently and says, "Come to my office tomorrow at 4:00 PM, and I will have a check waiting for you." The next day rolls around, and the poor man does not appear. It is already 6:00 PM and the poor man, who was in such dire need, is still absent. Another hour goes by, and the-would-be benefactor decides to go home.

The next day, the wealthy man walks down the street to be greeted once again by the poor man: "Please help me. I am starving. My family is starving. We cannot go on like this." He continues pouring out his tale of woe: "If you could only lend me a few gold coins, I could repay my debts and support my family."

The wealthy man looks into the poor man's eyes and says, "I do not understand you. We had made up to meet yesterday at 4:00 PM. What happened to you? I waited until 7:00 PM, and you did not show up, so I went home. Come again tomorrow, and I will bring the money."

The next day, the wealthy man waits at the appointed time for the poor man to appear. He does not show up until the following day, when they *once again* meet on the street and the poor man *once again* starts to delineate his litany of woes. Finally, the wealthy man says to him, "I do not think you are serious. Twice we have met, and you have poured out your heart to me, only not to appear the next day to retrieve the funds. You just want to beg, but you do not want to follow through!"

This analogy applies to us. Every day, we entreat Hashem during the *Ahavah Rabbah Tefillah* of *Shacharis,* "May You be equally gracious to us and teach us… instill in our hearts to understand and elucidate, to listen, learn…Enlighten our eyes to Your Torah…." We recite these and many other supplications daily. There is no doubt that Hashem is prepared to grant us our entreaty. After all, why not? It will certainly enhance our *mitzvah* performance and enable us to achieve greater understanding in Torah knowledge. There is only one thing that Hashem asks of *us*: to appear at the *bais ha'medrash* and learn.

Regrettably, our entreaties are only lip service which we pay to Hashem. We say the words; we talk the talk, but refuse to walk the walk. And even when we do go to the *bais ha'medrash*, do we apply ourselves to the learning — or do we spend our time bickering and indulging in other forms of idle conversation? This goes on until the next day, when we once again turn to Hashem with more requests.

✽ ✽ ✽ ✽ ✽ ✽

כי יקרא קן צפור לפניך בדרך....והאם רבצת על האפרחים...לא תקח האם
על הבנים. שלח תשלח את האם ואת הבנים תקח לך

If you encounter a bird's nest on the road... with young birds... and the mother is roosting on the young birds... you shall not take the mother with the young. You shall surely send away the mother and take the young for yourself. (22:6,7)

If the Torah's goal is to spare the mother bird, it would be more sensible to prohibit taking the young altogether. Surely when the mother returns, she will be anguished to discover that her chicks are no longer in the nest. What is the rationale for this *mitzvah*? *Horav Yosef Chaim Sonnenfeld, zl,* explains that the Torah is teaching us a powerful lesson in *menchlichkeit*, humanness and ethics: It is forbidden to take advantage of a mother bird's love for her children in order to catch her more easily. Usually, when a predator approaches a nest, the bird will immediately fly away. This bird does not leave, because she is a mother protecting her young. Her survival instinct is superceded by her motherly love, as she prefers remaining in the nest to protect her young rather than escape for her personal safety.

The Torah enjoins us to respect this motherly instinct and not take advantage to easily catch a devoted mother bird. The reward for obeying this command is *arichas yamin*, longevity. The lesson is clear and simple: When someone demonstrates sensitivity towards Hashem's creatures, Hashem reciprocates towards him.

Rav Yosef Chaim substantiates this thesis with the words of the

Rambam, *Hilchos Shechitah* 13:7 who writes: "If a person sent away the mother, but she came back, and after this he took her, this is permitted." The Torah forbids catching the mother only if she is incapable of flying away from her young, over whom she hovers to protect them from being taken. The *halachah* is applicable only if the mother remains out of love. The mother who does not place her young before her own safety does not necessarily deserve our protection. We may add that this idea should apply equally to the human arena. A child comes first. If we bring children into this world, we have a moral obligation to care for them — even if it might put us out. This problem often emerges with decisions concerning education. A parent chooses what is best for the parent, or what he believes is best for his child. What the parent thinks and the reality do not necessarily coincide. We may be so bold as to suggest that this applies also to the surrogate parent, the *rebbe*, whose decisions concerning the student are critical to his growth and development.

✹ ✹ ✹ ✹ ✹ ✹

כי תקצר קצירך בשדך ושכחת עמר בשדה לא תשוב לקחתו

When you reap your harvest in your field, and you forget a bundle in the field, you shall not go back to take it. **(24:19)**

As *Horav S.R. Hirsch, zl,* notes, the time of harvest is a milestone for the farmer. It is the culmination of a season's hard work of toil and overcoming challenges. It is a time when the farmer feels a deep sense of pride. It is precisely at this time that he is enjoined to share his success with the poor, to realize that what he has is in itself a gift from the Almighty to share with those who are less fortunate. *Shikchah*, the forgotten sheaf, applies to a single bundle that one has forgotten to gather — or even standing grain that a reaper inadvertently has passed by. This is an intriguing and fascinating *mitzvah* in the sense that one cannot prepare for it. One cannot have *kavanah*, concentration, since it is based on forgetting. The moment that he "remembers" to forget, it is no longer *shikchah*.

Horav Yaakov Dushinsky, explains that a significant aspect of this *mitzvah* is the Torah's admonition, "You shall not go back to take it." One's innate love of money should not begin to stir within him, convincing him to return for the grain. Once one forgets, it is to remain forgotten. He should pay gratitude to the Almighty for availing him of the opportunity to perform such a *mitzvah* — a *mitzvah* with grain that to him is insignificant, but to a poor man, might represent his life. The inherent joy in such a *mitzvah* should be incredible, since the benefactor hardly loses and the beneficiary gains so much.

The *Tosefta* in *Peiah* 3:12 cites an incident concerning a pious man who had forgotten a sheaf of grain in his field. He asked his son to sacrifice a calf for him as an *Olah*, Burnt-Offering, and a calf as a *Shelamim*, peace-offering. The son asked his father, "Father, what is there about this *mitzvah* that excites you so much, more so than any other *mitzvah*?"

His father replied, "Every other *mitzvah* in the Torah has been given to us by Hashem to be performed perceptively and with knowledge aforethought. This *mitzvah*, on the other hand, can only be carried out if one is unaware. The Torah blesses us for forgetting the sheaf. Now, if the Torah guarantees blessing for something which is the result of incognizance, how much more so will we be rewarded for a positive act of consciousness."

The *mitzvah* of *Shikchah* addresses the unknown within a human being. It teaches us how to react to a lapse of memory and the positive consequences that can result from it. The poor and the needy are the beneficiaries of one's failure to remember the sheaf of grain, and, indeed, the individual himself is blessed thereby. Everything, even forgetfulness, can be a source of blessing.

In contrast to the *mitzvah* of *Shikchah*, there is a *mitzvah* of *Zechirah*, remembrance. We are admonished to "Remember what Amalek did to you... Erase the memory of Amalek from beneath the Heaven. Do not forget" (*Devarim* 25:17,19). The *mitzvah* to remember and obliterate Amalek's name also awakens and educates our unknown dimension. Instead of forgetting what Amalek did to us, even to the point that some might find a place in their hearts to forgive his malevolence, the *mitzvah* functions as a reminder — do not forget! Do not forgive! Do not fall prey to false dreams and liberal rhetoric as if Amalek no longer exists. His miscreancy is alive and well and burning with a passion. The hatred that he generated in the world towards the Jew has germinated and developed. His evil must be expunged. This can only occur if we *never forget* what he had done to us.

The *mitzvah* to forget has its place in the service of Hashem when it involves helping the poor and needy. Likewise, the *mitzvah* of remembering also has its place when it addresses the needs of *Klal Yisrael* and its land.

✽ ✽ ✽ ✽ ✽ ✽

כי יהיה ריב בין אנשים... והצדיקו את הצדיק והרשיעו את הרשע

When there will be a dispute between people...and they vindicate the righteous one and find the wicked one guilty. **(25:1)**

*H*orav Yaakov Kaminetzky, *zl*, infers from here that the appellation of *tzaddik*, righteous person, is applied to one who is supported by the truth. This makes sense, since *tzaddik* and *tzedek*, justice, share the same root. Thus, a righteous person is one who adheres to the truth, whose actions and total demeanor reflect integrity, straightforwardness and honor. A *tzaddik* is not only pious — he is straight and principled, always using absolute truth as his barometer.

Rav Yaakov substantiates this thought with the words of *Chazal* at the end of *Mishnayos Oktzin* 13:12, "In the future, Hashem will bequeath to each *tzaddik* and *tzaddik* three hundred words." The *Tosfos Yom Tov* explains that the redundancy in the text (each *tzaddik* and *tzaddik*) is a reference to the various *shitos*, contending opinions throughout *halachic* dialectic. Why should the sages of the *Mishnah* be called *tzaddikim*? They should be referred to as *chachamim*, wise men. Moreover, the title *tzaddik* usually applies to one who acts righteously with his fellowman, such as Noach *HaTzaddik*, and Yosef *HaTzaddik*. Now, however, that we interpret a *tzaddik* as one who is the paragon of veracity and who seeks to establish his opinions only concerning that which he understands to be the absolute truth, we can understand why a *chacham* is a *tzaddik* — even disputing opinions in *halachah*. Since, *Eilu v'eilu divrei Elokim chaim*, "These and those are the words of the Living G-d," both *chachamim* have a parallel goal — the truth.

✽ ✽ ✽ ✽ ✽ ✽

Parashas Ki Savo

ולקחת מראשית כל פרי האדמה... וענית ואמרת לפני ד' אלקיך

You shall take of the first of every fruit of the ground... then you shall call out and say before Hashem, your G-d. (26:2.5)

The underlying motif for the *mitzvah* of *Bikurim* is *hakoras ha'tov*, gratitude. *Rashi* cites the *Sifri* that explains that the declaration which accompanies the *Bikurim* is an indication that we are not ingrates, a sign that we understand that Hashem has given us the land as a gift. David *Ha'melech* says in *Sefer Tehillim* 14:1, "The *naval*, degraded man, says in his heart, 'There is no G-d'; they have corrupted and made abominable their actions, there is no doer of good." *Horav Chaim Vital, zl*, explains that *naval* is a reference to he who is a *kafui tov*, ingrate. The *Sefer HaChinuch* also refers to the ingrate as a *naval*, abominable person. *Horav Avraham Schorr*, *Shlita*, suggests that the source of this name originates with Avigayil, who said about Naval, her husband, "For he is as his name implies — *naval* is his name and revulsion is his trait" (*Shmuel I* 25:25). The *Sefer Chassidim* explains that Naval was an ingrate to David *Ha'melech* who watched his sheep, because ultimately Naval refused to pay him. Thus, the term *naval* characterizes the individual who does not appreciate the benefits he receives from others. Hashem despises such a person, and He does not delay in remitting swift punishment to him.

In his commentary to *Sefer Tehillim*, the *R'am Almoshino* explains that the *naval*/ingrate denies the gifts that he receives from Hashem. He says, *ein Elokim*, "there is no G-d." In other words, he is saying that the various occurrences which have spared us throughout time were not from Hashem. Each was a *mikreh*, a chance incident, that had no connection to G-d. Therefore, these events do not obligate us to be grateful to Him. The *naval* substantiates his apostasy, asking why — if everything comes from Hashem — do some things have a bad ending? If there was a good and benevolent G-d, everything would culminate on a positive note. The ingrate cites the tragedies of life as proof that Hashem does not guide the world, in order to prove that he does not owe Him anything in return.

Rav Schorr cites the *Mechilta* in *Parashas Beshalach* that includes Amalek, the archenemy of the Jewish People, among those who personify *kefiyas tovah*, ingratitude. Amalek seeks to dismiss everything G-d does as a mere *mikreh*, chance event. He maintains that things do not happen by design, and there is no Divine *Hashgachah*, Providence; things "just happen." This is the meaning of the words *asher karcha baderech*, "that he chanced upon you on the road" (25:18). Amalek wanted to diminish the Jew's belief in Hashem by asserting that everything happens by chance.

The *yetzer hara*, evil inclination, seeks to create a sense of *shikchah*, forgetfulness, within the Jew, in order to make him forget Hashem and what He constantly does for us. If not for this *shikchah*, our passion to serve Hashem would retain its fire and verve. The *Baal Shem Tov* explains that Amalek's function is to generate *shikchas ha'Boreh*, forgetting the Creator. By *v'ram levavecha*, increasing the haughtiness in our hearts, we forget Hashem. Interestingly, the *gematria*, numerical equivalent, of *ram*, is 240, which coincides with the *gematria* of Amalek.

Rav Schorr concludes by explaining the juxtaposition of the *mitzvah* of *Bikurim* to the *mitzvah* of erasing Amalek's name, which concluded *Parashas Ki Seitzei*. *Bikurim* teach us the significance of *hakoras hatov*, recognizing and repaying the good we receive from Hashem. This is the antithesis and,concomitantly, the antidote for the evil that is represented by Amalek. Amalek seeks to infuse us with a lack of gratitude by causing us to forget about Hashem and view His Divine guidance as a chance occurrence. When one sees Hashem's guiding hand in every-day events, he fights the evil generated by Amalek and his modern-day counterparts.

✸ ✸ ✸ ✸ ✸ ✸

לא עברתי ממצותיך ולא שכחתי
"I have not transgressed any of Your commandments, and I have not forgotten." (26:13)

*R*ashi interprets *v'lo shochachti*, "I have not forgotten," as a reference to thanking Hashem through the blessing for the opportunity to perform the *mitzvah* of *Hafroshas Maasros*, separating tithes. Although the act of reciting a *brachah* is Rabbinic in origin, this *pasuk* is an *asmachata*, a Scriptural allusion, to a law destined to be enacted by *Chazal*. Indeed, the privileges that are afforded us to perform a *mitzvah*, to serve Hashem, should inspire within us a propensity to bless Hashem. It should be a natural response to a unique opportunity. The *Seforim* suggest that this attitude prevailed within the Jewish psyche until the period of *Chazal,* when they felt that the people were diminishing their sense of gratitude for *mitzvos*. Hence, the Rabbinic *obligation* to recite a blessing prior to performing a *mitzvah* developed.

How should one recite a blessing? What should be his focus of concentration? The *Yesod v'Shoresh HoAvodah* writes that when one begins the *brachah,* when he says, *Baruch Atah,* "Blessed are You," he should imagine in his mind that he is standing before the Almighty and speaking. He should say the words, *Elokeinu Melech haOlam,* "Our G-d, the King of the world," slowly, reflecting on its meaning, rejoicing in the fact that Hashem is our G-d and that His monarchy encompasses the entire universe. A *brachah* recited in this manner certainly has greater meaning.

I recently read a profound comment made by *Horav Avraham Yaakov, zl, m'Sadigur* to one of his *chasidim*. He said, "It is possible that a person travels to the city of Lemberg for a business purpose — or so he thinks. He does not realize that the Almighty, the *Mesabeiv Sibos,* Cause of all causes, wanted him in Lemberg for a different purpose: to recite a *Shehakol niheyeh bidevaro* on a glass of water in Lemberg!

We can derive two lessons from this statement: First, we have to remember that Hashem guides our life and everything happens in it for an underlying purpose. Second, *brachos* have great significance — to the point that they have a profound effect on the place in which they are recited. Perhaps the next time we take a drink of water, we might stop to think before we make the *brachah*. It might just make a difference.

❈ ❈ ❈ ❈ ❈ ❈

וראו כל עמי הארץ כי שם ד׳ נקרא עליך

Then all the peoples of the earth will see that the Name of Hashem is proclaimed over you. **(28:10)**

When *Klal Yisrael* raises the banner of its value and beliefs, the nations around them will understand that Hashem's blessing is upon them. *Horav Mordechai Sharabi, zl,* was a *Sephardic gadol,* Torah leader, who truly exemplified this concept. His total demeanor reflected Hashem's Divinity hovering over him. He was a saint who attempted to recluse himself. He had no interest in pursuing idle conversation with the members of the Muslim clergy. This, of course, did not please them. Furthermore, *Rav* Mordechai never touched a Muslim, and no one — not even a Jew — was permitted to touch the utensils used for his food.

When the Muslim sheiks noticed how *Rav* Mordechai rebuffed them, they decided to trump up a libel charge against him. They informed the Emir of their community, a noted anti-Semite, who was a close confidant of the Imam of Yemen. The Imam was also no great friend of the Jews, and he sent the *gendarme* to *Rav* Mordechai's home to arrest him.

As soon as the *rabbanim* of Yemen heard that the *gendarme* was dispatched to arrest their beloved leader, they declared a public fast and *Yom Tefillah,* day of prayer. When *Rav* Mordechai heard about this, he dissuaded them from fasting, saying that he would triumph with Hashem's assistance. He would not allow anyone to accompany him as he was taken to the Emir's palace. His *bitachon,* trust in Hashem, was echoed in everything he said.

There was an unwritten rule in the Emir's home that anyone who entered had to genuflect and say, "Peace to my master," and remain bowed until the Emir instructed him to rise. He then was to stand until the Emir offered him a seat. *Rav* Mordechai did exactly as Mordechai *HaYehudi* in Shushan did — he refused to bow down to the Emir. He also refused to greet him as "master." With great faith and trust in the Almighty, *Rav* Mordechai entered the room, sat down next to the Emir, and asked, "Yes, what is it that you want?"

The Emir, slightly taken aback, turned to him and asked, "Are you Mordechai?"

"Yes, I am," replied *Rav* Mordechai.

"We have a number of serious allegations against you," said the Emir. The Emir began to read the list of complaints, among which was the fact that he would not shake hands with the Muslim clergy.

Rav Mordechai patiently explained to the Emir that gentiles eat non-kosher food. When they travel, the sweat that is on their hands is the product of unclean, unkosher animals. He asked, "How can I, a servant of the Almighty G-d, touch these hands? I will defile my body! Also, I never leave my home except to pray in the synagogue. I study Hashem's Torah all day. How do you expect me to waste my time discussing religious philosophy with people that are not members of the Covenant of Hashem?"

Their interchange continued. Every time the Emir posed a question to *Rav* Mordechai, he received a quick and lucid response. The Emir saw that *Rav* Mordechai was pious, committed and sincere in his belief in Hashem. When people see that we are upright and sincere, they respect us. The Emir's attitude quickly changed, as he was enlightened about the level of conviction that was maintained by *Rav* Mordechai, the representative of the Jewish community. He sent him home with pomp and regalia, as befitting a man of distinction and a friend of the king. Respect from others is the result of the self-respect one has for himself. When we maintain pride in our heritage and commitment to our religion, we will achieve the respect of the outside world.

******

תחת אשר לא עבדת את ה' אלקיך בשמחה ובטוב לבב

***Because you did not serve Hashem, your G-d, amid gladness and goodness of heart.* (28:47)**

After a lengthy litany of frightening curses, the Torah states a reason for these terrible punishments: a lack of joy on our part in serving Hashem. The Torah seems to be emphasizing that joy is a primary obligation. Let us take a moment and reflect on this statement. Is it really possible to remain happy with so much suffering all around? To ignore the pain of others is callous and insensitive. Apparently, there is a deeper meaning of what joy is and its relationship to the Jew in this world.

First and foremost, we must understand that the greatest gift granted to us by the Almighty is the gift of life. Being alive is an intrinsic reason for expressing joy — regardless of the negative experiences one may encounter.

Life is an opportunity for growth and that in itself has the ultimate value. Life is everything: without life, one has nothing.

We are placed in this world for a purpose: to serve Hashem and earn ultimate happiness in the World To Come. The awareness that everything positive we do in this world earns us a portion in the World to Come should be a constant source of joy. The *mitzvah* to be happy is the knowledge that our sojourn in this world is a means of achieving ultimate pleasure and joy. The error of many is that they think that this world is an end in itself. No, it is only an opportunity, a means toward achieving the true goal.

Regrettably, many of us realize too late the value of the gift of life. It is only when our lives hang in the balance, when one almost loses life and then miraculously gains it back, that he discovers the wonderful opportunity that he has been given. We become complacent with what we are accustomed to having. Familiarity breeds neglect and a lack of appreciation. When that complacency is shaken, one quickly awakens from his slumber.

Let us go a step further in understanding the Torah's demand for joy. Upon carefully perusing the text, one gains a powerful insight into this *mitzvah*. The Torah does *not* say that we must constantly be happy, and always walk around with a smile on our faces, regardless of our mood or the circumstances with which we are confronted. The Torah does not say that we must <u>live</u> in happiness; the Torah says that we must *serve* Hashem amid joy. Serving Hashem has to be performed with happiness. It should be our reason for ecstasy. The source of joy is the ability and opportunity to carry out Hashem's command to be His servant. The pain does not hurt; the work is not difficult — because it is for Hashem. This is the true meaning of joy.

We worry when we lose sight of where we are and Who guides us. If we would take into account that everything in our lives is directed by the Almighty, we would not worry. A secular author once told the story of a ship at sea during a fierce storm. The passengers were in great distress. After awhile, one of them — against captain's orders — ascended to the deck and made his way to the pilot. The seaman was at his post, calmly carrying out his function at the wheel. When he saw that the passenger was agitated, he gave him a big, reassuring smile. The man then returned to the other passengers with the following words of comfort, "I have seen the face of the pilot, and he smiled. All is well."

It is all a matter of attitude. If one realizes that the challenges he encounters in life are directed by Hashem and that Hashem will be with him throughout the ordeal, he will view the situation through a different prism. I recently read the following story in *Touched By A Story 2,* by Rabbi Yechiel Spero. I believe it goes to the core of what we are saying.

This story is about a bus driver for a group of boys in a Buchari neighborhood. The boys were tough, and driving them every day was difficult. The respect they demonstrated to him left something to be desired. The driver decided that the job was no longer appropriate for him. At the end of the month, he informed the principal of his decision to seek employment elsewhere. The principal, being an understanding man, listened intently to the driver and commiserated with him. He assured him that he would speak to the boys, and he even offered him a raise for his troubles.

The driver, although appreciative of the raise, said that he had had enough. It was not because of the money. The boys were not really bad and were just acting in the manner of boys that age. He basically wanted a change, something different, something more relaxing. As they were walking towards the door, the principal made one last attempt, "Would you mind visiting with *Horav Ben Zion Abba Shaul?*" The driver agreed, thinking to himself that the great *Sephardic rav* could not say anything to him that would change his mind.

They walked together to the *Rav's* apartment and sat down to talk. The principal explained the predicament: how the bus driver had served the school faithfully for a number of years, and now he had decided that it was time to move on. While it would be upsetting to replace him, the bus driver insisted that he could go no longer continue. He was emotionally spent, and he desperately needed a change of scenery.

Rav Bentzion's eyes sparkled with warmth and sensitivity as he looked at the bus driver. In reality, he was focusing on his heart. He said, "My dear friend, you think that you are driving a simple van, but actually you are driving a mobile *Aron Kodesh*! The children are not just passengers; they are living *Sifrei Torah*! When you open the door to your mobile *Aron Kodesh,* you are being honored with *Pesichah,* opening the *Aron Kodesh*! Each and every child on that van is precious. He is our future!"

When the bus driver heard his vocation being interpreted in this way by the great *Rav*, he felt ashamed for having been so petty. He assured the *Rav* that he would continue performing his function with distinction and esteem. The next morning, the attitude he displayed to his young charges was visibly altered. "Good morning boys," he greeted them. "Thank you for granting me the privilege to drive you to *yeshivah* today, so that you can learn Torah."

As the last boy exited the van, he looked up at the driver and said, "Thank you." The driver smiled and countered, "No, thank *you!*"

It is all in one's attitude. The opportunity to live and serve Hashem should be our ultimate source of joy.

✿ ✿ ✿ ✿ ✿

Parashas Nitzavim

אתם נצבים היום כלכם לפני ד' אלקיכם

You are standing today, all of you, before Hashem, your G-d. (29:9)

T he *Midrash* explains the word *nitzavim*, standing. When the people heard the frightening curses enumerated in *Parashas Ki Savo*, they were overwhelmed with fear at what seemed to be a hopeless future. Hence, Moshe *Rabbeinu* comforted them, saying that despite their previous sinful behavior, they were still standing before Hashem. He had not eliminated them in the past, and He will continue to sustain them in the future. The *Tochachah*, Admonition, was there to inspire fear, as well as to indicate the punishments which would atone for their evil deeds. The commentators wonder why *Klal Yisrael* reacted so negatively to the curses in *Parashas Ki Savo* and not to the forty-nine curses enumerated in *Parashas Bechukosai*.

Horav Shmuel David Walkin, *zl*, suggests that there is one curse in the litany of ninety-eight curses that filled the Jewish People with overwhelming fear: "He will bring upon you all the sufferings of Egypt, of which you were terrified, and they will cleave to you" (*Devarim* 28:60). He cites the *Alter, zl, m'Kelm* who explains the significance of *machalas Mitzrayim*, the illnesses of Egypt, and relates why they are referred to with the unique term, *makah*, plague. He explains that the *makas Mitzrayim* did not accomplish anything in terms of atonement. Pharaoh continued along his sinful way, ignoring the punishment. If the illness does not effect a change, it is a *machalah b'li refuah*, an illness for which there is neither cure nor therapeutic effect. The *makos* that *Klal Yisrael* undergo bring about *teshuvah*, repentance, inspiring them to rise up from the depths of sin to correct their ways. This is the underlying meaning of the *pasuk* in *Shemos* 15:26, "If you hearken diligently to the voice of Hashem…then any of the diseases that I placed upon Egypt, I will not bring upon you, for I am Hashem, your Healer." In the *Talmud Sanhedrin*, 101, *Chazal* ask, "If He does not send illness, why is healing necessary?" They explain that if *Klal Yisrael* listens, then Hashem will not send illness. If they do not listen, He will send illness, but He will heal them, because the purpose of His punishment is not punitive, but restorative, to purge them of sin and influence them to repent. Hashem will never send against us an Egyptian form of distress, the focus of which is purely to punish. Whatever emanates from Hashem is to inspire us to return to Him.

We now understand why *Klal Yisrael* became so disconcerted when they heard the curse that Hashem would bring upon them the sufferings of Egypt. They could handle the punishment if it would stimulate *teshuvah*. The thought that they would have pain for the purpose of pain, punishment that was punitive — and not conducive to repentance — was frightening.

Incidentally, there is a powerful lesson to be derived herein, especially as we prepare to usher in a new year with its challenges, its opportunities for success, its trials and travails, and its symbol of hope. What Hashem does *to us* is really *for us* — to make us better people, to serve Him better — so that we can ultimately earn the true reward that is awaiting each one of us.

אתם נצבים היום כלכם...ראשיכם שבטיכם זקניכם ושטריכם כל איש ישראל

You are standing today, all of you...the heads of your tribes, your elders, and your officers — all the men of Yisrael. **(29:9)**

On the last day of Moshe *Rabbeinu's* life, he assembled all of *Klal Yisrael* and inducted them into Hashem's Covenant for the last time. In the *Yerushalmi* at the end of *Meseches Horayos, Chazal* make the following intriguing statement: "Why did Moshe *Rabbeinu* precede the *roshim*, heads of the tribes, before the *zekeinim*, the Torah scholars and elders, while Yehoshua, upon speaking to the people, preceded the elders before the leaders of the tribes? Moshe did not exert himself in the study of Torah. Hashem gave it to him as a gift, thus ensuring that he would never forget it. Yehoshua, in contrast, had to toil in order to retain the Torah that he had learned from Moshe. Thus, Yehoshua had a more profound appreciation of the *zekeinim* than did Moshe."

What an incredible statement! *Horav Moshe Shapiro, shlita,* adds that only *Chazal* could issue such a compelling declaration. *Moshe Rabbeinu,* our greatest teacher, the quintessential leader of *Klal Yisrael,* the *Adon v'Avi haNeviim,* master and father of all prophets, did not know how to value the toil expended by Torah scholars as well as Yehoshua did. He was the greatest scholar, but since his scholarship was not the result of *yegia,* toil and exertion, he was missing a vital component in his ability to hold the *talmid chacham,* Torah scholar, in the proper esteem.

Chazal are clearly asserting that in order to appreciate *ameilus ba'Torah,* toil in Torah, one must himself have studied Torah *b'ameilus.* Just as one does not reach the summit of Torah knowledge without prior exertion in studying Torah, so, too, is he not qualified to value and appreciate those who have achieved proficiency in Torah knowledge. To be *ameil ba'Torah* is to never interrupt one's learning. To paraphrase *Horav Elchonan Wasserman, zl,* "*Vihogisa*" means one must *tracht,* think, in learning. There should not be any cessation in one's relationship with Torah learning.

We may add that this concept applies to all endeavors. Unless one has "been there," he is not qualified to judge one who has. All too often, we make judgment calls and establish opinions based upon how *we* perceive an issue or a person. Yet, we forget to take into consideration how this issue or person evolved to this point. If there are reservations about *Moshe Rabbeinu's* capacity for evaluating, *yegias ha'Torah,* what should we say?

When a person is *ameil ba'Torah,* genuinely toils in Torah, he can reach unlimited heights, regardless of his ability. Furthermore, the rewards in store for those who toil in Torah — and the esteem in which they are held — are incredible. Toil is not just a lofty way of studying Torah; rather, it is an absolute requirement! *Horav Yisrael Gustman, zl,* was a *gaon* who exemplified *ameilus ba'Torah.* When he was only twenty-years-old, he was appointed as a *dayan,* judge, on the *bais din* of *Horav Chaim Ozer Grodzenski, zl,* the venerable *Rav* of pre-World War II Vilna, and the leader of world Jewry. *Rav* Yisrael served as *dayan* for twenty-five years. When he came to *Eretz Yisrael,* he was granted an audience with the Steipler *Rav.* The Steipler *Rav* could not hear well. Thus, he had his visitors write down their requests. *Rav* Yisrael wrote his request and signed his note, Yisrael Gustman. Upon reading the note, the Steipler queried, "Was your father the *dayan* in

Rav Chaim Ozer's *bais din?*" *Rav* Yisrael replied, "That is I."

"That is you?!" the Steipler asked incredulously. The Steipler was not well and hardly left his house. Yet, he stood up and <u>ran</u> to *Rav* Yisrael, hugging and kissing him. "You have no idea the esteem in which you were held by *Rav* Chaim Ozer!"

A similar incident occurred when *Rav* Gustman went to visit the Tchebiner *Rav, zl,* who donned his hat, stood up, and recited the special *brachah* one makes upon seeing an outstanding *talmid chacham.* One who toils in Torah achieves the greatest respect and reaches the zenith in Torah knowledge.

Horav Moshe Aharon Stern, zl, gives a practical analogy about toil in Torah. He asserts that one who is *ameil,* toils, is assured of *gadlus ba'Torah,* noble achievement in Torah. Hashem gives the Torah to each and every Jew but only if the person prepares vessels for containing it. Someone who comes with a "*shnapps*-glass," shot glass, will have his small cup filled. One who comes with a large barrel will have his container filled to the top. Every one of us should maximize the time we dedicate to Torah study. Those that do will reap rewards commensurate with their toil.

Parashas Vayeilech

הקהל את העם האנשים והנשים והטף

Gather together the people — the men, the women and the small children.
(31:12)

T he *mitzvah* of *Hakhel* took place once every seven years on the first day of *Chol HaMoed Succos* following a *Shemittah* year. Everyone was included in this *mitzvah*: men, women and even the small children. As *Chazal* state, "The men came to learn; the women came to listen; the children came to give reward to those who brought them." The *Malbim* explains the benefit the children had in attending the *Hakhel* experience. Although they could not understand the proceedings, their eyes would be glued to the awesome sight of millions of Jews gathered together for the sole purpose of hearing the *Dvar Hashem*, Word of G-d. This would leave an indelible impression on them, inspiring them to lead lives of *kedushah v'taharah*, holiness and purity.

While the *mitzvah* of *Hakhel* is not in effect today, *Horav Avraham Pam*, *zl*, suggests that its message is eternal and certainly worth contemplating. A child develops a love for what he sees his parents cherish. When a child sees his father learning, he develops a love of learning. When a child notices his father is not at home and, after asking where he is, he hears that his father is in the *bais ha'medrash* learning, he, in turn, also wants to learn. On the other hand, if he notices his father spending his time doing everything else but learning, the message he will derive is, regrettably, clearly negative. Parents have an enormous responsibility in raising their children in the Torah way. *Rav* Pam cites the *Viddui*, confession prayer, that we recite on *Yom Kippur, Al cheit she'chatanu le'fanecha b'prikas ol,* "For the sin that we have sinned against You in throwing off the yoke." The simple meaning is that this is a reference to the yoke of Heaven. *Rav* Pam understands this also as a confession for reneging on the yoke of parenthood. The responsibility is awesome; the challenge is formidable, but that is the essence of parenting. *Nachas* does not just happen. One has to work and work for it. At times, we allow our guard to slip, as we defer to the many pressures of life and child-rearing. Our children are our most precious possessions. It is up to us to make the correct decisions for them, not necessarily based upon what is easiest and best for us. All too often, our decisions are mired by the "What are others going to say?" syndrome. If we care for our children, we will do what is best for them and not what enhances our image. Parenting is an endeavor which does not allow much room for error, so it would be best that we make the correct and proper decisions the first time around.

✸ ✸ ✸ ✸ ✸ ✸

והסתרתי פני מהם... ואנכי הסתר אסתיר פני ביום ההוא

And I will conceal My face from them... But I will have surely concealed My face on that day. (31:17,18)

K lal Yisrael acknowledges that its troubles are the result of Hashem removing His Presence from their midst. Their acknowledgement does not suffice to effect Hashem's return. It is only through sincere *teshuvah*, repentance, preceded by *Viddui*, confession, that Hashem's concealment will end. How does one bring Hashem into his life? How does one make the *Shechinah*, Divine Presence, a factor in his daily life? *Horav Moshe Swift, zl,* cites a fascinating *Chazal* in the end of *Meseches Makkos* 24a, which sheds light on our query. David *Ha'melech* in *Tehillim* 15 describes the ideal Jewish personality: "Who shall sojourn in Your tent, who shall dwell upon Your holy mountain?" David *Ha'melech* goes on to detail the quintessential Jewish character — "Walking uprightly, working righteousness, speaking truth in his heart, having no slander on his tongue, nor doing any evil to his fellow." He concludes, "He who does these things shall never falter." *Chazal* relate that when *Rabban* Gamliel would approach this chapter in *Tehillim*, he would weep, saying, "Is it only he that does *all* these things who shall not falter? Does this imply that he who does only one of these, that he is moved?"

The reply was, "No, No, David *Ha'melech* does not say that he must do all these things. Even if a man observes only one thing, if he demonstrates one quality, but he does it wholeheartedly — because it is Hashem's command — then he shall not falter for eternity." In his *Peirush HaMishnayos,* the *Rambam* adds, "If a person fulfills any one of the *Taryag Mitzvos,* 613 commandments, as it should be fulfilled, without any ulterior motive or improper intention of any possible kind, but purely for the sake of the *mitzvah* and for the love of G-d's commands, he thereby becomes worthy of eternal life."

The *Rambam* asserts that *Rav* Chanania ben Teradyon, one of the *Asarah Harugei Malchus,* Ten Martyrs, earned his portion in *Olam Haba,* not because of his martyrdom, but, rather, because of one *mitzvah* that he performed *completely lishmah,* for the sake of Heaven, without any vestige of personal interest, only for the love of Hashem and fulfillment of His command!

What a powerful thought. If we want to bring the *Shechinah* into our midst, we just have to perform one *mitzvah l'shem Shomayim.* This brings G-d into our daily lives. It touches our homes and makes them a veritable *Mishkan,* Sanctuary. It permeates our lives as we cling to the Almighty. The Jew who acts *l'shem Shomayim* forges an unbreakable link between Heaven and earth.

Hashem conceals His Presence from us because we are not willing to repent. If we begin performing *mitzvos* in the correct and proper manner, however, we will merit His return, to bring Him back into our lives. Of course, we must observe <u>all</u> of the *mitzvos,* not just pick and choose what is most palatable. It is understood that we cannot maintain the correct *kavanah,* attitude, towards all *mitzvos.* If we take one *mitzvah* and perform it correctly, *l'shem Shomayim,* we will be privileged to bring Hashem into our lives, so that we can continue to perform the rest of the *mitzvos* properly — for Hashem.

הקהילו אלי את כל זקני שבטיכם ושטריכם

"Gather to me all the elders of your tribes and your officers." **(31:28)**

ashi comments that the *chatzotzros*, trumpets, were not used that day to assemble the people. These trumpets were made exclusively for Moshe *Rabbeinu's* use and Yehoshua did not have authority over them. Indeed, they were hidden by Hashem during Moshe's lifetime in fulfillment of *Shlomo Ha'melech's* dictum in *Koheles* 8:8, "And there is no rulership over the day of death." The *Midrash* at the end of *Sefer Bereishis* emphasizes that Hashem hid Moshe's trumpets to ensure that no one else would use them. *Horav Mordechai Ilan, zl,* explains that every leader is endowed with specific qualities, abilities and talents that will assist him in leading *his* generation. What works for his generation will not necessarily succeed in the next generation. His trumpets are for his use during his tenure as leader. With his passing, the baton is passed to the next leader who has his own trumpets which are suitable for use in his specific generation. Every generation has its Moshe *Rabbeinu*, and every Moshe has his singular trumpet.

✽ ✽ ✽ ✽ ✽ ✽

Parashas Ha'azinu

יערף כמטר לקחי תזל כטל אמרתי

May my Torah drop as the rain, may my speech flow gently like the dew.
(32:2)

Moshe *Rabbeinu* uses the simile of rain and dew to describe the Torah. The commentators, each in his own unique manner, expound on the comparison of Torah to these natural gifts of Hashem. *Sforno* emphasizes the relationship of the *mekabeil*, receiver/student of Torah, to the Torah. Both rain and dew have a beneficial effect on the earth, providing the water it needs so that the seeds may grow. Rain may come down to earth in torrents. Dew, in contrast, lands gently on the earth in a thin layer.

Sforno posits that both the average person and the erudite, brilliant scholar are capable of comprehending the Torah. The difference between the two is in their level of understanding and ability to grasp its lessons and profundities. The average Jew will absorb Torah on a superficial level. His grasp does not exceed his reach. He understands and appreciates Torah within the constraints of his intellectual acumen. This concept of Torah is compared to *tal*, dew, which benefits and enhances the earth on a gentle and limited level. The intelligent, advanced student of Torah, who plumbs its profundities and resolves its mysteries, is compared to the rain. Strong rain is driven to the earth with force, which, at times, overwhelms the land. The Torah overwhelms the mind of the scholar, just as it captivates and penetrates the soul of the wise man, who is capable of appreciating its depth and the wonders of Hashem's teachings.

How is it possible for the same item to have two distinct incongruous effects on people? How could Torah be compared to gentle dew and also to strong rain? *Horav Moshe Reis, Shlita,* cites *Ibn Ezra* in his preface to his commentary to *Sefer Koheles,* who compares Hashem's influence, His spiritual flow, to the rays of the sun. We see with our own eyes that some objects become brighter in the sun, while people turn darker from its rays. The sun is the same; the objects are different. Likewise, among people: There are those to whom Torah is overwhelming and compelling, due to its depth and wisdom. To others, Torah is simple and gentle. It all depends on the capabilities and attitude with which one approaches it.

Attitude plays a critical role in success in Torah. One must have a great desire to achieve success in Torah and be willing to work hard to achieve his goal. The individual who takes it easy — sitting back and waiting for the Torah to enter his mind — will only develop a peripheral knowledge of Torah. I recently read a powerful story about a young boy's resolve to study Torah, related in Rabbi Yechiel Spero's, *Touched By A Story 2*.

The story is about a thirteen-year-old survivor of the Holocaust. As a child, he did not have the opportunity to study Torah beyond the primary courses taught in the local *cheder*. His desire had always been to go to *yeshivah gedolah* to study Torah in depth, but his hopes were not realized as a result of the war. He spent his youth differently than others. As a young boy, he was witness to his parents' execution. He then became a victim of Nazi cruelty himself. Forced to run away and hide, he survived on grass and hay.

Following liberation, he was thrown into a new turmoil. With no home and no family, he finally made it to the American shore, alone and lonely. He was fortunate to be befriended by a family, who, albeit kind, could not really understand his plight. The next two years were at best bittersweet, filled with sadness and pain.

His dream to become a *talmid chacham*, Torah scholar, continued to burn fiercely in his mind. He visited a number of schools, hoping to be accepted as a student. Alas, no one was interested in teaching *Aleph-Bais* to a thirteen-year-old boy. He was frustrated. All he wanted was to learn Torah, and no one was willing to give him a chance. He was about to give up, but decided one more attempt could not hurt. He would try one more *yeshivah*.

He walked into the principal's office and presented his case. Giving it all he had, he mixed emotion with logic and a little begging. The principal seemed genuinely concerned, and the young boy felt he might finally have made a dent. He would be accepted as a student in this *yeshivah*.

Just as his hopes soared, however, the rug was pulled from under him, as the principal said, "We would love to have you attend our school, but there is nowhere that I could place a thirteen-year-old boy whose proficiency level does not extend beyond the *Aleph -Bais*."

Crushed, the young boy looked at the principal and, with dejection written all over his face and with tears streaming from his eyes, he said, "I accept the rejection. It is something I have become accustomed to hearing. I ask you only for one favor. Could you please write me a note stating that I came to you and asked to be accepted in your *yeshivah,* so that I could learn Torah, and you told me that it is ridiculous for a thirteen- year-old boy to be studying in the same class with kindergarten children. Please see to it that when I die the *Chevrah Kadisha,* Jewish burial society, buries me with that note in my hand. This way I can come before Hashem and tell Him that I at least tried to the best of my ability to learn Torah!"

When the principal heard this heartrending plea from the boy's mouth, he jumped up from his chair, embraced the boy and together they cried. The very next day, the thirteen-year-old boy was learning Torah with boys who were nine years his junior. He did not care. He finally was doing what he always strived to do — learn Torah. Today, he is a *talmid chacham* who, for almost a half of a century, has been teaching Torah to earnest young men in *Yerushalayim* who, like himself, want to achieve Torah scholarship.

קל אמונה ואין עול צדיק וישר הוא

A G-d of faith without iniquity, righteous and fair is He. (32:4)

I n the *Talmud Taanis* 11a, *Chazal* explain the meaning of *tzaddik v'yashar hu,* "righteous and fair is He"— Hashem metes out exacting justice to the righteous for their misdeeds, while He rewards the wicked for their merits, so that He does not deprive the *tzaddikim* of eternal life in the next world. They add that at the time of a person's departure to his eternal home, all of his earthly deeds also take leave of him. The Heavenly Tribunal then says to him, "Did you do thus and thus at such and such place on such and such day?" He responds, "Yes." He is then told to sign his name to attest to the veracity of the record of his deeds. Moreover, the individual is *matzdik es ha'din*, ratifies the judgment he will receive, telling them, "You have judged me correctly." This is the idea behind fairness and righteousness: everybody gets his due — and he accepts it.

Let us try to understand *Chazal*. This occurs in the *Olam ha'Emes*, World of Truth. There are no games there, no *shtick*, no lies. Why is a person asked anything? Is there a possibility that one might not recognize his own actions? Is it necessary to respond in the affirmative and to sign in testimony and agreement? What are *Chazal* teaching us with this idea?

Horav Baruch Mordechai Ezrachi, *Shlita*, explains that in this world our perspective is limited to time, place and sensory perception. Everything we do has an enormous effect on our surroundings, on the people with whom we deal and on those we influence. We do not realize this, however, because we cannot perceive anything beyond the boundaries that restrict a human being.

Horav Yisrael Salanter, *zl*, explains that only Hashem *Yisborach* can mete out justice in a righteous and just manner. Hashem's retribution, takes *every* variable into consideration. Every smile, every tear, every bit of joy, and every drop of sadness all factor into Hashem's accounting of a situation and His retribution.

This process is beyond man, given his physical limitations. In the World of Truth, our perception becomes eminently clear, the past and future are no longer incongruent tenses. They can now be viewed as parallel with the present. Suddenly, the actions that appeared "reasonable" from the earthly perspective have now taken on a completely new image. More people are involved, ramifications are magnified and extended. The individual no longer recognizes his actions for what they were before. Could these be his actions? Is it possible that what he sees now is the consequence of his actions? Against his will, he must accept the new reality, the picture perfect of his earthly activities. "Yes," he acknowledges, "these are my activities."

Likewise, when a person acts in a positive manner, whether it be carrying out a *mitzvah*, performing an act of lovingkindness, or any good deed, the picture in the *Olam ha'Emes* also changes. He will see the incredible long-term effect of his positive actions, whom they inspired, how their influence spread out in many ways.

He is then asked to affix a signature affirming *his* actions. That signature is the moment of truth. He now confronts the overwhelming reality of his actions. He sees the incredible good, and that is reassuring, but he also sees the extent of his misdeeds. The realization that <u>all</u> of the terrible consequences of his actions are before him — and they are <u>his</u> sins — is in itself the greatest punishment. When we are confronted with the truth — the extent — the effect — the overwhelming negativity resulting from our misdeeds, we realize the depth of our sins and recognize their severity. What we thought was a simple infraction has now become a sin of epic proportions.

As we begin a new year filled with aspirations, hope and renewed vigor to serve Hashem in the prescribed and correct manner, we should keep all this in mind. The good deeds that we perform are magnified beyond anything we can fathom. Regrettably, our negative activities have a similar effect. Our decision concerning which path we choose — that of reward or that of punishment — is a decision we must make <u>here</u> and <u>now</u>.

זכר ימות עולם בינו שנות דר ודר

Remember the days of yore, understand the years of generation after generation. (32:7)

Moshe *Rabbeinu's* theme is very clear: *Klal Yisrael* is an *am naval*, a vile nation, whose shortsightedness and ingratitude play a role in its malevolent attitude towards Hashem. The cure is equally simple — reflect upon the past; study the glorious history of a nation under G-d's direction and beneficence; and realize that what has occurred in the course of world history was all regulated by Hashem for His People. We wonder why the Torah focuses on *yemos olam*, the *days* of yore. Should it not have said *me'oraos olam*, the *happenings* of the world? What about the timeline during which these occurrences took place needs to be emphasized?

I think the Torah is teaching us a compelling lesson in history and gratitude. We must judge history corresponding to the backdrop of *yemos olam*, the time period during which the historical endeavors and occurrences took place. Upon judging the people of history, we must do so through the prism of the time frame of that period.

Having said this, I feel it is necessary to focus on a topic that has long been ignored. If Moshe *Rabbeinu* tells us that studying the past will cure our ingratitude and that lessons gleaned from a previous generation will be therapeutic for our shortsightedness, perhaps *we* should also follow this advice.

American Jews of the post-Holocaust period are the beneficiaries of a rich legacy of Torah that was transplanted on these shores by the *udim mutzalim me'eish*, "firebrands saved from the flames," survivors of the European conflagration known as the Holocaust. America today is replete with Torah from coast to coast: *Yeshivos* of every genre; Torah *chinuch* for girls; *kollelim;* Jewish outreach centers; Day Schools in most communities, even in some of those communities where years before a Torah school was nothing more than a dream — or a nightmare. But it was not always like this.

Sixty-five years ago, America was a spiritual wasteland, barren of Torah, bereft of schools, with a critical shortage of leadership that was capable and willing to lead. When the survivors of the Holocaust came to these shores, they did not concede to apathy and depression. They were acutely aware that they were spared for a reason — to build Torah in America. Together, with a handful of devoted rabbinic and lay leadership, they transplanted European Torah to American youth. They planted the seeds that have sprouted and flourished with unprecedented Torah study and *mitzvah* observance.

Do we know who they were? Do we care? Have we ever taken the time or interest to study their lives, to delve into the challenges, trials and tribulations they overcame to build Torah for *us*? Or, in contrast, have we attempted to distance ourselves from them, because they would probably not fit in our present day Torah milieu? *Zechor yemos olam!* Remember the backdrop of that time period. Reflect on with what our predecessors had to contend: Who were their adversaries? What was public opinion? What was the effect of the economy? Of what did the spiritual landscape consist? Now, after we have factored in all of the above, we will have a more profound appreciation of the vicissitudes they faced, the challenges they overcame, and the circumstances over which they triumphed. Whatever we have achieved in the area of Torah is in no small part attributed to their *mesiras nefesh*, self-sacrifice, blood, sweat and tears. Indeed, we stand on their shoulders.

✳ ✳ ✳ ✳ ✳ ✳

כי לא דבר רק הוא מכם
For it (the Torah) is not an empty thing for you. (32:47)

R ashi interprets this to mean that we toil in Torah for a good reason. "Much reward depends on it, for Torah is our life." In an alternative explanation, *Rashi* says that "there is nothing empty in Torah." Every word in Torah can be expounded upon. To substantiate this idea, he cites the *pasuk* in *Bereishis* 36:22, "And the sister of Lotan, Timna…and Timna was a concubine of Eliphaz, son of Eisav." *Chazal* ask, "Why would a noblewoman such as Timna, who was Lotan's sister, settle to become a concubine? They explain that she said, 'I am not worthy to become a wife to him. If only I could become his concubine!' Why did the Torah go to such lengths to inform us of this? It is to teach us the praise of Avraham, that rulers and kings would desire to cleave to his seed." This demonstrates how a few innocuous words in the Torah teach us a significant lesson.

It would seem that *Rashi* is implying that in order to become aware of Avraham's eminence, we need Timna's affirmation. Consider the facts that Hashem refers to Avraham as G-d-fearing and that the Torah records many episodes concerning Avraham *Avinu* that depict his exemplary character and virtue. What concern is it to us what Timna thinks?

Horav Eliyahu Meir Bloch, zl, cites his father the *Telzer Rav, Horav Yosef Yehudah Leib Bloch, zl*, who explains that while Timna's praise does not add anything to Avraham's stature, the Torah nonetheless takes human nature into consideration. Any respect given to a person, regardless of the source, means something to people. An individual's esteem is elevated in our eyes when we see the respect accorded to him by others. If Avraham's esteem was elevated in the eyes of people as a result of Timna's respect for him, then it is worthy of being recorded in the Torah.

Rav Eliyahu Meir adds his own thoughts to the matter. The Torah is not simply conveying to us Avraham *Avinu's* virtue, it is also teaching us the importance of relating the greatness of a *tzaddik*. While we are certainly aware of Avraham's righteousness, every incident adds to his distinction, and that is important to convey. When we see how far the Torah goes to relate the piety and character of a *tzaddik*, we will be inspired to give a *tzaddik* his proper esteem.

We see from here that the way *we* treat our *gedolei Yisrael*, Torah leaders, sets an example for others to emulate. Thus, before we point an accusing finger at the average Jew and demand a greater degree of *derech eretz* for our Torah leadership, we should set the standard.

✯ ✯ ✯ ✯ ✯

ויהי בישרון מלך בהתאסף ראשי עם יחד שבטי ישראל

He became King over Yeshurun when the members of the nation gathered — the tribes of Yisrael in unity. (33:5)

Rashi explains that Hashem is *Klal Yisrael's* King in the most complete sense only when the people unite to do His will. Just as *achdus*, unity, prevailed at *Har Sinai* when all of *Klal Yisrael* accepted the Torah, so, too, does Hashem reign only over a nation that maintains a sense of harmony in belief and action. The *Navi* writes in *Melachim* I 3:3, "And Shlomo loved Hashem, walking in the statutes of David, his father; only he sacrificed and burnt incense in high places." *Rashi* explains that while Shlomo acted in a manner similar to David *Ha'melech*, he deviated in one area from his father's practice: He delayed the construction of the *Bais HaMikdash* for four years, during which time he continued to offer his sacrifices in the "high places," a reference to the personal *Bamos*, altars, that each individual placed on top of his roof or in his yard. According to *Rashi*, Shlomo *Ha'melech* is criticized for delaying the construction of the *Bais HaMikdash*. This is not consistent with the *pasuk* that intimates that his only infraction was continuing to make use of the *Bamos*. Why do we have this apparent contradiction? As long as there was no *Bais HaMikdash*, offering sacrifices on a *Bamah* was totally permissible. If so, why does the *Navi* note the continued use of the *Bamah*, while it seems to ignore the primary dissatisfaction with Shlomo for having delayed the *Bais HaMikdash*?

Horav Shmuel Truvitz, *zl*, cites the *Netziv*, *zl*, in his commentary to *Shir HaShirim*, who writes that we would be wrong to suspect Shlomo of indolence concerning building the *Bais HaMikdash*. The reason that he took his time in building the *Bais HaMikdash*, is that as long as there was no *Bais HaMikdash* the people were free to use their personal *Bamos*, allowing for increased latitude of expression of one's love for, and gratitude to Hashem. The *Bamah* was available everywhere. Anyone could sacrifice in any place.

This is, regrettably, where Shlomo erred. While individual service is wonderful and meaningful, it is not the optimum that Hashem desires. Hashem does not want individual service, in which each person does his "own thing." He wants all of *Klal Yisrael* in perfect harmony and in total unity to worship Him collectively from one *Bais HaMikdash* through the medium of one service. As Moshe *Rabbeinu* told Korach, "We have one G-d, one *Aron HaKodesh*, one Torah, one *Mizbayach*, and one *Kohen Gadol*."

Hashem is one, and unity among His subjects is the precise manner in which He demands that we serve Him. Everything in our lives focuses on bringing together the various parts into a single, consolidated unit. While there is strength in numbers, this strength reaches its apex when all of its parts act in perfect harmony together, as one. This does not demean individual expression. On the contrary, every individual's personal contribution is significant, as long as each is focused on the same goal. *Horav Yaakov Kamenetzky, zl,* notes that Hashem divided *Klal Yisrael* into individual *degalim*, banners, each depicting the singular traits of its *shevet*, tribe. This was done, however, only after the *Mishkan* was erected and placed in the middle of their encampment. They first had to *all* be focused on one unified goal — then, they were free to express themselves individually.

✴ ✴ ✴ ✴ ✴ ✴

וללוי אמר תמיך ואוריך לאיש חסידך

Of Levi he said, 'Your tumim and your urim befit Your devout one.' (33:8)

First, Moshe *Rabbeinu* stressed Levi's position as the tribe from which the spiritual leadership, the *Kohanim*, of the nation emanated. Then, Moshe turned to the tribe as a whole, focusing on its bravery and steadfast loyalty in the desert. He then blessed the *Leviim* as the teachers of the nation. The commentators note the omission of Shimon from the blessings. This is due to the fact that Shimon was severely criticized by Yaakov *Avinu* for the tribe's later participation in the worship and consequent moral deviation concerning the Baal Peor idol. The *Sifri* notes that at one time, Shimon and Levi had equal status in the eyes of their father, Yaakov. After their reaction to Shechem's violation of their sister, Dinah, Yaakov was angry at them. Indeed, on his deathbed, he said, "Accursed is their *rage* for it is intense and their *wrath* for it is harsh" (*Bereishis* 49:7).

What ensued since that day, such that now Levi is extolled and Shimon is ignored? The *Sifri* compares this to two individuals who borrow from the king. After awhile, one repays the king his debt, while the other one not only does not repay his debt, but he even borrows again. Likewise, at Shechem, both Shimon and Levi acted in a manner that was censured. They lost it, and, therefore, Yaakov castigated them for their rage. Years later, in the wilderness, when Moshe *Rabbeinu* proclaimed, *Mi l'Hashem eilai*, "Whoever is for Hashem — to (join) me!" (*Shemos* 32:26), Levi came forward. Shimon did not. At that time, Levi reimbursed the "king" for his debt. Shimon did not. And again, years later in Moav, under the leadership of Zimri, Shimon's tribe resorted to a complete moral breakdown. It was Pinchas, from the tribe of Levi, who saved the day. Shimon "borrowed" again, while Levi, so to speak, lent to the "king."

We now understand what occurred, and how Levi corrected his problem, while Shimon magnified it. I think, however, there is a deeper meaning to *Chazal* than the aforementioned. In his *Haamek Davar*, the *Netziv, zl,* writes that when Shimon and Levi avenged their sister's honor, they did so for disparate reasons. Levi sharply felt the insult and profanation of Hashem's Name, the terrible slight to His honor. If people would lose respect for those who respect and serve Hashem, they would ultimately lose respect for Hashem Himself. Levi therefore acted for — and in the Name of — G-d. This is later demonstrated both when his tribe stepped forward in response to Moshe's clarion call of *Mi l'Hashem eilai* and when Pinchas slew Zimri in order to put a stop to the plague that was decimating the nation.

Shimon also avenged his sister, but for a different reason: he had intense feelings of family loyalty. The honor of his family was defamed. He felt compelled to do something about it. Both Shimon and Levi demonstrated extreme loyalty, but the foci of their allegiances were discordant.

Later on, during the incident of *Baal Peor*, their loyalties were divergently expressed: Levi's led to elevating Hashem's honor; Shimon's led to disaster. In the confrontation between Zimri, the *Nasi* of the tribe of Shimon, and Pinchas, scion of the tribe of Levi, Pinchas avenged Hashem's honor, while the tribe of Shimon resorted to moral degradation and open rebellion.

All of this indicated that these two brothers were not the same — in any way. Levi *acted* with rage and wrath, but his true character was expressed in his total commitment to Hashem. *Mi l'Hashem eilai!* aptly defines Levi's essence. Shimon, on the other hand, did not just act with rage and wrath; his response was an expression of a basic flaw in his character. Rage and wrath are necessary traits at times, which one must employ when contending with a vicious enemy whose goal is to undermine and usurp the Name of Hashem. When it pits one brother against another, however, for personal reasons, it is far from being worthy of a blessing.

✸ ✸ ✸ ✸ ✸ ✸

וימת שם משה עבד ה'
So Moshe, servant of Hashem, died there. (34:5)

According to one opinion in *Chazal*, the last eight *pesukim* of the Torah were written by Moshe, but, rather than using ink, he wrote the last words with tears. The Torah comes to an end with the passing of Moshe, the quintessential *rebbe* of the Jewish nation, the man who dedicated every fibre of his being to *Klal Yisrael*. This conclusion to the greatest volume that has ever been recorded is written with tears — Moshe's tears. It is very difficult to accept that Moshe wept over the words, "So Moshe, servant of Hashem, died there." Our leader led a perfect life. No man ever achieved the pinnacle of spirituality and the unprecedented relationship with the Almighty that personified his life. Moshe's place in *Gan Eden* was assured. Moreover, he was acutely aware that his stay in this world was coming to an end *before* the nation which he had so faithfully led would enter *Eretz Yisrael*. Why did he weep?

If I may use my homiletic license, I would like to suggest that Moshe cried over the words, *And no one knows his burial place to this day* (*Ibid.* 34:6). What is the significance of these words? I think that the Torah is conveying a powerful message. Throughout the millennia, millions of our people have been persecuted and put to death through the most cruel and inhuman means. For the Jew, however, there is something even worse than death: not having the opportunity to be laid to rest in a *kever Yisrael*. Throughout our history, millions of Jews have been deprived of a Jewish burial. This is a tragedy of epic proportion. Hashem *Yisborach* addressed this dilemma when He personally buried Moshe and concealed his burial site. Hashem was teaching us that every Jew who does not have a *kever Yisrael* is buried personally by the Almighty — and He knows the spot. Just like Moshe, whom He buried, so, too, have millions of our brothers and sisters been buried by Hashem.

Moshe *Rabbeinu* realized the implications of the words, *and no one knows his burial place.* He understood profoundly what these words would mean to the millions of Jews, who, like himself, would be buried by Hashem. So he cried. These were not tears of sadness. They were tears of pride in knowing that, regardless of what our enemies do to us, they will never triumph. Hashem will never forsake us. And this is how the Torah concludes.

ולכל היד החזקה ולכל המורא הגדול אשר עשה משה לעיני כל ישראל

And by all the strong hand and for all the awesome power that Moshe performed before the eyes of all Yisrael. **(34:12)**

The Torah records every significant moment of Moshe *Rabbeinu's* life that impacted his nation for all time to come. His activities — whether in the area of leadership or social justice, his relationship with the Almighty, or his character traits — are all presented either overtly or in the context of a subtle lesson. If we were to sum up his life's endeavor and search for the crowning lesson — that action for which he is to be remembered for posterity — it would be found in the closing words of the Torah. The words that seemingly serve as our quintessential teacher's epitaph are: *And by all the strong hand and for all the awesome power that Moshe performed before the eyes of Yisrael.* Moshe is to be remembered for his *yad chazakah*, strong hand. What does this mean, and what message does it convey to us?

The *Midrash* at the end of the *parsha* cites a fascinating dialogue that took place between Moshe and Hashem. Moshe asked Hashem, "The Torah which I received from Your Right Hand, perhaps when I leave this world, it will be called by another name?" (a name attributing it to another individual). Hashem replied, "Heaven forbid! It will always be called with your name." Hence the *pasuk, Remember the Torah of Moshe, My servant* (*Malachi* 3:22).

Horav Nissan Alpert, z.l., suggests that *Chazal* here underscore the overriding significance of *limud haTorah,* the absolute study of Torah. Veritably, we have 613 *mitzvos* and specific principles of belief, together with a host of exhortations concerning our interpersonal relationships and how we must act in every aspect of our daily lives. What is the *briach ha'tichon,* middle bar, that sustains and supports our lives? What is the most important aspect of Judaism? It is *limud haTorah.* Moshe was acutely aware that during his tenure as leader the focal point would be Torah study. What about after his death? What would be the agenda of his successors? Would the ensuing leadership underscore the primacy of other *mitzvos* and transform them into the cardinal principles of Judaism? Would they say that the most significant way to serve Hashem is through action, through endeavor, but not necessarily through Torah study? True, study is important — but not all-important.

Moshe feared that people would relegate those who spend their lives immersed in Torah study to a distant second place. Action! Doers! That is what *Klal Yisrael* needs — not "*bank kvetchers,*" bench warmers. They would not understand that Torah study is what maintains us. For forty years in the wilderness, they did nothing else but study Torah. Moshe taught them nothing else. They did not need anything else. In fact, the last *mitzvah* in the Torah, the one that he "squeezed in" shortly before his final farewell, was the *mitzvah* of writing a *Sefer Torah.* That was it: Torah, Torah — and more Torah! Everything else was secondary.

Now, as Moshe stood at the threshold of his grave, he asked Hashem, "Was it all for naught? Will Torah study be forgotten?" Hashem assured him that our people will never forget the significance of Torah study. It will always have primary status within the framework of Judaism.

This is the meaning of *U'lchal ha'yad ha'chazakah,* "and by all the strong hand." Moshe accepted the *Luchos* representing the Torah in his two hands, seeing to it that the study of this Torah would be imbued into the hearts and minds of *Klal Yisrael,* so that it would be their *yad ha'chazakah.*

Our *gedolei Yisrael,* Torah leaders, have exemplified this quality to the fullest. While many were gifted with exceptional minds, the common denominator has been their unparalleled and uncompromising love of Torah. Their diligence in studying Torah under the most brutal conditions has been the foundation of their greatness. *Horav Yisrael Gustman, zl,* one of the most brilliant *Roshei Yeshivah* of the past generation, was well known for his consummate love for Torah. During the Nazi destruction of Europe, *Rav* Gustman displayed his great love for the Torah that he so diligently studied. Rabbi Yechiel Spero in *Touched By A Story* 2, relates that when the Nazis invaded his village, *Rav* Gustman was forced to flee for his life. He ran deep into the forest on the outskirts of town. There, he was able to create a makeshift hideaway for himself and his family in a small alcove of a pigsty. He remained in this "hole" for six months. One can only imagine what such an experience can do to the mind and nerves of a person — but *Rav* Gustman was different. Despite the deplorable conditions, he was able to recite and review the Talmud *Zevachim* by memory over thirty times! Is it any wonder that we considered the novellae which he composed during that period as some of his most treasured?